The Messages of Holy *and* Divine Love

VOLUME 1
March 1, 1993 – December 31, 1997

Messages to the Visionary
MAUREEN SWEENEY-KYLE

Published by:
Archangel Gabriel Enterprises Inc.

DECLARATION

Unless otherwise indicated, all of the Messages contained in these Volumes were given by Heaven to the American Visionary, Maureen Sweeney-Kyle.

Current Canonical Explanation:
RESPONSE TO APPARITIONS AND VISIONARIES FOR ROMAN CATHOLICS

Since the abolition of Canon 1399 and 2318 of the former Code of Canon Law by Paul VI in AAS58 (1966) page 1186, publications about new apparitions, revelation, prophecies, miracles, etc., have been allowed to be distributed and read by the faithful without the express permission of the Church, providing that they contain nothing which contravenes faith and morals. This means, no imprimatur is necessary.

The Discernment of Visionaries and Apparitions Today
by
Albert J. Hebert, S.M., Page III

Published by:
©2015 Archangel Gabriel Enterprises Inc.
North Ridgeville, OH 44039   All rights reserved
ISBN 978-1-937800-54-3

Contents

Dedication

To the United Hearts
of the Most Holy Trinity
– Father, Son and Holy Spirit –
in union with the
Immaculate Heart of Mary

November 1, 2014
Feast of All Saints

Blessed Mother says: "Praise be to Jesus."
"This is the age of the realization of much of Scripture. These are times of fulfillment of ancient prophecies just as in the day when Christ came into the world. For that reason, God permits Scripture to be quoted with many of the Messages, as the Messages are supported by Scripture."

"Do not take Heaven's efforts here lightly – nor the abundance of apparitions and Messages for granted. Each one bears its own weight on the scale of God's call to be converted. You do well to listen sooner rather than later, for only the Father knows times and dates of specific happenings."

Read Isaiah 10:20-23
and 1 Thessalonians 2:13

Introduction to the Volumes

Maureen Sweeney-Kyle's visions, apparitions, locutions and messages from Heaven began in 1985 and continue today. Now, three decades later, Maureen has received over 30,000 Messages, including the large body of Holy and Divine Love Messages dating from 1993, which we present in these Volumes.

Through Maureen, Heaven has given the world the Holy and Divine Love Messages for the benefit of all people and all nations and all faiths, and it is Maureen's mission to make these Messages known.

With that end in mind, we are publishing the Holy and Divine Love Messages in this multi-volume set, so the Messages can be easily read and studied in-depth for years to come.

We caution the reader not to attempt to read the Volumes as you would a novel, but to read them as you would the Bible, taking time to listen and absorb and meditate on the Messages.

Use your Bible to look up the Scripture references which have been given by Heaven to increase our understanding of the Messages and the times in which they were given.

Use the Holy Love website (*www.holylove.org*) to search for Messages on specific themes and topics, such as the Chambers of the United Hearts, holiness, virtues, etc. A separate Index Volume will be published after the Messages come to an end.

Throughout the years, Heaven has repeatedly stressed that we should read, study, propagate, and then, live the Messages. You can do so if you take these Messages to heart, put them into action, and be the Message. We hope that these Volumes will help you to do just that.

—Holy Love Ministries

May 20, 1996

Our Lady comes in white. There is a gold cross at the top of Her mantle, and there are many gold crosses in the background behind Her. She says: "I tell you, My angel, it is not by happenstance I come to you. I come because of your inadequacies. Jesus allowed Me to choose you and your lack of knowledge concerning Church doctrine and spiritual matters at this particular time in history. Since your background does not reflect previous knowledge of the Holy Love Message, it is most obvious that the Message comes from an outside source – mainly Heaven."

About the Apparitions

The Visionary

Maureen Sweeney-Kyle is a very petite, shy, timid and frail wife, mother and grandmother, who was born and raised in the greater Cleveland, Ohio area. Maureen resides with her husband, Don, at the site of the miraculous Maranatha Spring and Shrine located in nearby Lorain County.

Don Kyle and Maureen Sweeney-Kyle

Maureen Sweeney was born on December 12, 1940, on the Feast of Our Lady of Guadalupe. The youngest of two girls, Maureen was raised in a Catholic family in Fairview Park, attending public schools and earning a college degree. As a lifelong Catholic, Maureen has been devoted to Our Lady and the Rosary since childhood.

ix

"Around the age of six or seven, I never remember being without a little statue of Our Lady in my room. I always had a little rosary after my First Communion. When I got in grade school, someone gave me a little book on Fatima."
       — Maureen Sweeney-Kyle on February 11, 2015

The visions, apparitions and messages began when Maureen was in her mid-forties. Even so, Maureen recounts having had experiences, even as a child, that seemed to anticipate the visions of her later life.

(Excerpt from a Talk on "Angels" given by Maureen Sweeney-Kyle on December 11, 2000) *"When I was about eleven or twelve years old, our family lived on an old family farm, and as the city encroached upon the country, a 4-lane highway ended right at their property and became two lanes, but you had to make a sharp turn to the left in order to get onto the 2-lane highway, and there were no signs – no traffic light. So, we had a lot of cars lined up in our front yard, and my dad was continually replacing the mailbox, replanting the flowers, replanting his tomatoes.*

Well, one night, there was a bad accident and, of course, we were there before the police, as usual, and I asked my mother if I could cross the street to see if anyone was hurt, and she said, 'Sure. Go ahead,' and of course there weren't any street lights either. I mean, this was really rural!

So, I was running along the tree lawn and I heard two voices which had to be angels, because there was no one else around, shout at me, 'STOP! LOOK UP!' So, I stopped and I looked up, and I was about to run into a live wire that was dangling.

That was my first encounter [with angels]."

The Apparitions Begin

Our Lady first appeared to Maureen in 1985 during Adoration of the Blessed Sacrament at St. Brendan Catholic Church in North Olmsted, Ohio. Our Lady came dressed in a light pink and smoky lavender color.

"I was at Adoration at a neighborhood Church and Our Lady was suddenly just standing to the [right] side of the Monstrance – She never puts Her back to Jesus or the Blessed Sacrament. She had a large beaded rosary in Her Hands and I thought, 'Am I the only one seeing Her?' People were getting up and leaving, or coming in and not paying any attention. All of a sudden, the fifty Hail Mary beads turned into the shapes of the fifty states [of the United States]. Then She left. I didn't know why She was there, but I thought, 'Maybe She wants me to pray for the country.'

There was one man who ran Adoration and I told him what I saw, but I didn't want other people to know. Then, later, I started getting messages – first from Jesus, then from Mary, but I didn't tell anybody about them.

At the time, though, I joined a charismatic prayer group. At one of the meetings, a man got up and said, 'There's someone here who is getting messages and not speaking them.'

I thought, 'Oh, no!' Then he said, 'We'll turn off the air conditioner in case you have a quiet voice, so everybody can hear you.' Well, they knew instantly that it was me because I was the only one who was being quiet at these meetings. I went out of there crying, and I quit the prayer group.

Then I went back to see the first man who ran Adoration. He said for me to just give him the messages and he would get up and read them. No one would have to know I was getting them. I said, 'Okay,' and that's when I first started to write them down."

— Interview with Maureen Sweeney-Kyle in July 2006

This is how Maureen described Our Lady's visits to her:

"Our Lady always appears in a very bright light, quite often floating on a cloud. Many times She has angels with Her. She brings a heavenly presence with Her. Our Lady's face is oval shaped and Her skin is a milky white. I see Her with brown [honey-colored] eyes. Her hair is medium brown, always parted in the middle and reaches just below Her shoulders. Usually most of it is concealed under Her veil. Her voice is melodic and velvety. I've never heard a voice like it on earth. As breathtaking as Her physical appearance is, Her real beauty comes from within. It is this inner beauty that makes you feel a sense of peace, even when She speaks about unpleasant things. Sometimes She cries and I would do anything to make Her happy again. She comes to reconcile mankind to God through Holy Love."

— Maureen Sweeney-Kyle in May 1996

Decades of Messages from Heaven

Since 1985, Jesus and Blessed Mother have appeared to Maureen on a nearly daily basis, along with visits from God the Father and numerous saints, angels, Poor Souls from Purgatory, and more.

Maureen remained anonymous for the first nine years, until Our Lady asked her to step out in faith and, with Holy Boldness, to speak publicly - a great trial for this shy and reluctant woman of frail health. Maureen and Don then traveled across the United States and to many parts of the world, spreading Heaven's Messages of Holy and Divine Love.

> *"My daughter, I am coming to you to recall hearts to Holy Love, a Love for which they were formed in the Will of God. Because this is vital, I continue to come to you, whereas in other areas of the world my public apparitions have ceased."*
>
> *"The thrust of My call to you, the Holy Love Message, is one that must be heard. Therefore you must represent Me - and your husband as well - near and far. Do not be mindful of opposition. My grace will decide for many what is Truth. Be joyful and at peace."*
>
> *(Our Lady - January 3, 1998)*

Over the past 30 years, Maureen has received more than 30,000 Messages from Heaven, which have been given either as Public Messages for all people and all nations or as Private Messages for the guidance of the Mission and Ministry.

Apostolic Missions

Jesus and Blessed Mother have given Maureen a series of missions to accomplish:

1986 – 1990

OUR LADY, PROTECTRESS OF THE FAITH
(Promotion of the Title and the Devotion)

1990 – 1993

PROJECT MERCY
(Nationwide Anti-Abortion Rosary Crusades)

<u>1993 – Present</u>

Promotion of:

- *The Revelation, Image and Devotion to the **UNITED HEARTS** (1991; 2007) combined with the **JOURNEY OF PERSONAL HOLINESS THROUGH THE CHAMBERS OF THE UNITED HEARTS** to the Divine Will (1999; 2003);*

- *The Revelation, Title, Image and Devotion to **MARY, REFUGE OF HOLY LOVE** (1997);*

- *The Revelation and Devotion to **ST. MICHAEL'S SHIELD OF TRUTH** (2006); and*

- *The Revelation, Image, Devotion and Chaplet to the **MOURNFUL HEART OF JESUS** (2013).*

Formation and promotion of Ecumenical Lay Apostolates:

- ***SECULAR ORDER OF MISSIONARY SERVANTS OF HOLY LOVE** (1995);*

- ***CONFRATERNITY OF THE UNITED HEARTS** (2000); and*

- ***CHILDREN OF THE UNITED HEARTS ASSOCIATION** (2012).*

Manufacture, distribution and promotion of:

- *The **CHAPLET OF THE UNITED HEARTS** (1996); and*

- *The **ROSARY OF THE UNBORN** (1997) and the **CHAPLET OF THE UNBORN** (2013) as designed by Our Lady to help end abortion.*

The Chambers of the United Hearts of the Most Holy Trinity and Immaculate Mary

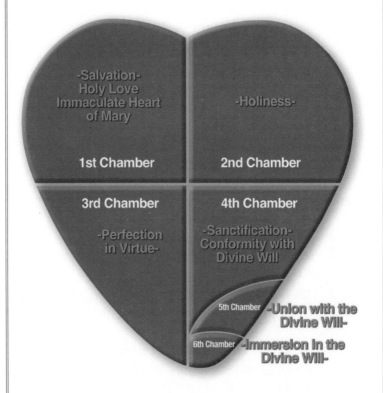

-Salvation-
Holy Love
Immaculate Heart
of Mary

1st Chamber

-Holiness-

2nd Chamber

3rd Chamber

-Perfection
in Virtue-

4th Chamber

-Sanctification-
Conformity with
Divine Will

5th Chamber -Union with the Divine Will-

6th Chamber -Immersion in the Divine Will-

The Door to Each Chamber is Deeper Surrender to Love – the Divine Will

In 1993, Our Lady began **Holy Love Ministries** and then requested that the Ministry procure property for a shrine in Lorain County, Ohio. This was accomplished in November of 1995. This 115-acre shrine is now known as **Maranatha Spring and Shrine**, the home of **Holy Love Ministries**, an Ecumenical Lay Apostolate to make known to the world the Chambers of the United Hearts.

January 7, 2013

"I am your Jesus, born Incarnate."

"The thrust of this Mission is to reconcile the heart of the world to the Divine Will of My Father in and through Holy Love. Since Holy Love is Truth, Heaven's call is for all souls to discover the Truth of Holy Love, thereby discovering My Father's Will."

"This Mission presents ways by which to live in Holy Love:"

1. *"Read, study and propagate - then, live the Messages."*

2. *"Begin, in every present moment, your journey through the Chambers of Our United Hearts."*

3. *"Pray the Rosary of the Unborn in an all-out effort to convict the heart of the world of the sin of abortion."*

"Plainly, you must see that this Mission is an ecumenical effort to conform the heart of the world to the Will of My Father. Unbelievers have not discovered the Truth of the state of their own heart."

Spiritual Directors:

Over the years, Maureen has been guided by various spiritual directors and advisors who have been experts in Marian Theology, including: the Rev. Frank Kenney (S.M., S.T.D.) a Marianist priest from Dayton, Ohio, with a doctorate in Marian theology, who served as Maureen's Spiritual Director from 1994-2004; and His Grace, Gabriel Gonsum Ganaka (O.F.R.), Catholic Archbishop of Jos, Nigeria, who served as one of Maureen's Spiritual Directors in 1999. All of Maureen's spiritual directors and advisors since Fr. Kenney have remained anonymous.

On August 11, 1999, Maureen and her husband, Don, accompanied by Archbishop Ganaka and Fr. Kenney, met with His Holiness, Pope John Paul II, to present him with the United Hearts and Holy and Divine Love Messages, and the Images of Mary, Refuge of Holy Love and the United Hearts.

On the joyful occasion of the visit by the Visionary, Maureen Sweeney-Kyle, with Pope John Paul II on August 11, 1999.

Maureen with Fr. René Laurentin—renowned author
and Marian theologian—and her Spiritual Director,
Fr. Frank Kenney (1921-2012)

Archbishop Gabriel Gonsum Ganaka
of Jos, Nigeria (1937-1999)

About the Messages of Holy and Divine Love

- "I come to invite each one of you into My Father's Kingdom of His Divine Will. **The way is through these Messages of Holy and Divine Love**. Do not reject it." *(Jesus - April 6, 2015)*

- "This Mission and **the Messages of Holy and Divine Love are the culmination of all the Messages Heaven has given to earth.**" *(Jesus - May 20, 2005)*

- "I desire the eternal salvation of all of humanity. **This is why I have willed that these Messages of Holy and Divine Love come into the world at this time.** They are an anchor for the Remnant Faithful and a sword of Truth thrust into the heart of the world." *(God the Father - March 9, 2007)*

- "These **Messages of Holy and Divine Love** and the path of spiritual holiness through the Chambers of Our United Hearts **are meant to strengthen hearts in the Truth**. Thus fortified in Truth, every soul and whole nations, as well, can move forward in holiness." *(Blessed Mother - July 1, 2013)*

- "Here at this site [Maranatha Spring and Shrine] I have given many graces to draw mankind back onto the path of righteousness. **These Messages are the bridge which spans the abyss between Heaven and earth, for the Messages lead souls in Holy and Divine Love.** Some readily set foot upon this bridge. Others foolishly hold back saying - the bridge may not be trustworthy or the right people may not approve."

"The Bridge of Holy and Divine Love is here before you. I have constructed it for you with each word of every Message. It is sound and safe. I, your Jesus, call you upon it. The more souls who accept My invitation to traverse this bridge, the stronger the bridge becomes, and the narrower the abyss between man's heart and the Heart of the Divine Will."

"Do not hold back, I tell you. Do not! Those upon this Bridge of Love will not experience the upheavals of land or sea but will be supported by My Hand. Once upon this bridge, do not look back but only move ahead in Holy and Divine Love. My Mother travels the bridge with you."

"The way to traverse the bridge is to live the Messages of Holy and Divine Love." *(Jesus - April 18, 2011)*

* "Today, I come to address those who believe in these Messages [of Holy Love], yet do not live in Holy Love. Such as these are more culpable before God than those who do not believe for false reasons. Hearing the Messages and believing the Messages carries with it the responsibility of changing that in your life which is not Holy Love. This very often means a change in attitude regarding relationships with people, trying to increase in virtue, and pursuing a deeper prayer life."

"How sad it is to hear the Truth and ignore it. The Messages call you to have childlike faith - a faith that does not seek its own advantage - an unselfish attitude in every situation. This is not easy and requires much effort while cooperating with grace."

"Dear children, do not make the mistake of hearing and believing, but not living the Messages. Each Message is for you." *(Mary, Refuge of Holy Love - February 3, 2015)*

- "Dear children, today I invite you to **read and listen to every Message I impart to you as though they were My last Words you will experience on earth.** This is the way it must be, and it is the way it should have been from the beginning."

   "Each Message is given for your welfare and offers guidance, informs, even redirects your efforts. Do not always wait for the next Message. One day there will not be a 'next Message'. Concentrate on and appreciate what I am giving you today." *(Blessed Mother - February 21, 2012)*

- "If you believe in the **Messages of Holy and Divine Love**, then in truth you must be in the foreground in the **fight against abortion**." *(Jesus - January 14, 2007)*

October 7, 2013
Feast of the Holy Rosary

Our Lady is here as Mary, Refuge of Holy Love. She is holding the Mournful Heart of Jesus with the Rosary of the Unborn wrapped around it. She says: "Praise be to Jesus."

"This is Heaven's Peace Accord with earth. Pray the Rosary of the Unborn for an end to abortion. This will console the Mournful Heart of My Son and resolve the differences which divide you. If you listen, dear children, you will have peace. If you continue on your path of self-destruction, I cannot protect you from the consequences. It is by your efforts the future can change. Please realize the passage of time brings the fulfillment of My Words to you ever closer."

"Abortion is the bad fruit of the compromise of Truth and the abuse of authority: the grievances which mourn My Beloved Son's Heart with intensity. It is by the Rosary of the Unborn this can change, hearts can change and the evil of abortion stopped. You must help Me. I beg your assistance."

"Dear children, if you pray the Rosary of the Unborn or the Chaplet of the Unborn against abortion, then you are doing all you can in the present moment to console My Son's Most Mournful Heart.* This is the sin that most epitomizes the narcissism of the heart of the world today and calls upon God's Justice."

"Your prayers can save lives."

"Dear children, your presence here today makes Me very happy and makes My Day special. Your prayers, dear children, are important to Me - most especially to end abortion."

"I tell you, once again, solemnly, that **you will not have peace in the world until you have peace in the womb.** God protects and honors the good, but He opposes all evil."

"Today, dear children, I am blessing everything on you, and with you, and I'm extending to you My Special Blessing."

* *More information on the Rosary of the Unborn and the Chaplet of the Unborn can be found in the Appendix at the end of this volume* **("Our Lady Gives the World the Rosary of the Unborn and the Chaplet of the Unborn to End Abortion")** *and on the Rosary of the Unborn website:*
                www.RosaryOfTheUnborn.com

About Holy Love

WHAT HOLY LOVE IS

"Holy Love is:"

- "The Two Great Commandments of Love – to love God above all else and to love neighbor as self."
- "The fulfillment and the embodiment of the Ten Commandments."
- "The measure by which all souls will be judged."
- "The barometer of personal holiness.
- "The Gateway to the New Jerusalem."
- "The Immaculate Heart of Mary."
- "The First Chamber of the United Hearts."
- "The Purifying Flame of Love of Mary's Heart that all souls must pass through."
- "The Refuge of Sinners and the Ark of these last days."
- "The source of unity and peace amongst all people and all nations."
- "Holy Love is God's Divine Will."

"Realize that <u>only evil</u> would be opposed to Holy Love."

(Jesus – November 8, 2010)

THE TWO GREAT COMMANDMENTS OF LOVE

When the Pharisees heard that Jesus had silenced the Sadducees, they assembled in a body; and one of them, a lawyer, in an attempt to trip Him up, asked Him, "Teacher, which commandment of the law is the greatest?" Jesus said to him, "You shall love the Lord your God with your whole heart, with your whole soul, and with all your mind. This is the greatest and first commandment. The second is like it: You shall love your neighbor as yourself. On these two commandments the whole law is based, and the prophets as well."

(Matthew 22:34-40)

THE VIRTUE OF LOVE

"I am your Jesus, born Incarnate. I have come to speak to you about the virtue of love. Holy Love is, as you know, the Two Great Commandments: love God above all else and your neighbor as yourself. It is the embrace of all Ten Commandments. Holy Love is the Immaculate Heart of My Mother. It is the Divine Will of God."

"Holy Love can be likened to the sun, which spills its rays over the earth enlightening the shadows of darkness. It is like the keys to the Kingdom I entrusted to My apostle Peter. It is the door to My Sacred Heart and union with Divine Love."

"Holy Love is the harmony between man, nature, and the Creator. It is the interpretation of the law and the means of all sanctification."

"The will of man must choose Holy Love. It is not open to debate, and stands undaunted in the face of discernment. Holy Love cannot be judged, for it is the judge."

"Holy Love is offered in every present moment and follows the soul into eternity."

(June 28, 1999)

THE EFFECTS OF HOLY LOVE IN THE HEART

Messages from St. Francis de Sales

"I have come to you to speak about the effects of Holy Love in the heart."

"Holy Love can transform the most mundane task into a powerful redemptive tool in the Hands of God."

"Holy Love, when it is accepted in the heart, can transform darkness into the Light of Truth."

"Holy Love can inspire victory over sin; therefore, Holy Love is the foundation of every conversion of heart."

"Holy Love is the vehicle of surrender of free will to accept God's Divine Will."

"It is Holy Love which helps the soul to recognize God's grace in every cross."

"These are sound reasons for souls to accept these Messages and to support this Mission of Holy Love by living the Messages. To do so is to allow your heart to be transformed by Holy Love. To do so is to follow the pursuit of Holy Perfection."

(January 14, 2012)

"Without Holy Love in the heart, good deeds, penance and reparation are hollow; for Holy Love is the foundation of holiness, righteousness and truth. It is impossible for the soul to comply with the Divine Will of the Father apart from Holy Love, for God's Will is Holy Love."

"Holy Love leads the soul away from focus on self to focus on God and neighbor. This leads the heart into balance with the Divine Will. The soul gradually loses sight of how everything affects him – to focus on how everything affects God and neighbor. Such a soul is a jewel in God's Eyes and mounts swiftly up the Stairway to Holiness. This is the path to perfection."

(January 16, 2012)

IT'S TIME TO CHOOSE HOLY LOVE

Our Lady comes as Mary, Refuge of Holy Love *[see Image on back cover]*. She says: "Praise be to Jesus."

"The first step to living in Holy Love is to choose it. This choice may need to be made over and over throughout the day. Entrance into the First Chamber encourages this."

"It is important that the soul determines the direction his thoughts, words and actions are taking him. Are they inspired by good or by evil? Certainly, it is clear that there are evil inspirations in the world today. It is also evident that evil is most often presented as good. The heart that does not fully accept this is easy prey for Satan."

"Dear children, you must not be complacent, for Satan knows the best way to infiltrate each heart. He knows your weaknesses and your strengths. Please recognize him in every anxiety, every weakness of virtue and every discouragement. **Read each Message I impart to you as though I am speaking directly to you.**"

"I desire our hearts beat in unison in every present moment."

(January 30, 2015)

"I am your Jesus, born Incarnate. Today I come to remind the world that the future of humanity rests on the degree of Holy Love in hearts. The fruit of Holy Love is peace and harmony with the Will of God. The fruit of hatred and love of self above all else is war, terrorism, famine, disease and every sort of natural disaster."

"The barometer of Holy Love in hearts is the acceptance or rejection of sins such as abortion, same-sex marriage and the sin of indecision concerning these issues. Government and Church leaders need to call these issues what they are – sins, not rights. The Ten Commandments may not be in vogue with some in the world, but they are still dictates from God to His people. No law can change that."

"If you want wars and violence to stop, then turn away from compromise and sin and choose Holy Love. Those who support politicians who are in favor of abortion are as guilty as the abortionist who wields the instruments of death. Those who support homosexuality and/or same-sex marriages in any way – for any reason – are guilty of sin, as well. Do not support sin because it is stylish or popular."

"Once again I come into the world to call sinners onto the path of righteousness. This is the path of Holy and Divine Love that leads you through the Chambers of Our United Hearts. As you progress through these Sacred Chambers, allow Me to penetrate your heart with My Divine Love. Love must be sanctified by reciprocation. It is only by allowing Me into your heart that you will be transformed according to the Will of God."

"Until now the heart of the world has been an empty chamber. But now, I offer you the warmth and security of My Merciful, Loving Heart. The more you empty yourselves of selfishness, the more I am able to fill you with Divine Love."

"I come to help you understand that the journey through Our United Hearts is a journey of Loving Trust. Therefore, do not fear the future. When you fear, dear ones, you lose your focus on Our United Hearts and think in human terms – 'what will happen to me, my family, my environment?' I am calling you to a greater reality – the spiritual reality of Our United Hearts where you will always be safe and secure when you lovingly trust in Me."

"The future of your country begins in the present moment. If, through your free will, you **choose Holy and Divine Love**, you will help to shape a secure future for America. The choice is up to each soul and to all souls."

"My brothers and sisters, how I long to fill each heart with My Divine Love. It is in this way that the Will of My Father will take up its reign over all people – every nation, and the whole world. When I return it will be in and through Divine Love. **You can hasten My Triumph by spreading the Messages of Holy and Divine Love."**

(September 5, 2004
Jesus' Monthly Message to
All People and Every Nation)

SELF-LOVE vs. HOLY LOVE	
Is motivated towards self-advantage in thought, word, and deed.	Is motivated in every thought, word, and action by love of God, and neighbor as self.
Sees only others' faults, not his own. Considers himself on the right path—perhaps even humble and virtuous.	Sees himself full of imperfections. Is always seeking to be perfected through love. Considers everyone more humble and holy than himself.
Holds a checklist in his heart of every wrong perpetrated against him.	Imitates Divine Mercy as best he can. Is compassionate and forgiving.
Is quick to anger and stands vigil over his own rights making certain they are not transgressed.	Is patient. Takes note of others' needs and concerns.
Hangs on to his own opinions refusing to surrender to another viewpoint.	Offers his own opinions but listens to others and lends them equal merit with his own.
Takes pride in his own achievements. May even take pride in his spiritual progress.	Realizes all things proceed from God; that without God he is capable of no good thing. All good comes from grace.
Sees himself and the world as the be-all/end-all. His only pleasure is thus achieved through the world.	Takes joy in storing up heavenly treasure, in growing closer to God and deeper in holiness. Knows the difference between earthly pleasures and spiritual joy.
Uses the goods of the world to satisfy self.	Uses the goods of the world to satisfy quest for holiness.
Objects to every cross. Sees trials as a curse. Resents others' good fortune.	Surrenders to the cross through love as Jesus did. Sees crosses as a grace to be used to convert others.
Prays only for himself and his own needs.	Prays for all in need.
Cannot accept God's Will. Becomes bitter over trials.	Accepts God's Will with a loving heart even when difficult.

(Given to Maureen Sweeney-Kyle by Blessed Mother on August 18, 1997)

1993 - 1997

1993 - 1997

Historical Guide
(1993-1997)

Mission and Ministry Timeline
(With Message Dates)

1993

1988 - 1994	From 1988-1994, **Mary's House of Prayer** in the city of Seven Hills, a suburb of Cleveland, housed the Ministry's offices and prayer services.
MAR 8	"Encourage My children to come to My **Blessing Point**, for it is here I will open My Heart to humanity" *(Our Lady – Mar. 8)*.
MAR 19	Our Lady asks that this Mission be known as **'Holy Love Ministries'**, an ecumenical Ministry for all people and all nations. *(Incorporation date – February 9, 1994.)*
SEP 27	Blessed Mother directs Maureen where on the Seven Hills property Her spring will be located *(Sep. 27)*. Jesus requests **the spring be named 'Maranatha'**, which is Aramaic for 'Come, Lord Jesus' *(Our Lady – Oct. 1; Nov 27)*. The Spring is unearthed on May 5, 1994.
OCT 24	Our Lady imparts Her Motherly Blessing *(Oct. 24)*, which is:

- "A blessing of Holy Love which will enable you to live in this virtue." (Our Lady – Jan. 24, 1994)

3

- *"The embrace of My Immaculate Heart."*
  (Our Lady – May 22 1994)

NOV 21   Our Lady describes the **Five Steps to Holiness** *(Nov. 21; Nov. 25; Nov. 28; Dec. 1; and Nov. 30, 1994).*

1994

JAN 16   • "Many will arrive [at Maranatha Spring] besieged and forsaken, but will leave encouraged and accompanied by a **special angel**, who will guard the soul against the adversary." *(Our Lady's Treatise to Pilgrims – Jan. 16, 1994)*

• The angel that each one is given at Maranatha [Spring] is the **angel of Holy Love**. This angel stands guard over the doorway to your heart, repelling that which is not of Holy Love, and preparing the heart to be part of the New Jerusalem." *(Jesus – Dec. 30, 1994)*

MAY 5 -   **Maranatha Spring** is unearthed at the House
Feast of   of Prayer on the **Feast of Holy Love**.
Holy Love
• "I desire the day that Maranatha Spring is unearthed be remembered always in hearts as: My Feast of Holy Love." *(Our Lady – May 3)*

• "The triumph of My Immaculate Heart will begin today at Maranatha." *(Our Lady – May 5)*

• "You do not comprehend what heaven has ordained today; for Maranatha is the threshold of Holy Love and the gateway to the New Jerusalem." *(Our Lady – May 5)*

• "The space around Maranatha will be filled with angels." *(Jesus – May 5)*

• "My presence is continually and always at Maranatha Spring and at the Blessing Point. For here I intend to grant many favors." *(Our Lady – May 23)*

MAY 20   "I invite all to join Me here on the **13th of every month**, anniversary of My Feast Day in Fatima." *(Our Lady of Fatima – May 20)*

JUNE   The city of Seven Hills obtains a temporary **restraining order against the Ministry** when a large crowd of 1,000 pilgrims gathers to pray at Maranatha Spring on June 13th.

AUGUST   The **court orders the Ministry to move by December 21st** and **imposes a maximum of 25 people on the property** at any one time. During the remaining months of 1994, the Ministry prays at various locations, including: Broadview Heights; the historic Little Red Schoolhouse in Middleburg Heights; picnic areas and parks; etc.

SEP 3   Graces attendant to the **Missionary Image of Our Lady of Guadalupe** *(Our Lady – Sep. 3; Nov. 22)*.

NOV 3   Formation of **Refuge of Mary Prayer Cells** *(Our Lady – Nov. 3; Nov. 14)*.

DEC 12   Invitation to commemorate the Twelfth of December by **meeting for a rosary on the Twelfth of each month**, beginning in January 1995 *(Our Lady – Dec. 12)*.

DEC 21   The House of Prayer in Seven Hills is closed. The grounds remain open to the public. The Ministry moves to a house in the nearby city of Parma.

1995

1995 –   Our Lady's **Monthly Messages to All Nations**
1998   **on the 12th of each month** commence in January 1995 and continue until December 1998.

APR 16   Our Lady dictates the three-day **'Consecration to the Flame of Holy Love'** *(Apr. 16 – Easter Sunday)*.

JUN –   On the 12th of each month, the Ministry prays
NOV   outdoors at Indian Hollow Park in Lorain County for Our Lady's Monthly Message to All Nations.

SEP 12   Formation of the Lay Apostolate – the **'Missionary Servants of Holy Love'** *(Our Lady – Sep. 12; Jesus – Sep. 14)*.

SEP 25   Vision of Our Lady with the **Two Hearts Scapular** *(Sep. 25)*. Jesus states the promises attendant to it *(Oct. 2)*.

NOV   The Ministry acquires an 83-acre farm in **Eaton Township** in Lorain County, located between the cities of Elyria and North Ridgeville, for the **new home of Holy Love Ministries**.

| DEC 12 | The **second Maranatha Spring is unearthed** on the Feast of Our Lady of Guadalupe on the grounds of Our Lady's site of predilection in Lorain County, at an area designated by Blessed Mother. Even though well-drillers estimated a 75-foot hole would be dug before striking any type of natural spring, Maranatha Spring was unearthed using a shovel and post hole digger and digging a mere 2-3 inches below the frost line. *(Dec. 10; Dec 12)* Our Lady states that all the same graces from the first Maranatha Spring in Seven Hills will be attendant to this Spring. |

1996

FEB 10	**'The Chaplet of the Two Hearts'** devotion *(Jesus – Feb. 10)* and Promises *(Our Lady – Feb. 29).*
MAR 15	Venerate the **Image of the United Hearts of Jesus and Mary** and propagate the devotion to the United Hearts *(Jesus – Mar. 15).*
MAR 21-23	Jesus and Blessed Mother impart the **initial Blessing of the United Hearts** *(Mar 21).* Promises of the Blessing of the United Hearts *(Jesus – Mar. 22; Mar. 23).*
MAY 5 - *Feast of Holy Love*	A **large crowd of 6,000 pilgrims** gathers at the Eaton Township prayer site for a promised apparition of Our Lady.
AUG 31	The Ministry closes the House of Prayer in Parma and **moves to its new home at Maranatha Spring and Shrine** in Eaton Township.

FALL / WINTER	The Ministry prays outside in all weather conditions until the new pole barn (prayer center) is constructed.
NOV	Construction of the **Immaculate Heart of Mary Prayer Center** (a simple pole-barn structure) begins *(Our Lady – Jan. 1).*
NOV 8	Our Lady's explanation of **miraculous photographs** *(Our Lady – Nov. 8).*
DEC 9	**The Bread of Holy Love Movement** *(Our Lady – Dec. 9).*

1997

JAN – MAR	Construction of the **Immaculate Heart of Mary Prayer Center** is completed in the spring *(Our Lady – Jan. 1).*
MAR 4	Maureen draws the miraculous **Image of Mary, Refuge of Holy Love** with Blessed Mother's assistance *(Our Lady – Mar. 4; May 15).*
APR 1	Formation of the **Allegiance of the United Hearts of Jesus and Mary** *(Jesus – Apr. 1).*
APR 3	The **Image of Mary, Refuge of Holy Love vanquishes a fire** in Maureen's apartment complex *(Apr. 3; Apr. 6).* The huge fire stopped just outside Maureen's apartment.
MAY 10	The **Immaculate Heart of Mary Prayer Center** is blessed by Fr. Kenney, Maureen's Spiritual Director, during a special 'Day of Recollection' on May 10th *(Our Lady – Jan. 1).*

JUN 18 **Patron Saints of the Mission**: Saints Pio of Pietrelcina (Padre Pio) and Thérèse of Lisieux (The 'Little Flower') *(June18)*.

SEP 5 **'Meditations for the Sorrowful Mother Shrine'** *(Mary, Refuge of Holy Love – Sep. 5)*.

SEP 14 **A Strand of Blessed Mother's Hair** is given to Maureen *(Sep 14)*.

SEP 15 **Dedication of Our Lady of Sorrows Shrine and Lake of Tears** *(The Sorrowful Mother – Sep. 15)*.

OCT 17 Vision of the **Rosary of the Unborn** *(Our Lady – Oct. 7)*.

NOV 12 **Graces and favors offered to pilgrims** who visit Maranatha Spring and Shrine *(Our Lady of Guadalupe – Nov. 12)*.

Mary's House of Prayer in Seven Hills, Ohio

Main entrance and parking

The corner of the room in the House of Prayer where Our Lady's Blessing Point is encircled on the carpet for pilgrims to venerate

Seating for prayer services and pilgrim visits

The original Maranatha Spring is unearthed on May 5, 1994 at an area designated by Blessed Mother on the grounds of the House of Prayer in Seven Hills

The grounds of the House of Prayer with the original Maranatha Spring and the Stations of the Cross

Mary's House of Prayer in Parma, Ohio

Interior of the House of Prayer

Our Lady's Blessing Point was brought from Seven Hills to the
House of Prayer in Parma

The Blessing Point encircled on a wooden frame

The Little Red Schoolhouse in Middleburg Heights where prayer services were conducted

Historical Marker for the Schoolhouse

Prayer service at Indian Hollow Park in Lorain County
on July 12, 1995

Prayer service at Indian Hollow Park in Lorain County
on September 12, 1995

The second Maranatha Spring is unearthed on
December 12, 1995 at an area designated by Blessed Mother
at the Eaton Township prayer site

Construction of the Immaculate Heart of Mary Prayer Center

Entrance to the Immaculate Heart of Mary Prayer Center

Interior of the Immaculate Heart of Mary Prayer Center

Messages of Holy *and* Divine Love

1993

MANIFESTATIONS OF PRIDE

Dictated by Jesus - March 1993

PRIDE
Root Sin

- JUDGING OTHERS
- HOLDING GRUDGES
- REFUSING TO LET GO OF OUR OPINIONS OR IDEAS
- WOUNDED EGO
- DISCUSSING OTHERS FAULTS

ANGER
Ripple Effect
Contagious
Emotion

WAR AGAINST LOVE
1 Cor. 13:4-7

Dictated by Jesus - March 1993

Judging Others......................	Love is kind - ready to make allowances.
Holding Grudges...................	Love does not store up grievances.
Hanging Onto Opinions/ Ideas...	Love does not seek its own advantage (self-seeking).
Wounded Ego.......................	Love is not boastful. Love is not jealous.
Talking Behind Others' Backs...	Love is patient - kind - ready to make allowances.

March 1993

■ **March 4, 1993.** "Dear children, to be truly consecrated to the Cross, you must be accepting of God's Will in your life, and to accept God's Will is to be holy. The hour of God's retribution is at hand, when all man's effort towards worldly gain will turn to dust. Therefore, My children, make ready your hearts in holiness through the Cross."

■ **March 4, 1993 / Thursday Rosary Service.** Our Lady came dressed in a grayish-white gown. There was an angel with Her and all around Her was a circular light. Our Lady gave a private message, then said, "There are many downstairs who have turmoil in their hearts, and all this over small things. I am concerned for how they will face greater problems in the future. I ask you to pray with Me now." We prayed. Then Our Lady said: "Let us pray each day for all people in such turmoil." Then She said, "I want to bless everyone here now, in the Name of the Father, and of the Son, and of the Holy Spirit. Amen. Go in peace." Then She left.

■ **March 7, 1993.** Our Lady was dressed in white and the lining of Her mantle was gray. She said: "Praise be to Jesus." I said, "Now and forever." She gave me a private message. Then She said, "Dear children, much of humanity and most countries have come to accept man's law above God's commandments. And so, I come to warn you that what you toil to produce will be of no avail. Come to value that which is everlasting. Pray, pray, pray." Then She blessed us and left.

■ **March 8, 1993.** From Our Lady: "Encourage My children to come to My Blessing Point,* for it is here I will open My Heart to humanity."

* Throughout the early 1990's, Our Lady appeared to the Visionary during prayer services held at Seven Hills, Ohio. Our Lady hovered over one particular area of the room at the prayer meetings. No matter where Maureen would sit, Our Lady always appeared in the same place. Eventually this area of the carpeting, over which Our Lady appeared, began to radiate the fragrance of roses. Our Lady advised the Ministry to mark off this area with a circle (representing eternity), and to place rosaries and other holy items there for special blessings. When the Ministry moved from the Seven Hills site, Our Lady directed the Ministry to cut out the carpeted area where "HEAVEN AND EARTH HAVE MET" so the blessings could continue for those who venerate this special area of grace.

■ **March 14, 1993.** Our Lady had on a long blue veil with a gold band around it. She gave a private message, then said, "Dear children, I come today especially to invite you to surrender to Me all of that which is keeping you from proclaiming My message amongst others. Ask me, and I will give you the grace to fearlessly spread My message amongst unbelievers." Then Our Lady blessed us and left.
Read Acts 4:27-31 and 1 Thessalonians 2:1-7

■ **March 18, 1993 / Thursday Rosary Service.** Our Lady came to the Thursday Rosary Service dressed in a blue mantle with a white veil. She was surrounded by a bright light and was accompanied by two angels. Our Lady said: "Praise be to Jesus." I answered, "Now and forever." Our Lady gave a private message, then She asked me to pray with Her for all the people present in the house tonight. Then Our Lady said: "Dear children, tonight I come especially to invite you to love God first, and then your neighbor as yourself. If you do this, My dear little children, you will answer My call to holiness." Then She blessed us and left, and in Her place for a minute

was St. Joseph. Then he, too, left.
Read 1 Peter 2:11-17 and 1 Corinthians 13

■ **March 21, 1993.** "I am Mary, Queen of Heaven and Earth - Queen of the Most Holy Rosary. All praise be to Jesus." I answered, "Now and forever." "My little child, the hour of great decision has come when those who seek to remain faithful to My Heart will need to prudently choose. Satan will divide My Son's Church upon earth. He will come clothed in reason and goodness. And you must be careful to remain faithful to Church Tradition as it stands now under John Paul II. The ensuing confusion will bring bishop against bishop, parent against child, husband against wife. Some Masses will not be valid under Church law, and many will be deceived. You will need to be strong. Persevere in Tradition as I have taught you. My mantle is over you. My Immaculate Heart is the Refuge of all who are faithful to Church Tradition. Therefore, be at peace."

■ **March 21, 1993 / Sunday Holy Hour.** Our Lady came dressed in aqua and white. She said: "Praise be to Jesus." Our Lady gave a private message, then said, "Help Me to pray now for unbelievers." We prayed. Then Her rosary beads turned into drops of blood. The Blessed Mother then said to all those present here, "Dear children, today I invite you to realize the only thing of importance is God's Will in your lives and how you respond to His Will. Do not be sidetracked by the allurements of the world, or by personal difficulties. This is all Satan's confusion. I love you, My dear children, and I continue to pray for you. I am blessing you now in the Name of the Father, and of the Son, and of the Holy Spirit." Then She left.

■ **March 25, 1993 - Feast of the Annunciation.** Our Lady was dressed in white brocade and She had a large angel with Her who arranged Her mantle where She came to stand. Our Lady gave a private message. Then She asked me to pray with

Her for all government leaders who held the fate of millions
of lives in their hands. Then Our Lady said: "I will address
all the people here tonight. Dear children, I come tonight to
teach you how to have peace in your hearts. You will achieve
this, My dear children, if you die to your own will, and only do
the will of God. Remember, God does not permit, or ordain,
anything that is not the best for you." Then Our Lady said:
"God the Father loves you, Jesus loves you, the Holy Spirit
loves you, and I love you." Then She blessed us and left.
Read John 5:25-30

■ **March 28, 1993 / Sunday Rosary Service.** Our Lady came
dressed as Our Lady of Grace, and She said, "Praise be unto
Him, Lord of lords, King of kings, Jesus the Christ." I answered,
"Now and forever." Then Our Lady said: "Dear children, in My
Heart is every grace you need towards holiness. Ask me, and
I will give you prudence, patience, wisdom, discernment and
understanding for every situation. If you do not come to me,
Satan has his entry, and you do not act according to God's
Will. I am blessing you now in the Name of the Father, and of
the Son, and of the Holy Spirit." Then She left.

April 1993

■ **April 1, 1993 / Thursday Rosary Service.** Our Lady
was dressed in a pearly-pink color with a gold band around
the mantle. She gave a private message, then said, "Dear
children, I have come to ask that you prepare your hearts to
be wellsprings of faith and trust, so that any onslaught that
the enemy conjures up will leave you in peace. Therefore, My
little children, die to your own will and live only for the Will of
God." Then Our Lady blessed everyone and left.
Read Psalm 23 and Psalm 32:10-11

■ **April 5, 1993.** *(After Communion)* Jesus says: "In this hour of decision, the smallest prayer or sacrifice can mean the difference between life or death for a soul."

■ **April 8, 1993.** "My child, My messenger, I come now in praise of the Holy Name of Jesus. I am Mary, Ever-Virgin. I come to petition the hearts of all humanity to pray, pray, pray. Never before in the history of the world has the need for prayer been so great, for the Arm of Justice descends upon earth. I can no longer restrain that which approaches. However, make your prayers copious and from the heart. Match each of My tears with fervent prayer that I may beg the Lord God to hasten His second coming, thereby shortening all that mankind must suffer. Appease My Son's already grieved Heart by bringing Him souls. Time is running out for many. The decisions made in the coming days will mean salvation or perdition to countless souls. I come to beg for them - pray, pray, pray."

■ **April 8, 1993.** Padre Pio says: "The greatest natural resource your country has at this time is prayer. But it needs to be refined, honed, and polished just like crude oil or a diamond in the rough."

■ **April 9, 1993 - Good Friday.** From Our Lady: "Dear children, I come to invite you to bring alive this Easter season in your hearts. As you meditate on My beloved Son's Passion, surrender your will to God and die to all sin in your lives. When you celebrate His glorious Resurrection, celebrate your freedom from the captivity of sin. On the feast of Jesus' triumphant Ascension into heaven, realize that your fervent prayers from the heart rise to heaven as fragrant blossoms. Then comprehend, My dear little children, that these same prayers return to earth as great graces, just as on Pentecost My heavenly Spouse returned to earth. Then you will truly be able to consecrate yourselves to the Cross, seeing in it victory."

■ **April 15, 1993 / Thursday Rosary Service.** Our Lady was dressed in gray and pink, and was carrying a golden rosary with her. She said: "All praise be to Jesus," and I answered, "Now and forever." Our Lady gave a private message, then asked me to pray with Her for the people that came tonight, and for the people She called to come but didn't respond to Her call. Then She said, "Dear children, tonight I come especially to offer you the hope of the Refuge of My Immaculate Heart which is the Ark of this age against the rising tide of apostasy that sweeps across the earth. Those that seek this Refuge will not be confused and will be at peace in the midst of confusion." Then Our Lady blessed us and left.

■ **April 21, 1993.** Jesus says: "Much of what the Church has traditionally stood for is about to be submerged. It is for this reason I will establish, through My Mother, refuges of faith. All of these are already formed in My Mother's Heart. They will be under attack from within and without, but they will stand firm."

■ **April 21, 1993.** *(9:45 a.m.)* "Make it known that the pockets of true believers will be scattered throughout the world." She is showing me a map with little white flowers on it. "These will be watered by the Holy Spirit and bloom in grace." At this point I asked Her to identify herself. "I am Mary, Mother of the Church. I come in praise of Jesus, King of Glory. Do not be afraid. Make it known."

■ **April 21, 1993.** *(1:30 p.m.)* From Our Lady: "The tide of popular opinion is about to flood the Church. Those who follow it will drown in it. But those who seek the Refuge of My Immaculate Heart will find herein a safe harbor of the true faith and dogma of the Church. See how close I am to those who cling to the true faith." She is wearing a blue mantle with white flowers all over it. These flowers represent the "pockets" of true believers She spoke about earlier.

■ **April 21, 1993.** "Just as you can never retrieve a *Hail Mary* once said, so you cannot retrieve a Eucharist once received. Do all with your heart."

■ **April 25, 1993 / Sunday Holy Hour.** Our Lady came in gray with a dark blue band around Her mantle, and She had on a pink gown and was holding a crucifix. She asked me to pray with Her for all unbelievers, some of whom were in the Church. She then asked me to pray for all those who were suffering in spirit. Then She said, "I desire that a devotion to My Son's Passion and death be developed here. I will personally consecrate the ground on which these stations will stand, and I will pray with those who recite the stations. Devotion to the Passion and death of My Son is more efficacious than any sacrifice." Then Our Lady said: "Dear children, I come today to invite you to come to trust in My Heart of grace, for it is herein you will find every goodness. Pray in child-like confidence for discernment and wisdom which you will so need in the near future." Then Our Lady blessed us and left.

■ **April 26, 1993.** After Communion, I saw in my heart a tabernacle with many roses coming out of it. Jesus said, "Know that all that is good originates with Me. It passes through My Mother's Heart and comes to you as grace. Satan tries to divide you through words and ideas. But he can only succeed in this if you open your hearts to pride first."

■ **April 30, 1993.** Our Lady says: "I am sending you the way for Mary's House to become a spiritual sanctuary. I give to you the way and the means so that this house will be a sanctuary of the true faith as it has been handed down through the ages and through John Paul II."

May 1993

■ **May 1, 1993 / Saturday May Crowning.** Our Lady came completely dressed in gray and She was holding a rosary, which was the exact duplicate of the one the statue downstairs held. Then Our Lady said: "Dear children, tonight you are praying for states, but I am here to tell you that soon you will be praying for countries." She blessed us and left.

■ **May 1, 1993.** From Our Lady: "I want to teach you to be disciples of the grace of My Heart. Dear children, realize that all things are a grace and dependent upon grace. See how little you are compared to this magnificent gift. When you come to realize your littleness, I will build you up in grace to accomplish God's Will through you. I will nurture your little hearts in My motherly grace so that you will be all God wants you to be, and then you will answer My call to you."

■ **May 2, 1993 / St. Casimir Rosary Crusade.** Our Lady came during the second decade of the Glorious Mysteries. She was dressed in white and She had a sword piercing Her Heart. There was also a light illuminating Her Heart. She gave a private message, then said, "Dear children, today the sword that pierces My Heart is Satan's deceit in the world. Each of your prayers helps Me to uncover him where he has remained hidden. Therefore, My little children, pray, pray, pray." Then Our Lady blessed us and left.

■ **May 6, 1993.** Our Lady came dressed in blue and white with a pink sash around Her waist. She said: "Praise be to Jesus." I replied, "Now and forever." Then She said, "My daughter, tonight, I ask that you pray for all priests, especially those who have compromised their vocations." We prayed together for that. Our Lady gave two private messages, then said, "Dear children, tonight, I implore you to pray for priests.

There are some who are priests but do not have vocations and have reached high ranks in Christ's Church on earth. It is for these My Son's Mercy is spent." Then Our Lady blessed us and left.

■ **May 9, 1993 - Mother's Day.** Our Lady was dressed all in white and was wearing the crown that the statue downstairs has on (the crown used for May Crowning last week). She said: "Praise be to Jesus, Son of the living God." I replied, "Now and forever." Our Lady gave a private message, then asked us to pray for souls that do not love. We prayed an *Our Father* and *Glory Be* with her. Then Our Lady said: "Dear children, today I invite you most especially to have hearts of love. If you love, My dear children, you will respect everyone. It is only through Satan's deceit and confusion that you do not respect and you do not love. All of this is an obstacle to grace." Our Lady blessed us and left.
Read Ephesians 4:1-4, 14-16; 5:1-3

■ **May 13, 1993 / Thursday Rosary Service.** Our Lady came dressed in gray and the edges of Her mantle were a scarlet color. She said: "All praise be to Jesus." I replied, "Now and forever." After a private message, Our Lady said: "Let us pray now for all hearts to be at peace." We prayed. Then She said, "Dear little children, these days I invite you especially to keep your hearts centered on holiness. For it is in the heart that all sin takes its root. Therefore, My dear little children, pray for holy hearts and hearts that are at peace." Our Lady then blessed us and left.

■ **May 16, 1993 / Sunday Rosary Service.** Our Lady came dressed all in white and had a great light coming from the area of Her Heart. She was also holding a pink rosary, exactly like the one I was holding. Our Lady said: "All praise be to Jesus." I replied, "Now and forever." Our Lady then asked us to pray with Her for the needs of all those intentions in our hearts and in Her Heart. We prayed. She then said, "Thank you for responding to My call. I come today, dear children, to ask you to surrender to your victimhood. Jesus is forming an army of victim souls, each soul surrendering his will to the Will of God in accepting all that God does bring. Do not allow discouragement to be a part of your crosses. Pray for courage and perseverance and pursue the path to My Immaculate Heart. I love you, My dear little children." She blessed us and left.

■ **May 20, 1993 - Feast of the Ascension.** Our Lady came in gray and gold in a material I had not seen before. She said: "Praise be to Jesus." I answer, "Now and forever." She said: "Littlest of My messengers, solemnly I inform you, Jesus sends Me to ask every heart to immerse themselves in response to My call. Satan is gripping the hearts of many and most in confusion and deceit. It is in this way, governments will be led into war and economies will collapse. Jesus desires souls to find their peace in My Immaculate Heart, soon the last Refuge of many."

"Further, I inform you, all countries that have been graced by My presence in the form of an apparition will suffer more or less in the coming retribution in proportion to their response to My call to holiness. Every site of My apparitions upon earth will continue to be a blessed fountain of grace and of peace throughout much of the purification, as Jesus gives souls every chance to respond to conversion. In all of this, I will be with you." (She seems to be talking more personally to me, now.) "My Heart will surround you, and you will know your Mother's presence and guidance. Do not be afraid, but pray, pray, pray. You know well now the fruit of obedience is to disarm Satan." She blessed me and left. Our Lady was very somber throughout this visit.
Read Luke 21:1-28

■ **May 20, 1993 / Thursday Rosary Service.** Our Lady was

dressed in white lace. She gave a private message, then said, "Dear children, tonight I invite you to seek always the Refuge of My Immaculate Heart and the peace herein. Do not be deceived to think that you can obtain peace without God's grace. Dear little children, you must forgive. Pray for the grace of forgiveness because it is only in this way you will be at peace and be able to love as God wants you to love." Then Our Lady blessed us and left.

■ **May 23, 1993 / Sunday Holy Hour.** Our Lady came dressed in white and gold and had a circle of stars over Her Head. She gave a personal message, then said, "Dear children, today I come especially to inform you the time fast approaches, indeed, the hour is here, when you must make a conscious choice to choose for the true dogma of faith. For Satan confuses many hearts to follow popular opinion rather than Church Tradition." Then Our Lady asked me to pray with Her for all God's children, that they not be deceived. Then She blessed us and left.
Read Ephesians 4:14-16

■ **May 27, 1993 / Thursday Rosary Service.** Our Lady came dressed all in white except that the lining of Her mantle was red. She was holding a rosary and had a rosary all around Her like an oval-shaped frame. Our Lady said: "Dear children, tonight I invite you to understand that prayer is the doorway to heaven. Please open your hearts to prayer, so that the Holy Spirit can fill you with the gifts He so much wants to give you. Little children, pray, pray, pray." Then She blessed us and left.

■ **May 30, 1993 - Pentecost Sunday.** Our Lady came from heaven with two angels. She was dressed in white like Our Lady of Fatima. She said: "All praise, honor, and glory be to Jesus, the King." I answered, "Now and forever." Then Our Lady said: "Dear children, today I come especially on this feast to invite you to pray each day that the Holy Spirit renews your heart in love. It is in this way that you will be able to accept the crosses in your life as My Son accepted His Cross, and you will be at peace." Then Our Lady blessed us and left.

June 1993

■ **June 3, 1993 / First Thursday Rosary Service - Message To Priests.** Our Lady came dressed all in white with a dark gold band around Her mantle. She said: "Praise be to Jesus." I answered, "Now and forever." Then She said, "Pray with Me for all sinners." We prayed an *Our Father* and a *Glory Be*. After we finished, Our Lady said: "I would like to address My priest sons." Then She said, "Dear sons, I invite you tonight to renew your hearts in the true Faith, and in so doing, call your flock back to the Sacrament of Reconciliation. Uncover Satan where he is hidden in the lives of the people Jesus has entrusted to you. The strength of your ministry is measured in the numbers of confessions." Then Our Lady blessed us and left.

■ **June 6, 1993.** Our Lady came as Our Lady of Guadalupe and She said, "Don't be afraid, I come in the name of Jesus. All praise, honor and glory be unto Him." I said, "Now and forever." A private Message was given, and then Our Lady said: "Dear children, I'm inviting you once again to become apostles of prayer. It is your prayers, My dear children, that are My ammunition against Satan's deceit. Therefore, little ones, pray, pray, pray." Then Our Lady blessed us and left.

■ **June 10, 1993.** Our Lady came dressed all in gray and was holding a gray rosary. She gave a private message, then said, "Dear children, I come especially tonight to encourage you to pray for world peace. You do not realize how powerful your prayers are and how much I need them. Satan tries to conceal all this from you. You have the most powerful weapon

on earth at your fingertips - the Rosary. But you must use it."
Then She blessed us and left.

■ **June 13, 1993 - Feast of Corpus Christi / Sunday Rosary Service.** Our Lady came dressed in a red gown with a white veil. She said: "Praise be to Jesus truly present in the Sacrament of the Altar." I answered, "Now and forever." Then Our Lady said: "Pray with Me please, little daughter, for all those who received the Eucharist unworthily today, and especially for priests who celebrated Mass unworthily." We prayed an *Our Father* and a *Glory Be*. She gave a private message, then said, "Dear children, today I invite you to understand God's justice is coming swiftly and completely. His justice has already been greatly forestalled through prayer and sacrifice, and so I ask you, spend many hours in front of My Son's Eucharistic Heart and pray, pray, and pray." She blessed us and left.

■ **June 13, 1993 - Feast of Corpus Christi.** After we prayed, Our Lady turned to everyone in the room and said, "I invite all here present today to offer the present moment to Jesus as a special gift of love."

■ **June 17, 1993 / Thursday Rosary Service.** Our Lady came dressed in a white gown and a cream-colored veil. On the veil there were red swatches. While She was talking to me, I noticed that these red marks were bloodstains that were in the shapes of countries. Our Lady gave a private message, then asked me to pray with Her for all souls to choose the path of light instead of the path of darkness. Then She said, "Dear children, tonight I come to remind you that you are called to a vocation of holiness. Some government leaders do not choose holiness, and the spirituality of these countries then becomes atheistic. To choose other than holiness is to choose Satan. Many countries have chosen this path to perdition. Therefore, My little children, you must pray that

every heart recognizes My genuine motherly call to holiness."
Then Our Lady blessed us and left.

■ **June 17, 1993.** Our Lady had a message for the people
in the apparition room. She said to "Trust God's Holy Will for
them."

■ **June 19, 1993 - Feast of the Immaculate Heart.** From
Our Lady: "Dear daughter, always have a heart full of love, for
love is never in error. Love is the path I call you upon. A heart
replete with love does not sin, but pursues God's Will in all
things. I, Myself was able to answer God's call so completely
because My Heart knew nothing but love. Forgive everything
and you will not be in error. Then you will be at peace."

■ **June 27, 1993.** *(Earlier that day)* From Our Lady: "Little
daughter, Jesus desires all souls seek the refuge of My
Immaculate Heart during this translation of apostasy that
is sweeping through the Church. In My Heart, you will find
defense of Church Tradition. Call on Me using these words:"

The Key To The Refuge Of Our Lady's Heart
*"Immaculate Mary, shelter me in the refuge of
Your Heart. Protect me and give me peace."*

"With these words Satan will find no hospice in your soul,
and I will afford you the refuge of My Immaculate Heart. Make
it known."

■ **June 27, 1993 / Sunday Rosary Service.** Our Lady came.
She was dressed all in white and was surrounded by a bright
light. She said: "All praise be to Jesus." I answered, "Now
and forever." Right away, She said, "Pray with Me for souls
to find the path of light that leads to My Heart." So we prayed
an *Our Father* and *Glory Be*. A personal message was given,
then Our Lady said: "Dear children, tonight I come again to

beseech you to pray fervently from the heart. The stronger your prayers, My little children, the stronger the weapon in My hand against evil." Our Lady blessed us and left.

July 1993

■ **July 1, 1993 / First Thursday Rosary Service – Message To Priests.** Our Lady came in white and She had a red lining on Her veil. She said, 'Praise be to Jesus." I answered, "Now and forever." Our Lady gave a private message, then said, "I desire that you pray with Me for all souls who do not love and do not follow the path of holiness to My Heart." We prayed an *Our Father* and *Glory Be.* Then Our Lady said, "I desire My priest-sons to understand that every sin is an act against love and a step away from holiness. Therefore, it is My desire that they lead their flock towards perfect Love and into the Refuge of My Immaculate Heart." She blessed us and left.

■ **July 4, 1993.** Our Lady came in white with Her Immaculate Heart exposed. She reverenced the Blessed Sacrament by bowing low before It. Then She said, "My child, My Heart is the last Refuge of the faithful. In My Heart is perfect submission to God's Will. Come to know the path to My Heart is paved with humility. For the humble, the little way to My Heart is short and without obstacle." Then Our Lady blessed us and left. In Her place for a minute was a sparkling cross in front of Her Heart.

■ **July 6, 1993.** Our Lady said, "Begin a novena in praise and thanksgiving for God's Mercy, and in petition for His continued Mercy upon earth. My daughter, you do not fully realize or comprehend what is coming when God's Merciful Hand is completely withdrawn from earth and His Arm of Justice descends." Maureen says, "Are you the Mother of

God?" Our Lady answers, "I am the Mother of Mercy, Jesus Incarnate." Maureen says, "Which novena should I say?" Our Lady answers, "Any prayer is good. Ask those around you to pray similarly."

■ **July 7, 1993.** Jesus says: "Pray first for a heart of love, for to love is to be holy. Then pray for a heart of courage to show this love. Anything contrary to this is from Satan, and is a distraction. Those who reject you, reject me."

■ **July 8, 1993 / Thursday Rosary Service.** Our Lady came dressed in pink and white and was standing on a globe of the world, and had many angels with her. Our Lady's smiling and says: "I know what's on your heart, but I've come tonight to pray for unbelievers, most especially those who have heard My messages but choose not to believe. They are not courageous in their fight against evil. My messages made them uncomfortable and they are choosing not to leave their old way of life." We prayed. Then Our Lady said: "Dear children, tonight I come especially to ask that you seek the path of holiness which is love. All the grace you need to love is in My Heart. Ask for it. I, as your Mother, desire so much to give it to you. There are many here who think they love, but are deceived, for they have not forgiven. Any thought, word or action that is against love takes you off the path of holiness. Therefore, My little children, learn to come to My Heart for all the grace you need to love and to forgive." She blessed us and left.
Read Luke 6:27-38

■ **July 9, 1993.** Before and after Communion I was given the following vision. There was a narrow road which I understood was the narrow path of holiness that leads to Our Lady's Heart. Branching off this road were many side roads. These side roads seemed to go up to Our Lady's Heart at first, but then took a sharp turn downwards towards earth and away from Mary's Heart.

Jesus said: "The side roads are the temptations of everyday life that each soul has. Satan's angels try to lure the soul from the straight and narrow path to My Mother's Heart. At first glance, the temptation looks good and the soul is deceived into thinking he is still on the good path. But as he is led farther and farther from holiness, he gets farther and farther from the Refuge of My Mother's Heart." *[See diagram]* He continued, "Pray to be shown the temptations in your life which are obstacles to holiness."

Mary's Heart

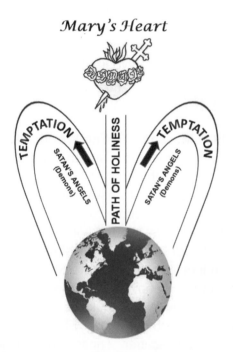

■ **July 9, 1993.** Our Lady comes in white, and bows before the Eucharist. "Dear daughter, pride is the root of unforgiveness. Pride nurtures unforgiveness in souls and makes it difficult to accept the faults of others. This is all contrary to love and is an obstacle to the grace of My Heart." After giving a private message Our Lady said: "If souls could forgive, they would be able to love. Then there would be peace in hearts and in the world. Atrocities such as abortion would be eliminated and holiness would flourish. Therefore, pray always for forgiveness and show others how to forgive."

■ **July 11, 1993 / Sunday Rosary Service.** Our Lady said: "I am Mary, Queen of Peace, all praise be to Jesus." I answered, "Now and forever." She asked us to pray with Her for unbelievers. We prayed. Then Our Lady said: "I desire all souls seek the Refuge of My Immaculate Heart." Then She said, "Dear children, I assure you, hearts that are divided cannot find their way along the path of holiness. Hearts that are full of self-interest cannot be filled with the grace of humility and cannot be brought to love. Therefore, My little children, love only God, and your neighbor as yourself." She blessed us and left.
Read 1 John 3:11-24

■ **July 15, 1993 / Message To The World.** Our Lady came and was dressed in gray and a cream color and had a rose pinned to Her robe slightly under Her neckline. She said: "Praise be to Jesus." And I answered, "Now and forever." Then She said, "Tonight I come to ask you to pray with Me for unbelievers, amongst whom I include the lukewarm." We prayed. Then Our Lady said: "Most especially I invite all government leaders to realize that the two greatest laws are: Love the Lord your God above all else, and love your neighbor as yourself. All earthly laws should be based on these two commandments. Remember, those who do not gather with the Good Shepherd, scatter. Those who do not legislate according to God's commandments will have much to answer for. It is not God who will judge, but the commandment that will judge them." Then Our Lady blessed us and there was a brown scapular with a cross in front of it in Her place for a minute.
Read Mark 12:28-34

■ **July 17, 1993 - Feast of the Humility of Mary.** From Our Lady: "Abandon all care to the Heart of My Son, trusting in His Divine Providence. Nothing depends on you, but everything depends on His provision. How foolish to spend time in concern for anything when all things are under God's domain. For this is true humility - to submit to the Will of God, which is always His provision."

■ **July 17, 1993.** As Our Lady and I recited the *Our Father*, a great light shone from Her Heart down to earth when we said *"Thy Will be done on earth as it is in heaven"*. Today She explained what it meant. She said: "Every grace of My Heart is the Will of God." Later She added, "The Will of God is always a grace."

■ **July 18, 1993 / Sunday Rosary Service.** Our Lady was dressed in a white material I've never seen before. She said: "All praise, honor and glory be to Jesus, now and forever." And I answered, "Now and forever." She said: "I come tonight to pray most especially for souls in darkness who purposefully reject the path of light that I call them to, through their own will." Then Our Lady said: "Please pray with me." We prayed. Then She said, "Thank you. I come in particular to ask prayers that souls recognize the crosses in their lives as graces, for they are graces for other souls. Each cross brings with it the grace to accept it and to offer it for sinners." She blessed us and left.

■ **July 19, 1993.** From St. Raphael: This morning when I was praying to the angel Raphael, he came and stood next to me. He had large wings, dark hair and features and was dressed in green. I asked him if he believed Jesus Christ was born in the flesh. He bowed so low his wings covered his head. He said, "I believe Jesus Christ was born of the flesh." Then he straightened up and looked right at me. He said, "And so do you." He continued, "You need to go deeper into the Mother's Heart. Do not give in to discouragement. Remember, God does not ask of you what you cannot give." I asked him how I could do this. He said, "Continually seek the Refuge of Her Heart and, in so doing, do not dwell on anything discouraging." Then he disappeared.

■ **July 20, 1993.** Jesus says: After Communion I saw a great light come out of Jesus' Heart in a vision. At the foot of the light were three white lilies which turned into three stars. Jesus said, "These are faith, hope and love. The more perfectly you practice these virtues, the easier you will be able to trust."

■ **July 21, 1993.** Our Lady told me in an interior locution, "Many times as My Son was growing up I was given to see the marks of the scourging and the nail prints on His flesh. I never dwelled on the sorrow I felt in My Heart, but I used these visions as an impetus. Each day I prayed for Him - for His public ministry and that He have fortitude and perseverance during His Passion. You must do the same for those you are praying for. Do not dwell on the lives they are leading now, but pray that their hearts be converted."

■ **July 22, 1993 / Thursday Rosary Service.** Our Lady came dressed in gray and a cream color and had the rose on that we picked for her. She gave a private message, then said, "Dear children, I come especially tonight to invite you once again along the path of holiness. Please surrender your will to holiness. Comprehend with God there is no half-measure. You cannot have your heart set on holiness one day and the world the next. Surrender your will completely to My call to holiness. The more complete your surrender, the more grace I can give you towards faith, hope and love." Then Our Lady blessed us and left.
Read Matthew 5:3-12

■ **July 23, 1993.** Jesus says: "For the humble, the path to My Mother's Heart is short and without restraint. For the proud, it is long and strewn with obstacles. The humble love easily. The proud are caught up in self-love."

■ **July 25, 1993 / Sunday Rosary Service.** Our Lady was dressed in gray and was standing in front of a large cross. She said: "All praise, honor and glory be to Jesus, the King and Prince of Peace." I answered, "Now and forever." A private message was given, then Our Lady said: "Dear children, tonight I come especially to encourage you to come to My Heart of grace. I, your Mother, desire to give you every grace so that you can more easily support your cross in life. I offer you every grace in love. Pray, pray, pray." She blessed us and left.

■ **July 29, 1993.** Our Lady came dressed all in white and She said, "All praise, honor and glory be to Jesus." I said, "Now and forever." She gave a private message, then Our Lady asked me to pray for all souls who forget to offer their suffering for sinners. Then She said, "Dear children, tonight I invite you to comprehend the only thing that keeps a soul from holiness is free will. Therefore, My little children, pray for the will to be holy." She blessed us and left.

August 1993

■ **August 1, 1993 / Sunday Rosary Service.** Our Lady came and said, "All praise, honor, and glory be to Jesus - Redeemer and King. I invite you to pray now for those who have not chosen holiness. For certainly they are numbered amongst the unbelievers." We prayed. Then She said, "Dear children, tonight I come especially to invite you to understand that you must make a choice between holiness and evil, for certainly those [who fail to make a choice] will find their indecision a condemnation. Therefore, My little children, pray to be holy." She blessed us and left.

■ **August 1, 1993.** I see Our Lady in black. She bows to the monstrance and turns to me. Her Heart is exposed and has several wounds in it that are bleeding. She says: "All praise, honor and glory to Jesus, risen and ever-present in the Eucharist." I answered, "Now and forever." She says, 'This will be the month of decisions in the world, in the Church, and in hearts. Therefore, it is wise to pray for discernment and wisdom. Satan is spreading confusion everywhere. He is trying to destroy all good. But you will be at peace if you come as little children to My Immaculate Heart."

■ **August 5, 1993 / First Thursday Rosary Service - Message To Priests.** Our Lady appeared and said, "All praise, honor and glory be to Jesus, the Word Incarnate." I responded, "Now and forever." Then She said, "My daughter, pray with Me now for all mothers who chose not to give birth today." We prayed. She spoke to me privately, then said, "I say to My priest sons: Dear sons, give Me your hearts, seek holiness with your whole heart. Come to love holiness. Please understand, My dear sons, your vocation is to bring the Sacraments to the people. If you are holy, you will understand this. Little children, always pray to be holy." She blessed us and left.

■ **August 8, 1993.** Our Lady was dressed all in blue and had a rosary in Her hands. She said: "All praise, honor and glory be to Jesus." I answered, "Now and forever." Then She said, "Please pray with Me for poor sinners." We prayed. A private message was given. Then Our Lady said: "Dear children, I come tonight especially to invite you to understand how much I need your prayers in order to combat evil. The adversary is busy trying to destroy the peace in your hearts. In so doing, he weakens your prayers and weakens the weapon in My

hand." She blessed us all and left.
Read Ephesians 6:10-17

■ **August 9, 1993.** From Our Lady: "There are many bitter trials ahead. There is no peace, save in the grace of My Heart."

■ **August 12, 1993 / Thursday Rosary Service.** Our Lady is dressed all in white and has a pink lining on Her veil. She said: "All praise, honor and glory be to Jesus." I replied, "Now and forever." She has angels all around Her and She has roses at Her feet. She said: "Little daughter, let us pray now for the Holy Father and that the message he brings will be planted in many hearts." We prayed. Then Our Lady said: "Dear children, tonight I come especially to invite you to realize the only path open to souls at this time is the path of holiness. All other paths lead to perdition. Remember there are no half-measures with God, and He will spew the lukewarm from His mouth. Therefore, My little children, rely on the provision of My Heart, for herein is all you need." She blessed us and left.

■ **August 14, 1993.** Our Lady came during the fifth Glorious Mystery. She was dressed in many pastel colors and with a crown on Her head. She venerated the Eucharist. Then She turned to me and said, "Let us give praise, honor and glory to Jesus, King of kings, Son of Man." We did this. Then She parted Her hands and said, "I have come to inform. The bitter trials ahead include spiritual, physical and emotional catastrophes for every soul."

"My Son's power to extend redeeming grace during these times is contingent upon each soul's acceptance of the crosses he is given to bear. For it is through the consecration to the Cross grace will come. Therefore, I urge My children to imitate My Son's acceptance of the Cross in love and peace." She traces a cross in the air with Her hand and leaves. A cross is left in the air momentarily.

■ **August 15, 1993 - Feast of the Assumption / Sunday Rosary Service.** Our Lady was preceded by St. Michael, who stated, "The Mother is coming." Then Our Lady came dressed all in gold. She said: "Pray with Me for the unbelievers." We prayed. Then She requested that the people gather here at the three o'clock hour, pray the Divine Mercy Chaplet, then proceed to the Stations of the Cross (outside) and pray the Stations (on Sundays). A private message was given, then Our Lady said: "Dear children, I have come to bring souls to salvation. Therefore, I ask that you consecrate your lives to the Cross. For herein lies the grace that unbelievers need to be holy." Then Our Lady blessed us and left.

■ **August 19, 1993 / Message To The World.** Our Lady was dressed all in white and said, "All praise and honor to the Lord God Jesus, King of kings." Then She said, "Dear children, I invite all nations to pursue the path to My Immaculate Heart, Refuge of Peace. This path is prayer. Learn to depend on this path now in times of little tribulations, so that at the hour of great adversity you will know well the way to My Immaculate Heart, haven of peace for all sinners." She blessed us and left.

■ **August 22, 1993 - Feast of The Queenship of Mary.** Our Lady came in pink with a great light around her. She bowed before the monstrance and said, "All praise, honor and glory be to Jesus, the King." I answered, "Now and forever." She said: "My daughter, I come especially today on My feast to encourage souls on the path of holiness and prayer, for this path is one and the same. This path is the path to My Heart My children, in order to be holy you must love God above all else, and in so doing choose to pray. To choose holiness is to love God more than yourself. In this way, you decide for His Will above your own will. Herein then, is the secret to holiness - the secret to the path to My Immaculate Heart. Indeed, the secret that opens the door to this most solemn Refuge of sinners. Therefore, I come to invite all of My children to

decide today to love God more than themselves and to pray, pray, pray. It is the only choice of value today."
Read Jude 17-25

■ **August 22, 1993 / Sunday Rosary Service.** Our Lady was dressed all in white with Her Immaculate Heart exposed. She also has a crown over Her head. A private message was given. Then Our Lady said: "Let us pray now as I have directed you for all souls having spiritual apathy." We prayed. Then Our Lady said: "Dear children, continue to pray from the heart, most especially for the lukewarm, for this is the greatest percent of the world's population and the greatest sword that pierces My Immaculate Heart." She blessed us and left.

■ **August 26, 1993 / Thursday Rosary Service.** Our Lady came dressed in gray and there are two angels with her. She said: "All praise, honor and glory be to Jesus." I replied, "Now and forever." Our Lady spoke privately, then asked us to pray for unbelievers. We prayed. Then Our Lady said: "Dear children, tonight I invite you once again to the path of holiness that leads to My Immaculate Heart. Jesus desires each soul be steeped in final perseverance. This grace is ready for everyone in My Heart of love. Please understand, dear children, in order to pursue the path of holiness, you must love God above everything and your neighbor as yourself." She blessed us and left.

■ **August 27, 1993.** *(1:00 a.m.)* From Our Lady: "All are called to a vocation of holiness, but few pursue it with sincerity. Little daughter, Jesus sends Me to invite you to be a prisoner of My Immaculate Heart - a captive of love. Reflect how each action would take on renewed meaning if you were thus confined. You would do nothing from a selfish motive but give everything to God. This is what true holiness is. And so I call all of My children to this lofty, yet attainable goal. It is here in My Heart that your crosses are transformed into grace. The deeper the soul is drawn into the recesses of this Heart, the sweeter and more pure the nectar of grace that is mediated. Therefore, I tell you, the more you love the more holy you become."

■ **August 27, 1993.**
The Virtue Of Holy Love
From Our Lady: "My child, I wish to cultivate in the garden of your soul the virtue of Holy Love. This virtue made it possible for the first Apostles to spread the Faith to foreign lands. It is through Holy Love the soul chooses to love God with the whole heart and neighbor as self. Holy Love enables you to look past obvious flaws of character in those you meet and see a soul journeying on the path of salvation much as your own. It is Holy Love that turns the soul away from the world and self and towards My Son."

■ **August 28, 1993.** From Our Lady: "Dear children, these days I call you to come to My Heart where I will dispense to you God's favor. I want to give you 'Holy Love' which is a love for the salvation of all souls. In this way, My little children, you will pray and sacrifice with greater fervor for all people towards their salvation. This holy, spiritual love is God's Mercy in action during this hour."

■ **August 28, 1993.** *(3:46 a.m.)* From Our Lady: "Do not flee to the mountains nor to the desert, but remain a faithful vigil where you are."

■ **August 29, 1993.** *(12:30 a.m.)* From Our Lady: "Dear children, I come still again to invite, to plead, and to implore. Open your hearts to Holy Love. It is through this magnificent virtue many can be won over to salvation rather than slipping to their perdition. This holy, spiritual love is the same love that enabled My Beloved Son, Jesus, to remain on the cross until His death. Holy Love is what enables Mother Theresa to extend herself to the destitute and the dying. My children, you cannot be complete in holiness without Holy Love, for without it all your works are empty - all your prayers mere words. Turn to the merciful Heart of Jesus and He will begin this journey of spiritual love with you."

■ **August 29, 1993 / Sunday Rosary Service.** Our Lady came dressed in a blue that I've never seen before and said, "All praise, honor and glory be to Jesus, Redeemer and King." She asked that we pray now for souls that do not love. We prayed. She gave a private message, then said, "Dear children, tonight I invite you to understand that the soul is like a tapestry. The two threads running through the tapestry are holy humility and Holy Love. Without these two threads the soul does not progress in holiness and they are dependent upon each other." She blessed us and left.

■ **August 29, 1993.** From Our Lady: "When the path you are climbing seems the most difficult, remember to place your eyes back on Jesus, My Son. Everything that is occurring in your life is by the hand of God."

■ **August 30, 1993.** Jesus says, after Communion: "The door to the soul is free will. It is through this door every grace and virtue flows from the Heart of My Holy Mother. When the intellect, which controls the will, decides to believe in Satan's lies, the door of the soul closes."

■ **August 30, 1993.** Jesus says: "The reason souls choose to believe Satan instead of My Truths is always pride."

■ **August 30, 1993.** *(12:08 a.m.)* "My child, let Me explain to you further. Holy Love is to love God with your whole heart and love your neighbor as yourself. But it never exists in the tapestry of the soul without holy humility. These two virtues knit together to form holiness and bring many other virtues with them, such as patience, meekness, perseverance, fortitude, joy and peace. Working together, these virtues strengthen the soul in all that is holy. It is impossible for humility to flourish in the soul without Holy Love, and vice versa. These are interwoven to design holiness. Make it known."

September 1993

■ **September 2, 1993.** From Our Lady: "My daughter, I want to pour out on humanity the grace of My Heart. Most especially, it is important souls pray for the grace of perseverance in the true faith. All manner of deceit will come against the faith in the end. It is by means of the solemn refuge of My grace-filled Heart that My children will persevere. Please comprehend, My daughter, no one is immune from Satan's attacks. Even the most holy will be severely put to the test. But I mean to defend those who call upon me."

■ **September 2, 1993 / First Thursday Rosary Service - Message To Priests.** Our Lady came dressed in gold and gray, and She said, "All praise be unto Him, Jesus, the Word Incarnate." I answered, "Now and forever." A private message was given, then Our Lady asked us to pray for all sinners. We prayed. Then She said, "I speak now to My priest sons and I ask that they come to realize that they must feed their flock spiritually and not intellectually, through administration of the Sacraments. They need to pray more and be examples of holy humility, Holy Love. Priests all over the world are failing in this, through Satan's deceit." She blessed us and left.

■ **September 3, 1993.** Our Lady came in gray and a gold color. She bowed before the Eucharist. She said: "Give praise, honor and glory to Jesus, ever-present in this Holy Sacrament of the Altar." I answered, "Now and forever." "My little messenger, what I most wish to convey to you is how much Jesus depends on souls who have sincerely consecrated themselves to the Cross. These souls are steeped in Holy Love and emulate the Heart of My Divine Son. Without Holy Love, souls reject the crosses in their lives, not seeing the beauty in the trials that are offered to them for the sake of others."

"It is Satan who hides all of this from souls who are not child-like. For with sophistication is sown confusion and doubt. Jesus had one apostle who was sophisticated. He did not possess Holy Love, but rather love of self. Holy Love is simplistic, unselfish and unassuming. This is how Holy Love allows the soul to see through worldly goals and seek only heavenly acclaim. It is most important these days that souls see the great value of the Cross, through which salvation continually flows. Therefore, pray to be child-like in every virtue but most of all Holy Love. Let your daily bread be the joy of the Cross through Holy Love."

■ **September 5, 1993.** Our Lady comes in gray and with Her Heart exposed. She said: "I am the Mother of Jesus Incarnate - the Mother of Holy Love. I come to ask My children once again to surrender completely to My call to holiness. There is no time to weigh the decision I solicit from you. Souls are in the balance. The wheat is being separated from the chaff. To choose for holiness is to choose life. Anything else is death. I come from Love to request this. Dear children, you do not realize how your decision affects the world and the future of the world."

■ **September 5, 1993 / Sunday Rosary Service.** Our Lady is here in gray, and She said, "All praise, honor and glory be to Jesus." I replied, "Now and forever." She asked us to pray for all souls in darkness, that do not choose holiness. We prayed. Then Our Lady said: "Dear children, tonight I invite you to the treasury of grace, that is My Heart. Herein weave for yourselves a vestment of humility and Holy Love. Then you will see that other graces and gifts come to adorn this garment. This is the way, My dear children, to choose holiness and avoid Satan's deceit." Our Lady blessed us and left.

■ **September 6, 1993.** *(5:30 a.m.)* From Our Lady: "My dear little daughter, I want to teach you how to live in My Immaculate Heart, for herein lies the secret to holiness. If you are in My Heart you will always be at peace. Your heart will be focused on God, His Omnipotence and His Will. You will realize God's Will is in everything, even though the reason is obscure to you while on earth. You will keep your thoughts on My Beloved Son, His Passion, His life on earth, His teachings. You will not feel alone or try to solve your own problems. You cannot solve your own problems. If you are in My Heart, you will realize everything is a grace. Everything depends on grace. You can accomplish nothing alone. When you accept this in your heart, you will no longer focus on the world. You will be in My Immaculate Heart, and you, in Holy Love, will be at peace."

■ **September 6, 1993.** Our Lady comes dressed as the Mother of Holy Love. She reverences the Eucharist and moves towards me. She says: "My angel, I have come to help you realize the depth of My message to you concerning Holy Love. Please comprehend that all virtues spring from holy humility and Holy Love. These two - holy humility and Holy Love - are always together in a soul. One does not exist without the other."

"The great mystery of My Son's Mercy is the offspring of His Holy Love for all souls. Holy Love never is nourished by the intellect, but only in the heart. These two greatest virtues are necessary in order for a soul to dwell in My Immaculate Heart and herein take its refuge. Both of these virtues are only possible if the child of God first dies to self. The more the soul gives up his own will, the greater these virtues will be in him and the deeper the soul will be drawn into My Immaculate Heart."

■ **September 9, 1993 / Thursday Rosary Service.** Our Lady is here in gray and pink and is holding a golden rosary.

She says: "All praise, honor and glory be to Jesus, Prince of Peace." I answered, "Now and forever." Our Lady then said, "Let us pray now for those who perpetuate the crime of abortion." We prayed. Then She said, "Dear little children, Jesus has sent Me to ask of you extra prayers, as many prayers as you can offer, for such is the need of our Hearts. Every prayer you offer is already used up by My Son, whose Heart is greatly offended. Therefore, My little children, pray, pray, pray." She blessed us and left.

■ **September 10, 1993.** Our Lady came in gray. She said: "Jesus has sent Me to ask you to offer everything you are suffering for the souls farthest from His Mercy. When He extends mercy to a soul and it is rejected, this places the soul farther from His mercy than ever. Then it is more difficult for the soul to accept the grace of conversion. It is only through Holy Love that the grace of conversion is effected. And it is through love that the soul opens the door to the grace of conversion."

■ **September 10, 1993.** Our Lady came in gray. She told me, "Please take this down. Tell everyone that all grace - all virtue - flows from Holy Love. God is Holy Love. My call to you to conversion is a call to be a reflection of God - a reflection of Holy Love. It is in this way you will be united with God. Make it known."

■ **September 11, 1993 / Saturday Evening.** Our Lady is here in white, and She says: "All praise, honor, and glory be to Jesus." She gave a private message, then said, "Jesus sends Me tonight especially to ask you to place in your heart the *Consecration to the Cross* and bring it to life in your lives. For it is this way that you will triumph and I will triumph through you." She blessed us and left.

Consecration to the Cross
(The Key to the Church of Atonement)

"My Jesus, I consecrate myself this day to Your Holy Cross. Just as You took upon Yourself that great Cross for the sake of all humanity, so I vow to embrace the crosses in my life. Everything I suffer I give back to You, my Sweet Jesus, to atone for my sins and those of all the world. I will begin and end each day at the foot of Your Cross, together with our most Blessed Mother and Saint John, our brother. My only pleasure will be to comfort You, my Sweet Savior. Amen." *(Blessed Mother – December 4, 1990)*

■ **September 11, 1993.** From Our Lady: "What objectives appear hopeless, in all truth, are not through the grace of My Heart. Therefore, give praise, honor and glory to Jesus, who sends Me with these words of hope and inspiration. Pray to be holy. Be mustard seeds amongst the brambles. Do not lose sight of the goal. My dear children, if you knew the power of your prayers, you would not cease praying."

■ **September 12, 1993 / Sunday Rosary Service.** Our Lady is here in gray. She says: "All praise be to Jesus, Redeemer and King." I answered, "Now and forever." Then She said, "Pray with me, please, for those who do not keep holiness today." We prayed. A private message was given, then Our Lady said: "Dear children, once again, tonight I come to invite you to climb the mountain with me, the summit of which is personal holiness. That which blocks Holy Love from entering the soul is love of self. Therefore, My little children, love God and love your neighbor, die to self and ascend the mountain with me." She blessed us and left.

■ **September 12, 1993.** From Our Lady: "Dear children, I

come to ask that you make of your hearts burning vigils of faith, ever mindful of Satan's attempts to undermine the true faith by means of his deceit. These days in the final struggle My adversary portrays black as white, and white as black. 'Freedom' has become slavery to sin. And My Beloved Son has been de-frocked of the dignity and awe due Him in His Real Presence on the altar. Only by the merit of your prayers and sacrifices can darkness come into the light. Therefore, My dear little children, pray, pray, pray."

■ **September 13, 1993.** Jesus says: "Without grace you can attain no good. All goodness and love flows through the Heart of My Mother. Her Heart is the perfect Refuge all must seek to attain holiness. And holiness is all you need seek today. It is the path - the height of eternal joy. Indeed, heaven on earth."

■ **September 15, 1993 - Feast of Our Lady of Sorrows.** From Our Lady: "The more the soul dies to self, the further it enters along the path of Holy Love, and the deeper it goes into My Immaculate Heart. Holy Love is the foretaste of eternal love in heaven."

■ **September 16, 1993.** Our Lady is here in dark blue and white, and says: "All praise, honor and glory be to Jesus, the Word Incarnate. I've come to ask you to pray with Me for souls who do not love." We prayed an *Our Father* and *Glory Be*. Then She said, "Dear children, I come tonight to ask you to perfect yourselves in obeying the commandments - love God with your whole heart, and your neighbor as yourself - for these commandments are the embodiment of Holy Love. If all would perfect themselves in obeying these commandments, there would be no war, no disease, no abortion, and God's Will would be done on earth." She blessed us all and left.
Read 1 John 3:11-18; 4:7-21

■ **September 16, 1993.** From Our Lady: "Remember, you are being called to be a witness to trust. The secret here is to live from moment to moment, never fearing the future, for that is from Satan, nor begrudging the past, for that too is from the adversary."

■ **September 17, 1993.** Our Lady came in blue and pink and stood at an angle next to the monstrance. She said: "All praise, honor and glory be to Jesus, ever-present in the tabernacles of the world." I answered, "Now and forever." She said: "My angel, draw souls into My Immaculate Heart by merit of your Holy Love. This Refuge is as close as the soul's own heart, and as accessible as the soul's will. It is here in My Motherly Heart the soul will take up its peace. Let your love for others reflect in your every thought, word and deed. In this way, they will be open to My words to you."

■ **September 17, 1993.** "Now I come to tell you, My dear little children, when you come to My Heart, you come as well to the Heart of My Most Beloved Son. No one can enter this Refuge of His Mother and be rejected by Him. These days of tribulation, all who come to My Heart suffer for the sake of those who have not found their way here. But, my dearest little children, you will have joy and peace in the midst of the greatest trials. No one abides in this refuge in fear." She looks at me now. Before, She was looking up to heaven. "The more you suffer, My little angel, the more hearts will be touched with these messages."

■ **September 18, 1993.** *(Saturday Evening)* Our Lady came and said, "All praise, honor and glory to Jesus." I replied, "Now and forever." Our Lady said: "My little children, please understand that it is the soul's own will that leads it away from the Refuge of My Heart."
Read I John 4

■ **September 18, 1993.** She came in white and She spread Her hands so I could see Her Heart and She said, "My daughter, the foundation of the New Jerusalem is within My

Heart." Our Lady came back (dressed in white) and She spread Her hands so I could see Her Immaculate Heart and said, "Within My Heart, My daughter, is the foundation of the New Jerusalem."

■ **September 19, 1993.** Our Lady is here in blue and white. She bowed toward the monstrance and then stood and waited for me to finish the Rosary. Then She folded Her hands and said, "Give praise and thanksgiving to Jesus, present in the Holy Sacrament of the Altar." I answered, "Now and forever."

"Child, come to understand that which I now impart to you. If the commandments 'Love God with your whole heart and your neighbor as self' are the embodiment of Holy Love, then Holy Love is the embodiment of every virtue. There is no virtue that does not flow from Holy Love. Every sin is contrary to Holy Love and leads you away from My Son and the grace of My Heart. Therefore, please comprehend, in order to turn to My Son and to holiness itself, you must first turn to Holy Love through your own will."

■ **September 19, 1993 / Sunday Rosary Service.** Our Lady is here in blue and white and says, "Praise, honor and glory to Jesus – Redeemer and King." She says, "Pray with Me tonight for all those who fail to see the path they travel." We prayed an *Our Father* and *Glory Be*. Then Our Lady said, "Dear children, tonight I come to invite you to search your souls to find the ways in which you fail in Holy Love. Please understand, My dear children, that when you consecrate yourselves to the Cross, you indeed consecrate yourselves to Holy Love." Our Lady blessed us and left.

■ **September 20, 1993.** Our Lady comes as I am finishing the Stations of the Cross. There are many flowers around Her Immaculate Heart. She says, after bowing to the monstrance, "And so, My daughter, realize the sweet fragrance of grace from My Heart disperses from the soul only when Holy Love leaves the soul's heart. For when Holy Love takes up its leave, sin enters and My grace departs. Then the soul is left to its own demise until, through free will, it turns to God once again. The Sacrament of Reconciliation opens the door of the soul to Holy Love once more. My words to you are no longer just messages, they are teachings. Go in peace."

■ **September 21, 1993.** Our Lady comes in gray with Her arms extended. She says: "Holy Love transcends all other love." I said, "Do you believe Jesus was born of the flesh?" She said: "I am the Mother of the Word Incarnate. Do you understand, My daughter, My words to you lay bare the path of holiness to My Heart and the Heart of My Son for His Remnant flock? It is through Holy Love you will be signs of joy and peace in times of adversity. You cannot trust if you do not first love." Our Lady blessed me and left.

■ **September 22, 1993.** Our Lady is here in white with a gray gown. She bowed before the Eucharist, then turned to me and said, "Praise be to Jesus, Creator and King." I answered, "Now and forever. Amen." She said: "My daughter, pray with Me for Father's special intention." [mentioned earlier at Mass] We did. Then She said, "To have Holy Love in your heart is to be selfless and to live only for God and for others. Make all your prayers for others, and God, who is all-knowing, will see to your needs. Remember, worry is only a distraction from Satan. God's provision is always perfect. The path of peace is Holy Love. Holy Love is the Refuge of My Immaculate Heart. The means of attaining this is forgetting self."

■ **September 23, 1993 / Thursday Rosary Service.** Our Lady is here in purple and a cream color. She says: "All praise, honor and glory be to Jesus." I replied, "Now and forever." Our Lady says: "Let us pray now for all those who have stumbled from the path of holiness." We prayed. She has a very bright light around Her now, and there are sparkles coming from the light. She says: "Dear children, it is My desire that the seed

of faith in your heart bloom to full capacity. Therefore, I have come to ask that you pray every day for the gift of Holy Love, so that you may proceed upon the path of holiness that I have come to call you upon." She blessed us and left.
Read Philippians 3:17-21

■ **September 23, 1993.** Our Lady comes with many angels and reverences the Eucharist. She turns to me and says: "My little daughter, to you is given the solemn task of praying for the remnant of faithful that even now I am gathering in the crucible of love that is My Heart. My words to you will be beacons of light that lay bare the path of holiness which leads to My Heart. Few will choose to follow. All are called. Hasten to understand, My angel, that to which you are summoned." She gave a private message, then blessed me and left. After She left, a cross of light was left in the air. I heard Her say, "I am depending on you."

■ **September 27, 1993.** *(Monday morning, about an hour after the spring was located)* Our Lady is here in white and does not have a veil over Her head but Her Heart is exposed. She says: "Let us give praise, honor and glory to Jesus." I replied, "Now and forever." Then Our Lady said: "Please understand, My dear children, God's timing is perfect and the spring is here to give glory to God and to lead souls along the path of holiness through My Immaculate Heart, which stands ready to free humanity from captivity. The water will heal souls. Tell them it [the fountain] is heart-shaped and will lead to My Heart."

■ **September 28, 1993.** I saw in a vision the Holy Spirit fly from a host suspended in the air upon a Bible. The Bible opened and the pages were being turned by some unknown force. First, as the pages stopped turning, they came to Acts 16 with the dove (Holy Spirit) pointing at it: then it stopped on Revelation 6 and then on Daniel 6.
Read Acts 16; Revelation 6; Daniel 6

■ **September 29, 1993 - Feast of St. Michael.** Our Lady is here with St. Michael - She prayed the *Glory Be* with us and St. Michael was kneeling in front of her. She had Her hands and eyes turned towards heaven. She says: "Dear children, I have come tonight especially to tell you that the spring will be a strengthening for the Church of Atonement,* and many who come here will be healed. But it is not for you to concern yourselves concerning any controversy. For in My Heart is all the grace you need. Remember, where there is great grace, there are also great trials."

* *Messages about the Church of Atonement can be found in the Holy Love publication, The Messages of Christ's Mystical Church of Atonement.*

■ **September 29, 1993.** Our Lady came in white. She was in a bright light. The belt around Her waist cascaded down to Her knees in many gold stars. She said: "Let us give praise, honor and glory to Jesus." We did this. Then She said, "Dear daughter, penetrate the depths of My Heart and realize this is a spring of fresh beginnings for many. I have come to invite souls to search out what is hidden and to quench their thirst for holiness." She leaves.
Read Matthew 5 and John 7

■ **September 29, 1993.** St. Michael came as all light except for his blue eyes. He said, "I am Michael, the precursor of grace. I am here to tell you what is about to spring forth will bear much fruit and many graces." I asked him for a Scripture passage. He told me, "Look in Acts, Chapter 17." The Scripture opened automatically to this passage because it was marked with some rose petals and a picture of one of the Medjugorje visionaries *(apparitions to 6 visionaries in Bosnia-Herzegovina from 1981–present)* speaking at Our Lady of Lourdes Shrine.
Read Acts:17

■ **September 30, 1993.** *(At the site of the spring)* From Our Lady: "My daughter, this is the [Maranatha] spring of new beginnings. For some it will be a sign of dispute. Jesus wants you to know this. For others it will be a conviction of heart. For most it will be a certain blessing. I am leaving two angels at this site until it is completed. This way the work will be hastened. Be pleased to know this is an endless source of grace."

■ **September 30, 1993.** *(Interior locution)* "Pilgrims that come here will have their hearts convinced. They will be given the choice of conversion. By this [Maranatha] spring, your life will be completely changed."

■ **September 30, 1993 / Thursday Rosary Service.** Our Lady is here in light gray and pink, and She says: "All praise, honor and glory be to Jesus, My Son. Let us pray now for those who are spiritually blind." We prayed. A private message was given. Then Our Lady said: "Dear children, I come tonight once again to call you on the path of holiness. It is impossible to proceed along this path if you are not trusting. Persevere in prayer, for you can only trust one whom you know and love." Our Lady blessed us and left.

October 1993

■ **October 1, 1993 - Feast of St. Thérèse of the Child Jesus ("The Little Flower").** After Mass, Our Lady came and said, "It would please Jesus if you would name the spring 'Maranatha'. It is a strengthening and a completion of the remnant church. Let us give praise, honor and glory to Jesus." *[According to the message of 11/27/93, 'Maranatha' is Aramaic for 'Come, Lord Jesus']*

■ **October 2, 1993.** After Mass, Our Lady came with Her

arms outstretched and said, "Pray with Me for the remnant church." We prayed a *Glory Be*. She asked me to pray the *'Pour forth, we beseech Thee...'* prayer. She gave me the following message: "It is important that My children know Jesus asks this spring be named 'Maranatha', for He IS coming. It is through the grace that flows from My Heart that the remnant church will be strengthened and protected."

■ **October 2, 1993.** *(1:00 p.m.)* Our Lady came in white. She said: "Together let us give praise, honor and glory to Jesus." She turned to the monstrance and we praised Him. Then She turned back to me. She said: "Do not fear, My angel. But be aware that Satan is on the prowl. He tries to bring one against the other and comes in the guise of good. But you can uncover him in your inmost spirit. He is not peace and joy, but agitation and worry. Lay these battles at My feet. I am able to disarm the adversary through your Rosaries, and truth will spring forth. Every day include the remnant church in your works of mercy." She blessed me and left.

■ **October 3, 1993.** *(4:30 p.m.)* Our Lady came in white. She said: "All praise be to Jesus." I answered, "Now and forever." She said: "Just as the grace is spilling from My Heart, so it shall pour forth from the spring, 'Maranatha'." She had Her Heart exposed. Golden rays of light seemed to be pouring out of it. She said: "Each one that comes that is to be part of the remnant church will receive a special angel for protection." She blessed me and left.

■ **October 3, 1993.** From Our Lady: "Dear child, I have come to give glory to God. Let us pray together for the Remnant church." We said a *Glory Be*, and Our Lady was radiant. She then said, "My child, please understand, you need to make yourselves little so that God's grace will be great. I am leading many, many to this spring, through which the grace of My Heart will pour. Jesus wants the people to know that they must be united in the grace of My Heart for the Remnant church to flourish. And so, He chooses to teach them through this spring how great the grace of My Heart truly is. You see many people coming. I tell you, threefold what you imagine will come. But your trials will multiply. Accept everything in humility and do not fear."

■ **October 3, 1993 / Sunday Rosary Service.** Our Lady is here in gray and mauve. She says: "Let us give praise, honor and glory to Jesus." I replied, "Now and forever." She says: "Pray with Me for those who do not pursue their own salvation." We prayed. Then Our Lady said: "Dear children, tonight I come to invite you to surrender your will daily to the Father. You can do this, My dear children, by continually pursuing His Will and not your own gain in any situation. Pray for the remnant church, who Jesus seeks to shepherd through the grace of My Heart." Our Lady blessed us and left.

■ **October 4, 1993.** From Our Lady: "My daughter, proceed with the [Maranatha] spring as I have told you. Do not concern yourself with funds or know-how. In holy boldness, give them the plans as I have inspired you. That is your job. All else leave to me. The grace flowing from this spring [water] will cover a multitude of errors and bring peace wherever it is taken. None can prevail against the grace of My Heart. All praise be to Jesus."

■ **October 4, 1993.** *(Locution from Our Lady)* "You are not to concern yourself with depth or breadth, but let others determine this. Only proceed with the design as I have shown you. The [Maranatha] spring is for all faiths, all nations, all people."

■ **October 4, 1993.** Our Lady came in gray. She asked me to join Her in giving thanks and praise to Jesus, truly present in the Blessed Sacrament. We did this. Then She said, "Dear little daughter, I wish to lead you along the path of holiness and still deeper into the refuge of My Immaculate Heart. Please try to consciously live every moment in Holy Love. This is how to unite your human will with the Divine Will. Everything My Son did on earth was motivated and performed in Holy Love: His Incarnation, His hidden life, His preaching, His healings, even His suffering. You can accomplish this if you live in the present moment. When Satan takes your will into the past, he conjures up grudges, which is always contrary to God's Will and Holy Love. To willfully think of the future allows Satan to bring up worries. This, then, is not trusting in God's Will. Come to comprehend, little daughter, God's Will is Holy Love. The best way to pray is to ask Jesus to let your prayers be born from Holy Love. Then He will send the Holy Spirit to engulf your heart with this precious gift." She blessed me and left.

■ **October 5, 1993.** Our Lady came in gray and pink and was seated on a throne. She had many angels around her. She said: "Let us give praise, honor and glory to Jesus, Redeemer and King." We did this. Then She asked me to pray with Her for the remnant church. We said an *Our Father* and *Glory Be* together. Then She said, "My little child, come to understand everything in God's permitting Will is an opportunity to grow in holiness. If you are impatient or do not trust, God allows opportunities to arise where you can practice patience and trust. If the soul lacks humility or is self-seeking, he will be given opportunities to grow in the virtues needed. All things are God's Will and every soul is given the chance to enter the portal of sanctity. The more the soul cooperates with the grace of the present moment, the deeper they are drawn into My Heart. Make it known!"

■ **October 6, 1993.** "Often you do not see the grace that accompanies trials because you are looking only at the trial. Today I invite you to see the path of holiness you are being called upon. Each trial is accompanied by grace and the opportunity to go deeper into My Heart through your response to My call to holiness, which is the practice of virtue."

■ **October 7, 1993 - Feast of the Holy Rosary / Message To Priests.** Our Lady is here as Our Lady of Fatima. She says: "All praise, honor and glory be to Jesus." Then She said, "Pray with Me now for all those souls who are spiritually apathetic." We prayed. She says: "I desire very much that My priest sons universally accept the encyclical* of My Pope, for it dispels darkness that has cast its shadow upon the Church." She has three rosaries. One does not have any beads, one has just a few beads, and the third rosary has all its beads. Our Lady then stated, "The one [rosary] that does not have any beads represents the Rosaries that are never said. The one [rosary] that has just a few beads are Rosaries that are not prayed from the heart, and these two are the same as giving Satan power. But Rosaries that are prayed from the heart are a great, great weapon in My hands against all evil. Dear children, pray, pray, pray." Our Lady blessed us and left.

* ***Veritatis Splendor*** *("The Splendor of Truth" - Regarding Certain Fundamental Questions of the Church's Moral Teaching. Encyclical by Pope John Paul II, August 6, 1993)*

■ **October 10, 1993 / Sunday Rosary Service.** Our Lady is here in white. She says: "Dear child, I have come to ask you to help Me pray for those who have already joined the Great Apostasy, for they have not accepted the Holy Father's encyclical in their hearts. Please pray with Me now." We prayed. Then Our Lady said: "Dear children, with great eagerness I call you along the path of holiness into My Immaculate Heart, so that I can lead you to the Eucharistic Heart of My Son, where you will be at peace and not fear the future or God's Justice, which advances around the world with certainty. Little children, pray, pray, pray." She blessed us and left.

■ **October 11, 1993.** *(12:45 p.m. - Adoration)* Our Lady comes in white with two angels who support Her mantle as She bows to the Eucharist. She drifts towards me, nods and says: "My angel, it is good to see you here again so soon. Please pray with Me for those who choose their own will over God's Will." We prayed. As She prayed, a bright light shone around her. Then She said, "I want to help you to further understand the mystery of Holy Love. God is Holy Love! Therefore, God's Will is Holy Love. All good proceeds from Holy Love. Without Holy Love, no good can exist, only darkness. Therefore, souls who live according to their own will live contrary to Holy Love and salvation."

I asked Our Lady how can we tell if we're choosing God's Will. "God's Will for you is always Holy Love. And so, all your actions must be based on the two great commandments - Love God above all things and love your neighbor as yourself. You cannot be holy unless you live by these commandments. I cannot put holiness in simpler words. The path is now laid bare. Make this known!" She leaves.

■ **October 11, 1993.** Jesus says: "You can only be at peace if you are doing My Will and living according to Holy Love in thought, word and deed. Souls that reject Holy Love, reject Me."

■ **October 12, 1993.** *(5:30 p.m. – Adoration)* Our Lady was standing to one side of the altar as I prayed the rosary. She prayed the *Glory Be* with me. Then She said, "My child, I want to share with you a portion of the love I felt for Jesus when I carried Him in My womb. It is a love that overshadows all other desires and will not allow you to take an alternate path away from holiness. God's presence was always with Me as I carried My Son beneath My Heart. Therefore, I was never disturbed by trivialities of earth. I saw in each person I met the soul My Son would live and die for. I was embraced in Holy Love and I, in turn, embraced this love myself. If you love in this way, little child, you will be at peace and bring peace wherever you go. This is what all are called to. This Holy Love is in the refuge of My Immaculate Heart."

■ **October 14, 1993 / Thursday Rosary Service.** Our Lady is here as Our Lady of Fatima. She says: "All praise be to Jesus." I answered, "Now and forever." Then She says: "Pray with Me for all those who have been deceived by Satan and do not turn to prayer." We prayed. A private Message was given. Then Our Lady said: "Dear children, I come tonight to ask you to continue to pray for all My intentions. My intentions today are the same as they were when I appeared at Fatima. The serpent is on all sides preparing for war, and you must pursue the path of holiness with both feet and with your whole being. For now is the time to pray, pray, pray." She blessed us and left.

■ **October 14, 1993.** Our Lady is here in blue and white. She is holding a rosary. She says: "Let us give thanks and praise to Jesus Incarnate, for all He has given us." She raises Her hands and looks up to heaven. Together we praised Jesus, and She is bathed in a light, as She always is when She prays. She lowers Her hands and looks at me. "You see, little daughter, Jesus has allowed the Maranatha spring to be uncovered so that those who come will be strengthened in their faith. In this way, His remnant will be stronger and of firmer conviction. It will be easier for the remnant to attest to the true faith and withstand opposition. But not all that come will believe or even remain faithful to Church Tradition. The apostasy is Satan's last attempt at destroying My Son's Church. But the spring will dilute the adversary's potent lies against the faith. Please be at peace." She leaves.
Read Amos 9

■ **October 17, 1993.** Our Lady is here. She is dressed as Our Lady of Fatima and says: "All praise be to Jesus." I replied, "Now and forever." She says: "Let us pray now for those who have chosen the path of perdition." We prayed the *Our Father* and *Glory Be*. Then Our Lady said: "Dear children, I have come tonight to invite you to understand that My invitation to holiness is not singular, but from moment to moment. You must surrender your will to the Will of the Father and, in so doing, proceed along the path that I call you upon, that leads to My Immaculate Heart the Refuge of sinners." Our Lady blessed us and left.

■ **October 19, 1993.** Our Lady came in gray and gold. She said: "Let us glorify God through this prayer." She parted Her hands and raised them to heaven. As we prayed the *Glory Be*, angels supported her. She was completely absorbed in prayer. Then She looked at me and said, "My angel, please pick up your pen."

"Dear children, the path I call you upon moment to moment, the path of holiness that leads to My Heart, is the path of holy perfection. The tool and the measure given to attain this holy perfection is Holy Love. You will only be as perfect and as holy as you love. The obstacle to Holy Love and, consequently, holy perfection, is always self-love. Therefore, My dear children, in order to progress along the path of holiness - the path of holy perfection - you need to ask the Holy Spirit to reveal to you all the areas of self-love in your lives. Perhaps you love your reputation. Perhaps you love your ideas and opinions. Perhaps you love your appearance. None of these are lasting. Only Holy Love is eternal. Surrender to the Father all that self-love, so that He can fill you with Holy Love. Then you will be given a greater love of God and of souls. Then you will progress along the path of holiness to holy perfection."

■ **October 21, 1993 / Thursday Rosary Service.** Our Lady is here in blue and pink, and She says: "All praise, honor and glory be to Jesus." I replied, "Now and forever." Our Lady gave a private message, then said, "Please let us pray now for all those who have failed in holiness today." We prayed. Then She said, "Dear children, learn to live in the present moment, appreciating always that which is everlasting - the pursuit of holiness. Please comprehend, My dear little children, all that which you see, all that is around you is temporary and passing. Therefore, make holiness your only pursuit your only joy, and your only peace." She blessed us and left.

■ **October 22, 1993.** From Our Lady: "I render unto you the Refuge of My Heart, remedy of all affliction, safety against the foe."

■ **October 23, 1993.** *(Saturday Morning)* Our Lady came in a radiant light in white. "All praise, honor and glory be to Jesus, Redeemer and King." I answered, "Now and forever." She says: "My child, I invite you to realize that Satan's only entry into a soul is through any imperfection in Holy Love. Knowing this, I extend to you, and to humanity through you, this prayer:"

Prayer For Holy Love
"Dear Jesus, through the Immaculate Heart of Your Mother, perfect me this day in Holy Love! Keep me mindful that every thought, word and action should come from and lead to Holy Love. Bring me along the path of holiness by means of this love, so that by loving God and my neighbor, I will attain holy perfection. I ask this in Your Name, Lord Jesus. Amen."

■ **October 23, 1993.** Our Lady is here. Her Heart is exposed and She has tears coming out of Her Heart. She says: "All praise, honor and glory be to the Eucharistic Heart of My Son. My child, you need to penetrate the depths and the truths of My Heart, just as you need to penetrate the earth deeper to find the [Maranatha] spring. You need to be patient. You will know when you have reached the depths of My Heart, and you will be certain when you have found the spring."

■ **October 24, 1993.** *(11:30 a.m.)* Our Lady came in gray with a red lining in Her mantle. She spreads Her hands and says: "All praise be to Jesus. I am the Mother of Jesus crucified. My angel, My little child, I invite you to further understand in your heart that Holy Love is a selfless love. It opposes the world and self In like manner, holy perfection is a selfless perfection in that the soul chooses to perfect himself in holiness to please God. My daughter, as I, your Mother, stood beneath the cross, I suffered everything for love of God and for souls. I suffered this way in Holy Love and it was holy suffering. Holy suffering has no regard for self, but sees only what is being accomplished for souls. The more the soul is steeped in Holy Love, the more holy his suffering. So then, even at the darkest moment, the soul sees God's purpose and unites himself to God. I am showing you all of this in the light of truth so that as error spreads, as it will, you can be light to others. Pray for the love of souls."

■ **October 24, 1993 / Sunday Service.** Our Lady is here in blue and says, "All praise be to Jesus." I answered, "Now and forever." Then Our Lady said, "Pray with Me tonight, My dear children, for all those who do not love." We prayed an *Our Father* and *Glory Be.* Then Our Lady said, "The Remnant of the elect is constructed with the bricks of Holy Perfection, the mortar of which is Holy Love. All that comes against this Remnant is love of self. Little children, pray to love God and to love souls – this is the way to perfection. I am giving you My Motherly Blessing which is the Blessing of My Immaculate Heart." Then She left.

■ **October 25, 1993.** Our Lady comes as Our Lady of Holy Love. She says: "All praise to the crucified Jesus, Redeemer and King." She raises Her hands to heaven as She says this. Then She looks back to me. "My angel, it is important you comprehend the meaning of the 'Consecration to the Cross.' When you pray in this way, you are uniting all of your suffering, big and little, to Jesus on the cross. In this way you remove self from all your suffering. Then all your trials become holy suffering and have eternal value. Jesus has sent Me to tell you He wishes to make of you a particular sign to others of holy suffering. Therefore, learn to be a conduit between heaven and earth of redeeming grace. And in all of this, the remnant will be strengthened. This remnant will flourish in hearts that persevere in the true dogma of faith. If you do not persevere in holy suffering, Satan will sow confusion amongst those in the ministry. It will be easier for him to foster lies, and resentments will abound. Already he has infiltrated hearts that do not know Holy Love - hearts whose every motive is self-seeking. If you are strong, you will readily uncover him. I give you now My Heavenly Blessing."

■ **October 27, 1993.** Our Lady comes, but I can see only Her face. She says: "All praise be to Jesus." I answer, "Now and forever." "My little daughter, you are beginning to understand. There is a way of living and there is a way of living in holiness. There is love, and there is Holy Love. There is suffering, and there is holy suffering. There is patience, and there is holy patience - perfection, and holy perfection. The difference always being the willingness of the soul to practice the two great commandments: Love God above all else, and your neighbor as yourself. These two commandments separate the wheat from the chaff. These are the embodiment of the Ten Commandments - indeed the embodiment of holiness. To live contrary to these two greatest commandments is to leave the path of holiness that leads always to My Heart. Make it known!"

■ **October 28, 1993.** From Our Lady: "You're close to the source of the spring. You have only to probe further, and I have marked off the site of Maranatha. The front of the shrine can be designed by those in charge, for I have no preference. Only that the people be permitted to proceed on their knees at some point in prayer."

■ **October 28, 1993 / Thursday Rosary Service.** Our Lady

is here in gray with a pink gown and says: "All praise, honor and glory be to Jesus." I replied, "Now and forever." She said: "Pray with me, dear child for all priests, that their vocations be strengthened in Holy Love." We prayed. Our Lady gave a private message, then said, "Dear children, I come tonight to remind you to have recourse to My Immaculate Heart so that I can aid you in living in Holy Love. I want to lead you to the source of Holy Love, which is the Heart of My Son. He is the source of all good, all holiness, all love, all mercy. I am only a reflection of His most Sacred Heart. Come in confidence and I will lead you." She blessed us and left.

November 1993

■ **November 2, 1993.** *(5:10 a.m.)* Our Lady says, "All of the other virtues - holy humility, holy suffering, holy obedience, holy purity, holy patience, holy perfection - every virtue comes to naught without Holy Love. For it is through love of God and love of man, virtue becomes holy virtue. There is no virtue unless it is motivated by Holy Love."

■ **November 4, 1993.** *(Afternoon)* Our Lady comes in gray. She bows towards the Eucharist and moves towards me. She says: "All praise be to Jesus." I answer, "Now and forever." She says: "My little daughter, I come once again to invite you along the path of holiness. To choose holiness is to begin to practice holiness, which is Holy Love. When you once begin to turn to holiness, God will give you the grace that you need to succeed. Holy Love, My daughter, is God's Will for you, and His Divine Will is Holy Love. They are one and the same. God will always extend to you the grace you need to cooperate with His Will, and so with Divine and Holy Love. Please understand, all that has happened to you so far in your life has been ordained or permitted as a means of drawing you along the path of holiness and deeper into My Heart. Let this be the moment you begin your 'yes' to Holy Love, and so, God's Will for you. Say 'yes' in a way that you are able to choose holy forgiveness. Forgive your own imperfections and forgive others' faults, as well. If you begin to choose this, God will help you through the grace of My Heart. Every thought contrary to Holy Love has its origin in evil. Make all of this known!"

Read John 4:34-38 and John 15:1-17

■ **November 4, 1993.** Padre Pio came before Our Lady. He told the visionary, "If you are praying for someone for conversion, pray to the soul's guardian angel. Ask their guardian angel to immerse their soul in DIVINE MERCY."

■ **November 4, 1993 / Thursday Rosary Service - Message To Priests.** Our Lady is here in white and gold and says: "All praise be to Jesus." I replied, "Now and forever." Then She said, "My daughter, please pray with Me for all priests and religious who lack confidence in their vocations." We prayed. Then Our Lady said: "To My dear priest sons, I respectfully suggest they must uncover evil around them, for in every instance, to avoid this is to sanction this. Dear children, I come tonight most especially to invite you to continue along the path of holiness you are being called upon. The Alpha and the Omega of this path, this path of holiness and of Holy Love, is Divine Love." She blessed us and left.

■ **November 5, 1993.** Our Lady is here in white and says: "All praise, honor and glory be to Jesus." I replied, "Now and forever." She says: "Pray with Me now for those who have not chosen the Will of God in their lives." We prayed. Then She said, "Dear children, I wish to infuse into your souls Holy and Divine Love so that you will be better instruments in My hands. Give to Me all your misgivings and imperfections." She blessed us and left.

Then, as I rested in the spirit, I saw [in a vision] a number of white tongues that were at the feet of Our Lady. Then I saw these tongues come together to form a flaming sword. Then Our Lady said that the water in the spring would be a decisive force against evil and would separate the wheat from the chaff, the remnant from the apostasy.

■ **November 6, 1993.** *(Locution from Jesus)* "Messenger of She who bore Me, I come to appeal to the hearts of all humanity. It is through Divine Love that the little way of Holy Love is given. This little way of Holy Love is the path of holiness laid bare for these times. Once called upon, as all are, the soul should make himself little - God and his neighbor big."

"This is the path that circumvents evil and the most intricate plans of Satan. This holy simplicity finds its way as a flaming arrow to My Divine Heart, burning in its wake all self-love. Then, in Divine Love, I can mold the soul into a true instrument of grace to bear witness in the world to the truth. How I love the souls that pursue this path! It is the 'yes' of this age that will bring about My Eucharistic Reign. It is the triumphant chorus of the remnant. It is the path of victory of My Mother's Immaculate Heart. Make this known!"

■ **November 6, 1993.** Jesus says: "Divine Love is God in your midst. Holy Love is a reflection of Divine Love and a foretaste of heaven. My remnant church is being molded in Holy Love. Hearts that are thus formed will find their peace in Me. Though they will suffer, it will be holy suffering and I will be their strength."

■ **November 7, 1993 / Sunday Rosary Service.** Our Lady is here in red and gold and has a cross around Her neck. She says: "All praise be to Jesus." I replied, "Now and forever." She says: "Pray with Me now for all souls in darkness." We prayed. Our Lady gave a private message. Then She said, "Dear children, tonight I come especially to invite you anew upon the path of holiness. I desire very much that you lay bare this path to others. Do not hold My messages to you captive in your hearts." She blessed us and left.

■ **November 8, 1993.** Our Lady is here with Her Heart exposed. She says: "I am Mary, Ever-Virgin, Mother of Jesus the Prince of Peace. All praise be unto Him." I answer, "Now and forever." She says: "My angel, multiply by a trillion what you feel today for *(blank)* and you will know a fraction of the anguish I feel for souls who choose darkness. Do not let his failure be your failure. Come to know, there will always be opposition to every good until Satan is defeated. But half the battle is won when you recognize the adversary at work. The victory is won when you pray against the evil. God always has a plan to overcome evil. Sometimes, much can be accomplished just by offering up not knowing God's plans in advance. This trust in God's provision can save many souls. If I can console you further, it is to say that *(blank's)* choices, have not been your choices for him. So do not let his failure be your failure. And this maxim holds true in all interpersonal relationships. Guilt is Satan at work. Prayer is grace at work. I encourage you to pray, pray, pray."

■ **November 9, 1993.** *(To Our Lady's Prayer Group)* Our Lady came dressed all in white and is holding a fifteen-decade rosary. She says: "All praise be to Jesus." I replied, "Now and forever." She spoke to me privately, then asked me to pray with Her for our countries' leaders. We prayed. Then She said, "Dear children, tonight I invite you to understand the Rosary is your armor. You are letting your personal opinions and habits take over your lives, instead of your prayers. Remember, Christ is the Center of your lives. If He isn't, then Satan is." She blessed us and left.

■ **November 11, 1993.** All at once I saw St. John Bosco delivering a sermon. "My brothers and sisters in Christ, it is only through forgiveness that we are led on the path of holiness and brought deeper into the Heart of Jesus. Forgiveness summons forth God's mercy and so His love. Then He is pleased to lead the soul according to His Divine Will since there is nothing to hinder Him. Unforgiveness is like a cloak of darkness, shrouding the soul from passing into light and truth. Pray that the Holy Spirit lead you in forgiveness of others and forgiveness of yourself, so that this foreboding obstacle to holiness be forever removed from your life."

■ **November 13, 1993.** Our Lady comes with many stars around her. She says: "All praise be to Jesus." I answer, "Now and forever." She asks me to pray first with Her for the remnant church, then for all the lukewarm souls who, She says, "do not realize the path they follow slips to perdition." Then She asks me to pray with Her for all cardinals, bishops and priests, most especially those who make "conscious decisions each day against faith and morals." Then She says: "My daughter, the remnant church will take its structure within the ark of My Immaculate Heart. Already, the apostasy has formed in hearts that compromise Church Tradition according to their own whims. These souls place their own will above God's Will which, in the end, will be their condemnation. Even as I speak to you the hour has struck and God's arm of justice descends toward earth. This justice will expiate every abomination and will be complete in its coming."

"But you have nothing to fear if you pursue holiness with every breath. Holiness is the vindication offered a beleaguered world. Therefore, My little daughter, it is necessary that you remove every distraction from your daily routine, insofar as is possible. Be attentive to the voice of the Holy Spirit. Do everything in Holy Love for the sake of holiness. Then God, in His mercy, will take what He needs from you and add what He sees you need from Him. I am ever your Refuge in heaven and on earth. I come from Love to bring you to love, and so to joy and peace."

■ **November 14, 1993.** *(Locution from Our Lady)* "Dear children, today I invite you to understand that when you are relying completely on the grace of My Heart you are the strongest. It is then that you are in the Refuge of My Immaculate Heart, and I am using you in My plan of salvation. Comprehend, My children, the great love the Father has for you that He would invite you to such a call."

■ **November 14, 1993 / Sunday Rosary Service.** Our Lady is here dressed all in white, and was holding in Her extended arms a large gold key. Then She said, "All praise be to Jesus." I replied, "Now and forever." Our Lady gave a private message, then said, "Pray with Me now for the bishops." We prayed. Then She said, "Dear children, your prayers are as a bridge of light which crosses the abyss between heaven and earth. You do not see their strength or know their power. You also do not see the great opposition Satan thrusts into your lives to destroy the peace in your souls, so that you cannot pray. Let your hearts be like flowers that open to the sun, so that God can fill them with peace and love and joy." She blessed us and left.

■ **November 16, 1993.** Our Lady comes in gray. She says: "All praise be to Jesus." I say, "Now and forever." "Please understand, My daughter, Satan does not come into your life as himself, but in the guise of others' needs, others' judgments, others' anger. Anything that attacks your peace is not from God, but from the adversary." Here I was distracted and She left.

■ **November 18, 1993.** *(Morning)* Our Lady comes in white. She says: "All praise be to Jesus." I answer, "Now and forever." "My angel, do not judge yourself so harshly. Let God be your judge. Relinquish to Jesus all the imperfections in your family. Let the incense of your soul be Holy Love so that it is evident to all around you. Let Holy Love pour from you, engulf you and become you. I am forever your intercessor before the throne of God. I impart to you My Motherly Blessing."

■ **November 18, 1993 / Message To The World.** "Dear children, tonight I invite you to realize that the division in the Church which fast approaches is already the division that is in hearts. It is the choice that is not a choice. It is the division between Church dogma and Traditions, and contemporary opinions. Make it known."
Read Ephesians 4: 14-16

■ **November 18, 1993 / Thursday Rosary Service.** Our Lady is here in white and says: "All Praise be to Jesus." I answered, "Now and forever." She says: "My angel, please join Me in prayer for all governments who are deceived by Satan." We prayed. Then Our Lady said: "Dear children, I invite you once again to abandon sin and pursue the path of holiness. For it is only through holiness that salvation comes. I need your prayers, dear children, for they are My weapons against all evil, and all which takes you off the path of holiness." She blessed us and left.

■ **November 19, 1993.** Our Lady comes in white. She says: "Praise be to Jesus, My angel." I say, "Now and forever." She says: "Please do not despair the decisions made by others. For while they are offered life and choose death, there are those who choose life and are put to death (now She is weeping tears of blood), and slavery to atheistic points of view presented as freedom has become the government's undoing in the majority of nations."

■ **November 20, 1993.** *(Locution from Jesus)* "God is Divine Love. Holy Love is the imitation of Divine Love. In order to practice Holy Love, you must emulate all the other virtues, for it is impossible to possess Holy Love and not the other virtues. The sanctification of a soul comes from the Great Sanctifier, the Holy Spirit Himself. To practice Holy Love is to open our hearts to the Holy Spirit and so to sanctification."

■ **November 20, 1993.** Our Lady is here in white and says: "Praise be to Jesus." I replied, "Now and forever." She has these flowers that are cascading down in front of her. The ones that are closer to Her Heart are larger, then they get smaller as they go down. She says: "This is to illustrate the farther you are from My Heart, the weaker the grace, and so when you depend on the grace of My Heart you are receiving all you need. I am using each of you as tabernacles of My messages on holiness, and I desire that you spread this message and be this message to all you meet. For it is here the grain will be separated, the wheat from the chaff; those who choose holiness and those who choose not to abandon sin; those who decide for the true faith, those who decide for contemporary opinion." She's showing me a long path of people - some are traveling straight, some to the right and some to the left. She says: "Only the path that goes to My Heart leads to the Heart of My Son." She blessed us and left.

■ **November 21, 1993.**
First Step To Holiness
I heard the angels say, "Our Lady is here." I looked up and saw Our Lady in pink and white. She said: "Praise be to Jesus." I said, "Now and forever." Our Lady said: "My little daughter, I have come to infuse into your heart knowledge which you are incapable of grasping at this time. It is so the call to holiness will be complete that Jesus sends to humanity through His Mother. Each step you will be shown in subsequent messages will be complete in its entirety. Today, I invite you to open your heart as I reveal the first and tantamount step in holiness."

"The first step in any journey is the person's choosing to take the journey. And so it is with My call to holiness. The soul must choose holiness. This decision is a progressive choice and yet it begins anew each day, each moment, indeed, with each breath the soul takes. This decision for holiness is the umbilical cord that links the soul to My Heart, which is Holy Love. My Heart is Holy Love (holiness). My Beloved Son's Heart is Divine Love. When the soul chooses Holy Love, he chooses to be in the Refuge of his heavenly Mother's Heart. Do not be distressed if you do not understand all I am revealing to you at this time. I do invite you to comprehend, My child, there is no salvation outside of Holy Love. Holy Love is holiness. Make all of this known!"

■ **November 21, 1993 / Sunday Rosary Service.** Our Lady is here in gray and has many angels with her, and she's weeping. She says: "All praise be to Jesus." I replied, "Now and forever." Then She said, "My sorrow is that the strength of My Son's Church is hidden in disbelief and scorned, so pray with Me now for those who do not believe in His Real Presence." We prayed. Then Our Lady composed herself and said, "Dear children, tonight I invite you to understand that grace and free will must blend together in order for a soul to say 'yes' to holiness. Little children, pray that souls will consent to holiness." She blessed us and left.

■ **November 25, 1993.**
Second Step To Holiness
Our Lady comes in white and pink. She looks down at me. Her mantle is blowing as the air stirs. She says: "My daughter, let us give all praise, honor and glory to Jesus." I say, "Now and forever." "Understand, My daughter, the guardian of the soul is free will. Through free will the mind, heart, senses and members make decisions from moment to moment for

or against holiness. When the soul chooses to be holy, he must at the same time choose to abandon sin. Sin is anything contrary to Holy Love. It is holy wisdom that enables the soul to see the value of holiness and to choose for Holy Love. I am opening the grace of My Heart upon humanity that more will choose for salvation, and sin will be purged from their lives. Make it known."

■ **November 25, 1993.** She has a globe of the world around Her neck, suspended by two chains. Our Lady says: "You see these chains that hold the world close to the grace of My Heart. One of these is the Rosary. The other is faith-filled reception of the Eucharist. Both of these chains are weakened the more the soul chooses his own will over the will of God. I invite you today to understand the portal to Holy Love and holiness is free will."

■ **November 25, 1993.** Our Lady comes in white and pink at the end of a Holy Hour. She says: "To Jesus, the praise and the glory." I say, "Now and forever." "My daughter, it is important to realize that the world is being lulled to sleep by a false sense of peace. For what appears as secure is, in reality uneasy. Errors are multiplied by errors in the Church and in hearts. Prayer is more important today than yesterday, as any appeal to you is itself more urgent. This is a war only won by consecrated lives of faith. For this reason, Satan comes against faith on all sides and tries to chase Holy Love from hearts. You will need to be a bastion of faith, hope and love in the future, and so prepare now. Put all doubts to rest, realizing the course of My call. Bring Me souls through the strength of your prayers. I am bringing those to you for you to comfort. Remember, the key to the future is trust in the present moment."

■ **November 27, 1993 / Saturday Rosary Service.** Our Lady is here as Our Lady of Grace. She says: "All praise, honor and glory be to Jesus." I answered her, "Now and forever." She says: "Pray with Me now for those who do not follow the path of salvation." And we prayed an *Our Father* and *Glory Be*. She's turning to the people here and She says: "Pray much for the souls in darkness, who surround them in their daily lives. Pray and trust. Your prayers will be heard. Dear children, tonight I come especially to remind you that you live in an age of Advent, preparing for My Son's Second Coming. As you prepare for this Christmas, offer each day small sacrifices as straws in the manger; and on Christmas, He will truly flood your heart with grace. And I am blessing you now with My Motherly Blessing."

■ **November 27, 1993.** *(Locution from Jesus)* "All hearts will be made whole and be made one at the [Maranatha] spring if they come in faith."

■ **November 27, 1993.** Our Lady comes on a cloud. She is in bluish-gray. She spreads Her hands and says: "It is time to set all foolish goals aside and pursue holiness. All praise be to Jesus." I say, "Now and forever." Our Lady says: "Consider the goal of heaven - to bring all hearts together in the peace of the Refuge of My Heart. My daughter, all else pales in comparison. My plea to humanity now is more strong, more urgent than ever before in the history of man. Only pray that ears and hearts open in response to the grace that now waters earth in its every need." Throughout the vision there is something written beneath Her feet that I cannot make out. I ask Her now what it is. She says: "The word is 'Maranatha' (Aramaic for 'Come, Lord Jesus.')." She blesses me and leaves.

■ **November 28, 1993.**
Third Step To Holiness
From Our Lady: "I want to take you deeper into My Heart

to renew your soul and refresh your spirit. Little daughter, let us give praise to the living Christ, present in the Sacrament of the Altar. My daughter, to choose holiness is to choose God's Will and to abandon your own will. The soul abandons his own will and chooses God's will when he chooses to love in thought, word and deed. It is one step, and yet it is many steps each day. Every grace of My Heart comes from and leads towards the Will of the Father. For I am the gateway to holiness and to the Will of the Father."

■ **November 28, 1993.** *(Early Morning)* "Do not lend heed to doubt or discouragement." I turn over and see Our Lady. She says: "All praise be to Jesus." I answer, "Now and forever." She shows me a field of grain. The grain parts [separates] and there is a little weed growing in the midst of the grain. Our Lady says: "This is how Satan plants doubts. They begin small and grow bigger. His [Satan's] plan being to choke out My work at the House of Prayer. Always the malefactor comes to twist and deceive and cause misunderstanding concerning My messages. But I am sending angels to pluck him from your midst, so that the harvest will ripen and flourish. In all you suffer, unite it to Jesus on the cross. Never forget your vocation to bring souls with you along the path of holiness, and so to the benevolent and merciful Heart of My Divine Son."

■ **November 29, 1993.** Jesus says: "Everyone has the same opportunity for grace. It depends upon their response to the graces in their lives as to the amount and depth of graces given on a continuing basis. So then, when you pray for the conversion of souls, pray that they respond to the graces in their lives."

■ **November 29, 1993.** Our Lady comes in white, with many gold stars all over Her mantle. As She speaks, I understand in My heart that every nation of the world is represented by one of these stars. She bows to the Eucharist and turns to me, saying, "All praise to Jesus, truly present in the Most Holy Sacrament of the Altar." I say, "Now and forever." "My little child, please realize your Mother's most urgent need. That is the salvation of every soul. It is My prayer that when the great universal moment of truth comes, souls will open their hearts to this grace. Make this your petition, as well." She blesses me and leaves.

December 1993

■ **December 1, 1993.**
Fourth Step To Holiness
From Our Lady: "My daughter, I am the Mother of Mercy and of Holy Love. All praise be to Jesus." I answer, "Now and forever." "This, My little child, is the final step in holiness. When the soul is able to surrender his will to the Will of God, he is on the path of holiness. Then the soul makes his will one with God's Will. He accepts everything in the present moment as the Will of the Eternal Father. He views the past and the future only in terms of Holy Love, trusting in Divine Providence which is perfect in God's Will. Every sin opposes Holy Love and God's Will, and distracts the soul from the path of holiness. Therefore, ask for the grace of seeing your sins more clearly and you will better be able to avoid these pitfalls. Make this known."

■ **December 1, 1993.** *(Locution from Jesus)* "I need you to mark this down. I come in this way, in these times, to tell you a moment of decision is fast approaching. All will be given knowledge of their sins. Those who do not recognize this as My Mercy pouring out on humanity will not be reconciled with Me. It is most important that you make this known!"

■ **December 2, 1993.** *(Locution from Our Lady / Strong scent of roses)* "This is My last significant apparition site. These are the last significant messages extended to humanity. For this reason, My little child, it is important these messages be put in book form so that their distribution be more prolific. I am the Mother of All Mercy, the Mother of All Love. Praise be to Jesus."

■ **December 2, 1993 / First Thursday Rosary Service - Message To Priests.** Our Lady is here in white and Her mantle is lined in pink. She says: "All praise be to Jesus." I reply, "Now and forever." She says: "Please thank everyone for coming tonight to pray with me. Pray with Me now for souls who make gods of their own will, and so are not at peace." We prayed. "To My dear priest sons: I ask that they always keep their eyes on My Son, for His Will for them is the true dogma of faith. If their foot slips from the path to the left, they find the weeds of apostasy; to the right, the thorns of disbelief and many rocks which represent popular opinion. But I am calling them to support the true dogma of faith as it stands under Church Tradition as handed down through John Paul II. Anything else is from Satan."

"To those here tonight: Dear children, tonight I come once again to ask you to make your will the Will of God, by accepting the present moment in Holy Love, and I leave you with My Motherly Blessing."
Read Luke 8:4-8, 11-15

[Note: Our Lady's Motherly Blessing is "a blessing of Holy Love which will enable you to live in this virtue." (01/24/94)]

■ **December 3, 1993.** Our Lady comes seated on a throne. "Let us give praise to Jesus." I say, "Now and forever." She says: "My dear little daughter, I have come today to ask you to tell everyone that too much emphasis is being placed on what is to come by God's hand of justice. People need to concern themselves with what is eternal and not what is passing. All that souls accomplish towards holiness lives forever. This is why Jesus sends me to seek publication in book form of my messages leading souls to holiness. He wants this widely circulated in book stores, and promoted both here and in other countries. The hour grows late and the need for this book is manifest by the evil which pervades earth. Therefore, I come as a mother with a final plea to Her errant children. Please make this known."

■ **December 3, 1993.** *(9:30 p.m.)* Our Lady is here on a cloud. She has on a gown and mantle that are two different shades of purple, and a white veil. She had an archangel with her. She says: "All praise be to Jesus." I answered, "Now and forever." She's looking at all of us and says: "Pray with Me now for the remnant." We prayed. "My daughter, you need not fear now, for many doors and corridors which have remained closed to you in the past will now open and God's messenger [an angel] will take My words to you to the farthest point of earth. Use all My messages concerning holiness. Make prudent use of time. Do not go over past messages. I am calling many from all points, and this will be the center for many graces." She blessed us and left.

■ **December 4, 1993.** Our Lady is here in two shades of blue and white, and She says: "Praise be to Jesus." I answered, "Now and forever." She asks me to pray with Her for those who are not discerning God's Will in their lives. We prayed. She has this sash around Her waist that has stars on it. She says: "They represent the countries of the world, and that the ones farthest from My Heart are receiving less grace, because they have not pleased God and they have chosen atheistic legislation." Then She says: "Dear children, tonight I invite you to understand that as you prepare for Advent you must also prepare your hearts for My Son's Second Coming. I wish for all of you to become apostles of love, living and spreading My message of Holy Love to the world, thereby converting hearts." Our Lady blessed us and left.

■ **December 5, 1993.** "People who come here will be

spiritually hungry. I will feed them with the grace of My Heart. The grace will multiply according to their response to My call to holiness."

■ **December 5, 1993.** Our Lady comes as the Mother of Holy Love. She says: "Give praise to Jesus, who is Holy Love." I say, "Now and forever." She gives a private message, and then says: "Further, I come to encourage you in holy trust, which is the way to faith in all that is God's Will. I am building a temple in the recesses of My Heart composed of every fragment of the remnant Church. It is in My Heart I will instruct and guide them through you, and so do not concern yourself with details on how the path will be laid. My Heart is eternal. Many areas of earth will be consumed by the fire of the Holy Spirit, and safe will be the Refuge of My Heart. I am putting many things in place to begin what Jesus asks in love."

■ **December 8, 1993 - Feast of the Immaculate Conception.** From Our Lady: "My children, I am calling you to a deeper understanding of Holy Love, so that you will know better the Father's Will. Holy Love desires holiness for everyone. It does not injure in thought, word or deed. It prescribes no action against love of God and neighbor. It harbors no contempt. Holy Love needs to be all-consuming and inspiring. The way to Holy Love is through the door of the soul, which is free will. It is surrendering your will until it becomes one with God's Will."

■ **December 9, 1993 / Thursday Rosary Service.** Our Lady is here in white and gold and says: "Praise be to Jesus." I replied, "Now and forever." She says: "Thank you for surrendering your will. This surrender is sweet and will save many souls." Our Lady gave a Private message. Then She said, "Dear children, I desire every nation be reconciled to the Will of God through Holy Love, and so I will facilitate the spreading of My words to you throughout the world. Every heart is important. Jesus desires every soul find the path of holiness that leads to salvation. Therefore, little children, continue to pray, pray, pray." Our Lady blessed us and left.

■ **December 11, 1993.** I saw Our Lady in gray. She was holding a globe of earth in front of her. Half of the world was all dark. The other half was light. Then I saw that the half that was light was being illuminated by Her Immaculate Heart. Our Lady said: "An eclipse of darkness is grasping and embracing the world." (I thought by darkness She meant evil.) She continued, "But see how the souls that pursue the refuge of My Heart will remain in the light. Praise be to Jesus."

■ **December 12, 1993 - Feast of Our Lady of Guadalupe / Sunday Rosary Service.** Our Lady is here as Our Lady of Guadalupe. The stars on Her mantle look like lights. She said: "Praise be to Jesus, My angel." I replied, "Now and forever." Our Lady then said, "Pray with Me now for those who do not choose life." We prayed. Then Our Lady said: "Dear children, choose always Holy Love in every moment and you will be in Father's Will. Remember, His Provision is always perfect. Therefore, you need not fear the future. Let Holy Love be the measure of your every thought, word, and action." She blessed us and left.

■ **December 13, 1993.** *(Locution from Jesus)* "The reason people do not trust is they do not know My strength and My power. If they believed in My omnipotence, they would trust Me."

■ **December 15, 1993.** I saw many angels coming from the Eucharist, floating towards me and past me with what seemed to be pieces of bread. Then I saw Our Lady come towards me holding a loaf of bread. She said: "Let us give praise to Jesus." I said, "Now and forever" She said: "This is your daily bread. It is all the grace you need towards Holy Love in the present moment. It is the strength you derive from the Eucharist, the peace you receive through prayer. Let it permeate your soul as yeast permeates this bread, and swell your soul with Holy Love, so that everywhere you go the fragrance of grace is spread."

■ **December 16, 1993 / Thursday Service - Message To The World.** Our Lady came in gray and a cream color and Her Immaculate Heart was exposed. She said: "Praise be to Jesus." I replied, "Now and forever." I recommended to Her all those who had asked for special prayers. She said: "This was in My Heart before the petition formed on their lips." Then She asked me to pray with Her for those petitions. We did. Then She said, "Dear children, tonight I invite you to be warriors of Holy Love. Spread Holy Love wherever you go, by word and by example. For I tell you that nations shall march against nations, and one country will skirmish for boundaries against another country. But God's justice comes without discretion to every area of earth. Therefore, little children, pray, pray, pray." She blessed us and left.

■ **December 17, 1993.** Our Lady is here in pink and blue, and says: "All praise be to Jesus." I answered, "Now and forever." She says: "Whenever you gather consecrate yourselves to the Cross ['Consecration to the Cross' prayer]. It is in this way that you will come to love the Cross as My Son desires. Pray with Me now for those who are not attracted to holiness." We prayed. Then Our Lady said: "My children, it is important that you realize the remnant must gather in My Heart, Refuge of all sinners, just as the shepherds gathered next to the manger on the first Christmas. For it is in My Heart, and only in My Heart, you will be able to reach the pinnacle of holiness, which I tell you today is love of God's Will for you. This is what will see you through every trial, every disaster." She blessed us and left.

■ **December 18, 1993.** An archangel was here first and was holding up a book that said - *Be of stout heart, prompt to forgive and slow to anger.* Now Our Lady is here in white and says: "Praise be to Jesus, My angel." She says: "I've come to ask for prayers for the world situation, which is deteriorating as we speak." We prayed. Now she's turning to the pilgrims and says: "I invite you to persevere in all you pray for. Heaven is attentive to your prayers. Dear children, tonight I come to invite you to the pinnacle of Holy Love, which is love of God's Will for you. Few reach this way of holiness. All that is needed is the grace of My Heart and practice in the present moment of Holy Love." She blessed us and left.

■ **December 19, 1993.** Jesus says: "I am calling the remnant to unite in the unadulterated Refuge of My Mother's Heart. It is here they can cling to the true dogma of faith and stand away from Satan's confusion."

■ **December 21, 1993.** *(3 a.m.)* From Our Lady: "There is no salvation outside of Holy Love. This is the truth My Son came to earth to reveal. All praise be to Jesus, the Word Made Flesh."

■ **December 22, 1993.** *(10:45 a.m.)* Our Lady is here in gray with a white veil over Her head, and She has Her hands extended with a pearl-colored rosary in one hand. She says: "All praise be to Jesus." I reply, "Now and forever." Then Our Lady said: "My little daughter, I come to extend to mankind the invitation of understanding the benevolence of My Son's Divine Heart. It is a great grace that He comes to Seven Hills, and that He sends His Mother to Seven Hills to instruct and to guide the remnant Church. I will draw pilgrims here, through the grace of My Heart from all points of Earth, and you will see many changes. Begin to understand the extent of My call, the timeliness, and the call to love that Jesus sends Me with. Through Holy Love, I am calling all of My children into

My Immaculate Heart, solemn Refuge of the True Dogma of Faith of the Roman Catholic Church. Make it known!"

■ **December 22, 1993.** *(4:45 a.m.)* "Please write down what I have come to tell you. Let all the world give praise to Jesus." Our Lady is here in gold and white. "Dear children, in order to uncover Satan in the world, it is necessary to uncover him first in your own lives. The adversary is everywhere. He is in all self-love. He is in every thought, word, or action that is contrary to Holy Love. He opposes your every effort in this regard, trying to obstruct your journey on the path of holiness. Therefore, little children, you must live in Holy Love in the present moment. This will require effort and a conscious choice, as your will becomes Holy Love." She leaves.

■ **December 23, 1993.** Our Lady is here in pink, gray and gold. She says: "Praise be to Jesus." I answer, "Now and forever." She says: "I have come tonight to tell you how to make your Christmas especially pleasing to My Son. I invite you to make of your hearts a manger where My beloved Son can take up His rest. Just as the star was a beacon in the night for the wise men and shepherds, let your souls be light in the darkness drawing souls to My Son. Let your gifts of gold, frankincense and myrrh be your prayers and sacrifices towards peace in the world. Then, My dear children, your Christmas will be a gift to My Son. I impart to each one of you My Motherly Blessing."

■ **December 25, 1993 – Christmas Morning.** *(5:55 a.m.)* *(Locution from Jesus)* "The path (of holiness) is strewn with obstacles, all of which are pride in various disguises. But when a soul pursues holiness with sincerity, he has everything."

■ **December 25, 1993 – Christmas Day.** After Communion, I saw Our Lady in an interior vision. She had on gold and white, and was holding the Infant Jesus. She handed me the Infant.

As She did, I saw that a silhouette of the Infant had been left on Her gown where She held Him against her. The silhouette was in blood. Our Lady said: "This represents what My Son suffers in the Blessed Sacrament, those who are martyred for the faith, and those who die in abortions."

■ **December 26, 1993.** *(After Communion)* Jesus says: "When the soul chooses to love as I commanded, he chooses holiness. Love and holiness are one and the same. Therefore, anything contrary to love is contrary to holiness. Make it known."

■ **December 26, 1993.** Our Lady is here in white and gold, and has the Baby Jesus in Her arms. Saint Joseph is here also, standing to Our Lady's right. She says: "All praise be to Jesus." Then She said, "Pray with Me for poor sinners." We prayed. Then Our Lady said: "Dear children, I invite you here tonight especially to make known the Refuge of My Immaculate Heart, the resting place of all souls. God desires that you make known this Refuge, the peace and the trust herein. For it is only by God's grace that you accomplish anything. Alone you are nothing; in My Refuge you are the strongest. I impart to each of you now, My Motherly Blessing."

■ **December 27, 1993.** Our Lady is here in white and holding a rosary. She says: "Praise be to Jesus." I answer, "Now and forever." Our Lady says: "When you are uniting your will to God's Will you are pursuing the path of holiness. It pleases Me to see you accept this. The world is about to experience every kind of misfortune. Your country will experience political and economic upheavals such as it has never known, and chaos will ensue. But those who have chosen the path of holiness and pursue it in the midst of misfortune will be at peace. I was sending many to the House of Prayer who are in the midst of turmoil, all because they are not trusting, and they do not see God's Will for them. Grace will come to them, and the House of Prayer will be a balm of peace for many."

"Do not be distressed over your own situation, which I tell you is in the hands of God, Who even now foresees the outcome. Once again I draw you to the reality of the present moment. It is in the present moment that you will find God's presence most profoundly affecting your life and that of those around you. Therefore, I implore you, prayerfully seek the path of holiness in the midst of each new trial. Love and pray."

■ **December 30, 1993.** Our Lady is here in gray and white and says: "All praise be to Jesus." She gave a private message, then said, "I am asking prayers now for all countries who have not seen the path of holiness, or worse, do not choose to follow it." We prayed. Then Our Lady said: "Dear children, I come tonight to encourage you once again along the path of holiness, the path which the Father has laid for you from the beginning of time. To pursue holiness is to act upon the gifts of faith, hope and love infused in your souls at Baptism. Practice these gifts, My dear children, for they are your salvation." She blessed us and left.

■ **December 31, 1993 - New Year's Eve.** From Our Lady: "Dear children, as you begin the new year adoring My Jesus lying in the manger, I have come to ask that you surrender completely to holiness, by abandoning everything that is prideful. Holy Love, which is holiness, is the opposite of self-love, which Satan makes so attractive. Think only good of each other. Love each other as you love yourselves. This is the path of conversion and peace. I have come to ask the world to recognize and to choose. This is the year when indecision is decision. My Heart will triumph through your 'yes' to Holy Love. If you choose holiness you are already defeating Satan, who wants every soul to fall into perdition. I am imparting to each one of you My Motherly Blessing and special grace to help you to choose each minute good over evil." She motions towards Her Immaculate Heart with both hands, then leaves.

■ **December 31, 1993.** *(Second Message)* Our Lady is here again in white. She's radiant. She's bending over me and says: "Let us give praise to Jesus. My little daughter, I have come once again to reveal to you the sure path of holiness. Holiness is love in the present moment, loving God above all else and neighbor as self. What hinders the soul from the path of holiness is pride. Pride is from Satan, pride is self-love. When the soul can surrender the past to love, and the future to love, and live in love, he is holy. Make it known."

Messages of Holy *and* Divine Love

1994

January 1994

■ **January 1, 1994.**

Holiness

Our Lady was here in pink and said, "All praise be to Jesus. My little angel, I see your eagerness to pray much for the conversion of Russia and hearts around the world. Therefore, I reveal to you My Special intention and I ask your prayers for it. I desire very much that My messages to you, revealing the path of holiness, be made known around the world. Satan vehemently opposes this, as he opposes all spiritual growth. Therefore, My little daughter, pray often for this intention, that My messages to you revealing the path of light be made known around the world. Make it known.

■ **January 1, 1994 / Saturday Rosary Service.** Our Lady came with many roses. She said: "The new year holds many opportunities for grace. Let us give praise to Jesus." I said, "Now and forever." She continues, "Dear children, today, on My feast, I invite you to understand that My words to you are a thread in the tapestry that is the Triumph of My Heart, just as your prayers are. Satan opposes the publication and dissemination of My messages leading souls to holiness. Therefore, it is My special intention that you pray that all obstacles in this regard are overcome. I am drawing all souls to the Refuge of My Heart, solemn sanctuary of Holy Love. Each of you has a special part to play in this Divine Plan. Make it known."

■ **January 3, 1994.** Our Lady is here wearing a blue a blue gown and white veil. Her Heart is exposed and She says, "Praise be to Jesus. You are experiencing the coldness that is in hearts." (There was no heat in the Old Schoolhouse - temperature at 20 degrees.) "Which combined with the value of your prayers and your meritorious sacrifices, melts away the ice that is around hearts. Pray with me now for hearts to decide to change." We prayed. She continued, "Dear children, your sacrifices to Me are as priceless treasures. I need them to change the course of human events, for unless hearts change, the world will bring about its own chastisement. I ask you tonight to give Me extra prayers and sacrifices, so that hearts will change and governments will be swayed. It is My Message to you on Holy Love that can change the world. Therefore, My little children, pray that it is propagated. I am blessing you now." She leaves.

■ January 6, 1994 / Thursday Rosary Service.
Call To Conversion

Our Lady is here in peach and white. She says: "All praise be to Jesus, My little angel." I replied, "Now and forever." Then Our Lady said, "Pray with me, please, this evening for souls who have heard My message of Holy Love but have not held it in their hearts and pursued the path of holiness." We prayed. Then Our Lady said: "Dear children, tonight I invite you to realize that conversion is the first step of holiness. Not all souls that are converted pursue the path of holiness and of Holy Love. Therefore, My little children, I ask you to keep in your hearts My special intention that all souls find and pursue the path of holiness. Pray, pray, pray." She blessed us and left.

Read Luke 8:4-8, 11-15

■ January 6, 1994.
Our Lady came in gray and gold. She asked if I slept well. She then asked me to pray with Her for the remnant Church. She said: "Some will leave it and fall into compromise." We prayed an *Our Father*. Then we prayed a *Glory Be* for those who at this moment were considering compromise. Then She said, "Dear children, today I invite you to comprehend that the path of holiness is a continuum. It is as an unfinished symphony each sacrifice and prayer being a note. My Beloved Jesus is the audience Who listens to this

symphony of holiness at the final judgment. Dear children, understand you are not finished striving for holiness until eternity. Open your hearts to My call."

■ **January 8, 1994.** Our Lady is here in white and is holding a black rosary. She says: "All praise be to Jesus." I reply, "Now and forever." Then Our Lady said: "Pray with Me now for those who are struggling to stay on the path of holiness." We prayed. Then She looked over to the two pilgrims and gave a private message. Then She said, "Dear children, once again tonight I remind you to give the present moment to holiness. Choose always Holy Love. Pray, pray, pray." She blessed us and left.

■ **January 9, 1994.** Our Lady is here in gray and pink and is holding the 'Rosary of the States.' She looks around the room at those here and says: "I have come to tell you that this year is special, for within the next few months, two things will come to light - my messages to you and the shrine. And so, please pray with loving hearts, dear children, for these intentions." We prayed. Then She said, "Thank you. Once again I welcome you and thank you for your prayers. Holiness, My dear little children, is cooperation between the soul, its will, and the grace of My Heart. Without love you cannot be holy," Our Lady blessed us and left.

■ **January 10, 1994.** After Communion I had the following vision. I saw a large key floating in the air towards me. Coming behind it were many smaller keys, floating one after the other. Jesus said, "The key then to holiness is the surrender of the will to the Will of the Father. But each day holds many small opportunities for re-commitment to holiness." [smaller keys]. "Indeed, any moment in time not given over to Holy Love is wasted."

■ **January 11, 1994.** *(To the Dayton Marian Prayer Group)*

From Our Lady: "Dear children, the Triumph of My Heart is in Holy Love. Therefore, My little ones, pray to love God first and above all else, and your neighbor as yourself."

■ **January 13, 1994.** Our Lady is here in two shades of gray and pink and is holding a black rosary. I asked Her to pray for those who had asked for prayers. She points to Her Heart and a cross comes out. Then the cross changed into roses, and they fell towards earth. Our Lady said: "I am holding them in My Heart. Dear child, please understand every cross is a grace in disguise. Pray with me, please, for those who have chosen not to follow the path of holiness." We prayed. Then She said, "You are looking at My black rosary, and I reveal to you now it is such a color for those graces which die because souls do not choose Holy Love. Dear children, tonight I come to invite you to understand that I am always with you. The grace of My Heart is the remedy for every situation. You are never alone. I give you peace, resignation, and even a new path to follow where you think there's no hope. Pray, pray, pray." Our Lady blessed us and left.

■ **January 14, 1994.** Our Lady is here in blue and pink and white, and She has many rose petals falling from Her Immaculate Heart, which is exposed. She says: "I have many graces yet in store for those who pursue the path of Holy Love and so the Refuge of My Immaculate Heart. Let us pray now for all those who choose holiness, that they persevere." We prayed an *Our Father* and a *Glory Be*. Then She said, "It is only when you rely on people, places and things of the world that you begin to fear. But when you trust in the grace of My Heart, you have everything. For nothing lies outside this grace, which changes all hearts to good and brings about God's Will in all situations." The rose petals falling from Her Heart have turned to droplets of blood. She continues, "It is through the error of abortion, which is termed 'freedom', that duplicity has seduced hearts of men. Today, freedom has been used to describe slavery to sin. It is in such cases that the grace of My Heart is rejected, and My Heart weeps tears of blood. You do not clearly see, nor understand, the grace I desire each of you to have. Only now I seek all your prayers to reveal that which Satan tries to cover."

■ **January 15, 1994 / Saturday Rosary Service.** Our Lady is here dressed in pink and gray. She was preceded by many rose petals. She says: "Praise be to Jesus. Pray with Me now for those who unconsciously choose the path of perdition." We prayed. She says: "Thank you. Dear children, tonight I come to remind you that all of your decisions, moment from moment, are important. It is when you choose against Holy Love that you are choosing your own will over God's Will. This is how people, groups, and whole nations fall to perdition." Our Lady blessed us and left.

■ **January 16, 1994 / Treatise To Pilgrims.** Our Lady comes in gray and pink. There are many crosses on Her mantle and She is holding a pearlish-pink rosary. She first tells me to head the message 'Treatise to Pilgrims'. Then She says: "Praise be to Jesus." I answer, "Now and forever." She looks back to me, as She was looking up to heaven, and seems to compose herself. "My daughter, I have come as Jesus has sent me, especially to speak to the pilgrims."

"Dear children, thank you for answering My call to come to My House of Prayer and to Maranatha Spring. It is here, the faith of the remnant will be nourished and replenished. It is here, I appoint you to be apostles of Holy Love, so that the path of holiness is laid bare to many. It is here, those seduced by the powers of darkness will find the Light. No one comes who will not be touched. I invite all to come and to pray. Many will arrive besieged and forsaken, but will leave encouraged and accompanied by a special angel, who will guard the soul against the adversary. I leave My presence amongst you. Come in procession to My spring of grace."

■ **January 19, 1994.** *(To the Dayton Marian Prayer Group)*
St. Michael is here. He says: "There is much more merit in placing all in the Mother's Heart, there to gain grace for souls undeserving."

Our Lady is here with a white veil, a blue mantle and a white gown. She says: "Praise be to Jesus." I answer, "Now and forever." She says: "Pray with Me for peace in all hearts." We say an *Our Father* and *Glory Be*. She says: "Dear children, tonight I come to inform you, there is no merit in any cross unless it is accepted by the soul. Struggles against any cross are inspired by the evil one. All conflicts, all wars, are against Holy Love and inspired by evil. Therefore, little children, pray to have Satan revealed in your lives so that you can be filled completely with Holy Love. Pray, pray, pray."
Read Ephesians 6:10-20

■ **January 20, 1994.** Our Lady is here with several angels. She says: "Praise be to Jesus." I reply, "Now and forever." Our Blessed Mother says: "Pray with Me now for the remnant." We prayed. Then Our Lady said: "Dear children, tonight once again I invite you to abandon yourselves to My Immaculate Heart, the grace of which is all-encompassing, all-powerful, and everlasting. Pray for governments, many of which are led astray by the great seducer. I tell you, if governments would lend themselves to legislate according to Holy Love, there would be peace in all hearts!" She blessed us and left.

■ **January 22, 1994 / Saturday Rosary Service.** Our Lady is here dressed in dark navy with gold trim, and has a cross on the top portion of Her veil. She says: "Praise be to Jesus." I replied, "Now and forever." She says "Dear children, pray with Me for all priests, that they recognize and pursue the Refuge of My Immaculate Heart." We prayed. Then Our Lady said: "Dear children, Jesus sends Me tonight to invite you to abandon your old ways and anything that is opposite Holy Love. Come to love the Will of the Father. For this is true holiness." She then blessed us and left.

■ **January 22, 1994.** Our Lady is here in a white gown with a periwinkle veil. She said: "Pray with Me now for souls who waste suffering on self-pity." We prayed. "My child, those that accept the Cross, accept God's Will. They are one and the same. Remember, nothing escapes the grace of My Heart. Therefore, ask for the grace to accept each new cross."

■ **January 23, 1994.**
Prayer And Sacrifice
Our Lady is here dressed all in white and She is holding a rosary that looks like lights. She says: "Praise be to Jesus. Dear children, I come to invite you to place all of your needs in My Heart." She's looking at each of us. "Dear children, I need your prayers more than you'll know in this life. For each one helps Me assist a soul from the path of perdition to the path of holy perfection. The hour has come, indeed is already here, when this ministry will pass from patient waiting, to trials and intensified 'graces. Therefore, My little ones, pray, pray, pray." She blessed us and left.

■ **January 23, 1994.** *(Locution from Our Lady)* "Child, please comprehend, Mary's House of Prayer emulates the Refuge of My Immaculate Heart on earth. Here there must be no fear, no conflict, only peace. It is a refuge of sinners where I will pour out My grace. Just as I reject no one so you must welcome all. Just as My Heart is Holy Love, so you must be apostles of Holy Love. I desire that Mary's House of Prayer be a turning point in the lives of the lukewarm, the unforgiving and the apathetic. So you must be my instruments in helping souls to choose holiness through Holy Love."

■ **January 24, 1994.** *(Our Lady describes Her Motherly Blessing)* "A blessing of Holy Love which will enable you to live in this virtue."

■ **January 24, 1994.** Jesus says: "Do you know why My Mother came and Her rosary was engulfed in light last night?" I answered, "No." He said, "Because prayer sheds light on the path of holiness."

■ **January 26, 1994.** From Blessed Mother:

MEDITATIONS ON THE MYSTERIES OF THE ROSARY

THE FIVE JOYFUL MYSTERIES

1. **The Annunciation**
   Sorrowful and Immaculate Heart of Mary, perfect me in Holy Love so that, just as You said 'Yes' to the angel and became the handmaid of the Lord, I too, will say 'Yes' to God's plan for me.
2. **The Visitation**
   Sorrowful and Immaculate Heart of Mary, perfect me in Holy Love so that I will show love of my neighbor through corporal works of mercy, as you exemplified when You visited Your cousin, Elizabeth.

3. **The Nativity**
   Sorrowful and Immaculate Heart of Mary, perfect me in Holy Love so I may take as an example the Word Made Flesh, Your Son, Jesus, and live in the world but have my heart in Heaven.

4. **The Presentation**
   Sorrowful and Immaculate Heart of Mary, perfect me in Holy Love and help me hold in high esteem Church Tradition, as You and St. Joseph did when You presented Your Infant Son in the Temple.

5. **The Finding of Jesus in the Temple**
   Sorrowful and Immaculate Heart of Mary, perfect me in

Holy Love so that I will never lose sight of God, but be diligent in the pursuit of holiness, just as Your Son was about His Father's business in the Temple.

THE FIVE SORROWFUL MYSTERIES

1. The Agony in the Garden
Sorrowful and Immaculate Heart of Mary, perfect me in Holy Love by helping me to surrender my will to the Will of God, just as Jesus did in the Garden of Gethsemane.

2. The Scourging at the Pillar
Sorrowful and Immaculate Heart of Mary, perfect me in Holy Love through all the 'scourgings' I suffer throughout the day by fasting from my own will, just as Jesus did when He was scourged.

3. The Crowning with Thorns
Sorrowful and Immaculate Heart of Mary, perfect me in Holy Love so that I am able to surrender to you my reputation, as Jesus did when He was mocked and crowned with thorns.

4. The Carrying of the Cross
Sorrowful and Immaculate Heart of Mary, perfect me in Holy Love so that I willingly accept the crosses in my life out of Holy Love, just as Jesus accepted His cross.

5. The Crucifixion
Sorrowful and Immaculate Heart of Mary, perfect me in Holy Love so that in dying to myself I am able to live for others, as Jesus showed us in His passion and death.

THE FIVE GLORIOUS MYSTERIES

1. The Resurrection
Sorrowful and Immaculate Heart of Mary, perfect me in

Holy Love that I may be victorious over the death of sin in my life, just as Jesus was victorious over the death of the grave.

2. **The Ascension**
   Sorrowful and Immaculate Heart of Mary, perfect me in Holy Love so that through the love of God and love of neighbor, I will be worthy to share Heaven with You and Your Son.

3. **The Descent of the Holy Spirit**
   Sorrowful and Immaculate Heart of Mary, perfect me in Holy Love and invoke Your Heavenly Spouse to infuse in my soul Holy Boldness, so that I may be a worthy apostle of Holy Love.

4. **The Assumption**
   Sorrowful and Immaculate Heart of Mary, perfect me in Holy Love so that placing God first in my heart, I will not fear death but see it only as a transition - a passport to Heaven.

5. **The Coronation of the Blessed Virgin Mary**
   Sorrowful and Immaculate Heart of Mary, perfect me in Holy Love, so that through Holy Love, I can help bring about the triumphant victory of Your Immaculate Heart here on earth.

■ **January 27, 1994 / Thursday Rosary Service.** Our Lady is here dressed in a blue gown and white mantle. She has many golden roses under Her mantle and by Her hands. [Note: roses signify graces.] She says: "Praise be to Jesus." I replied, "Now and forever." Our Lady then says: "Please pray with Me for those who are unillumined and choose evil over good." We prayed. She gave a private message, then said, "Dear children, I have come tonight to help you find peace in your hearts, by surrendering to God all that is in the present moment in choosing Holy Love. For it is in the present moment that you will find holiness and peace. Tonight, I impart to you My Motherly Blessing. Pray, pray, pray." She blessed us and left.

■ **January 27, 1994.** Our Lady is here in white and has a palm branch in Her hand. She says: "Praise be to Jesus. Dear children, the Triumph of My Heart is not only in your pursuit and your choice of holiness, but in your moment-to-moment decision to live in Holy Love. For when you are not living in Holy Love, you are living according to your own will, and it is then that it is difficult for Me to protect you in the Refuge of My Heart. Continue to pray for your families and your friends who are not close to the faith and who do not choose holiness. Satan conceals from you the strength of your prayers, most especially My Rosary."

■ **January 28, 1994.** Our Lady is here as Our Lady of Grace. She is all sparkling. She says: "Let us give praise to Jesus, truly present in the tabernacles of the world." I said, "Now and forever." Then Our Lady said: "My angel, these days, the light to pursue is the light on the path of holiness. Do not waste time pursuing earthly refuge, but pray and you will find the Refuge of My Heart. I am with you whenever you turn your heart over to prayer. You have no petition I do not lay before the throne of God by My own hand. What is in your heart, is as well in My Heart. Jesus desires that all understand these things, for so many live in fear and overlook the grace of the Refuge of My Heart. I speak to you as a mother who desires only the best for Her children. I hold many favors in My Heart for those who pursue in earnest this path - this viaduct I call you upon - of Holy Love. Make all of this known."

■ **January 29, 1994 / Saturday Rosary Service.** Our Lady is here dressed in a navy blue gown and a white mantle, with Her Immaculate Heart exposed. She says: "Praise be to Jesus." I reply, "Now and forever." Then She said, "Pray with Me now for those who are enemies of the cross and enemies of Holy Love." We prayed. Then Our Lady said: "Dear little children, tonight I come to inform you that when you are able to love your crosses and give them back to Jesus with love, you are well on the way to Holy Love, and into the depths of My Immaculate Heart. For it is in this way you bring to Me many souls, and I give back to you many graces." Our Lady blessed us and left.

■ **January 29, 1994.** Our Lady is here dressed in white brocade. She has a circle of stars over Her head, and has many gold roses all around her. She says: "Praise be to Jesus, My angels. Please understand, My dear children, My victory is not in great important acts; but in your small acts of love that you give Me from day to day, your humble prayers that you hold in your hearts, and in your gracious acceptance of your everyday crosses."

"Do not be discouraged, but trust. Remember, I am accomplishing everything through this ministry by means of the grace of My Heart, and so human imperfections will not play a part in My victory. I am extending to you tonight My Special Blessing. Be at peace." She blessed us and left.

■ **January 30, 1994.** Our Lady is here dressed all in gray, while the lining of Her mantle is navy blue. She says: "Praise be to Jesus." Then She said, "Pray with Me now for all those who have fallen from the path of light." We prayed. "It is good that you are here. Dear children, I am calling you as a mother. As lambs come into the sheepfold, come through the sheepgate of My Heart. Always be willing to be messengers of Holy Love wherever you go. Ask for the grace not to be afraid - not to live in the future, and I, your Mother, will see that you have it."

■ **January 31, 1994.** Our Lady is here as Our Lady of

Guadalupe. She says: "I come in Praise of Jesus." I answer, "Now and forever." Our Lady says: "My dear daughter, I am about to impart to you the reason Satan is opposing all I will accomplish through Holy Love. Please understand, Holy Love is the last hope of the sinner, for it is only through Holy Love that the heart opens to contrition. Therefore, please see that Holy Love is the last portal of salvation to the dying, for outside of Holy Love there is no salvation. Without a contrite heart, the soul is lost forever. Therefore, come to realize Holy Love is the hope of salvation and the last true thread I pass to humanity to cling to. Satan is anxious to undo all My plans, but it is through Holy Love My Heart will triumph. Make it known."

February 1994

■ **February 2, 1994.** From Our Lady: "Acceptance of the crosses in your life is light and helps Me to snatch from the adversary, souls already in his grasp. In regards to your own dilemma, God's Provident Hand often is not readily seen, but is nonetheless omnipresent. Therefore, be of stout heart." As I watched Her, some of the pearls around Her Heart fell into Her hands and She placed them in Her Heart. She looks at me again and says: "For it is through My Heart, I pour the grace of final contrition." She leaves.

■ **February 3, 1994 / First Thursday - Monthly Message To Priests.** Our Lady is here in a white mantle with a blue lining. Her gown is either pink or has a warm glow to it. Her Heart is exposed. Around it are five or six rows of tiny pearls. Our Lady tells me, "These are the souls I am praying for in My Heart as we speak, for they are about to slip to perdition in their last breath." Then She lowers Her eyes and says: "Let us give praise to Jesus." I answer, "Now and forever." She continues, "My angel, souls in darkness include many. They are the bishops who compromise Church teachings. They are priests who do not hold as their priority bringing the sacraments to the people. Anyone who ignores the Commandments in their entirety is in darkness. Those who live contrary to Holy Love - these, too, are in darkness."

■ **February 3, 1994 / Thursday Rosary Service.** Our Lady is here dressed in gray with a mauve-type of sash around Her waist. She says: "You must continually pray for the spiritually apathetic, for they number in the millions. Pray with Me now." We prayed. Then She looked around the room and said, "I welcome you, and I invite you to pray always for this intention. Dear children, all that you accomplish in Holy Love is towards salvation. Therefore, please see that in the cross there is victory when it is accepted in Holy Love." Our Lady blessed us and left.
Read 1 John 4:17-21

■ **February 5, 1994 / Saturday Rosary Service.** Our Lady is here dressed in a white gown and a blue mantle. There are stars all over the mantle. She says: "Please continue to pray with Me at this time for the spiritually apathetic. For these are the lukewarm, whom God will spew from His Mouth." We prayed. Then Our Lady said: "Dear children, these days - these times of confusion - free will has become its own god. I, your Mother, am here to tell you that when you are not loving and you are choosing your will, you are slipping from the Refuge of My Heart. Call upon My name and I will come to your aid and quickly guide you back to this solemn Refuge. I love you, My dear children. I'm anxious to spend paradise with you." Our Lady blessed us and left.

■ **February 5, 1994.** *(Afternoon)* Our Lady is dressed in gray and mauve. She has many roses all around Her. She says: "Do not be disturbed by what is happening around you. See, My daughter, this is only Satan who contradicts My every plan. He brings hopelessness where there is faith. But move continually forward with the certitude of the grace of My Heart."

■ **February 6, 1994.** Our Lady is here dressed in a cream-colored gown and a red brocade mantle. She says: "My daughter, I'm sending two angels with you to do your bidding, and to help in special circumstances that will arise on this journey. Do not presume what the future holds, and I caution all those in the ministry not to allow opinions to separate them from each other, for this is how Satan destroys My plans. Where God is, so too, are peace and unity."

■ **February 6, 1994.** Our Lady is here in three shades of gray. She says: "Pray with Me, dear children, that My messages on Holy Love will be well received and convert hearts." We prayed. "Dear children, you have sensitive souls. You know well your smallest faults. Tonight I invite you to offer these imperfections to My Immaculate Heart, thereby changing them into sacrifices which I beautify through the grace of My Heart."

■ **February 8, 1994.** Our Lady is here in blue and white. She has golden rays coming from Her Heart which I understand are graces. There are purple rays coming from earth into Her Heart. She told me, "These are all your prayers and sacrifices which I use to call souls to conversion. Dear children, petition My Heart and I will anoint you with Holy Love which is love of God and love of neighbor. Be united in this petition, for it is My call to holiness."

■ **February 9, 1994.** Our Lady is here as Our Lady of Guadalupe. The stars on Her mantle are like lights. She says: "I am with you, and the favor of My Heart rests upon you. Dear children, tonight I invite you to live the present moment in Holy Love. When you are loving, My dear little children, you are in the Refuge of My Heart, and it is then you are doing God's Will. I wish to impart to you at this time My Motherly Blessing."

■ **February 10, 1994.** Our Lady is here as Our Lady of Fatima. She asked me to kneel. She said: "It pleases Me that you have chosen to turn your hearts over to prayer tonight. Please know that the victory over every sin is Holy Love." She looked around the room at everyone and said, "Tonight I impart to you My Motherly Blessing."

■ **February 10, 1994.** Our Lady came in blue and white. She said: "Dear children, I come once again to remind you of My call to be apostles of Holy Love. My call to conversion and to Holy Love are one and the same. It is man who separates these two in his heart. Not all who are converted choose to continue on the path I invite them to follow - the path of holiness through Holy Love."

■ **February 11, 1994.** From Our Lady: "My children, dear children, today I give praise to Jesus. Today He leads you out of the desert. Let your hearts be united in Holy Love. Thus, I will bring you into the Refuge of My Heart where you will be at peace. My triumph is in your answer to My call."

■ **February 11, 1994 - Feast of Our Lady of Lourdes.** Our Lady is here as Our Lady of Lourdes. She says: "Dear children, My grace is your merit, joy, and every good measure. The present moment is made into eternal good when spent in love."

■ **February 12, 1994.** *(Our Lady's Chapel, St. Jude Cathedral, St. Petersburg, Florida)* Our Lady is here as Our Lady of Guadalupe. She says: "My daughter, the greatest grace is in surrendering the future to God's Providence. Humbly embrace this cross of not knowing the next step. Then you will see the merit of the present moment. For when you decide to embrace the cross, you cease to suffer."

■ **February 12, 1994.** Our Lady is here in white with pink roses falling down from Her waist. She asks us to pray an *Our Father* and *Glory Be* for the spiritually weak. Then She says: "Dear children, please understand all evil forms first in hearts - just as wars begin as unrest in hearts - so the apostasy has taken form in hearts as rebelliousness against the Church hierarchy. Therefore, My children, pray, pray, pray."

■ **February 13, 1994.** *(Cape Coral, Florida, 5:30 a.m.)* "Today I want you to give Me the whole day, moment to moment in Holy Love; not looking back; not looking ahead. Immerse your heart in Mine in this way, so that our hearts are one and beat as one. For in eternity this is how it will be, My angel. Such joy you give Me in this act of confidence such resplendent joy. Sustain your peace in this way. I am Mary, Queen and Mother. All praise be to Jesus!"

■ **February 13, 1994.** "My angel, I want you to remember this. Holy Love does not recount past mistakes. It holds no memory of error. Holy Love does not form conclusions concerning the future. Holy Love is always in the present. I am praying for you that you can comprehend this truth, for herein lies peace and joy." I commanded this vision to leave in the Name of Jesus, if it was Satan, or sent from Satan, but Our Lady smiled and then I felt peace. After She left, I realized that every thought we have about the future, or the past, is in the present. The future is according to God's Will.

■ **February 13, 1994.** Our Lady is here in a blue mantle and pink gown. "Dear children, I am with you always when you pray, and in every moment you choose Holy Love. Most especially, I need your prayers for those who do not choose holiness. Your prayers lend light to the path I call them upon. All praise and glory be to Jesus."

■ **February 13, 1994.** Our Lady is here in blue and white. She says: "Dear children, I love your prayers. It is your prayers that help Me to take souls from the path of perdition so that they can choose holiness. The more you do God's Will, the more powerful your prayers."

■ **February 14, 1994.** *(Cape Coral, Florida)* Our Lady is here as Our Lady of Mt. Carmel with the Infant Jesus. She gave me a private message and then asked us to pray an *Our Father* and *Glory Be* for souls to find the way to the peace of Her Immaculate Heart. "Dear children, I come especially tonight to invite you to understand that when you are living in Holy Love in the present moment, you already have the New Jerusalem in your hearts. I love you, My dear children, and am happy when you gather to pray. I want to share paradise with you." They blessed us and left.

■ **February 14, 1994.** Our Lady is here. She asks me to pray an *Our Father* and *Glory Be* with Her for the remnant Church. Then She says: "Dear children, I come today, most especially, to help you understand that this is to be a stronghold of faith and a spiritual refuge. I come as your Refuge and Protectress, and I ask you to help Me to draw the remnant into My Immaculate Heart. Realize, My children, your salvation is in the present moment. Today I extend to you My Special Blessing."

■ **February 15, 1994.** Our Lady is appearing in white and gold by the tabernacle. Her Immaculate Heart is exposed and bleeding. She says: "Praise be to Jesus, ever present in the tabernacles of the world. My Heart weeps tears of blood, My dear children, for all who move away from the Cross. The Cross is your salvation and strength. You cannot choose holiness and reject My Son's Cross. Dear children, your prayers and sacrifices are My triumph."

■ **February 15, 1994.** From Our Lady: "My daughter, mark this down so to give praise to Jesus. I desire to draw souls into My Immaculate Heart and then to the Eucharistic Heart of My Divine Son. Within the next few days, I desire to dictate to you a consecration to this Eucharistic Heart."

■ **February 16, 1994.** Our Lady is here in gray with a light-colored veil. She says: "I welcome everyone. Dear children, these days I need each of your prayers, for without them I cannot extend grace to souls." Now She has rose petals falling from Her Heart, but some of the petals are withered by the time they reach earth. Our Lady says: "See how unclaimed grace goes to waste! I come to ask you to petition My Heart each day for the grace you need. My dear children, pray, pray, pray."

■ **February 17, 1994 / Thursday Rosary Service.** Our Lady is here in all gray and says: "Dear children, pray with Me now for all those who, through apathy, insult My Son in the Blessed Sacrament." We prayed. "Dear children, tonight I invite you to understand all that obstructs the path to My Immaculate Heart is your pride, which comes in various forms. Little children, I am eager to draw you into My Immaculate Heart, for this Heart is a conduit to the Eucharistic Heart of My Son." Our Lady blessed us and left.

■ **February 18, 1994.** Our Lady is here in white, and She prayed the *Glory Be* with us. She says: "Little children, pray to have the Will of God in your hearts. Make this your prayer every day, then your heart will be pressed against Mine, and our needs and petitions will be the same. Remember, nothing is impossible, for nothing is outside the Will of God."

■ **February 19, 1994.** Jesus says: "No one is drawn into the Refuge of My Mother's Heart that is not drawn into My Eucharistic Heart as well. It is here in My Heart I will nourish the soul through My Divine Love and bring into full bloom the Holy Love that My Mother plants in each soul, that seeks out

Her Heart. The fullness and completeness of holiness is in My Eucharistic Heart."

■ **February 19, 1994 / Saturday Rosary Service.** Our Lady is here in purple and white and says: "All praise be to Jesus." She continues, "Pray with Me now for all those who are spiritually weak and choose not to be holy." We prayed. Then Our Lady looks around the room and says: "I am praying for all your intentions. You must pray to accept the Will of God. Dear children, tonight I come to invite you to understand you can be as holy as you choose to be holy. Place all your burdens and petitions at the foot of the altar where they will be absorbed by the Eucharistic Heart of My Son, which is Divine Love. Pray, pray, pray." She blessed us and left.

■ **February 19, 1994.** Our Lady is here in gold and white. She says: "Dear children, pray to have the will to accept the graces I want to give you each day. For without your will, I cannot lead you, and you will stumble. Grace is the vehicle that moves you along the path of holiness and around every obstacle. When you are opening your hearts to grace, you are opening your will to holiness."

■ **February 20, 1994.** From Our Lady:

Consecration To The Eucharistic Heart

"Most Sacred, Eucharistic Heart of Jesus, Eternal Victim, truly present in the tabernacles of the world, to You I consecrate my entire being - body and soul. I place in Your Heart - burning ember of Divine Love - my every burden and petition. Take me and use me according to Your need and bring about the Glorious Reign of Your Eucharistic Heart on earth. Amen."

■ **February 20, 1994.** Our Lady has little circles of light all around her. They are like little hosts. She says: "Let us pray now for those who do not pray." We prayed. "Dear children, I continue to appeal to you to pray often and from the heart, most especially for peace in the world. Know that My mantle of protection is about you, and it is composed of a myriad of angels to assist you." She blessed us and left.

■ **February 20, 1994.** "Your vocation now is prayer. For without prayers, Satan is strengthened and I am weakened."

■ **February 22, 1994.** "My flower of grace, look here." Our Lady is here in gray with a white flower over Her Heart. "I invite you to understand the truth of My call, for it is Satan who tries to throw you off and cause bewilderment. My daughter, please know that My Son is the Alpha and the Omega. Every good, every grace, comes from Him and flows through My Heart. Therefore, no one advances in holiness unless they pass through Me to Him. Salvation is in Him. My call to you in Holy Love is to move towards Divine Love, that is My Son."

■ **February 24, 1994 / Thursday Rosary Service.** Our Lady is here in a blue gown and a white veil. I am seeing Her from the waist up. She says: "All praise be to Jesus, My angel. Pray with Me for those who have fallen away from the TRUE FAITH." We prayed. "Dear children, tonight I come especially to invite you to understand the present-day Manna, God sends to earth is His Own Son, ever-present in the Sacrament of the Altar. Unlike the Manna of the Old Testament, this Manna brings with it eternal life." Our Lady blessed us and left.

■ **February 24, 1994.** Our Lady was here before the Rosary Service. She was dressed in two shades of blue and said, "Praise be to Jesus, little heart. I come to call souls into the folds of My mantle. For unless souls accept Me as their Mother, they cannot seek the Refuge of My Heart." At this time She has many hearts that seem to be falling out of Her Heart. I asked why. Our Lady answered: "These are the hearts that seek every pleasure in the world instead of eternal bliss."

■ **February 25, 1994.** Jesus says: "Often your own crucifixion comes from within for sins committed in the past. Forgive yourself as I have forgiven you. Know that My Mercy is all-encompassing and everlasting. There is no sin I have not forgiven. Do not allow Satan then to carry you into the past, robbing you of the present moment. It is the present moment that I desire so much. Give it to Me in Holy Love."

■ **February 26, 1994 / Saturday Rosary Service.** Our Lady is here dressed in pink and has many white flowers all around her. She says: "Pray with Me for souls to open their hearts to the grace heaven wants them to have." We prayed. All the flowers around Her have now turned into angels. "Dear children, tonight I invite you to place your petitions in My Heart so that, purified and made whole through the grace of My Heart, I can present them to My Son. It is in this way, My dear children, I desire you place your souls within My Heart, so that in like manner, I can present your souls to My Son." She blessed us and left.

■ **February 27, 1994.** Our Lady is here in purple. She wants us to pray with Her so that we can live Her messages on Holy Love. We prayed. She wants us to pray now an *Our Father* and *Glory Be* for those who will come, but will not believe. We prayed as asked. Then Our Lady said: "Thank You. Dear children, I come tonight to invite you to strengthen your prayer lives, so that you will be better messengers of Holy Love for those who will come to My shrine, for they will have many problems, many tribulations. If you are not strong, you will not be able to lead others to My Heart. Pray, pray, pray." She blessed us and left.

March 1994

■ **March 1, 1994.** Our Lady is here in blue. She says: "My child, open the garden of grace that is your heart. Souls who surrender their hearts completely to Holy Love, need to be apostles of Holy Love to those who do not surrender, and will not listen. So many listen only with their ears and not with their hearts. These souls are already walking in the ash of purgatory and slipping to perdition. For to hear the message of Holy Love and not to live it, is to close your heart to the grace of salvation. Pray, My daughter, that in the final moments of life, souls choose Holy Love." She spreads Her arms and a great light comes from Her Heart before She leaves.

■ **March 2, 1994.** *(With the Dayton Marian Prayer Group)* Our Lady is here as Our Lady of Mt. Carmel and is holding the Infant Jesus. She says: "Pray with Me now that all souls surrender to Holy Love." We prayed. "My dear children, tonight I encourage you once again to open your hearts to Holy Love, for Holy Love is the triumph of My Heart and the Gateway to the New Jerusalem. Therefore, My little ones, be prompt to answer My call." The Infant Jesus blessed us and They left.

■ **March 3, 1994 / First Thursday - Monthly Message To Priests.** Our Lady is here in pink, gold and a cream color and says: "Pray with Me now for all those who are slipping to perdition, because they have neglected their spirituality and saw only the world." We prayed. "Dear children, tonight I invite My Priest Sons to understand that love casts out all fear. Therefore, please understand and comprehend, you must uncover sin in the lives of your flock, in Holy Love."

■ **March 3, 1994.** *(In Dayton)* I had a visitor at 5:30 this morning. Our Lady came. She bent over me and said, "Do not begin to fear because the flower of grace that is your heart begins to wilt and droop." Then She smiled at me. I asked Her why She came as Our Lady of Mt. Carmel at the prayer group last night. And She said: "I desire the people be vested in this scapular, for the coming times are so difficult, and the priests should take this upon themselves as a responsibility." I thanked Her for coming and asked Her if She would identify Herself. She said: "I am Mary, Ever- Virgin, Holy Mother of God, and I come in praise of Jesus. Continue to trust as you have been."

■ **March 5, 1994.** Our Lady is here as Our Lady of Guadalupe and says: "My child, the reason I come under this title of Our Lady of Guadalupe is this: when I appeared to Juan Diego hundreds of years ago on Tepeyac, it was a decisive point in the history of Mexico and an hour of conversion for millions. My messages to you on Holy Love can affect millions of lives if they are taken to heart and lived. So it is appropriate that I come under this title to effect a conversion of hearts through Holy Love. It is important that those who have accepted this message and are living it, pray that those whose lives are touched by the messages of Holy Love, also accept them and begin to live them. I am Holy Love and I proceed from Divine Love. I offer you My Motherly Blessing."

■ **March 5, 1994.** Jesus says: "You can be certain of My Love. I am the length and breadth, the height and depth of your joy. Your response to My Divine Love is Holy Love and the key that opens the door to your will and salvation."

■ **March 5, 1994.** *(2:00 p.m.)* Our Lady is here as Our Lady of Guadalupe and says: "Dear children, these days, as Satan's time grows short, he is using the best of people to confuse and collapse My plans and to bring one ministry against the other. Therefore, I come to tell you, use Holy Love as your measure of God's Will for you and he (Satan) will not be able to bring indecision in your midst. Dear children, pray, pray, pray."

■ **March 6, 1994.** Our Lady is here in a white gown and a dark blue mantle with a gold band around it. She says: "Little children, join Me in prayer for all those who do not value spirituality." We prayed. "Dear children, I come especially tonight to refresh your souls and renew them in Holy Love. Do not allow Satan to carry you into the past or project you into the future. Instead, find Jesus in the present moment, and you will be at peace."

■ **March 9, 1994.** From Our Lady: "Dear children, please understand that as I lead you along the path of Holy Love, I am leading you along the path of salvation. For no one enters paradise who does not love. My invitation to you to pray, pray, pray is in itself an invitation to love, love, love. For all your prayers need to be born from Holy Love.

■ **March 9, 1994.** Our Lady comes as Our Lady of Grace. She says: "My little child, it is important to know that soon My physical presence will be made manifest on the grounds at the House of Prayer. Hearts will become contrite at the site of the spring. Past sins left unconfessed will come to mind. Life situations and errors in judgment will be made known. But most importantly, souls will be given the grace of final perseverance in Holy Love. It is here I wish to heal souls of self-love. Make this known."

■ **March 10, 1994 / Thursday Rosary Service.** Our Lady is here in a white brocade and has a pink lining to Her mantle and is holding a large pearl-colored rosary. She's smiling and says: "Pray with Me now for My ministry of Holy Love." We prayed. "Dear children, tonight I come to ask you for your most difficult sacrifices, for your prayers on the days when it is hard to pray, for your Holy Love towards those whom it is difficult to love. For time is growing short, and the world is suspended by a thread. Dear children, I love you, and I desire to share paradise with you. Pray, pray, pray." Our Lady blessed us and left.

■ **March 10, 1994.** *(7:30 a.m.)* Our Lady comes and sits on the edge of My bed. She is dressed in blue and white. I closed My eyes and commanded the spirit to leave in the Name of Jesus. When I opened My eyes, She was smiling and said, "All praise be to Jesus. Never cease praising My Son, even in time of trial. Do not fear humiliation, but in love, offer this to Our United Hearts. When you see errors in others, give praise to Jesus for this insight and then pray for them. If everything is given to My Heart, so much good can be accomplished in My ministry of Holy Love. Please pray with Me for the ministry." We prayed. "Every soul you encounter is imperfect in Holy Love and needs to be instructed. Those who would say they are perfect in Holy Love are only fooling themselves and are deceived by the evil one. Those who cannot see their own sins have also been deceived by the adversary. My daughter, humility is the basis for every virtue. It is My desire you make all of this known."

■ **March 10, 1994.** *(Description of Vision)* Our Lady came as Our Lady of Mt. Carmel this morning and stood next to the bed. She didn't speak, but as I prayed the rosary, the beads of the rosary She held passed through Her fingers. The beads were like a flat oval shape and a seashell pink color. As She held them in Her fingers, they glowed in a bright light. Once She had held them, the beads continued to glow. I understood She was taking My prayers and making them more beautiful in the eyes of God as they passed through Her.

■ **March 11, 1994.** Our Lady appeared to the right of the monstrance during adoration. She was in pink and gold, and there were jewels all over Her mantle. She said: "These (jewels) are the many souls saved by the recitation of the Rosary. Give praise to Jesus. My daughter, silent messenger of My Heart, when a soul pursues perfection through Holy Love, he is pursuing love of God's Will in his life. The more perfectly the soul loves, the more perfectly he loves God's Will. Holy Love deepens every virtue so that the soul can more perfectly imitate Divine Love - My Son. The soul is at peace who loves. It is the struggle against God's Will that brings unrest. The soul that desires to love should practice Holy Love. Then he is already opening his heart to grace." She leaves.

■ **March 11, 1994.** While I was sleeping, Our Lady appeared in a dream I was having and said, "Dear children, pray, pray, pray. I need your prayers, for without them, Jesus does not allow Me to touch souls."

■ **March 12, 1994 / Saturday Rosary Service.** Our Lady is here dressed in pink, navy and white. She has four or five angels with Her. She says: "Praise be to Jesus." My child, pray with Me at this time for those who do not have peace in their hearts." We prayed. "Dear children, tonight I come once again to remind you to pray, pray, pray. While you wait for a particular time to pray, the hours are slipping away, and soon there will be no time. While you are busy thinking about the future or the past, you are failing to give God the present moment." She blessed us all and left.

■ **March 13, 1994 / Sunday Service.** Our Lady is here as Our Lady of Grace and says: "Pray with Me now, dear children, for those who make pilgrimages through life, but never find their goal - which is salvation." We prayed. "Dear children, Holy Love is the fruit of the choice you make towards holiness. The grace of My Heart is the means of reaching this choice. My little ones, you must pray for I can only touch souls when you pray. I impart to you My Motherly Blessing."

■ **March 13, 1994.** Our Lady is here in gray and purple. She spreads Her hands and says: "My angel, I come as Jesus sends Me to reveal further My call to Holy Love. Where the soul begins the journey of Holy Love, the state of his own soul is laid bare so that every flaw seems abhorrent to him. Here it is important to remember that there are three parts to Holy Love: The love of God, which is first and foremost; the love of neighbor; and the love of self. It is impossible to love your neighbor if you do not first love yourself. The soul needs to keep his feet firmly planted in the Refuge of My Immaculate Heart at this time as Satan tries to sweep him down the river of discouragement. Please tell My children, God loves each one more than they can comprehend in human terms. His love is constant and unchanging despite any sin; and you need to realize that this step on the path of holiness will take place at Maranatha Spring. It will be as though souls who open to Holy Love will see themselves before the eyes of My Jesus. What a merciful grace has come to earth! It pleases God that you will make this known."

■ **March 14, 1994.** Our Lady came in purple. She said: "Pray, pray, pray for all those who do not recognize the path of holiness I call them upon."

■ **March 15, 1994.** Our Lady is here in white with a pink lining on the mantle. She is surrounded by roses. She says: "Where are your writing implements, My angel?" I went and got them. "I come as Jesus sends Me to invite you to understand a great fruit of Holy Love is joy. It is the joy you feel in making others happy - in putting others' needs first. It is the joy that comes from serving others and from nurturing the faith of others. This is Holy Love in action. Holy Love is never jealous or selfish with its time, but is always open to extending self for the needs and desires of others. This is even so in extending self to spend time in prayer for others. What limits you place on yourself needs to be examined carefully, for God asks souls to give all they can give in prudence. When you are always seeking the best interests of others, you will be joyful."

■ **March 16, 1994.** Tonight I had the following vision. A pink rose seemed to drop in front of me. I was told by Our Lady: "The rose is Holy Love."

"The rose is holy love."

Love of God

Love of Neighbor

Love of Self

Each thorn was selfish love.

The stem was labeled Humility.

■ **March 17, 1994 / Third Thursday - Monthly Message For The World.** Our Lady is here in pink and lavender and says: "Tonight I come to ask your prayers for My ministry of Holy Love. Pray with Me now, please." We prayed. "Please understand, Satan is trying your patience and your courage, and you need to seek often the Refuge of My Heart. Dear children, tonight I come once again to invite you to let Holy Love shape your hearts and your lives for Holy Love is the containment of every virtue. Once again, I invite governments to legislate according to Holy Love, allowing peace to transform their lives and their countries." She blessed us and left.

■ **March 17, 1994.** Our Lady is back in pink and white and says: "Heaven desires very much that the Bible verse that is framed on the wall along with the locution from Jesus *(see inside front cover)* be printed on holy cards to be passed out at the House of Prayer. For this is the essence of Holy Love. All for the greater honor and glory of Jesus." Then She left.

■ **March 18, 1994.** "There are three great gifts to be given on the grounds of the House of Prayer. One is knowledge of the state of the soul. The second is contrition for past sins, and the last is Holy Love. Make this known."

■ **March 19, 1994 - Feast of St. Joseph.** Our Lady is here in blue and white and says: "Dear children, each of you is a means of the triumph of My Immaculate Heart and a way to the reign of the Eucharistic Heart of My Son, and I impart to you My Motherly Blessing."
(Five minutes later)
St. Joseph is here with the Infant Jesus. The Infant blessed us.

■ **March 19, 1994.** Our Lady is here with St. Bernadette Soubirous. She has on a white gown and a pale blue mantle. From the inside of the mantle extends a stream of light. She says: "Pray with Me for all those who have hearts of stone." We prayed. "Dear children, tonight I come especially to ask you to fast from all self-love and to embrace Holy Love. For it is in this way I will hold you in the Refuge of My Immaculate Heart." Our Lady blessed us and left.

■ **March 19, 1994.** *(1:00 p.m.)* Our Lady came and said, "Just as the grace of the spring will penetrate the hardest of hearts, you must penetrate the rock to find the spring." We had struck rock upon digging for the Spring.

■ **March 19, 1994 – Feast of St. Joseph.** Jesus says:

"Hearts will be opened at the spring. Holiness is loving God's Will." *(Our Lady advised us to dig for the spring on the feast of Her spouse.)*

■ **March 20, 1994.** Our Lady is in purple and has white trim around Her mantle. She says, "Praise be to Jesus. I want you to tell them how you first saw Me." I saw Her with a mantle that was made up of money. She continues. "I have shown you this to help you understand that humanity has taken money as its god and mantle of protection, but I come to ask you to consecrate your hearts to the Passion and Cross of My beloved Son. Please stay in the present moment, pursuing holiness with your whole heart so that I can embrace your hearts and fill you with every grace." She blessed us and left.

■ **March 22, 1994.** Our Lady is here in blue and white. She says: "The full measure of My Heart is Holy Love for herein is the fulfillment of Scripture. Holy Love is the path of choice for those who choose holiness. No one can be led upon this path against his will, nor step further along the path than by consent. Every choice, when measured by Holy Love, is a step upon the path. I come in the Name of Jesus, Most Holy. All praise be unto Him. Let the measure of each one's holiness be his choices in Holy Love."

■ **March 23, 1994.** *(To the Dayton Prayer Group)* Our Lady is here in pink, white, and gold. She says: "I come to thank all those who have labored towards the completion of this book, most of all, those who have prayed for this intention. Dear children, prayer - fervent prayer - is the fullness of My call to you. It is the way of salvation and is the unadulterated milk of the grace of My Heart. Little children, pray, pray, pray."

■ **March 24, 1994 / Thursday Rosary Service.** Our Lady is here as Our Lady of Guadalupe and says: "Pray with Me now for those who do not have joyful hearts." We prayed. "Dear children, tonight as you answer My call to prayer, I invite you to have joy, peace, and love in your hearts. Unite your heart to My Immaculate Heart and the Sacred Heart of My Jesus. Remember God is peace, and anything that destroys your peace is from the adversary." Our Lady blessed us and left.

■ **March 26, 1994 / Saturday Rosary Service.** Our Lady is here in pink and white and says: "Pray with Me now for those who do not practice Holy Love." We prayed. "Dear children, tonight once again, I call you to Holy Love. You can only practice Holy Love in the present moment. When the present moment is spent, it becomes the past. Therefore, My little children, do not wait for a big opportunity to love, but love always." Our Lady blessed us and left.

April 1994

■ **April 2, 1994 / Saturday Rosary Service.** Our Lady is here as Our Lady of Fatima (dressed all in white) and has many lights all around Her. She says: "Pray with Me now for all those who do not acknowledge the existence of sin." We prayed. "Dear children, tonight, I invite you once again to realize that your victory is through the grace of My Heart, which I extend to all those who will accept. Know that My Mantle of protection is comprised of your prayers. Therefore, My children, I encourage you to pray, pray, pray." She blessed us and left.

■ **April 6, 1994.** From Our Lady: "My child, this hour I come especially to embrace you in the Mercy of My Son's Heart. When you live according to Holy Love, you are also receiving the fullness of His Mercy, and so you live in Holy Mercy. Both of these, Holy Love and Holy Mercy, proceed from Divine Mercy and Divine Love. Love embraces Mercy and Mercy embraces Love. These are inseparable. No one can love who is unforgiving or stores up grievances. Similarly, no one forgives who does not first love. Therefore, see that My call to Holy Love and Holy Mercy are one and the same. You will please make this known."

■ **April 7, 1994 / Thursday Rosary Service.** Our Lady is here and has many roses and crosses suspended in the air all around Her. She is dressed in a blue and gold brocade. She says: "Pray with Me now for those who do not love and do not pray." We prayed. "Dear children, tonight I have come to invite you to realize that the Cross is Divine Love, and Holy Love is a cross. Each cross brings with it grace to bear it. These days I raise up an army of victim souls - the heel that will crush Satan's head. Further, realize, the remnant which is now being formed in hearts is built on Holy Love. I extend to you My Motherly Blessing." She fades away.

■ **April 7, 1994.** Jesus says: "As the springtime is awakening the earth, so I invite you to awaken your hearts to Holy Love. The full complement of Holy Love is salvation. The call to Holy Love excludes no one, but convicts hearts in every failure to love as I command."

■ **April 9, 1994 / Saturday Rosary Service.** Our Lady is here wearing a cream-colored gown and a blue mantle, the edge of which is glowing. She says: "Pray with Me now for those sinners who never pray." We prayed. "Dear children, I come tonight to invite you into the Refuge of My Immaculate Heart. All you need, dear children, is in God's Provision and in God's Will for you, which is perfect. The recompense of My Heart is Holy Love, the path of holiness that I call you upon. I offer you tonight My Motherly Blessing." Our Lady blessed us and faded away.

■ **April 10, 1994.** Our Lady is here in white with a crown of stars in a circle over Her head. She says: "I come especially today to draw you deeper into My Heart of Grace, few so penetrate. I advise you with Motherly Love, do not allow Satan to trouble you concerning decisions already made, or that will be made. This is his device he uses to keep you in conflict. My angel, today I am teaching you the fullness of God's love for all souls. Come to know the Divine Will, Divine Mercy, Divine Love and the Cross are all one. Holy Love is the means by which you attain these. The Holy Trinity embraces souls that so aspire. The grace of My Heart is the means of attaining Holy Love and is offered to each soul every moment. Those that accept Holy Love in thought, word and deed choose holiness. If you are loving, you will pray, pray, pray."

■ **April 12, 1994.** Jesus says: "The key to trust is keeping your heart in heaven instead of in the world."

■ **April 13, 1994.** Jesus says: "When you are in quandary, choose for holiness."

■ **April 13, 1994.** Our Lady comes floating in a misty cloud. Her rosary is made of lights (maybe stars). Her crown is of the same lights. She says: "I come in praise of Jesus, Alleluia!" She says to me, "Dear child, messenger of My Heart, you can conceal nothing from Me. I know your every concern. I hold in My Hand the means of every solution." She motions to Her rosary of lights. "Remain faithful to the present moment tendering every moment with Holy Love. Let your most mundane tasks be accomplished in Holy Love. In this way, I am able to give souls to My Son through your fidelity."

■ **April 14, 1994 / Thursday Rosary Service.** Our Lady is here in blue and white and She has lights all over Her mantle. She says: "Pray with Me now for those who do not choose holiness." We prayed. "Everything you need is a grace from My Heart freely given when you choose it. Remain faithful to your commitment towards holiness. Dear children, tonight I come especially to invite you to understand your perfection is in God's Divine Will. You are living in God's Divine Will when you choose Holy Love. My children, pray always for countries who are steeped in confusion and do not know the choice of holiness." She blessed us and left.

■ **April 15, 1994 / Treatise To All Nations.** Our Lady is here in white with golden lights all around Her. She says, "My little one, I come in praise of Jesus." I answer, "Now and forever."

"Tonight I come to appeal to all nations to embrace Holy Love. War is always conceived first, in the hearts full of self-love with little regard for God or neighbor. When war is in hearts, it is also in governments and so in the world. My Son has sent Me as emissary of Holy Love to invoke hearts to turn away from evil and choose good. No war comes without loss. No country goes to war that does not lose. Tonight I ask you let the Blood of the Lamb suffice. Do not allow lack of love to annihilate the human race. Pray, pray, pray."

■ **April 16, 1994.** Our Lady is here in navy blue and white. She says: "Dear children, tonight I desire you comprehend the completeness of My call to Holy Love. Holy Love is the fullness of redemption and God's Kingdom on earth. Often you look with worldly eyes for small reasons and answers. My invitation to Holy Love is an invitation to look with spiritual eyes and see God's Will which calls you to Holy Love. Please make it known."

■ **April 18, 1994.** Our Lady is here in white holding a scepter and with a crown on Her head. She says: "I come as Victorious Queen. I have shown you the path of victory, the path of sanctity, the path of salvation. It is Holy Love. All sin is the opposite of Holy Love. Solemnly I inform you, every manner of affliction, every natural disaster, famine, disease, or conflict is a direct result of lack of Holy Love and, consequently, sin.

Mankind calls all of these things down upon earth and upon himself and his neighbor, when he closes his heart to love and God. When you suffer, turn all of it to good through Holy Love. Then you will not suffer but bring souls to the path of salvation. I impart to you My Motherly Blessing."

■ **April 21, 1994 / Thursday Rosary Service.** Our Lady is here dressed all in white and says, "Praise be to Jesus. Pray with Me now for souls who do not choose holiness." We prayed an *Our Father* and a *Glory Be.* She gave two private messages, then said, "Dear children, tonight I come once again to ask you to pray. When you pray, dear children, My mantle of protection is around you, for it is comprised of your prayers. Pray for faith and trust so that you will be courageous in every battle against evil. I impart to you My Motherly Blessing." Our Lady blessed us and left.
Read 1 John 4:18-21

■ **April 23, 1994.** I saw Our Lady in the air with many roses in front of Her. She said: "My child, ascend higher on the path of holiness. When you die to your own will and embrace Holy Love, you are ascending the path of Holy Love and so to My Heart and the Benevolent Heart of My Son."

■ **April 23, 1994.** *(Saturday 12:30 p.m.)* Our Lady is here in white. She says: "All praise be to Jesus, Risen Lord. Alleluia. Today I come, My angel, to solemnly assure you that you are one with My Heart. As you embrace the cross, I am supporting you with the grace of My Heart which transforms the cross into grace. I desire souls realize that My invitation to Holy Love takes them to the threshold of holiness. It is their will that takes them across the threshold. Through Holy Love, all virtue takes on new definition. Today I seek especially your prayers for those souls who do not search their conscience towards every error in Holy Love. Some speak much, but in their heart God sees a multitude of falsehood. These are the souls that deceive themselves through self-righteousness. Remember, God sees only what is in the heart, and He measures according to Holy Love. You will please make this known."

■ **April 23, 1994 / Saturday Service.** *(8 p.m.)* Our Lady is here as Our Lady of Lourdes and says, "Praise be to Jesus. Pray with Me now for those who do not choose Holy Love." We prayed an *Our Father* and a *Glory Be.* She continues, "Dear children, tonight I come to remind you, your conversion is not from day to day but from moment to moment. Your conversion is in Holy Love. Thank you for responding to My call." Our Lady blessed us and left.

■ **April 24, 1994.** Our Lady is here in blue and a cream color. She opens Her hands and says: "All praise be to Jesus." As She says this, a great light shines around Her. "In all things, trust in the harbor of provision that is the grace of My Heart. The path that I call souls to ascend, the path of holiness that leads to My Heart, is Holy Love. It is a path only traveled through self-effacement. Holy Love is the hope and salvation of the world. My call to Holy Love is the promise given to Abraham. Child, continue to pray as you do, and I will be allowed to touch many, many souls to pursue Holy Love."

■ **April 26, 1994.** *(At Shrine Site)* Our Lady is here all in white. She asks us to pray with Her now for all those who will come to this site. We prayed. "Dear children, tonight I invite you to be instruments of Holy Love. When you pray, your crosses are transformed into grace through the grace of My Heart. Your rosary is the path of Holy Love for here in these mysteries you see Divine Love. Tonight, I am imparting to you My Special Blessing. Please return often." Our Lady blessed us and left.

■ **April 26, 1994.** Our Lady is here in white and is smiling. "My angel, I can use your prayers most easily if they originate in your heart. When you just say words, it is like you are handing Me a key that does not fit any heart. But when you begin your prayer first in your heart, then on your lips, you give to Me a key that I can open any heart with and fill it with grace. I come to you in the plenitude of God's goodness and mercy. Place in My Heart your every need for there is no greater trust." I asked Her about the well digger. She motioned to the list next to me. "One will be found today who is capable and trustworthy."

■ **April 26, 1994.** Jesus says: "Every treasure of My Heart is laid bare in the world today, and most especially, at Maranatha Spring. Here, I will free hearts of the burden of sin and lift them up to heavenly aspirations. By My own Hand am I forming this from the clay of the earth."

■ **April 27, 1994.** Our Lady is here in white and is totally encircled by many sparkling lights. She says: "Pray with Me now for Holy Love Ministries." We prayed. "Dear children, tonight I invite you to realize that conversion requires two steps. First, to choose holiness and Holy Love. Second, to reject your past sins and failings and to recognize them. Souls that are steeped in unforgiveness and bearing grudges have not effected either of these steps. For unforgiveness is a barrier to holiness and Holy Love. Make it known."

■ **April 28, 1994 / Thursday Rosary Service.** Our Lady is here in a pink gown and a silver brocade mantle and pink lining. She says: "I invite you to pray with Me now for those who do not convert." We prayed. "Dear children, you can only trust when your heart is in heaven. Trust is the key to conversion and to love. When you love with Holy Love, then you are living in God's Will. It is then that I can take your heart into My own Immaculate Heart. It is then you can embrace the Cross. I impart to you My Motherly Blessing." Then She left.

■ **April 29, 1994.** *(9 p.m. at Spring Site)* Our Lady told me to pray at the spring site this evening after dark. At the spring - there is a lighted cross on the ground (where we will drill for the spring next week), and Our Lady is above it floating on a cloud. She is dressed in two shades of blue. She says: "Pray with Me now for all those who will come (to the spring)." We prayed. "Dear children, you are kneeling where many will come, where many will find contrition and repentance. It is a resolute area of grace from My Heart. Untold graces are coming to earth at this site soon."

■ **April 30, 1994 / Saturday Rosary Service.** Our Lady is here in pink and has radiant lights all around Her. She says: "Tonight, I desire you pray with Me for pilgrims who will come, that they will open their hearts to My message of Holy Love." We prayed. "Dear children, tonight I come to invite each of you to be saints. There is no sanctification outside of Holy Love. Therefore, dear children, be little and humble, die to self, love God and your neighbor. I am drawing you into My Heart." Our Lady blessed us and left.

■ **April 30, 1994.** *(At Spring Site)* After Communion I asked Jesus about the cost of the spring. He said, "The cost is many prayers and much faith which you are already giving Me." Then I asked Him about the depth. He said, "The depth is the deepest recesses of My Mother's Heart, which is readily accessible at this blessed site."

■ **April 30, 1994.** *(7 p.m. before the Rosary Service)* *(Our Lady was crying)* Our Lady came in gray with a rosary in Her hands that seemed to be made of large, heavy, black stones. She said: "These are the rosaries left unsaid which weigh as a heavy burden upon My Heart. Most especially, I ask you to pray for those who know the rosary but do not put it to use."

May 1994

■ **May 2, 1994.** Our Lady comes as Our Lady of Grace. "I come in praise and honor of Jesus. My angel, I am pleased to come and reveal to you that the hour is at hand when the grounds at the House of Prayer will be sanctified through grace. My presence which is there will now intensify. The abundance of grace that will flow from My spring will reveal truths, heal, and bring peace. But no grace will be so great as the numbers who will find conversion. And so, prepare your heart. Heaven will ask much of you - those of earth, more. You will endure if you remain in My Heart as you are. I desire that our hearts beat as one so that alike, we will attract many souls to Holy Love. Let your heart be a tabernacle of Holy Love. Little child, you are only beginning to comprehend the depth of My call to you. Pilgrims are coming as numerous as raindrops in spring. The more who come in faith, the more grace will unfold. For it is the faith of those who will come that will multiply heaven's favors."

■ **May 2, 1994.** From Our Lady: "The multitude that is coming will be fed with the loaves and fishes of grace. They will come from the desert of the world to the oasis of Maranatha to quench their thirst for faith." She blessed me and a great light came from Her Heart which remained for a moment after She left.

■ **May 2, 1994.** An archangel spent most of the day with me. Our Lady helped me pick out fabric for my May Shrine. I was going to move the shrine from the center of my living room to the corner of the room, next to the TV, when the angel told me not to move the May altar out of the center of the room, because Our Lady is put in corners and hallways and so many other places. She should be venerated and honored.

■ **May 2, 1994.** *(Spring Site)* Our Lady has been here the whole time we've been praying. She just moved and floated over that spot where we first dug. She says: "My children, Maranatha Spring is to be a testament to Holy Love. I am bringing many from all parts and with every affliction - spiritual and temporal. You feel in your hearts the excitement for all of which is about to happen. But I tell you, the magnitude has not yet been told to you. My spring is coming soon and swiftly. All praise be to Jesus."

■ **May 3, 1994.** From Our Lady: "Please write down what I am telling you. I desire the day that Maranatha Spring is unearthed be remembered always in hearts as: My Feast of Holy Love."

■ **May 3, 1994.** Our Lady is here all in white and has white lilies all around Her, and is holding a golden rosary. She says: "Dear children, today I come to inform you, the spring is evidence of the Refuge of My Immaculate Heart on earth. Holy Love Ministries will be a catalyst of grace and will draw souls into My Immaculate Heart. It is for these reasons you will be under attack, as well as, all those who work towards this end; but you must be examples of those who seek the Refuge of My Immaculate Heart during difficult trials. I am coming tonight to manifest the desires of heaven."

■ **May 3, 1994.** *(Spring Site)* Our Lady is here as Our Lady Queen of Heaven and Earth. She is seated on a throne that is atop a globe of the earth. She is wearing a pink gown, a satin light-gray mantle; She is holding a scepter in one hand, a rosary in the other with a beautiful golden crown on Her head. The vision then moved forward until the globe of the world came to rest above the spring site. Our Lady said: "Pray with Me now for all priests and religious who will come seeking to renew their vocations." We prayed. "Dear children, these days, nothing in the world is secure, not nature nor man himself. The only security is My Immaculate Heart. Therefore, I reveal to you - I am raising up an army of Holy Love to encapture hearts and lead them into this Immaculate Refuge. You dear children, must decide to lead. Given every grace you need, submit humbly to My call." She then looked at me, smiled and said: "Do not be afraid. You'll lead by suffering." She blessed us and left. As Our Lady left, the globe of the earth floated over the area of the spring above the fiery cross. An Archangel then appeared and said: "Every word in the message has particular meaning."

■ **May 4, 1994.** I awoke at sunrise and suddenly Jesus was standing in My room. He was almost in a silhouette, but I could see His Face. He said: "Do you see this sunrise? This is how I will enlighten souls at Maranatha Spring, taking them from darkness and leading them into the light."

■ **May 4, 1994.** *(Spring Site)* Our Lady was present as we were praying the *Magnificat* this evening at the future spring site. A fiery cross lay on the ground where we will drill tomorrow. Our Lady says: "Welcome dear children. I am coming, especially tonight, to call into your hearts the prayer for all pilgrims who will come in the multitudes, and who will be fed from the Spring of love and mercy. Dear children, do not expect every issue to be resolved smoothly; but within the grace of My Heart, God's Will will come to pass; and all I desire accomplished in you will be accomplished, because you have answered My call. I am blessing you now." Our Lady left, and the fiery cross remained over the drill site for a while then, disappeared.

■ **May 5, 1994.** When I opened My blinds this morning, the rising sun to the east was very bright. It began to change colors - first a pink then a green. Then it started to grow large, then small, and dart around in the sky.

■ **May 5, 1994.** From Our Lady: "The triumph of My Immaculate Heart will begin today at Maranatha."

■ **May 5, 1994 – Feast of Holy Love / Thursday Rosary Service.** Our Lady is here in white and has pink roses all around Her. She says: "Pray with Me now in thanksgiving for Maranatha and those who will come." We prayed. "Dear children, tonight I come to invite all nations to Maranatha - wellspring of grace. You do not comprehend what heaven has ordained today; for Maranatha is the threshold of Holy Love and the gateway to the New Jerusalem." Our Lady blessed us and left.

■ **May 5, 1994.** Jesus says: "The space around Maranatha Spring will be filled with angels. If you look tonight, you will see them." *(We are drilling for the Spring this afternoon.)*

Maranatha Spring was unearthed today!

■ **May 6, 1994.** From Our Lady: "It is a wellspring of grace flowing from My Heart. These days, where so many are deceived seeking security in the world, the multitude who come to Maranatha will find peace, love and joy."

■ **May 6, 1994.** From Our Lady: "Dear children, I welcome you to this resolute point of grace, and I anoint your hearts in love, peace and joy." She blessed us and left.

■ **May 7, 1994 / Saturday Rosary Service.** Our Lady is here all in white with a golden sash around Her waist. She has many angels with Her and says: "Pray with Me now for those seeking Holy Love." We prayed. "My children, dear children, tonight I come to celebrate with you Maranatha for it is here that I will dispense every favor of My Motherly Heart. It is here I call you to the foot of the Cross to be glorified. Dear children, embrace Holy Love." Our Lady blessed us and left.

■ **May 8, 1994 - Feast of Our Lady, Mediatrix of All Grace /
Mother's Day.** Our Lady is here in a radiant white light. She is
dressed all in white and says: "Pray with Me now for those who
weaken the Church and reject motherhood through abortion
and artificial birth control." We prayed. "Dear children, today
I joyfully tell you the grace tendered at Maranatha Spring will
exceed even what you imagine. I am drawing souls to the
grace of conversion and to wholeness of mind and body. My
children, celebrate with Me for such a grace is given to earth."
Our Lady blessed us and left.

■ **May 9, 1994.** Our Lady is here in blue and white. She
says: "My daughter, messenger of My Heart, today I ask
you to realize that when you answer My call to come to
Maranatha Spring, you are also coming to the foot of the
Cross. At Maranatha, the grace to accept Holy Love is readily
dispensed, bringing the soul to also accept Divine Love,
Divine Mercy, God's Divine Will, and the Cross. All of these
come together at Maranatha Spring, and pour out as grace
upon those who allow themselves to be touched. So then,
begin to comprehend the magnitude of My call to you."

■ **May 11, 1994.** Jesus says: "Please write down what I
am telling you. Earth is engaged in a battle - good against
evil. The battle is lost and won in hearts. At Maranatha,
through the grace of My Mother, I intend to uncover what lays
hidden in hearts. I will awaken sleeping consciences. I will
make known My Mercy. I am preparing souls for My Second
Coming. Alleluia!"

■ **May 12, 1994 / Thursday Rosary Service.** Our Lady is
here in white. There are three angels kneeling at Her feet, and
they are holding Her mantle. She says: "Pray with Me now for
those who do not recognize the path of holiness that I am
so urgently calling them upon." We prayed. "Dear children,
tonight I invite you to understand these three great virtues -

Faith, Hope and Love - are readily given to hearts that open to God's Will. For it is surrender of self that nurtures Faith, Hope and Love. Faith and Hope remain aloof unless the soul opens to Holy Love." She had three little white flowers above Her Heart. They represented Faith, Hope and Love. Our Lady took them from Her Heart with Her right hand and extended them to me. Our Lady then blessed us and left.

■ **May 12, 1994.** "Some will be touched just by the water. Others will need to make the sacrifice of coming to Maranatha. You cannot decide which is which."

■ **May 12, 1994.** "Prayer begins in the silence of hearts."

■ **May 13, 1994 - Feast of Our Lady of Fatima.** Our Lady has come as Our Lady of Fatima. The border on Her mantle is a bright light. She says: "Dear children, I am leading you by means of gentleness and love. Every measure of My Heart comes to earth now to bring hearts into the fold of Holy Love. Each moment, dear children, is a new opportunity to choose love and so, holiness. Once it is spent, it cannot be retrieved but only surrendered to God's Mercy. Today, I call unceasingly for hearts to choose Holy Love so that governments and whole nations will choose love." She blessed me and left.

■ **May 14, 1994.** "Love is like a glowing ember in the soul. When fanned with the surrender of free will, it becomes a flame that consumes every fault."

"Love is like a sapling fruit tree that, when watered by the choice of free will, grows straight and tall towards heaven. It bears fruit a hundred fold in the form of every virtue."

"Love is the measure of God's judgment."

"Holy Love is the fiber of every soul that is saved and the choice of every heart that is converted."

■ **May 14, 1994.** Our Lady is here as Our Lady of Fatima. She says: "Dear children, I have come especially to ask you to be Holy Love to those around you and to all who come seeking the truth. This is the way hearts will open to My messages to you, for they are living messages not just words in a book. It is your response to My call to Holy Love that is opening hearts. Make it known."

■ **May 14, 1994.** From Our Lady: "My angel, I want to speak to you about unforgiveness. So many come to My Son seeking many needs when what they really need is to forgive." She advances closer to me. "In order to forgive, souls need to surrender their pride, remembering nothing occurs outside of God's Permitting Will. Souls who cannot forgive have the pride of self-centeredness. They want to know 'why'. But God alone holds the reasons in His Benevolent Heart. Often the reasons are not revealed until eternity. And so, My angel, to forgive, each soul needs to pray to accept God's Will even though he may not understand God's Will in this life. God's reasons are His own. There is so much I want to reveal to you. My Heart is always enveloping you. I have only begun to pour into you My love, and the secrets of My love for all humanity. Maranatha is a means of My opening hearts and touching souls." She bows Her head and leaves.

■ **May 16, 1994.** Our Lady is here in sparkling white and says: "My angel, you need to understand the world is plunging itself into darkness through lack of love. This is why I call souls to Maranatha - to bring about a renewed commitment to love and allegiance to the Roman Catholic Church. I am invoking the aid of all the heavenly court in this effort. Make it known."

■ **May 17, 1994.** Jesus says: "It is impossible to consecrate yourself to the Cross without also consecrating yourself to Holy Love. For the Cross is love."

■ **May 17, 1994.** Our Lady is here in a white satin gown,

mantle and veil. She says: "Dear children, the more you surrender yourself, the more I will be able to use you, and the more complete will your response be to My call."

■ **May 17, 1994.** Our Lady comes in white and is holding a rosary of lights. She has a crown of stars over Her head which also looks like lights. She says: "I want you to write this down in praise of Jesus. Dear children, I come especially to help you understand that Holy Love is a reflection of Divine Love, and so of the Divine Will. Holy Love holds no memory of wrong doing for that is all past. Come to see the value of loving in the present moment, for this is your salvation and the deliverance of the world. Holy Love in the present is heaven on earth - the New Jerusalem. Make it known."

■ **May 18, 1994.** Our Lady comes in a mist. She has many little hearts floating around Her that are light pink. She is in white. She says: "Take up your pen and paper. Let us begin. You see these hearts. These are the ones truly consecrated to Me, who not only listen to My messages but bring them alive in their hearts. Such souls are lights in a world of darkness though, through Satan's deceit, the world does not accept them as such. No one can be consecrated to My Immaculate Heart without living in Holy Love, which is also God's Divine Will. I pour every grace through such hearts and through them into a love-parched world. These are My instruments - My hands, My feet, My mouth. The grace of My Heart will reflect in their lives and influence their work, their prayers, their thoughts, and every virtue in their soul. Herein, you see why it is so much My request that souls allow themselves to become My message of Holy Love. For it is in this way My Immaculate Heart is already beginning to triumph. Make it known."

■ **May 19, 1994 / Thursday Rosary Service.** Our Lady is here in a blue gown and a white mantle. She says: "Pray with Me now for those who do not embrace Holy Love." We prayed. "Dear children, you must understand that all nations have become tools in Satan's hands. They slip to perdition through lack of Holy Love. My victory begins in hearts that embrace Holy Love. My victory is Holy Love."

■ **May 20, 1994.** Our Lady is here as Our Lady of Fatima. She says: "My angel, I am calling all nations to join Me at the foot of the Cross at Maranatha Spring. It is here mankind will find reconciliation with God, just as humanity was reconciled with God on Calvary. For here I will call to mind sins left unconfessed and convict souls through Holy Love. I invite all to join Me here on the 13th of every month, anniversary of My Feast Day in Fatima. Come in procession. Begin at twilight for the hour grows late. I will be with you as you pray for the universal Roman Catholic Church. Those who will come will find the favor of grace accompanies them. Pray, for three-fold what you presume are coming. You must make this known."

■ **May 22, 1994 / Saturday Rosary Service.** Our Lady is here in blue and white. She spread Her hands and said: "Tonight I ask you to pray with Me for those who are starving, most especially, those who are starving for Holy Love." We prayed. "Dear children, tonight I come especially to commemorate the anniversary of My Spouse coming to earth. Please understand, He is with you always. In thankfulness, give Him your own holy will. Tonight, I give you My Motherly Blessing, which is the embrace of My Immaculate Heart." She blessed us and drifted away.

■ **May 22, 1994.** Our Lady comes in pink and white. "I reveal to you now that if hearts and nations continue to idle in their embrace of Holy Love, a war of great magnitude will ensue. Your country will suffer greatly in the loss of lives, resources and esteem. Heaven extends to the world through the Holy Love messages the recourse to escape. Pray that hearts open to this. I will send you the means of propagating Holy Love." She blessed me and faded away.

■ **May 23, 1994.** From Our Lady: "My angel, I reveal to you this day that Holy Love Ministries began when Jesus gave the two great commandments to the world - Love God above all else - Love your neighbor as yourself. He only sends Me to you during these times to re-emphasize these laws. I call all My children to understand Holy Love in one heart is as a pebble cast on a pond which brings to the pond many ripples. Just as the little stone affects the water, so Holy Love in one heart affects many hearts around it. In joy, give praise to Jesus."

■ **May 23, 1994.** From Our Lady: "Please make it known My presence is continually and always at Maranatha Spring and at the Blessing Point. For here I intend to grant many favors."

■ **May 23, 1994.** Our Lady came in bluish gray. She said: "Disregard your latest health problems. When you are in heaven, they will seem minuscule while your rosaries will be known as great victories for God." She extends a rosary towards me. "This is the way to bring peace into hearts and into the world. It is the victory of Holy Love in hearts. In this give praise to Jesus." She spreads Her hands and leaves.

■ **May 26, 1994 / Thursday Rosary Service.** Our Lady is here as Our Lady of Fatima and says: "Pray with Me now for those who do not believe in My Son's real presence in the Tabernacles of the world." We prayed. "Dear children, tonight I come to beg you to feed the hungry. These days there is a famine in every corner of the world, for hearts are famished for Holy Love. The heart that embraces Holy Love is also a carrier of Holy Love. Dear children, once again I invite you to pray, pray, pray." She blessed us and faded away.

■ **May 27, 1994.** From Our Lady: "Dear children, I come especially to help you realize that My call to Holy Love is the same call of John the Baptist in the desert. I desire to baptize hearts in Holy Love so as to prepare them for My Son's Second Coming. Through Holy Love, My Immaculate Heart will triumph, and My Son's Eucharistic Heart will reign. I impart to you always, at Maranatha, My Motherly Blessing."

■ **May 27, 1994.** Our Lady is here in white with flowers in Her hair. She extends Her arms and turns the palms of Her hands towards heaven. "Dear child, this is why I desire so much, many rosaries from the heart. The fifteen-decade rosary exemplifies Holy Love. Each prayer is as a gentle drop of dew falling on My impoverished Heart that pleads for conversion of humanity. My heart withers when souls turn away, and your prayers replenish what lukewarm souls take from it. My heart is opening as never before to humanity. Pray, pray, pray."

■ **May 28, 1994.** Our Lady comes in a light blue satin and white. She says, "Praise be to Jesus." I answer, "Now and forever." She says, "Pray with Me now for those pilgrims who are coming tonight with a multitude of needs." We prayed an *Our Father* and *Glory Be*. She moved closer during the *Glory Be*. "Dear child, messenger of My Immaculate Heart, Heaven desires you make it known, when I come to you at the wellspring on the thirteenth, the grace of My Heart will be made manifest amongst those who gather. This is God's favor upon earth and His punctuation and verification of the importance of Holy Love. Expect miracles, most especially conversions." She leaves and a cross is in the air for a second in Her place.

■ **May 28, 1994.** Our Lady is here all in gold and says: "Embrace the Cross, embrace the Cross. Praise be to Jesus. Pray with Me now for those who are spiritually apathetic." We prayed. "Dear children, tonight I come especially to help you realize that your cross is your crown of glory in heaven. When you pray, I am with you embracing you in My Immaculate Heart. Your prayers are already used up in these times of sorrow. Therefore, My little ones, pray, pray, pray." She blessed us and left.

June 1994

■ **June 2, 1994.** Our Lady came in pink and gold and prayed with me this morning. The beads of the rosary seemed to float through Her fingers. They became illuminated as they passed through Her hands. She only moved Her lips on the *Glory Be*. She spoke, "Pray. I do not call My children together at Maranatha in error, but through God's Mercy and His Grace. The provision of My Heart will be made manifest at Maranatha." She drifted back towards heaven - fading away. A sparkling cross was left in Her place momentarily.

■ **June 2, 1994 / Thursday Rosary Service - Message To Priests.** Our Lady appeared standing next to me in a mist. I can see Her from Her waist up. She is in pink. There are tears coming down Her checks. She says: "My daughter, My Son's Church is entering upon its crucifixion. It is false freedom which, in reality, is slavery to sin that crucifies it. I want My priest sons to begin to call souls to Holy Love. If they are apostles of Holy Love, many can be saved. I come to tell you these things in this hour of need as Jesus sends Me. You will please make all of this known."

■ **June 2, 1994.** Our Lady is here in a pink gown and silver mantle and says: "My angel, tonight I desire to pray with you for all those who oppose My ministry of Holy Love." We prayed. "When you pray for your enemies and those who oppose you at every turn, you earn merit towards their conversion. Dear children, tonight I come to invoke you to unite all your crosses with every cross and suffering now present in the world and united to the suffering Heart of My Son. In doing so, you will win many souls for the Kingdom. Remember, one *'Hail Mary'* can convert a soul so do not negate its importance. I'm imparting to you now My Motherly Blessing."

■ **June 2, 1994.** St. John Vianney was with Jesus. Jesus said: "The warning I give to earth at this time is Holy Love, which should be the conviction of every heart. At Maranatha I will refresh souls with the waters of Truth, which will dispel fears and lay bare deceptions."

■ **June 4, 1994.** Our Lady is here in white and blue. She has Her hands out, and She has lights coming out of Her hands. She says: "Pray with Me now so that souls will embrace the new *Catechism [of the Catholic Church]*, and it will dispel confusion." We prayed. "Dear children, tonight I come as a loving mother to call you to holiness and lead you away from darkness. Dear children, with each cross comes the grace to carry it. Only through Holy Love can you accept God's Will and so embrace your cross. I impart to you now My Motherly Blessing."

■ **June 5, 1994.** Our Lady comes and drifts towards me. She is in white. Her Immaculate Heart is exposed. She says: "Today I wish to reveal to you the secret of Holy Love. It is taking the focus off yourself and placing it on God and others. You love yourself only in a detached way knowing God created you. All your thoughts and motives, however, are centered on God, His laws, and the well-being of your neighbor. Satan likes to attack the love in your hearts by tempting you to see how each situation affects you personally. This is a form of pride. If you try to love, My grace will be present in your hearts to assist you. But first, you need to choose to love. You need to be good to yourselves insofar as it will enable you to be good to others. I extend to you now My Motherly Blessing."

■ **June 9, 1994 / Thursday Rosary Service.** Our Lady is here in pink and white and has gold crosses all over Her pink gown. She says: "Pray with Me now for those who know Jesus but do not love Him." We prayed. "Dear children, tonight I come seeking peace in all hearts. The way to peace is to surrender your will to God's Will. When you want things your own way, you are not at peace; and you allow Satan to cause turmoil in your hearts. Surrender always to God's Holy and Divine Will which is Holy Love, and you will be at peace." Our Lady blessed us and left.

■ **June 9, 1994.** Our Lady comes in a blue mantle and a white gown. I asked Our Lady if we were going to have a war with North Korea. She said: "The enemy is aligning his forces. Your president is unprepared and ill-suited for such a conflict. Therefore, you need to pray, pray, pray for peace in all hearts." She blessed me and drifted back up to heaven.

■ **June 11, 1994 / Saturday Service.** Our Lady is here in a pink gown and a white mantle. She has Her Heart exposed, and there are many rays of light coming from Her Heart. At the end of each one of these rays are little hearts. She says: "These are the hearts that I am calling into the ministry in a special way, and I am praying for them. Please join Me now and pray for this intention." We prayed. "Dear children, I do not come in your midst to spread fear concerning the future but to spread Holy Love in the present moment. Please understand, My children, there is no salvation outside of Holy Love. Holy Love is the conformity to God's Divine Will." She blessed us and left.
Read 1 John 4:7-8, 18-21

■ **June 11, 1994.** Our Lady is here in peach with a white veil. Her Immaculate Heart exposed. She is floating on a cloud. "My angel, today I come with many graces, ready to call souls out of the world and into My Immaculate Heart -

Refuge of Sinners. There is no safe refuge in the world. The world concedes all that is life giving to that which destroys life. So today, I want to give souls the grace of looking beneath the surface which is worldly, to that which gives eternal life. Those souls who embrace Holy Love have received this grace. Holy Love is the foundation of salvation." She drifts back up to heaven, and a great light comes from Her Heart as She leaves.

■ **June 11, 1994.** Our Lady is here in white lace and pink brocade. "I want you to pray with Me for those who have traveled great distances and are still on their way." We prayed. "Please understand, My children, Holy Love Ministries is moving souls into the New Jerusalem. Therefore, you must prepare your hearts with much prayer." She blessed us and left.

■ **June 12, 1994.** Our Lady is here all in white and has two angels with Her. She says: "I invite you to pray with Me now for those who are coming [6/13/94] in need of conversion." We prayed. She says: "Thank you. Dear children, your prayers and sacrifices are opportunities of grace for the hundreds who will come. Holy Love is the final call to conversion and surrender to the Refuge of My Immaculate Heart. Therefore, My little children, you must pray, pray, pray." Our Lady blessed us and faded away.

■ **June 13, 1994.** Jesus was suddenly standing at the foot of My bed with His hand raised in a blessing. He said: "Peace be with you! Today the ministry will have its re-birth as many, many hearts open to the message of Holy Love. By My Own Hand have I formed this - just as I have formed every heart. I will bring good out of every effort today. Rejoice! As I am preparing, through the heart of My Mother, great grace and many favors for those who come. Alleluia!"

■ **June 13, 1994.** Our Lady is here in a pink gown and gray mantle. She says: "All praise be to Jesus. You see, when all is said and done, Satan has arranged for you to pray before the Blessed Sacrament. All of these trials are temporary, and your prayers disarm the enemy. *(Regarding Our Lady's above statement, the City of Seven Hills issued a court order against our praying at Maranatha Spring or any gathering on the property. A gracious priest across the street at St. Columbkille Church let us pray in church as a severe thunderstorm began.)* Our Lady then said, "Please pray with Me now for the universal Roman Catholic Church." We prayed. "Thank You. Dear children, tonight I come to warn you. The world is propelled towards the war of the century which will affect every nation and even nature itself. But the way out of this is Holy Love. Dear children, Holy Love is the final call to conversion and peace in all hearts. Pray, pray, pray. I impart to you My Special Blessing." Our Lady then faded away.

■ **June 14, 1994.** From Our Lady: "Build your shrine in the cathedral of My Heart. Here, in this impregnable fortress against all evil, I will call great numbers to Holy Love. Take up your solace in the enterprise of fervent prayer. This will bring the correction of erring spirits. God's plan is greater than any plan of earth."

■ **June 14, 1994.** Our Lady is here with the strong scent of roses. She says: "Praise be to Jesus." She is in white with roses on Her mantle. I ask Her: "When do you want us to meet?" She replied: "Strong advice is coming through another later today. Pursue it. The House of Prayer will be open for visitors to pass through. Some services will continue there, but some will be held elsewhere." I asked: "Where?" She replied: "You will be led. Follow. The ministry is growing. Often what appears to be a cross is in reality a grace. The healings will continue at Maranatha. You will come in procession soon, and I will be with you." She spreads Her hands and many rose petals fall to the floor as She drifts up to heaven.

■ **June 14, 1994.** Our Lady is here in white and says: "My children, pray with Me now for all city officials." We prayed. "My children, dear children, do not allow human issues to cloud God's Divine Will. For here I am telling you what city officials desire, and what God desires, are two different things; and you must decide who you serve. You are in My Heart when you pray from the heart. It does not matter where you are on earth. Now you are fleeing from Herod, but soon you will find within My Heart a safe dwelling." She blessed us and left.

■ **June 14, 1994.** Our Lady is here in gray and a cream-colored gown. She says: "If all you can see is the battle, and not the victory, how can you pray for the victory? For I tell you, even the battle itself is a victory when it is relinquished to My Heart of grace. Every victory is in this Immaculate Refuge." She bows Her head and spreads Her hands. "Let us give praise to Jesus. My daughter, the enemy is already defeated. This ministry is in hearts not in a dwelling on earth. And the hearts that so embrace Holy Love can pray anywhere. Tonight, go to the picnic area. I will be with you. Pray for those who confuse church and state and those who do not pray. My angel, every apostasy begins when souls stop loving in Holy Love." She leaves.

■ **June 16, 1994.** Our Lady was standing next to me at the sink. She said: "The ministry is growing too big for the House of Prayer and the great numbers I will draw into My Heart through Holy Love Ministries."

■ **June 16, 1994.** Our Lady is standing in front of me with Her hands out and Her Heart exposed. She says: "My Heart weeps tears of blood for the rosaries left unsaid due to these complications. My angels, every path has obstacles. You need to unite and pray for the grace to overcome them. Satan knows you are discouraged. Every door I open for you, he will attempt to close through conflicts in ideals. This is why you need neutral grounds." I asked: "Are you the Mother of God?" "I am She, Mother of the Word Incarnate, Jesus. You need to pray, for in prayer is every answer."

■ **June 17, 1994.** From Our Lady: "Have faith in the ministry that is in hearts and not in buildings. Seven Hills will be a sign of contradiction between God's Kingdom and the world."

■ **June 17, 1994.** Our Lady came with Her Heart exposed. She said: "You need to begin the new complex soon, for St. Columbkille [Church] is only a temporary solution." I started to cry and tell Her I felt like Moses wandering in the desert without direction. She said: "It is now you need to be the strongest and have a firm purpose of amendment. Do not fear for Maranatha. I am calling you out of the desert and into My Heart."

■ **June 18, 1994.** *(Before Mass)* From Our Lady: "I invite you to understand, My daughter, that God's message of Holy Love is not just for this area. For this reason, My visit will take on a national and even international spectrum. Holy Love is God's final message of mercy."

■ **June 20, 1994.** Jesus says: "I am most intimately at one with souls who are devoted to My Passion and Death. It is these souls I allow My Mother to flood with grace that overwhelms all opposition. Then have all hope in My Mercy. Unceasing is My suffering. Unceasing is My glory."

■ **June 20, 1994.** Our Lady is here in a light pink mantle and a gold and white gown. Her Heart is exposed. She is holding a rosary. She extends Her hands and says: "My daughter, complete your consecration to the present moment by realizing each moment in time includes the choice between the spirit and the world. If your heart is in heaven, most often your choice will be of the spirit, which is Holy Love. This is the way of perfection I call you upon. So, too, it is the way out of every situation that would destroy your peace."

■ **June 22, 1994.** Jesus says: "Pray for My Church! Pray for My Church! It is being fragmented by the god of free will." Then I had the following vision. I saw a peach, sliced in half, with the stone exposed. Jesus said: "The peach is My Church. I am the stone. The half of the peach you do not see, that is peeled off of the stone, are those who do not follow Church doctrine. This fruit will wither and die. Pray that all be reconciled to My Will."

■ **June 22, 1994.** Our Lord came to me with His Sacred Heart exposed. He said, "I want My Mother restored to Her rightful place in the Church. Just as Her shrine has been rejected in Seven Hills, so She is rejected in the Universal Church. Her place by My side cannot, and should not, be disputed. My priests should not be classified as Marian or non-Marian. This wounds Me. Too many have little regard for Her grace-filled Heart which I Myself fill to overflowing. You see this by way of Maranatha Spring. What takes place in My Church will take place in the world. Where My Mother is rejected, there too I am rejected."

■ **June 22, 1994.** Our Lady is here in a pink gown and gray mantle. She is standing on a cloud that has a banner under it which says: *"Mary Refuge of Sinners Protect Our Faith."* She says: "Pray with Me now for the Universal Church." We prayed. "You're forgetting, My children, that often grace comes in the form of a cross. And so, as we begin over, remember that it is grace that has brought you to this point." She says: "Make it known that Seven Hills has been an apparition site and that heaven desires that the public have access to the Spring [Maranatha]. It is only human will that is obstructing the way to this important goal. When I speak to you on the thirteenth, it will be a means of bringing My Son's Church on earth and all people under My mantle. My mantle is Holy Love. Make it known."

■ **June 23, 1994.** From Our Lady: "Dear children, My ministry is in your hearts, your sacrifices, your prayers, and in your moment-to-moment decision to live in Holy Love. All of these make up My mantle of protection against which no court can legislate."

■ **June 23, 1994.** I asked: "Blessed Mother, why are we being forced off the property where Your presence is?" Our Lady comes in a silver blue. She is on a cloud and spreads Her hands. "I am the Mother of the Word Incarnate, Jesus Christ. I come to reassure you, no legislation or court can overrule My presence. The opposition that has come against you is only the adversary. At Maranatha, his power is rendered useless. It is the evil of these times that pervades public opinion, and so, the judicial system as well. Do not form human expectations towards this ministry. Accept all that occurs in peace, knowing the victory is in the grace of My Heart." She leaves in a bright light.

■ **June 23, 1994.** Our Lady came as Our Lady of Grace. She parted Her hands and said, "It is necessary that you suffer in this way so that My messages to you about Holy Love will be propagated. Your prayers tonight from this place are more meaningful than if you prayed from the halls of a great palace, for God sees the sincerity of the intentions in your heart. Tonight, I ask prayers most especially, for the great needs I hold in My Heart." Our Lady then asked us to pray with Her. When Our Lady prayed the *Glory Be*, She ascended higher toward heaven with Her arms fully outstretched, and a large light came down upon Her. She continued: "Dear children, tonight I ask your perseverance and trust in the way that I lead you. Perhaps you do not see the path I call you upon clearly. But I tell you, it is Holy Love. Therefore, My little children, live each moment in Holy Love and continue to pray, pray, pray for all of My needs." She blessed us and faded away.

■ **June 28, 1994.** Our Lady came in white on a cloud. There is a pink stripe around Her mantle. She says: "I am with the Thursday night prayer group more profoundly than if they prayed in a great cathedral. I call them to persevere in trust and to believe in the graces most abundant at Maranatha. Keep all the commandments by living in Holy Love. It is through sin My children become separated. I desire all to be united in the Immaculate Refuge of My Heart through Holy Love. Every error, every injustice, every misconception that is in the world, was accepted in hearts first. This is why I am calling you to guard well your hearts against every evil and to pray, pray, pray. My daughter, make this known."

■ **June 29, 1994.** After Communion Jesus showed me a shoe stepping on a little flower. He said the flower was the ministry, the shoe was Satan. Then I saw Our Lady's hand come in and pick the flower. She said She was moving it to safer ground.

■ **June 30, 1994.** This morning Our Lady told me that the flower was picked and not transplanted, because the roots would still be at the original site.

■ **June 30, 1994.** Our Lady is here as Our Lady of Grace. She spreads Her hands, looks up to heaven and says: "Praise be to Jesus. Dear children, pray with Me now that there be peace in all hearts." We prayed. "Tonight, dear children, I invite you to understand the world has an uncertain peace, and a false peace. I invite all My children to be united in Holy Love, and to reconcile themselves to the cross by accepting everything that comes into their lives as God's Will and in Holy Love. I am with you tonight, dear children, praying with you; and I am carrying your prayers to My Son's Throne in heaven. I impart to you now My Motherly Blessing." She fades away.

July 1994

■ **July 6, 1994.** Our Lady comes with Her Heart exposed. She looks up to heaven, opens Her hands and says: "Praise be to Jesus. I will come tomorrow with many graces. I desire the people who come pray for those who oppose the ministry. Yes, I do call you upon a difficult path but not without grace. Please love the way upon which I lead you. For when you are loving, we are united. Every provision comes through My Heart." She leaves. Her Heart is left in the air. I understand we are to name the Prayer Center after Her Immaculate Heart.

■ **July 6, 1994.** Our Lady is here in blue and She says: "Pray for hearts hewn in stone - and they number in the millions. Grace can transform all hearts if the soul is willing. The spring is already convicting hearts. All that you suffer in these recent trials is for those who most need the spring. You will patiently endure." She left.

■ **July 7, 1994 / Thursday Rosary Service - Message To Priests.** *(At the new prayer site in Broadview Heights, Ohio)* Our Lady is here in white and says: "Pray with Me now for all priests, bishops and cardinals that they embrace courageously the new catechism." We prayed. When we said the *Glory Be*, She ascended higher, Her arms raised and outstretched, and She had many angels all around Her. "My daughter, the new catechism is the embodiment of the Faith. Those that are not for the Church are against it. Dear children, tonight I do not call you here in defeat, but in victory. For it is when your heart embraces Holy Love that My Heart is victorious. It is because your prayers are so meaningful that you are opposed at every turn. Dear children do pray, pray, pray. Tonight, I am consecrating these grounds towards the victory of My Immaculate Heart in the world, and I am blessing you now." She fades away.

■ **July 8, 1994.** Our Lady is here in two shades of blue. She says: "Dear children, it is impossible to embrace Holy Love and still sin, for Holy Love is the embodiment of God's commandments. Through Holy Love, I intend to lead souls into the New Jerusalem. No one enters the Kingdom of Heaven who does not first love God and then his neighbor as himself. Therefore, My children, see that in Holy Love you find your salvation."

■ **July 9, 1994.** Jesus says: "Each person will find his own truth in what is written about the ministry, but the reality of Truth is in the messages and the fruits they bear."

■ **July 10, 1994.** From Our Lady: "I am calling each one to remember the great value heaven places on one *'Hail Mary'*. It is the price of a soul. Once prayed, it cannot be retrieved. Therefore, come to see the value of prayer from the heart. I give to you now, My Motherly Blessing."

■ **July 13, 1994.** Our Lady is here wearing a white gown, a blue mantle, and a white veil. She says: "I have called all My children together tonight to pray for My Son's Church on earth, which is much maligned and divided by compromise. Dear children, if you do not accept the catechism that has been given you by My Pope, then you cannot call yourselves Catholic. Further, I invite you to understand, you do not have peace in the world because all hearts have not made peace with God's Will. Go to the well on this property which is abundant, which has abundant grace for you. I impart to you now My Motherly Blessing."

■ **July 14, 1994 / Thursday Rosary Service.** Our Lady is here in white. She has a crown on Her head and has many angels with Her. She is welcoming everyone. She says: "Dear children, when you return to your communities, make the message of Holy Love known and bring it alive in your hearts so that, in this way, you are My special missionaries of Holy Love. Pray with Me now for those who have not heard the message." We prayed. She says: "Thank you. Dear children, I desire that your hearts be united in Holy Love. I am with you always when you have prayer in your heart. I take your petitions directly to My Son. Dear children, be examples of Holy Love. It is through Holy Love I am leading souls along the path of holiness, then into the New Jerusalem." (A fiery cross is now in front of Our Lady.) "Please embrace the crosses Jesus gives you. For the cross is Holy Love and earns many graces for souls. I am blessing you now." She leaves.

■ **July 17, 1994.** Our Lady is here in a white gown and blue mantle. Her Heart is exposed. She says: "Please pray with Me for souls in darkness." We prayed. "I'm sorry I need to reveal to you some of the sorrow of My Heart. You do not see the darkest motives in hearts that I see. You are only seeing a trifle of what is real and present in hearts. This is why all your prayers need to be for hearts: that they change, that they choose holiness, for time is so short and God's justice so complete. Do not fear for how, or why, only step forward in faith. It is pride that asks reasons and questions, but humility only says yes."

■ **July 19, 1994.** Our Lady is here. She says: "My children, be pleased to know, this is where the grace from Maranatha Spring will be carried. Every promise attendant to Maranatha will be present here and come to fulfillment. I desire you keep this area as pristine (unspoiled) as possible. Pray here often for the many pilgrims who will come in need, and know that I am always with you at this sight. You have many roads ahead of you, but they are all covered by My mantle of protection. Therefore, My little children, be at peace and know I am with you."

■ **July 21, 1994.** Our Lady is here as Our Lady of Grace. She says: "Dear children, pray with Me now for those who have hardened hearts." We prayed. "Dear children, you see with what difficulty you meet to pray. This is how precious grace is rejected in the world. Come to know, I am with you wherever you meet to pray and whenever you have prayer in your hearts. Seek always the safe Refuge of My Immaculate Heart. I, your Mother, bid you, do not be discouraged. Continue to pray, pray, pray."

■ **July 21, 1994.** Our Lady comes back in white. "You have suffered and you have prayed. Come to realize God's Kingdom is now in your hearts. It is when you most need, I am presenting all your needs to the Father. Your needs do not go unanswered. I do not speak to all nations tonight, but to those who pray for My intentions. Make it known."

■ **July 22, 1994.** Our Lady is here in a bright light, dressed in white. She says: "Dear children, these days you view cosmic events with great awe and anticipation. Do you not see what great power God has over the universe? It is He alone that determines the course of every heavenly body. How can such a God continue to tolerate the sacrileges against life, and the rebellion against His laws in the world today? In all of this, please realize it is only by way of God's Mercy you still exist in His universe. It is through prayer and many sacrifices grace continues to sustain you. One day there may be no time left for prayer. Therefore, My little children, if you are listening, pray, pray, pray." She leaves.

■ **July 23, 1994.** Jesus says: "These things are of one accord, My Father's Will and the course laid bare in Holy

Love. Anything - thought, action or otherwise - that separates you from this chosen path is from Satan. The hearts that follow this path do not follow singularly but united with all the ones who follow. Do not say: this one follows well and so he is chosen, for not all come along the path with equal ease. All that takes a soul from the path is his own will. Such a one becomes known through his own actions. Therefore, trust everyone until he proves himself untrustworthy, but love all - all whom are coming."

■ **July 23, 1994.** There is a rosary of lights around the statue of Our Lady and She says: "My dear little children, see with what great compassion I pour the grace of My Heart onto this ministry." [When She said this, a great light projected outward from the heart of the statue.] "Continue to follow the path I lead you upon in holy obedience and do not allow Satan to rupture the line of trust you have obtained through prayer, much prayer. It is he alone who disrupts every effort, but through grace you will find the path once again. Remember, today's persecution is tomorrow's grace. In all of these trials, give praise to Jesus."

■ **July 25, 1994.** "Place the stations [of the cross at Maranatha Spring] where they are most naturally suited." Our Lady is here in blue and white. She spreads Her arms and light comes from where Her Heart would be. She says: "Tonight, I invite you to pray My Prayer Center into being, for it is not through human effort but by grace alone that this will come to pass. My children, many will come here seeking the refuge of My Heart, and you must become Holy Love to each one. Let this effort be one of love, so that when all is said and done, it can be said all was accomplished in love. I invite you now to be prisoners of My Heart, engaging always in prayers which will last for all eternity." She blessed us and left. All the while Our Lady was here, the birds were singing in the background.

■ **July 26, 1994.** After Communion Jesus told me, "Pray for unbelieving hearts for this is where all the opposition lies. Each time My Mother comes to you, She will pray privately with you for unbelievers."

■ **July 29, 1994.** Our Lady appeared in white. She said: "Further, I come to inform you My visit to you on August 13 will hold significant meaning and bring to earth many graces. But you, My daughter, need to prepare with many sacrifices for My coming. It will be the first time you will see the broader spectrum of My visits. I am telling you these things now, so that you will be ready and open to all heaven will give. Do not fear but give praise to Jesus."

■ **July 30, 1994.** Jesus told me after Communion: "There are many paths around the same obstacle. They all lead to My Heart. All are Holy Love. Anything accomplished outside of Holy Love does not lead to Me."

■ **July 30, 1994.** Our Lady told me in a locution that the reason She most often appears to children, and in remote areas, is because; these people are simplistic and ready to believe. She said the more our hearts are ensnared in the world, the harder it is to believe in Her apparitions. [Two young boys, ages 6 and 7, saw Our Lady when She came for last Thursday's Rosary Service.]

■ **July 30, 1994.** Our Lady came at the end of holy hour. A light shone from the Host onto Her. She said: "My angel, you must make very many sacrifices now, most especially for unbelievers. So many believe in the world but not in God. They place value on everything but their soul. These are the ones who do not realize the choices they are making. It is a grace Jesus allows Me to come and tell you this. Place all concerns in My Heart and pray, pray, pray."

■ **July 31, 1994.** I was thinking of something in the past that I was sorry for. Jesus came and said: "Do you not know all your iniquity has been consumed in the eternal flame of love that is My Heart? My Divine Mercy is My Divine Love. Nothing remains but My Love."

August 1994

■ **August 2, 1994.** Our Lady is here. She wants us to pray with Her for unbelievers. She says, "My children, the reason I persevere in coming to you on Thursday evenings is to reconcile the world to love and to call them away from the path of self-destruction. Therefore, when you suffer great difficulties on account of these meetings, remember the great need in My Heart for your prayers and your sacrifices. Do not be impatient, but in love, pray the harder."

■ **August 4, 1994.** Our Lady is here with St. John Vianney. She is dressed in blue and white. She says, "Dear children, it is necessary that you endure these hardships for the sake of unbelievers. Pray with me now for their conversion." We prayed an *Our Father* and *Glory Be*. She continued. She says, "Thank you. Dear children, I invite you tonight to realize that every sin is a failure in Holy Love, and every conversion is a result of the choice towards Holy Love. Therefore, My little children, please realize that Holy Love is the path to your salvation. I impart to you now My Motherly Blessing." She leaves.

■ **August 7, 1994.** Our Lady is here in blue and white. She says, "Pray with Me now for the unbelievers." We prayed. She continues, "Tonight, dear children, it is My joy to tell you when I come Saturday, My hands will come full of gifts. After this thirteenth, My visits to you will take on a national and even international scope. Prepare your hearts for what is coming. I am loving you and praying for you." She blesses us and leaves.

■ **August 9, 1994.** "Dear children, I invite you once again to please God by deciding for holiness. Overcome the evil that is in your hearts first so that you can help the world to overcome evil. If you are envious or unforgiving, choose to love. Then My victory can begin in you. Pray and ask God to reveal to you your faults so that you can be closer to heaven. I am coming soon to bring many favors, and prodigies will abound. But you, My children, must not pray because of miracles but pray because you love."

■ **August 11, 1994.** Our Lady is here dressed all in white. She has a bright light all around Her and a light coming from Her Immaculate Heart. She says: "My children, dear children, I am encouraged by your presence and your perseverance. Pray with Me now for those who have hearts of stone." We prayed. "Thank you. I cherish your prayers." Now there is a cross of light coming from Her heart. "Dear children, tonight I invite you to realize and understand in your hearts that sin is committed only in the present moment. Therefore, consecrate your hearts to holiness so that in this holy possession, you give every thought, word and deed to God. Dear children, I am loving you into eternity." She blessed us and faded away.

■ **August 12, 1994.** From Our Lady: "I desire that under the Protection of this Image [Our Lady of Guadalupe] - 'Mother of the Americas' - you place the Roman Catholic Church in America, so that I will protect it against sacrilege, apostasy and the worship of false idols. In this way, I will place under My Mantle of protection My Son's Church in the Americas."

■ **August 12, 1994.** Jesus says: "When My Mother comes tomorrow, one hand will be filled with power, the other, with might. It will be proof of My Mother's coming to you. None will leave untouched by grace. Do you not know that in obedience you accomplish more than in many sacrifices? If the people pray outdoors, they will be protected in the Refuge of My Mother's Heart which is greater than any shelter on earth. Have them face the statue that has been erected. Mark this down."

■ **August 13, 1994.** *(Servants of Mary Center in Windsor, Ohio, with a 50-foot-tall statue of Our Lady of Guadalupe.)* A bolt of lightning and a loud clap of thunder preceded Our Lady. She comes as Our Lady of Guadalupe and She is holding the Eucharist in Her hands. She says: "Pray with Me now for unbelievers." We prayed. "I am pleased you are all here together, here praying and loving. My Son, Jesus, sends Me under this title, Our Lady of Guadalupe - 'Patroness of the Americas', for He desires there no longer be apostasy, sacrilege or worship of false idols in His church on earth. Under this title, He desires that I protect the Roman Catholic Church, most especially in the west where it is much maligned. He desires to be esteemed and honored in the Blessed Sacrament and recognized in every tabernacle in the world. Dear children, it is My joy to tell you all the water on this property is truly blessed and holy. For I have touched it Myself. Tonight, I am imparting to you My Motherly Blessing and asking you to pray, pray, pray." She blessed us and left.

■ **August 15, 1994 - Feast of the Assumption.** Our Lady is here as Our Lady of Guadalupe. The stars on Her mantle are like lights. She says: "I am Mary, Mother of the Lord Jesus Christ."
I ask: "Blessed Mother, why are you coming under this title?" "I come as Patroness of the Americas to draw the Holy Roman Catholic Church under My Mantle of Protection. Time is short and soon the malefactor will fasten his grip around My Son's Church. Most especially, I come to maintain the faith in the Americas. Already, the seed of apostasy is in hearts that

will influence the faith of a multitude. My Son is already too greatly put to shame in the tabernacles around the world. He is truly present and little esteemed, in most churches. It is the outpouring of prayers that brings Me to you. My presence in your midst on the thirteenth of September, October, and on December Twelfth, comes amidst great prodigies and signs, so that hearts will return to devotion of My Son in the Eucharist."

She is crying now. "I can no longer console My Son. You must console Him through your love. I do not come to bring prestige to earth, but to return love and faith to hearts." She opens Her hands, and a light comes from where Her Heart would be. "I desire souls come to Me now, and always, under this title." She leaves.

■ **August 15, 1994 - Feast of the Assumption.** Our Lady comes in white. She says: "My angel, I come today from love. Dear children, let this be the moment, the day, you decide to love. Take everything from your hearts that is not love. Do not think ill of each other. When you nurture such thoughts in your hearts, you begin to judge. These thoughts are from darkness and do not come from God. My Son calls each of you to a special mission, where you are right now, in this present moment. My victory will begin in you according to your response to My call to Holy Love. All that God asks of you begins now in love. Make it known."

■ **August 18, 1994.** Our Lady is here dressed in a pink gown and white mantle. She is holding a scapular in Her right hand and a rosary in Her left. Both hands are extended out towards us. She says: "Pray with Me now for the conversion of all sinners." We prayed. Then She asked us to pray for those who do not recognize the sin in their lives. We prayed. "My children, these two - the scapular and the Rosary - are symbols of Holy Love for it is impossible to have devotion to either without embracing Holy Love in your heart. I desire very much through your prayer group that these two be made known and brought to light in these times, for herein is My victory. Unite your hearts in Holy Love, dear children, and place all your burdens in My Immaculate Heart. It is in this way I can enlighten you, and My victory can begin in you. I impart to you tonight My Motherly Blessing." She leaves.

■ **August 20, 1994.** Our Lady is here in a sky-blue mantle with gold stars and a gold border on it. She has a bright-gold crown on Her head. Her gown is white. She says: "Today especially, child, I come to help you understand that all that takes place in the world, even nature itself, is a consequence of what is in man's heart. Hearts that do not align their will with the Will of God change and alter human events. This has been true from the beginning of time. So then, when you pray, ask that people choose the Will of God. Remember, it is a special grace to accept change easily. It is also a grace to accept reality and to perceive where hearts are. Be assured, Jesus and I are with you. My mantle is over you. The Prayer Center is God's ordaining Will and, therefore, will materialize. Continue to pray for faith and courage. I desire very much to share My Heart with you." She leaves and a lighted heart is in the air.

■ **August 21, 1994.** Our Lady comes in gray, floating on a cloud. She says: "My children that assemble to pray, most especially on the thirteenth, come because of miracles. I so much desire they come in Holy Love. When I next come to you on the thirteenth, I will bring My Son. I am petitioning My Son to allow even greater signs wherever I appear. Make it known."

■ **August 24, 1994.** Our Lady comes in white with green plants (they look like palm leaves) around Her. I ask: "Blessed Mother, I thought you were coming with all the heavenly court." She replies: "I will come in this way on the thirteenth. It is with great, great joy I come to announce to you the special graces Jesus is placing in My hands to extend to the faithful who assist in prayer on Thursday night. One hand will overflow with physical, the other with spiritual healings. I will manifest God's love and gratitude this Thursday to those who assemble. Watch for changes in hearts. Do not fear the greatest trial which is indeed grace in disguise. What has been dealt to you unjustly will be turned to mercy and grace soon. For God sustains those who trust in Him." She seems to throw me a kiss with both hands, and a great light comes from Her Heart as She leaves.

■ **August 25, 1994.** Our Lady is here in pink and gray. She says: "Pray with Me now for unbelievers." We prayed. "Dear children, tonight I come especially to allow the nectar of grace that is Holy Love to penetrate your hearts. It is this love, dear children, that enables you to carry your cross. Each one has a cross particularly suited to his own life. I'm inviting you, dear children, to follow Me and consecrate your hearts to Holy Love so that I can take you to paradise." She blessed us and faded away.

■ **August 28, 1994.** *(4:30 a.m.)*
Our Lady's Invitation To Holy Love
Our Lady comes in blue. Her Immaculate Heart is exposed. She says: "Pick up your pen, My angel. Jesus sends Me this day to instruct souls on the spiritual annuity that is the Flame of Holy Love. This is the purifying Flame of My Heart. When souls choose to enter My Heart by this portal, they are consumed with Holy Love. Their imperfections burn away, and they are made most perfect and easily led to the Divine Love that is My Son's Heart. Though I hold every sinner in the refuge of My Heart, it is these souls especially who desire to purify themselves through the Flame of Holy Love, that I am embracing most profoundly and plunging deepest into My Heart. This Flame of Holy Love is all-consuming and does not permit the soul to retreat from its embrace. This is the

sanctification I desire all souls aspire to. Make this known to all of My little children."

■ **August 28, 1994.** Our Lady is here in a red mantle and a blue gown. Her Heart is exposed. She bends over me and says: "Oh, that souls would long to be purified in the Flame of Holy Love that is My Heart! Oh, that they would plunge themselves into the depths of this Refuge in this way! This Flame cleanses the soul of all that obstructs the path to holy perfection. My child, call My children into this Flame of Holy Love, which so long has sought to sanctify the world through love. My Son sends Me over and over to call souls from the path of perdition through this Consuming Torch that is My Immaculate Heart - Holy Love. Give praise and homage to He who so sends Me."

■ **August 30, 1994.** Jesus says: "Bring all of My Mother's children into the Eternal Flame of Holy Love that is Her Immaculate Heart. It is the Refuge of Salvation and Sanctity."

■ **August 31, 1994.** Jesus says: "Let your existence be fuel to the Eternal Flame of Love that is My Mother's Heart of Holy Love."

■ **August 31, 1994.** From Our Lady: "My daughter, ask My children to assemble at the East Mill Apparition Site, Sunday afternoon, to pray against Satan's tactics in Cairo.* Man is attempting to negotiate God's Providence. My Heart draws all sinners into this Flame of Holy Love. It is an eternal flame and the means of salvation Heaven extends to humanity. Let it be all-consuming and all-encompassing. I desire by means of this Flame to lead souls to Divine Love, which is the Eucharistic Heart of My Beloved Son. There is no path to supersede this path. I impart to you now My Motherly Blessing."

International Conference on Population and Development in Cairo, Egypt from Sept. 5 – 13.

■ **August 31, 1994.** Our Lady is here in white with gold reflections on Her mantle. She says: "My daughter, do not let your heart be troubled over opinions. Let the grace of My Heart resolve obstinate issues. If My messages to you are challenged, it is because My words to you are challenging hearts - even hearts who consider themselves in judgment over the Ministry. Do not allow Satan the victory of destroying your peace in the present moment. Today it is My special joy to reveal to you that there will be three apparition sites connected with My appearances to you. Just as we planned three faucets at Maranatha Spring for the Father, Son and Holy Spirit, now there will be three springs instead. My Son will not be outdone in generosity. So you will have a grace-filled spring in Seven Hills, the East Mill Apparition Site, and a third site as yet to be revealed, where Immaculate Heart Prayer Center will be built. The veil is being lifted now, and this is the hour to give praise to Jesus. Do not pay heed to confusion for in My Heart is the clarity for every situation. I am drawing sinners into the Flame of Holy Love - that vibrant Flame that is My Immaculate Heart. It is not without effort we must persevere in each trial remembering Satan only opposes that which is good. It is My loving joy to be with you." She leaves and a light is in the air momentarily.

September 1994

■ **September 1, 1994.** Jesus says: "Stay with Me. Abide in Me. In Me is every token of good. The property you are being drawn to is not out there. It is here in My Heart, burning ember of Divine Love. Others seek nostalgia, but you need nothing but Me. Place all fractured relationships in My Heart. I do not lay blame. That is Satan. If you are praying for them, you are seeking the fullness of My provision. I came into the world to give witness to the truth. It is the same truth My Mother bears to you. In the truth you will not perish. Therefore, let this anchor you. I am coming on the thirteenth with manifold grace and infinite wisdom. I am your peace and your confidence. The property you are seeking lays barren, awaiting the architect to plant the seed. There is no measure of human law laid claim against it. It is private but accommodating - fertile but forsaken."

■ **September 1, 1994.** Our Lady is here in a pink gown and a gray mantle. She has many angels with Her and says: "Pray with Me now for unbelievers." We prayed. "Dear children, tonight I desire more than ever to be united to you in Holy Love. Therefore, it is My pleasure to ignite in your hearts a Flame of Holy Love, which will help you along the path to the Divine Love that is the most Sacred Heart of My Son. It is by your efforts that I am able to thwart Satan's plans in the world. Therefore, My little children, persevere." She blessed us and left.

■ **September 2, 1994.** Jesus says: "All souls are judged according to their response to Holy Love. It is Holy Love that is My Kingdom. My Heart is a continual libation poured out to souls that Holy Love will inflame their hearts and lead them to salvation."

■ **September 3, 1994.** Our Lady comes as Our Lady of Fatima. She says: "I come especially today to inform you that My image from Guadalupe is bringing many graces with it to Holy Love Ministries. It is through this image souls will be engulfed in Holy Love, the eternal flame of My Immaculate Heart. My mantle is covering the hearts that comprise the Ministry. Peace will prevail. Each heart will find new depths in holiness. It is not long until you make long-range plans - both in and out of the Ministry. Any plan is acceptable as far as it is according to Holy Love. One amongst you is making decisions outside of Holy Love, but My mantle (Guadalupe image) will return this heart to the path of Holy Love. I reveal this to relieve concern not to condemn. The Prayer Center is already under My mantle and in My Heart. So many doors, so many doors, are about to open and reveal hidden treasures long awaiting you. Today, I give you the joy of faith and peace." She leaves.

■ **September 4, 1994 / Address To All Nations.** Our Lady is here in white with a blue border around Her mantle. Blue stars keep appearing and disappearing all over Her mantle. She extends Her hands and says: "My Son sends Me especially to address world leaders as they assemble to negotiate God's gift of life (Cairo Conference). Dear children, you have lost sight of God's purpose for life - mainly salvation. It is not yours to determine who lives and who does not live. You concern yourselves with numbers of people in the world when your concern should be lack of love in the world. The abyss between God and man widens each time a life is taken. Today, you have reached the point of absence of right reason. I solemnly tell you, you will not be capable of legislating against God's justice. The only recourse left is love - Holy Love, which is capable of reconciling souls to God. To those who listen, I say pray, pray, pray."

■ **September 7, 1994.** Our Lady is here in white and has a gold border around Her mantle. She says: "Pray with Me now for all those whose pride enters their faith." We prayed. "Dear children, when you consecrate yourselves to the cross, you are consecrating your lives to Holy Love. I come to you tonight to ask you to make every moment a special gift, to My Son, of Holy Love. On the thirteenth it is My great desire that My children come in procession to My image, and there I will bless them - one hand with miracles, the other with grace. I impart to you now My Motherly Blessing."

■ **September 8, 1994.** Our Lady is here as Our Lady of Grace. "I ask you now to pray with Me for all those who are meeting at the Cairo Conference." We prayed. "Dear little children, it is by your prayers My Heart will be victorious. Do not let Satan distract you by keeping you busy with many things and taking you away from prayer. By My efforts, evil will be turned back. Dear little children, once again I invoke you to pray, pray, pray." Our Lady blessed us and left.

■ **September 10, 1994.** "Great graces are coming to this Ministry - untold graces. For through you I am sending My love to the world, and those who once doubted will believe."

■ **September 10, 1994.** I saw St. Thérèse of Lisieux before Communion. She said: "Many things will come to completion in the month of October."

■ **September 13, 1994.** Jesus is here. He has the banner in His hand as He did at the Resurrection. Our Lady is now next to Him. She is in white. She says: "Dear children, please understand that your glory and your resurrection are in the cross. Therefore, do not reject the cross. Pray with Me now for those who have lost their faith." We prayed. I asked Our Lady to heal the people here today. She said: "All who have assembled are in My Heart of grace, and God knows best their needs. Dear children, tonight I tell you that My joy is in your prayers and your presence here together in Holy Love. My Son's Church is being pierced close to its heart through apostasy and controversy, and I ask your prayers most especially for the church upon earth. I am taking into My Immaculate Heart, the deposit of faith, that all might believe and that it will be safeguarded from evil. Dear children, you are My joy and My love. Continue to pray, pray, pray. I am blessing you now." Then She fades away.

■ **September 14, 1994.** Our Lady is here in two shades of blue and has a crown of stars above Her head. She parts Her hands that are folded, and a lighted cross is where Her

Heart would be. She says: "Child, in the acceptance of every cross is the victory of Satan's defeat. The cross is the light on the path of Holy Love. The more you embrace the cross, which is God's Will, the deeper you are plunged in My Heart to be nourished and guarded. No cross comes to you against God's Will."

■ **September 15, 1994 - Feast of Our Lady of Sorrows.** Our Lady is here as Our Lady of Sorrows. She says: "Please join Me and give praise to Jesus as we pray for sinners farthest from conversion." We prayed. "Dear children, tonight I come especially to ask your cooperation and your acceptance of the cross. It is through your yes to the cross, dear children, that My Heart is victorious. Therefore, My little ones, in every trial see My victory. Continue to pray, pray, pray. I'm blessing you now with My Motherly Blessing." Our Lady then faded away.

■ **September 17, 1994.** Jesus comes forward out of the Host at adoration. The Host becomes His Heart. He says: "Behold My Heart, burning Ember of Divine Love, poured out in libation for the sins of humanity. It is in imitation of Divine Love I draw all peoples through Holy Love. I am Eternal Love, constant beacon to the world that pursues confusion. I call to you now to be pilgrims of Holy Love in the midst of an evil age. Steady your hearts in love. Do not despair. I am with you always."

■ **September 17, 1994.** I asked: "Are you the Mother of God?" She replied: "I am Mary, Immaculate, Mother of Jesus made flesh. I come seeking, as always, your prayers. Through prayer hearts are opened, wills are moved, and heaven opens doors. Nothing is attainable outside of God's Holy and Divine Will. When you are called to Holy Love, you are called to His Will, for they are the same as one. Refuge in My Heart is at once Refuge in God's Will, which is peace. Outside of this

Holy Refuge there is no peace - only confusion. I will lead you into the way, the truth, and the life." She leaves.

■ **September 17, 1994.** Our Lady comes with three angels. "My daughter, My angel, the hour of sorrow has come when the adversary, aware of his defeat, is striking out at My littlest, humblest children. Do not lose courage, but give praise to Jesus as one who is chosen to suffer interiorly as a consequence of devotion to My Immaculate Heart. It is the assessors of My Immaculate Heart in the world that will comprise this army of victim souls who will engage in battle with the evil one. Always, the grace of My Heart is your mantle and refuge. Therefore, be courageous. Spread confidence in My grace which in the end will be triumphant. I am with you, watching over your fortitude, watching your prayers."

■ **September 18, 1994.** Jesus says: "The reason souls lose patience in any situation is they have not sufficiently died to self. This fault lets them view things only in the way it affects themselves. The soul then loses sight of any eternal value of suffering. Every soul falls victim to this fault at times, but serious effort should be made to recognize this selfish love. It is the same spirit that puts war in hearts and so in the world. True, holy perseverance comes from placing self last, and God's Will first. Pray to be strong spiritually and leave all other factors to Me."

■ **September 20, 1994.** Our Lady comes as Our Lady of Guadalupe. She says: "Child, precious angel, please know your 'yes' to Holy Love is your martyrdom. For it is through Holy Love, which is God's Will, you die to self. This is a martyrdom of the will. For your 'yes', just as My 'yes', leaves no room for self. The souls that completely surrender in this way are the army that I am using to come against Satan. Do not fear any petition, for to such a one I cannot refuse. Go in peace."

■ **September 22, 1994.** Our Lady comes and asks me to write down the following prayer:

Missionary Prayer Of Holy Love

"Immaculate Mary, Virgin and Queen of Heaven and Earth, consume my soul in the Flame of Holy Love that is Your Heart. Help me to be Your love in the world and to hasten Your victorious reign through my prayers and acts of Holy Love. Spread Your mantle of protection over Holy Love Ministries. Lead us and guide us. Intercede on our behalf before the throne of Jesus, Your Son. Amen."

She then said: "In this prayer is the future and the present of Holy Love Ministries. Praise be to Jesus."

■ **September 22, 1994.** Our Lady is here as Our Lady of Guadalupe. She says: "I invite you to pray with Me for unbelievers." We prayed. "Dear children, tonight I invite you once again to make prayer your joy. When you pray, dear children, you are united in My Heart; and My grace is overflowing upon you. I desire that you pray for your country and for all countries who legislate anti-Christian laws. Dear children, I want to lead you to My Son. I want you to adore Him in the Blessed Sacrament where He waits for you. I extend to you now My Motherly Blessing."

■ **September 24, 1994.** Our Lady comes with a crown on Her head, in a dark blue mantle with gold stars on it. She says: "These days, please realize nothing depends on you; everything depends on grace. Everything is a grace. Most especially, see the grace in every cross which passes to you by way of Divine Love. These two - Divine Love and Divine Mercy - are inseparable. Evil has easy access to hearts full of self. Such hearts fall easy victim to evil forces and their designs. But always pray for the grace to see Satan at once before his snares entangle you and take hold. His plans are so intricate, at times it is difficult to sort good from evil. It is then you need to use Holy Love as a maxim. Dear daughter, always remember, I am sending My Love to the world through you. Pray, pray, pray."

■ **September 25, 1994.** From Our Lady: "Dear children, I want to make your hearts vessels of Holy Love, for it is through your hearts I send My love to the world. The way out of every situation is grace through prayer. Therefore, My dear little children, persevere and pray, pray, pray."

■ **September 27, 1994.** Jesus comes like He looks in the Divine Mercy picture. He says: "Transcribe this in your notes. My Love and My Mercy are inseparable. My Father will come to you through Holy Love. When you are living in Holy Love, you are living in God's Divine Will, Divine Love, and Divine Mercy. All of these are in My Mother's Heart, for Our Hearts are united. In these there is no injustice."

■ **September 27, 1994.** Our Lady comes in white. She parts Her hands and says: "These days, My child, stumbling blocks to holiness are being removed. It is not without pain this occurs but through grace. I am supporting each soul. Find in My Heart the desire to be the littlest of the little, the least of all, and God will use you to the fullest. No one who desires recognition will be first in the Kingdom. Those who seek after the world will be forsaken spiritually. In this hour, find joy in how God is molding those closest to Me and deepest in My Heart. Often what is taken away is only what stands between the soul and God. It is in such times of confusion and darkness, the soul needs most to trust in Holy Love by plunging himself into the Flame of My Immaculate Heart. I am extending to you now My Motherly Blessing."

■ **September 29, 1994 / Thursday Rosary Service.** Our

Lady is here in blue and white. She says, "All praise be to Jesus. Pray with Me now for all those who have not followed the path of conversion." We prayed. She continues, "Dear children, tonight I want to draw you into the temple of My Heart and lead you before the tabernacle, where My Divine Son awaits you, forsaken and lonely. What a treasure the world passes by. How sad, when they discover what they have missed. Dear children, untold graces await you before the tabernacle, where My Son is always loving, always waiting unattended. I impart to you my Motherly Blessing." She fades away.

■ **September 30, 1994.** Jesus says: "Holy Love is the Tenth Station of the Cross. It is stripping yourself of all that stands between you and salvation. It is dying to your own will. In Holy Love, there is only one will, one opinion that matters, and that is God's. Sanctification comes when the soul can see what stands between himself and God, and he strips himself of it. It is My Tenth Station."

October 1994

■ **October 1, 1994.** Our Lady comes in blue with a white gown. She says: "My dear, dear child, your mission today and always is to embrace Holy Love in the present moment. Therefore, do not find fault with those around you. Look for the positive points in everyone. Make allowance for their errors, for no one is perfect. Even when My Son hung on the Cross, He begged forgiveness for those who were killing Him saying; "They know not what they do." If He was so merciful in that most agonizing moment, how can you but strive to imitate Him in this present moment and every subsequent moment. No one has wronged you to the degree that My Son was wronged. Love, love, love, My angel. For herein is your perfect joy."

■ **October 3, 1994.** From Our Lady: "Dear children, when you pray, ask Jesus to unite priests in My Immaculate Heart for this is the way to avoid schism in My Son's Church. Only if priests are so united will such difficulties be averted. Dear children, pray, pray, pray. And I am blessing you."

■ **October 3, 1994.** From Our Lady: "I am coming on the Thirteenth up here, as well as in Georgia,* to show that God has made Me Queen of Heaven and Earth. I can be anywhere in His power and through His choice without regards to time and space."

* *Apparitions of the Blessed Virgin Mary as 'Our Loving Mother' to Nancy Fowler in Conyers, Georgia from October 13, 1990 – October 13, 1998.*

■ **October 4, 1994.** Our Lady was preceded by St. Michael. She was dressed in a pink gown and blue mantle. She says: "Pray with Me now that all church hierarchy and priests be united in My Immaculate Heart." We prayed. "Dear children, tonight I invite you once again to come into My Immaculate Heart by means of its purifying flame. This Flame, which burns away all iniquity, leads the soul to choose only Holy Love in all thought, word and action. Dear children, continue to pray as I direct you. I love you, My dear little children." Our Lady blessed us and left.

■ **October 5, 1994.** From Our Lady: "Dear children, these days when you suffer much, I tell you it is for My pain that you suffer. It is for priests who betray their vocation. Every uncertainty about the future is for those who do not recognize the path of holiness. Always, and continually, I invite you into the Refuge of My Immaculate Heart. Here, I will purify you in the Flame of Holy Love and present your needs to My Son. Therefore, persevere, My dear little ones. Pray, pray, pray."

■ **October 5, 1994.** Jesus says: "The beauty and simplicity of My Mother's messages to you escapes the proud heart but is readily perceived by the humble heart. I do not send Her to you to influence the favor of those who place themselves in important positions in the world, but to change the hearts of sinners."

■ **October 6, 1994.** Our Lady is here in white. There are sparkling lights around Her. She tells me to get something to write on and almost seems to shoo me away as I was caught up in the vision. She says: "I am Mary, Mother of Jesus Christ. My children, dear children, I want your hearts to be on fire with love so that they are little flames of Holy Love. I want you to imitate My Motherly Heart which is aflame with Holy Love. You think too often it does not matter what you have in your hearts - that it is hidden. You think no one knows. I am telling you, Jesus and I know your hearts; and We know when you are not loving. Then all that is in your hearts is spilled out into the world. If it is anger or bitterness, then this is all around you. If it is deceit, then the world around you is deceitful. If you choose love, joy, and peace, then Jesus and I are in the world close by and helping you. This is why Jesus sends Me to you - to help you choose love. The present moment is the time God gives you to love, and when you are loving, My dear, dear children, your hearts are already in heaven." She leaves.

■ **October 7, 1994 - Feast of the Holy Rosary.** I heard angels singing, "O Queen of the Holy Rosary." Then Our Lady came in glistening white with a crown on Her head and holding a rosary. She said: "Begin to see, My humble servant, the rosary is the weapon against evil, but Holy Love is the ammunition. Without Holy Love in the heart, all prayers are stripped of power. Your free will must stand guard over your heart so that you decide in every moment to love. This is how to make your prayers in your heart first, for when your heart is full of conflict and ill will, your prayers are rendered useless. I am calling you always to love first and then to pray. Then, I will crush the head of the dragon by your efforts. Your love is always My joy. It is through your love I am victorious." She leaves.

■ **October 7, 1994 – Feast of the Holy Rosary.** *(8 p.m.)* Our Lady is here all in white. She has a rosary framed all around her and has the barn of the future site property of her prayer center in front of her. She says, "Your prayers are bearing good fruit, therefore be at peace. Pray with Me now for peace in all hearts." We prayed. She continues, "Praise, Honor and Glory be to Jesus."

"Dear children, when you are praying, you are united in My Heart. Tonight I invite you to pray for all those who make gods of their free will. That they will unite in My Heart through your prayers and your sacrifices. All around you is discord and disunity, in your families, in your prayer communities and even in countries. All the more I invoke you to pray, pray, pray." She blesses us and leaves.

■ **October 9, 1994.** Our Lady is here in white and has a gold sash. She says: "My prayer tonight is for those who come in pilgrimage on Thursday seeking holiness. Please join Me." We prayed. "Dear children, accept your crosses just as My Son accepted His Cross though innocent. The Cross is love, strength and salvation, and the guiding hand into the future. Your prayers, My dear children, are the light on the path. Place all your needs at My Son's feet where He remains in the tabernacles of the world. I will join you and petition His Heart for your every need. Dear children, I am extending to you My Motherly Blessing."

■ **October 10, 1994.** Our Lady comes in two shades of blue. She says: "Behold My Son, always and truly present in the tabernacles of the world though little esteemed. Commend to

His Benevolent Heart your every need in the present, as well as, the future." Now Our Lady has white flowers falling from Her Heart. "My angel, you do not see the graces you merit with each trial when you accept all in Holy Love. This acceptance is your peace. It is only when the soul opposes God's Will for him that he loses peace. So it is humble submission to God's Divine Will that earns for the soul swift passage on the path of holiness and advancement towards holy perfection. I am sending a certain joy to you soon, which some would consider a cross but you will recognize as My grace. It will convert many. Do not speculate its nature. The grace will not announce itself but arrive unexpectedly." She smiles because She knows I'm curious. "Be at peace in the present moment."

■ **October 10, 1994.** Our Lady is here with a crown on Her head, and She is in white and gold. She says: "Dear children, during this age, this hour of chastisement that weighs upon the earth, please know the Holy Spirit is convicting each heart towards good and evil. It is so that souls will come to terms with their own salvation and their conversion in the present moment. Dear children, you are always in My Heart - in My Heart of grace - deep within the boundaries of My Motherly love. Dear children, I am blessing you now."

■ **October 13, 1994.** *(5:30 a.m.)* Our Lady comes in white with many lights around Her. She says: "Are you awake?" I nod. She continues: "Today, I am coming asking once again that the people love. For in love is faith, and Satan is attacking faith on all sides. He comes as good, clothed in progress and change. But he is prying the Roman Catholic Church from the people who seek change. If My children return to prayer through a deep love for Jesus in the Eucharist, they will begin to see how the adversary attacks the faith. This is why I come - for love."

■ **October 13, 1994.** Our Lady is here as Our Lady of

Guadalupe. She says: "Dear children, pray with Me now for the Church in the Americas." We prayed. "Dear children, My dear little children, tonight I invite you more than ever to have hearts filled with Holy Love. It is only through love, My dear children, that your faith will be strong; and I will be able to lead you into the New Jerusalem. These days Satan attacks on every side with compromise and change, and tries to lead you away from the Holy Father, but I am calling you back to the Eternal Love - My Son in the Eucharist. I invite you to make Him the center of your lives and your prayers. I extend to you My Motherly Blessing."

■ **October 14, 1994.** Our Lady comes as Our Lady of Guadalupe. She smiles and parts Her hands. She says: "Please understand, My child, the miracle is in hearts that love and not in special signs. Signs are newsworthy, but the fruit is in hearts. And so, when you pray, pray for hearts to embrace Holy Love. What is given beyond this is initiated in heaven and through no call of your own. But your prayers and sacrifices serve to open hearts to Holy Love. Therefore, be at peace." I asked: "But wouldn't more believe and live the message if special signs were given?" She replied: "God works in each soul according to His Will. If a soul needs a certain grace to believe and God chooses to work in this way, it will happen." I remarked: "It just seems so many more would believe if there were more signs." She responded: "The message should be proof of heaven's presence in itself. Please surrender your will here. Pray to be a good messenger and for hearts to love. That is enough." She parts Her hands again and a bright light comes from where Her Heart would be. She leaves.

■ **October 15, 1994.** Our Lady is here in blue and white. She says: "Dear children, the hour has come when you need to pool your resources just as the apostles did, all for the greater glory of God. If it is time you can give alone, then you can give time. If it is money, money. If it is prayer, then give prayer. All towards the effort of this Prayer Center which will serve the flock. Dear children, the Hour of Justice has arrived. There is no more time to waste. Therefore, search your hearts, find your assets, and contribute generously."

■ **October 18, 1994.** Our Lady is here in a mist - floating on a cloud. She is in white. She says: "My daughter, My angel, in this hour of decision that weighs upon the world, Holy Love must be the fruit that tips the scales in favor of conversion. For this reason, it is as though the Ministry will return from exile to grow and flourish in hearts. The property that you have negotiated on will be a hospice of spirituality if hearts are willing. You need to pray now that hearts open and unite toward this end. Remember, in the end all that remains is love; and love alone determines your eternity. Satan is intent on opposing this message."

■ **October 20, 1994.** Our Lady is here in blue and white. She has gold roses [Roses signify graces] at Her feet, and She is dropping rose petals on the people here. Our Lady then asked us to pray with Her for unbelievers. We prayed. "Dear children, tonight I come once again to ask you to be apostles of Holy Love, for the salvation of so many rests upon this. I reveal to you tonight that God's Will is My Immaculate Heart and Holy Love. Therefore, My little children, you cannot afford not to spread this message of salvation. I impart to you tonight My Motherly Blessing."

■ **October 21, 1994.** Jesus says: "The Holy Love in your heart is a reflection of My Divine Love. My Divine Love is unconditional. Therefore, see that what keeps your love from being unconditional is what obstructs your progress in Holy Love. Holy Love and holiness are one. I love you despite every imperfection in Holy Love."

■ **October 23, 1994.** From Our Lady: "Do not dwell on

solutions to your problems. These are always and forever, in the grace of My Heart. Therefore, do not feel the solutions are within your comprehension."

■ **October 24, 1994.** *(During Holy Hour)* Jesus says: "To give of yourself means to open your heart to insult and rejection. But Holy Love does not weary of giving. Look at Me in the Blessed Sacrament. Here I offer My Presence over and over - continually. How many come? How many love and respect Me? But I do not withdraw. My love is unconditional. I do not fear rejection nor spurn those who hurt Me. I continue to love for My love is a humble love. I do not store in My Heart the names of those who insult Me through apathy. I continue to wait for their return. In Me is the way to love."

■ **October 25, 1994.** Jesus says: "All that the world holds in esteem - money, power, pleasures - is convicted by Holy Love. It is the humble heart that loves most ardently, and desires most profoundly, union with Me. See then, all that opposes Holy Love is pride. It is Holy Love that will lead souls into the New Jerusalem. It is Holy Love that will rule all hearts."

■ **October 27, 1994.** Our Lady is here in blue and pink with many roses on Her gown. She says: "Pray with Me now for those who will make the pilgrimage to Windsor on December Twelfth." We prayed. "Dear children, each time I come to you it is so that you will love more. The more you love, My dear children, the more fragrant the aroma of your prayers as they ascend to heaven; and the deeper I take you into My Immaculate Heart. The more you love, the longer I can stay the Arm of Justice. Dear little children, love, love, love." Our Lady blessed us and faded away.

November 1994

■ **November 1, 1994 – All Saints Day Rosary Service.**
Our Lady is here in grey and white. She says, "All praise be
to Jesus. Pray with Me now for unbelievers who will come
on December 12th." We prayed. "Dear children, once again
tonight I come as My Son permits, to invite you to have loving
hearts. When you have love in your hearts, My dear children,
you are more easily united with My Son, through prayer and
the sacraments. Dear children, I never tire of asking you to
spread Holy Love in the world around you. For this is the way
to hold back the Arm of Justice. Tonight I am extending to you
once again My Motherly Blessing."

■ **November 3, 1994.** From Our Lady: "Make no mistake, My
angel. This mission is souls. I desire so much that you become
a missionary of Holy Love, thus spreading the conflagration
of love that is My Heart to the most distant points. Thus, it
will be necessary to take upon yourself the cross of many
journeys, so that souls can sojourn to My Heart. When you
pray with a heart overflowing with Holy Love, all things are
possible. Bring souls to Me in this way. Make known this:
My desire for the formation of Refuge of Mary Prayer Cells
around the world, because My Heart is the spiritual refuge
all must seek during this tribulation. I desire these prayer
cells be lights on the path of Holy Love. You will need to be
ambassadors, traveling from one group to another, lending
incite and encouragement. A format of prayer will be handed
over to you soon. Be at peace, and do not question the 'why'
or 'wherefore'. I am loving you."

■ **November 6, 1994.** Jesus says: "My Heart is an oblation
of love poured out for humanity. I held nothing back for Myself.
I gave all, unconditionally. Holy Love is an imitation of My
Divine Love. It holds no record of wrongdoing. It carries no

promise of reward for love tendered. Holy and Divine Love have no self-interest at stake. This is how to live then. This is the doorway to sanctity."

■ **November 7, 1994.** Our Lady comes in white with many sparkling lights around Her. She says: "Today, I come to help you understand that in order to have Holy Love in your heart, you must first remove from your heart all that is not loving. This is any anger or bitterness which stems from the pride of unforgiveness. When you pray, ask Me, and I will help you to overcome these faults. I want to help you. I want you to let go of all that stands between us. Therefore, do not sulk about errors and wrongs done to you in the past. It only comes between us. Recognize unforgiveness as Satan's tool. I desire our hearts beat as one. Please make this known, as I want to uncover Satan where he lies hidden in hearts." She leaves.

■ **November 9, 1994.** Jesus says: "Write this down. It is a special favor of My Heart that extends this knowledge to you. Every heart is offered the Flame of Holy Love to burn within it. The more the soul perfects itself in Holy Love, the more intense and greater the flame that burns in the heart. Satan's efforts are spent in extinguishing this flame in every heart that accepts Holy Love. If the flame is smothered, then the world around that soul is not lit up by love. Satan uses the person's own faults to extinguish this Holy Flame. Therefore, see that the more the soul perfects himself in Holy Love, the more difficult it becomes for Satan to extinguish the love within the heart."

■ **November 10, 1994.** Our Lady comes as Our Lady of Fatima. She says: "Pray with Me now for all unconverted hearts. Dear children, tonight I solemnly invite you to open your hearts to the Kingdom of God. When you have Holy Love in your hearts, you already have the reign of God within.

This is the greatest miracle. This is your conversion. Dear children, I love you, and I desire that you give to God the present moment. I extend to you now My Motherly Blessing."

■ **November 13, 1994.** From Our Lady: "I know before you speak what is in your heart. It is so in every instance. Every fault stems from pride which opposes Holy Love. This is why perfection in Holy Love takes much courage and introspection. Any fault can be overcome when it is met head-on, dressed in the grace of My Heart. In the same way, you can come to accept the faults of others. Satan tries to bring division by intolerance of other's faults. But you cannot change others. You can change yourself and the way you respond to others. Think of it as a contest between you and Satan, for this is what it is. Satan points out to you the aggravating traits of others. You know you are commanded by God to love everyone, and your peace is destroyed. Do this: Cover yourself with the Precious Blood. Command the pride of perfectionism to leave in the Name of Jesus. Then look for the good in that person. Everyone has positive characteristics. When the malefactor sees you no longer harbor negative thoughts about others, he will gradually withdraw. Then there will be unity through love. Pray for the grace of patience with the path of perfection in Holy Love. It is a path I call you upon. Not all answer or have the courage to answer. I am with you, leading you."

■ **November 13, 1994.** *(To the Texas Group)* Our Lady is here as Our Lady of Guadalupe. She says, "Praise be to Jesus. Pray for Me at this time for all those who are spiritually blind." We prayed. She continues, "Today I invite you in a special way to be a light on the path to others leading them to My Heart through Holy Love. Dear, dear children, the cross is love and grace in disguise. How special you are. How dear to My Heart. Be ambassadors of Holy Love, leading them always to the light. I extend to you My Motherly Blessing."

■ **November 13, 1994.** *(To the Texas Group)* Our Lady says, "Tell them I desire that they lead souls into the New Jerusalem through Holy Love, and I extend to them My invitation to form a prayer cell."

■ **November 14, 1994.** Our Lady comes in white holding a rosary of lights. She says: "Dearest daughter, My message to you on Holy Love must be planted in hearts as a seed of conversion. I desire the Refuge of Mary Prayer Cells form after you speak as a means of cultivating this seed. Please understand, Holy Love is the Refuge of My Immaculate Heart. I am coming as a grace to bring grace to the flock and to lead them into the sheepfold of My Heart." She leaves.

■ **November 15, 1994.** Our Lady is here in white. She says: "Pray with Me now for all those who remain in disbelief." We prayed. "Dear children, once again tonight, I come to invite you into the Refuge of My Immaculate Heart where there is no tribulation, only love, and the fruits of love which are peace and joy. Let your hearts and your lives, dear children, be consumed with the Flame of Holy Love that is My Heart. I am blessing you now."

■ **November 15, 1994.** Our Lady comes in white, bows before the monstrance and says: "Dearest child, listen well. Take this message to all of My children. The more you surrender to Holy Love, the deeper I draw you into the Refuge of My Heart. At last, when you have given everything over to love, our hearts will beat as one. Then the adversary holds no confusion or deceit over your heart. All is laid bare in love. Satan is the opposite of Holy Love and does not want you to surrender to Me. He tries to pull you away through your own pride. But I tell you, this is how you will recognize him. Discern through Holy Love. All that opposes Holy Love and tries to take you from Me is evil. Make it known."

■ **November 16, 1994.** Our Lady comes as Our Lady of Guadalupe. "Those who will come on the Twelfth (of December) will be edified. Dear child, My angel, Satan is bringing confusion into the lives of all who are instrumental in propagating My messages. Most will endure through the grace of My Heart. A small number will submit to discouragement. My grace can always overcome evil. It is only when souls reject grace that they succumb. Take the power of the attacks as a sign of the power of My messages to you."

■ **November 16, 1994.** Our Lady is here in a light-blue gown and a white veil and says: "Please pray with Me now for those who are deceived to believe they are in grace and following the church doctrine when they are not." We prayed. "These are many free thinkers, intellectuals, and theologians who have deceived themselves through pride; and some wear the collar. You must continue to pray for them. I tell you, Satan's throne is composed of sins that have been unrepented, and of faults that have not been overcome. My Son's throne is composed of perfection through Holy Love. Always work toward this end."

■ **November 17, 1994 / Thursday Rosary Service.** Our Lady is here in white, Her Immaculate Heart is exposed. "Dear children, pray with Me now that your own failings each of you have in your hearts against Holy Love be revealed to you." We prayed. "Dear children, My dear little children, the door to My Heart is always open to you when you pray with hearts full of Holy Love. These days Satan's cohorts are everywhere and often disguised as good. Therefore, I beseech you, offer many prayers that he be revealed in your life and in the lives of those around you. I am with you, My dear little children, always loving, always praying for your intentions." Our Lady blessed us and left.

■ **November 19, 1994.** Our Lady comes as Our Lady of

Guadalupe. She says: "I have come, and I continue to come, under this title in order to call souls back to the faith through Holy Love in their hearts. No one is converted who does not embrace the two great commandments that are Holy Love. It is what is in the heart that determines the life or death of the soul. It is what is in hearts that determines the course of human history. Therefore, forgive Me if I do not come with the warnings of great catastrophes and Armageddon. Here, I come not to threaten but to invite hearts to change. It is only in this way the world around you will change. It is free will that is choosing the future. God does not choose to prepare great punishments and purifications for humanity. These things are chosen by people who decide against love. See that the Refuge of My Heart is all you need. Choose this good over all that is evil. It is in My Heart I will mediate love, peace, and joy."

■ **November 20, 1994.** From Our Lady: "I am the Mother of the Word Incarnate. I call all people into My Heart to be reconciled in Holy Love. Most especially, I invite those with opposing ideologies to be reconciled. Make it known."

■ **November 20, 1994 - Feast of Christ the King.** Jesus says: "Lead My people into My Mother's Heart. I will go ahead of them and meet them there, for Our Hearts beat as one."

■ **November 22, 1994.** After Communion Jesus said: "My Mother desires to speak to you." Our Lady said: "I desire My children know that there are many graces attendant to this Image [Missionary Image of Our Lady of Guadalupe]. It is through this Image many will be converted. I desire My children be called back to the faith and away from false gods; and so, I continue to come to you under this title and through My image. Lay your petitions at My feet."

■ **November 22, 1994 / Thursday Rosary Service.** Our

Lady is here in gray and white and says: "Pray with Me now for those who call themselves Catholic but do not support church tradition." We prayed. "Dear children, there are many who call themselves Catholic but support only the magisterium of free will. These take the form of choice that is placed above God. Dear children, I am calling you to pray, pray, pray for My Son's Church on earth, and for My Pontiff, John Paul II." She blessed us and left.

■ **November 24, 1994.** "Dear children, today I invite you not only to personal holiness in the present moment but to be crusaders for Holy Love. Do not give in to Satan's discouragement and accusations. Let your weapons be your communions and your rosaries. I am with you in every test. My victory is in your response to My call."

■ **November 29, 1994.** Our Lady is here in white. She has Her Heart exposed, and there is a great light coming from it. She says: "Dear children, pray with Me now for those who will come in pilgrimage on the Twelfth." We prayed. "Dear children, tonight it is My desire to draw you closer to the Child Jesus as He lay in the manger. With each act of Holy Love, with every sacrifice, I am removing obstacles from your path so that on that great day - Christmas Day - you will be standing next to the crib that holds Divine Love. Dear children, I am praying with you, for you, for this great gift; and I extend to you tonight My Motherly Blessing."

■ **November 29, 1994.**   Our Lady is here in white with golden lights on Her gown. She says, "Praise be to Jesus, My angel. I come to speak especially to our prayer group tonight. Dear children, tonight I invite you to understand you are in the Refuge of My Heart in a special way, for you are the first Refuge of Mary prayer cell. To each of my prayer groups I entrust the Message of Holy Love. I ask that you live the Message and that you propagate Holy Love through prayer, sacrifice and My words to you. When you have Holy Love in your hearts, My dear, dear children, you possess the Kingdom of God on earth. I am always with you when you meet to pray. Invoke My assistance under the title of Our Lady of Guadalupe. This is why I come, just as I did over 400 years ago. I come to convert hearts. Please assist Me by being My hands, My feet and most especially My Message of Holy Love to the world." She blesses me and leaves.

■ **November 30, 1994.** From Our Lady: "Dear children, Holy Love, the flame of My Heart that I desire to pass on to humanity, is God's Mercy upon earth. It is when love is in all hearts that earth will be transformed into the New Jerusalem. This is God's purifying flame of mercy for these last days of tribulation. Each one who hears this message of Holy Love needs to bear it to the world. The message itself bespeaks this dictate. Make it known."

■ **November 30, 1994.**
Fifth Step To Holiness
From Our Lady: "The ultimate step towards holiness - one few reach - is that of perfect union. Here the soul has no obstacle between himself and God. He has passed from the Refuge of My Immaculate Heart, which is Holy Love, and is embraced and illuminated by the true light of Divine Love that is My Son's Heart. Seldom is a soul so graced."

■ **November 30, 1994.** Jesus says: "The flame of love in your hearts needs to be great and all-consuming so that those whose lives you touch will be set on fire with Holy Love."

December 1994

■ **December 4, 1994.** From Our Lady: "Dear children, thank you for your prayers and your obedient response to My call,

all for the greater glory of Jesus My son. I call you to unite in Holy Love so that through Holy Love, faith will be restored in hearts. Dear little children, these days too many worship the false god of self. I call you to love God, and each other, and let self-love be last. Always, I am leading with My Motherly Heart away from evil and along the path of holiness. Dear children, pray, pray, pray."

■ **December 8, 1994.** I was thinking about how hard it has been and how many places we have looked at for a temporary alternate site for the office and for the prayer center. Jesus answered and said: "How many places did My Mother and Joseph look before they found the stable. That was at the last minute, wasn't it?"

■ **December 8, 1994 / Thursday Rosary Service.** Our Lady is here in white. She has lavender and pink highlights on Her dress. She is holding a cascade of white lilies. There is a rosary floating in the air in front of Her. She says: "Dear children, please join Me in prayer once again for all those who will come on the Twelfth." We prayed. "Dear children, once again I invite you to the most pure Immaculate Refuge of My Heart. When you are in My Heart dear children, you are also in the Divine Heart that is My Son's, for Our Hearts beat as one. Tonight, I invite you to flee the false god of love of self, just as Joseph and I embraced the Child and fled from Herod. Dear children, once again I am with you in a special way when you pray. I desire that you give Me all your intentions, most especially on My feast day, and I will bring them to the Heart of My Son." Our Lady blessed us and left.

■ **December 10, 1994.** From Our Lady: "When you decide [about where to move the offices and Blessing Point], I will render fruitful your choice. Do not fear failure. The Ministry needs an interim location between Seven Hills and the new Prayer Center. Hearts need to unite in this realization.

Compare this to the flight into Egypt - temporary but safe. The school house continues to suit our needs at this time. During the warmer months you will overflow. My angel, I am covering My ministry with the Heavenly Court and the Nine Choirs of angels come to do your bidding. Do not fear, I am with you."

■ **December 10, 1994.** Our Lady is here in white. She is holding a green rosary and says: "Please pray with Me now for those who are en route and are coming on the Twelfth." We prayed. "Dear children, the love that is in your hearts tonight is the gift I desire to give all mankind. This love is My joy, My hope in the salvation of the world. Dear children, let your every action, thought, and word come from, and lead to Holy Love." Our Lady blessed us and left.

■ **December 11, 1994.** Our Lady comes as Our Lady of Guadalupe. She says: "I come for the greater honor, glory, and praise of Jesus. I come as the Woman of the Apocalypse - 'the Woman Clothed with the Sun". I continue to come to you in this posture as a sign to humanity of My continued call to conversion. Only when you are living in Holy Love - which is conversion - do you understand My call to you. Do not waste time fearing opposing ideologies, other countries weaponry or even God's retribution. It is evil that is in hearts you must oppose. Take on the cloak of apostleship of Holy Love, and spread the message to the most distant points of earth which are all hearts steeped in darkness. Take as a sign of My call to you, this Image of Guadalupe. [A bright light comes around Her.] Be the light that shines in darkness. Be the rays of the star leading souls to My Son. Dear children, I come because I love you. Pray, pray, pray."

■ **December 11, 1994.** Our Lady is here as Our Lady of Guadalupe. She says: "At this time, My dear children, I find it necessary to request your prayers for My Son's Church which is undergoing her passion." We prayed. "Dear children,

I come tonight to remind you that you are in this place at this time, in God's will, in His Divine Love. Even the simplest act, My dear children, can merit great good if done in Holy Love. And so, tonight, I ask you to persevere in Holy Love, for in these times I come in this title to convert billions." Our Lady blessed us and left.

■ **December 12, 1994 - Feast of Our Lady of Guadalupe.** *(Servants of Mary Center in Windsor, Ohio, with a 50-foot-tall statue of Our Lady of Guadalupe. The Sun danced in the sky for one and a half hours.)* Our Lady is here as Our Lady of Guadalupe. She has two angels with Her and says: "All praise be to Jesus, My children. Pray with Me now for the unbelievers." We prayed. "Dear children, tonight I come to you with great love in My Heart for each of you. I ask that you turn away from evil and choose good. Do not allow the sacrilege to continue in the womb. This is more erroneous now than in the days of Juan Diego, for today, it is not ignorance and paganism, but Christians who perform such acts. Dear children, I am calling you to unite in love, in Holy Love. I will return to you soon, on this spot, on May Twelfth. Dear children, I come because I love you so much." She blessed us and left.

■ **December 13, 1994.** From Our Lady: "Commemorate the Twelfth of December by meeting for a rosary on the Twelfth of each month. In the winter, we will meet at our school house. In the warmer months, at a location as yet undisclosed. I reserve the month of May for Windsor."

■ **December 15, 1994.** Jesus says: "It is by virtue and merit of My Mother's coming to you that the Holy Love message will be propagated. Commemorate My Mother's feast of December 12 every Twelfth of the month. She will lead souls from darkness to light. She will speak profoundly to all nations and issues."

■ **December 15, 1994.** Our Lady is here as Our Lady of Guadalupe. She says, "Praise be to Jesus, My dear little children. Pray with Me now for all the lukewarm and the unbelievers." We prayed. She continues, "Dear children, your presence here tonight with Me, will warm many cold hearts who have turned away from the truth. I tell you the apostasy is already in hearts that do not support My Pope John Paul. For he is the true Vicar and the only one to follow. These days I come to you so often under this sign of Guadalupe, as so many worship false gods in the form of self-comfort and allurements of the world. This is how Satan enters hearts. Dear children, you must continue to pray, pray, pray. I extend to you My Motherly Blessing."

■ **December 17, 1994.** From Our Lady: "It takes many prayers to accommodate My Son's Heart bereft by souls who will not pray."

■ **December 20, 1994.** After Communion Jesus told me: "To procure a big benefactor without strings is like trying to catch a bird by putting salt on its tail." Then He showed me a vision of some birds being thrown bird seed. They all gathered around it. Jesus said: "If you feed them, they will come to you. Feed them with My Mother's words." (I had shared with some friends that when I was about 8 or 9 years old, My mother told me that, if you put salt on a bird's tail, then you could catch it. I believed her so I tried it.)

■ **December 21, 1994.** Jesus says: "Is My Heart not merciful as well as loving? Embrace the cross for it is tomorrow's grace."

■ **December 22, 1994.** Our Lady is here as Our Lady of Guadalupe. She says: "Pray with Me now for the unbelievers." We prayed. "Let us give praise to Jesus, truly present in all the tabernacles of the world. Dear children, tonight I want to teach you the importance of Holy Love in your hearts. My 'yes', to Archangel Gabriel, was born from Holy Love in My heart. The Holy Love in your hearts is the straw beneath My Son's fragile body. It is the swaddling clothes that warm Him. It is the gifts of the Magi. Dear children, come to understand the importance of loving with Holy Love. Pray, pray, pray for this love to be present in your hearts." Our Lady blessed us and left.

■ **December 22, 1994.** Jesus says: "Do not remain attached to the House of Prayer in bitterness. Live in the joy of the grace of the present moment. Allow the retribution to be Mine. The future of the ministry is in the grace of the future. I am that grace!"

■ **December 23, 1994.** *(Locution from Jesus)* "Maureen, you had childlike faith and trust in all your earthly mother told you. Otherwise, you would not have tried to salt birds tails as a means of capturing them [See December 20, 1994 message]. Have the same trust in what I impart to you now. The cross of all the misfortunes in Seven Hills is as much a part of My ministry as the grace of My Mother's visits to you. Therefore, accept this cross with love so that My plan will be complete in you. I need your childlike faith. I rejoice in it."

■ **December 25, 1994.** *(Christmas Morning)* Our Lady came as I was reciting the third Joyful Mystery. She was holding the Infant Jesus. There was straw that was still clinging to His swaddling clothes as Our Lady must have just picked Him up out of the manger. Our Lady said: "I come to enlist your aid in the formation of My Holy Love army. The hour so desperate, the conscience of man so obtuse; I desire My apostles of Holy Love to follow Me in this war against evil. So I am able to lead souls into My Immaculate Heart. Make all your communions in reparation to Our most grieved Hearts. In this way, My Son places grace and mercy in His outstretched hand and reserves His justice. I impart to you today a special Christmas Blessing of Holy Love."

■ **December 29, 1994.** Our Lady is here in white and has a gold band round Her waist. She is holding the Infant Jesus. She says: "Pray with Me now for all unbelievers, most especially, those who hold prominent positions in the world." We prayed. "Dear children, as this new year begins, I especially ask that you pray to keep Holy Love in your hearts. Let this be the year that you decide to love, My dear children. Many world leaders will make important decisions this coming year and I tell you much of the future weighs in the balance. Dear children, continue to pray, pray, pray. I impart to you tonight My Special Blessing." She faded away.

■ **December 30, 1994.** *(Locution from Jesus)* After Communion Jesus said: "The angel that each one is given at Maranatha is the angel of Holy Love. This angel stands guard over the doorway to your heart, repelling that which is not of Holy Love, and preparing the heart to be part of the New Jerusalem."

Maureen Sweeney-Kyle with the
Missionary Image of Our Lady of Guadalupe

Messages of Holy *and* Divine Love

1995

January 1995

■ **January 1, 1995.** Our Lady said: "Angel, take up your pen." I wished Her a happy feast day. She nods and says: "In this let us give praise to Jesus, born Incarnate. I desire that this be the year that hearts unite in Holy Love; in families, My ministry, the Church and the world. It can only be so if hearts open to love. The human heart is where every battle between good and evil is waged. Satan does not wish this to be made known. It is free will that determines the destiny of the world. I call you to love, just as I call you to holiness, so that evil will be overcome and My Son can return in glory." I asked, "Are you happy with the new offices?" "Please understand, small daughter, My ministry is in hearts that love, not in any accommodation of the world. My message to you on Holy Love is the key that pries open stubborn hearts. This is why you need to concentrate every effort towards this end - living and propagating Holy Love. It is only in this way you will succeed. Your illness is a means of bringing grace to the ministry, which is true of every cross of those who serve Me. Satan's discouragement is not a cross but spiritual warfare. I will give to you now My first blessing of the new year."

■ **January 3, 1995.** Our Lady is here wearing a blue gown and white veil. He Heart is exposed and She says: "Praise be to Jesus. You are experiencing the coldness that is in hearts. (There was no heat in the old schoolhouse; temperature at 20 degrees.) Which, combined with the value of your prayers and your meritorious sacrifices, melts away the ice that is around hearts. Pray with me now for hearts to decide to change." We prayed. She continues, "Dear children, your sacrifices to me are as priceless treasures. I need them to change the course of human events, for unless hearts change, the world will bring about its own chastisement. I ask you tonight to give me extra prayers and sacrifices, so that hearts will change and governments will be swayed. It is My Message to you on Holy Love that can change the world. Therefore, My little children, pray that it is propagated. I am blessing you now." She leaves.

■ **January 9, 1995.** From Our Lady: "I come to reconcile hearts to the Will of God through Holy Love. Dear child, every sin is a result of failure in love. Empty your heart of all that is unloving. This is your sanctification in the present moment. Do not look at how you differ from your neighbor, but how you are alike. This oneness is unifying. Holy Love divides the wheat from the chaff, but it unites those who embrace love. Therefore, once again, see that each moment presents the opportunity to choose sanctity through love. Those who do not love, do not choose salvation."

■ **January 10, 1995.** Jesus says: "I am sending My Mother to you on the Twelfth of each month to speak especially to this nation. If hearts do not change; if the lack of love in hearts is not resolved; your nation will continue to suffer internal strife."

■ **January 11, 1995.** From Our Lady: "I come especially today, to request of all My children true sanctity in the present moment through Holy Love. Consecrate the present moment to holiness as though you were about to stand before My Son in judgment. I love all My children and do not wish to loose one of you to eternal fire. I want each one to pray for the wisdom to choose for good over evil. Too often, the adversary comes clothed in goodness and positions himself in prominence where he is most dangerous. You, My children, need to look wisely at hearts and not actions. Pray to be aware of the cost of the present moment, for it is all you have and of the greatest value to My Son. I come as always to call you back to Him."

■ **January 12, 1995.** Our Lady is here as Our Lady of Guadalupe. Her Heart is exposed and has drops of blood

coming from it. She says: "Pray with Me please at this time for all those who hear My words in their ears but do not live My message in their hearts." We prayed. "Dear children, the whole and entire reason I come to you is to return hearts to God. Know for certain, there are many hearts of leaders in your country and in the populace, that are like the heart of PHARAOH - obstinate and unbending. It is for this reason many tribulations have come to your country by way of natural disasters. These events follow one after another and will come closer together unless your nation abandons the cause for abortion and alternate life styles. Dear children, My coming to you is a grace. I ask your prayers that hearts open to My messages to you, and read the signs of the times." Our Lady blessed us and left.
Read Exodus Chapter 7

■ **January 13, 1995.** *(8:00 a.m.)* Our Lady is here in white and gold. She says: "Come and write this down for posterity. I come as Jesus sends Me, to call your country away from paganism - the paganism of abortion. Unless your country responds to My call it will suffer much at the Hands of God. Many will die in their sins. The Church will embrace much compromise and become a sign of dispute. This already is at hand. Hearts must be restored to love. If they are not, the majority will bear these consequences. It is lack of love that causes so much pain to My Son's Heart and My own Immaculate Heart. You must make this known. Love is your liberation."

■ **January 13, 1995.** *(Temperature – 70 degrees in January)* Our Lady comes as Our Lady of Guadalupe. She says: "My daughter, for three seasons I have come to you and accurately predicted the weather. Though these forecasts were unusual, you listened, took heed, and prepared. You even spread the news to others who likewise paid heed and prepared. Now, I come to you in the same way, to prepare you for this season of tribulation. I ask only that you respond in a similar way, for I come out of love."

"The time fast approaches, My daughter, when your country will be under siege by nature. I tell you now, nature has no motive or cause in what comes. It is God who will allow these things, for He desires all hearts be restored to Holy Love. It will come to pass that waters will not know boundaries. Those in low lying areas will flee to the mountains. Storms will blow with great force from one end of the country to the other. The mountains will erupt and the earth will shake and shift. Foods of many kinds will become scarce and highly priced. People will try to blame nature, but once again I tell you, it is lack of Holy Love in hearts that will cause these things. As these events begin to unfold, My visits to you on the Twelfth of each month will take on added meaning. It is so I can encourage hearts in Love. There will be national attention here. Expect a multitude. Unresolved issues will be brought to light. I tell you all of these things out of great love, and so My angel, prepare your heart. There is no time for doubt." She leaves.

■ **January 14, 1995.**   Our Lady comes as Our Lady of Guadalupe. A great light comes from Her Heart. She says: "I come as always to bring souls to the salvation of Holy Love. Now, today, in this tribulation, I come to reveal to you that the greatest trial is already upon you. It is the confusion and compromise that is in hearts. This is how Satan destroys peace and love in hearts. Firmly plant yourselves in the true faith, for not even My Son's Church is exempt from this trial. Seek the Refuge of My Heart which holds itself away from all error. Do not let anything disturb your peace. The seasons will reverse themselves. The days and nights will be one. But, dear children, even these trials are passing, and you are safe if you remain in My Heart. All of this is revealed to you with unbounded love."

■ **January 16, 1995.** Our Lady is here in light blue. She smiles and says, "Dear little daughter, I come today to reassure you, what I predict in this, the season of tribulation, is contingent upon the number of hearts that open to Holy Love. My Son does not wish to permit any of this, but it is by this means earth will be renewed and made whole. Your country can be a sign of conversion or a sign of devastation and ruin. The choice is made in hearts. But, My Son will not be satisfied with half choices or indecision. These are choices against Holy Love. This is why people must see how important it is to love in the present moment. When My Son comes He will not look at what was in your hearts in the past, or what might be in the future. He will look into your heart in the present. Your hearts must not be compromised by unforgiveness or pride. Your country is moving with great haste towards grave consequences. Large numbers could be annihilated in seconds, and hearts have not begun to love. It is this reason I come to you so often and with such gravity to My tone. Please pray and make My words known."

■ **January 17, 1995.** Our Lady is here in blue and white. There is a blue light around Her and coming from under Her mantle and from where Her Heart would be. She says, "Let us give praise to Jesus. I am Mary ever-Virgin. It is important that you know this, as you will be approached by doubters and believers alike. Beware of those who bandy about times and dates of specific happenings. This is Satan's confusion to discredit the genuine, and cloud reality. Further, I tell you, some claim specific knowledge as to 'safe areas'. The safe refuge is My Immaculate Heart. This is not a dispute, but a fact. Remember, 'Those who would save their lives will lose them' *(Luke 9:24)*. Let your future be in heaven and do not cling to earth as though it was an end not a means."
Read Luke Chapter 9: 24

■ **January 17, 1995.** Our Lady is here as Our Lady of Guadalupe. She says: "Dear child, it is especially during this time of tribulation, I come to invite souls to take up the Refuge of My Immaculate Heart. In this Humble Refuge, find the same shelter Joseph and I found in the stable - a shelter of peace amidst trial. If you are living in Holy Love, you are already in the Refuge of My Heart. Holy Love is this Refuge. My Heart and Holy Love are one. In every trial avoid the trap Satan lays for you, which is the pride of self-pity. This is an obstacle to My Heart and to living in Holy Love. The more you submit to Holy Love, the easier it will become to avoid this obstacle. I am showing you the path to My Heart now, in easier times, so that when difficulties come, you will know the way. Pray, pray, pray that hearts accept this path."

"Now My daughter, Jesus desires that these latest messages be set apart from the rest. He wants them printed separately and entitled, 'Our Lady's Messages on the Coming Tribulation'. Include them in the reprint of the book as well, for these happenings are imminent. I leave you now in Holy Love."

■ **January 19, 1995 / Thursday Night Rosary Service.** Our Lady is here in gray and has a white veil. She says: "I come in praise of Jesus. Pray with me now for all those who have been spiritually apathetic." We prayed. She continues. "Dear children, do not suppose the path ahead can be made smooth by wishful thinking, for I tell you there are many ruts and obstacles in the road you must travel. But, I come to tell you that when you pray with love in your hearts, all is made easier and bearable. I am always with you. Do not imagine that Satan does not exist, for he scratches and claws to maintain his rule in many hearts. Dear children, when you pray you will recognize the enemy. I am with you always holding you under My Mantle of Protection. Dear little children, remember to pray, pray, pray." She blessed us and left.

■ **January 20, 1995.** Our Lady comes as Our Lady of Guadalupe. She says: "My daughter, pray with Me now for those who do not know or do not accept Holy Love." We prayed. "Through Holy Love, let us give glory and praise to Jesus. My daughter, it is during these hours of tribulation in the world, I am forming the remnant in My Immaculate Heart. Do not suppose that the tribulation is the promised chastisement spoken of in Revelations. No, it is God's purification and last call to conversion. The final chastisement can still be mitigated in accordance with the response to My call to Holy Love. It is for this reason I desire all I tell you be made known."

■ **January 21, 1995.** Our Lady says, "I reveal to you today, the reason most people compromise their faith is they desire to be esteemed and loved in the world. Today more than ever, faith is assailed on all sides. Allegiances to Rome and to my pope is controversial within the Church itself. The apostasy so often spoken of, is alive in hearts. Many who consider themselves good Catholics practice birth control. There are many priests and church hierarchy who question My Son's Real Presence! But what fuels the flame of apostasy, is the denial of those who embrace it. There is a strong spirit of self-righteousness, which has no place in My Son's Church. Position within the church hierarchy needs great humility such as the Holy Father has. What grieves me greatly is the lack of openness by some in authority to My authentic apparitions. But time and good fruits will bear the truth. Pray for the Holy Father." She leaves.

■ **January 24, 1995.** Our Lady comes in blue and white. She says, "Dear children, today I invite you to realize the power of Holy Love in your hearts. It is through Holy Love My Immaculate Heart will triumph. Please begin to understand, My victorious reign is first in your hearts and then in the world. Therefore, it is necessary that my victory begins in your heart in the present moment as you embrace Holy Love. Behold, every measure of grace is afforded you towards this end. Make it known."

■ **January 25, 1995.** Our Lady comes in blue and white. She says: "Dear children, today, I invite you to realize the power of Holy Love in your hearts. It is through Holy Love My Immaculate Heart will triumph. Please begin to understand, My victorious reign is first in your hearts, and then in the world. Therefore, it is necessary that My victory begins in your heart in the present moment as you embrace Holy Love. Behold, every measure of grace is afforded you towards this end. Make it known."

■ **January 26, 1995 / Thursday Night Service.** First, St. John Bosco was here, and he blessed the crowd. His dog Grigio (the angel) was with him. Our Lady came dressed in gray and white, and had a pink sash around Her waist. She says: "Pray with Me now for unbelievers who have hearts of stone." We prayed. "Dear children, tonight, please open your hearts, and realize that the stairway to heaven is Holy Love; each step being a virtue. The grace of My Heart leads and draws you along this path - the stairway to eternity. Satan tries to block your ascent through selfishness, spiritual smugness, and lack of confidence in the grace of My Heart. Dear children, please realize these days My Son allows Me to give to earth every grace possible. Dear children, never tire of praying."

■ **January 26, 1995.** Yesterday I had the following vision: There was a great light coming from Blessed Mother's Heart. There were little hearts rising and falling along this path of light. Our Lady told me tonight, that the hearts that were slipping back towards earth on this path were hearts that gave into self-will. She said: "See, My daughter, they never leave the light, but they are farther away from My Heart when they think only of themselves."

■ **January 26, 1995 / Thursday Night Rosary Service.** First, St. John Bosco was here, and he blessed the crowd. His dog Grigio (the angel) was with him. Our Lady came dressed in gray and white, and had a pink sash around Her waist. She says: "Pray with Me now for unbelievers who have hearts of stone." We prayed. "Dear children, tonight, please open your hearts, and realize that the stairway to heaven is Holy Love; each step being a virtue. The grace of My Heart leads and draws you along this path - the stairway to eternity. Satan tries to block your ascent through selfishness, spiritual smugness, and lack of confidence in the grace of My Heart. Dear children, please realize these days My Son allows Me to give to earth every grace possible. Dear children, never tire of praying."

■ **January 31, 1995.** Our Lady is here as Queen of Heaven and Earth. She says: "Pray with Me now for those who are in My Son's Church but are spiritually apathetic." We prayed. "Pray with Me now for priests who are considering leaving the priesthood." We prayed. "Dear children, once again tonight, I invite you into the light that is Holy Love. As children of this light, you need to draw others along this path. Let Holy Love uncover what lays hidden in your lives, and in the lives of those around you, but has remained in darkness. Dear children, you are the example that I want spread amongst all of My children. Further, I tell you, when you hear of startling events around the world, know that it is My Son calling all souls into the light. Tonight, I impart to you My Motherly Blessing."

February 1995

■ **February 9, 1995.** Our Lady is here in white. She is holding a rosary with black beads. As they pass through Her fingers they turn white. She says: "Tell them this means that Prayer gives life to souls. Pray with Me now for the conversion of sinners." We prayed. "Dear children, tonight, I invite you to realize that your country has lost its innocence through the pursuit of many pleasures. Dear children, I come to restore

Holy Love in hearts and the kingdom of God, which is Holy Love. Dear children, continue to pray, pray, pray for this and all My intentions."

■ **February 12, 1995 / Monthly Message To The Nation.** *(Naples, Florida)* Our Lady is here as Our Lady of Guadalupe. She says: "I come not to frighten, but out of loving concern. I desire very much that we now pray for the conversion of all sinners." We prayed. I asked Our Lady what does She want of all the people here today? Our Lady responded: "I desire very much their reparation to Our Loving Hearts, already most grievously wounded by the sins of mankind. I desire their acts of love in reparation to Our Hearts, their communions of reparation, their holy hours, and their prayers."

"Dear children, Jesus sends Me as a loving Mother in order that the eyes of the conscience of your nation may have the scales removed from them. Dear children, the tempter is already in the sanctuary, concealed in hearts full of compromise, and you do not see the grievous errors. Dear children, seek always the certain Refuge of My Maternal Heart. Pray, pray, pray." She blessed us and left.

She returned and said: "Dear child, today Satan takes dominion over many hearts clothed in goodness so as to confuse and confound the holy. Your country will suffer the grace of many misfortunes as a means of revealing and correcting her errors."

■ **February 14, 1995.** *(Cape Coral, Florida)* Our Lady is here as Our Lady of Mt. Carmel. She says: "Pray with Me now for all the faithful departed." We prayed. "Dear children, it is through the grace of My Heart every good is accomplished, and the accommodation of My Heart is Holy Love, always Holy Love. Once you place your foot upon the path of Holy Love, it is by your efforts, and the co-operation of the grace Jesus sends you through My Heart, you will increase in holiness. Dear children, I impart to you tonight My Motherly Blessing."

■ **February 15, 1995.** *(Naples, Florida)* Our Lady came as Our Lady of Guadalupe, She had a rosary in one hand and a cross made of light in the other hand. She says: "Dear children, tonight, I ask your assistance and your efforts in helping Me to return souls to God. Dear children, when you pray and when you sacrifice with Holy Love in your hearts, you give Me invaluable weapons against evil. My dear little children, pray, pray, pray. I impart to you tonight My Motherly Blessing."

■ **February 16, 1995.** *(Cape Coral, Florida)*
A Warning From The Blessed Mother
Our Lady is here as Our Lady of Fatima. She says: "Praise be to Jesus, My little children. It is My joy to be with you tonight, and to pray with you. Please join Me now and pray for the conversion of sinners." We prayed. "Dear children, tonight, I desire to make it known, that soon, as quickly as lightning flashes across the sky, souls will be illuminated as to their state before God. And so, you must make this known, My dear children, for the Hand of Judgment falls rapidly and certainly. It is of great love I come to warn you of these events. My dearest little children, you are in the light. Please assist Me in bringing souls out of the darkness. Pray, pray, pray." She blessed us and left.

■ **February 16, 1995.** Our Lady came as Our Lady of Mt. Carmel on a throne, holding Jesus. She said: "I desire that you be My message of Holy Love to the world." The infant Jesus blessed us and they faded away.

■ **February 17, 1995.** Our Lady is here in white. She says: "Please pray with Me for all those considering abortion." We prayed. "Dear children, tonight, it is My solemn desire and invitation, that you allow your hearts to become conduits of Holy Love, so that by your efforts, I can convert and save souls. I extend to you My Motherly Blessing."

■ **February 19, 1995.** Our Lady is here as Our Lady of Lourdes. She spreads Her hands and says: "Peace be with you." She now has a white rosary around Her waist, but the chain links between the Hail Mary beads are black. She then says: "It is by your efforts, and through your acts of love, that you make the time between the Hail Mary's efficacious. The greatest miracle is your salvation."

■ **February 19, 1995.** Our Lady is here as Our Lady of Grace. She says: "My call to you is to understand, dear children, that when My Son comes, all will be restored to Holy Love. The new heaven and the new earth will be Holy Love; and I will be with you; and there will be peace in your hearts. Dear children, abandon yourself to Holy Love. I am blessing you now."

■ **February 20, 1995.** *(Cape Coral, Florida)* Our Lady is here in white. She has many flowers and angels all around her. She says: "Pray with Me now if you would, for the propagation of the Holy Love message." We prayed. "Dear children, tonight I urgently invite you to be Holy Love in action. Be the rays of light that lead to My Heart, and do not hide My call to you under a bushel. I tell you, My summons to you is one of great urgency. Therefore, see that Satan is the complacency that tries to take over your hearts in this regard. My children, I love you, I pray for all your intentions and intercede for you before the Throne of My Divine Son. Tonight, I impart to you My Motherly Blessing."

■ **February 20, 1995.** From Our Lady: "I desire that all your thoughts, words, and actions, be towards the favor of My Heart, which is Holy Love. See that any impediment in this regard is an obstacle to the grace God intends for you in the present moment."

■ **February 21, 1995.** *(Florida)* Our Lady is here as Our Lady of Mt. Carmel. She says: "Dear children, pray with Me please for all unbelievers, especially the lukewarm." We prayed. "Dearest little children, place your petitions in My Motherly Heart, which is your protection and trust in the provision of My Son's Heart. Your every need is already in My Heart. Every concern must be your joy, for it helps to turn souls towards God. Dear children, I love you and I am calling you to be apostles of Holy Love. Through you dear children is My hope for all souls." Our Lady blessed us and left.

■ **February 22, 1995.** *(Florida)* Jesus says: "Make it known. The gateway to the New Jerusalem is the Flame of My Mother's Heart which is Holy Love. No one can enter, save through this Purifying Flame, for Holy Love is the New Jerusalem."

■ **February 23, 1995.** Our Lady is here as Our Lady of Guadalupe. She says: "Pray with Me now for sinners who are farthest from God." We prayed. "Dear children, tonight, I invite you to understand the reason I come under this title so often is that the need for conversion has never been so great in the history of the Church. Under this title, dear children, millions have been converted, and today, I need your prayers more than ever so that those who seek their every pleasure in the world will turn to God. Dear children, Holy Love, the Refuge of My Heart, is the gateway to the New Jerusalem. Pray, pray, pray." Our Lady blessed us and then left.

■ **February 25, 1995.** Our Lady is here as Our Lady of Guadalupe. She says: "Praise be to Jesus - King of Heaven and Earth. My daughter, the time is approaching when events in the heavens and on earth will arouse, awaken, and proclaim with certainty My Son's return. It is then, My children will need to choose for Holy Love, for herein lies the Refuge of My Motherly Heart. How else can I summon souls to this Refuge except out of love. Some will be unable to enter in time. Some will not know the way. For these reasons, enlighten the world with Holy Love. Make it known."
Read Luke 21:25-28

■ **February 25, 1995.** From Our Lady: "You need to be aware that Jesus desires all apostolates co-operate towards the final victory of My Immaculate Heart, and that My Beloved Son wants it made known that the gateway to the New Jerusalem is the Refuge of My Heart. Further, no one enters this Refuge outside of Holy Love. This is how much I desire My words to you be made known. Without Holy Love there is no remnant."

■ **February 25, 1995.** From Our Lady: "My victory lies dormant in hearts that do not love. So then, see that propagating My words to you is a means of calling souls into the gateway of the New Jerusalem."

■ **February 25, 1995.** Our Lady is here as Our Lady of Guadalupe. She says: "Pray with Me now for Holy Love Ministries." We prayed. "Dear children, I invite you to understand, that your mission is to MAKE KNOWN THE REFUGE OF MY IMMACULATE HEART AS THE GATEWAY TO THE NEW JERUSALEM, THROUGH HOLY LOVE. The means by which you accomplish this in Holy Love are: the PRAYER CELLS, the MEDIA, your PRAYERS, your SACRIFICES. All these combined will accomplish MY VICTORY. Dear children, please be careful not to confuse the means with the end. I extend to you today My Motherly Blessing."

■ **February 27, 1995.** Our Lady is here in white and Her Immaculate Heart is exposed. She says: "Praise be to Jesus My little children. Pray with Me now for all sinners." We prayed. "Dear children, tonight, I am advising you concerning the distribution of My monthly message. Do not attempt to contact each person individually concerning My monthly message, or concerning any special message. But if you contact each prayer group, the message can then be disseminated within the group, and in close proximity to the group. My dear children, I am drawing all into My Heart of Love, and you are the vehicles by which I am bringing souls into Holy Love."

■ **February 28, 1995.** Our Lady is here with two angels and She is here as Our Lady of Guadalupe. She says: "Please know My daughter, My coming to you continues to be a call to conversion. Understanding this, let us pray together for the conversion of all hearts." We prayed. "Dear children, you need to let your moment-to-moment conversion be the most important call of your life. Let your sacrifices during this penitential season be the cloth that wipes the bloodied Face of My Son. Let your prayers be the hand that aids Him in carrying the cross. Dear children, I am always with you, loving you, and protecting you. This season, I ask your most sincere efforts to pray and sacrifice with Holy Love in your hearts. Tonight, I am blessing you with My Motherly Blessing." Our Lady blessed us and left.

March 1995

■ **March 1, 1995.** Our Lady is here as Our Lady of Guadalupe. She nods and says: "I am Mary, Mother of Jesus Incarnate. I desire you make known My desire that the Prayer Cells serve as a distribution point for My messages. I encourage the guardian angels to form Prayer Cells themselves, and become more powerful in their service to Me. Take the time each day, My daughter, to pray for the formation of these groups. It is important the names of the leaders of each cell be filed at the Ministry for easy accessibility. The Prayer Cells are the complete unfolding of My plan."

■ **March 1, 1995.** Our Lady is here in white. She says: "Let us give praise to Jesus."

"Today, I reveal to you, not all will be converted by the

enlightenment of conscience that is to come. Satan will convince many to discount what is given as grace, and to disregard My Sign and Miracle. These are the ones farthest from the Light and most especially in the world. This is why I come now, previous to these events. I come to inform and warn. Make it known." She leaves.

■ **March 3, 1995.** Jesus says: "Stay with Me. Remain with Me. I am your Victor, your King. Place all your hopes and fears in My Eucharistic Heart. See in My Heart a burning passion for souls. Here is the Flame of Divine Love that desires to consume mankind. Do not look with uncertainty. My love for you never fades. The fire that is to come is My Justice. The fire here now is My Divine Love. Let this love be your fulfillment. It is what will remain."

■ **March 4, 1995.** When I entered the chapel, Our Lady was already waiting for me. She was dressed in two shades of blue. She said: "Let us begin by giving praise to Jesus. My daughter, these days it is necessary that I come to you with more and more urgent requests for prayer and sacrifices. As many souls are attracted to the Refuge of My Heart, so too, many are slipping to perdition. Satan would have it that most souls do not recognize the path of darkness they wholeheartedly pursue. This is because they allow their hearts to be anchored down in the world. My daughter, I desire that My call to holiness be as incense that fills the soul and lifts it up to heaven. Today, you do not see the urgency of My call to you. Tomorrow, you will."

■ **March 5, 1995.** Our Lady is here in gray. She says: "I am the Mother of the Word Incarnate. My angel, I am with you today to help you realize that the fulfillment of Holy Love will be the New Jerusalem. This is why Jesus names My Immaculate Heart the Gateway to the New Jerusalem, for no one can enter without first passing into and embracing Holy Love. Any gate is an entrance to a different environment. So it is with My Heart which leads to the Divine Love. Divine Love is God's Kingdom on earth - the New Jerusalem. Today I invite you to make this known."

■ **March 5, 1995.** Our Lady is here as Our Lady of Guadalupe. She says, "Let us give praise and honor to Jesus born Incarnate. Pray with Me now for your detractors and your supporters." We prayed. She says, "My children, come to realize that often your detractors and supporters are one and the same. Allow the Holy Spirit to set hearts on fire with the purifying Flame of My Heart. In other areas you will receive favorable press in different parts of the country. Dear children, continue to pray that My Message to you is disseminated liberally."

■ **March 6, 1995.** Our Lady comes as Our Lady of Mt. Carmel. "Let us give praise to Jesus by praying for all those who do not follow Holy Love." We prayed. "Thank you dear children, tonight I invite you to understand deep in your hearts, that prayer is the support of this ministry. It is through your prayers, your Rosaries, and your sacrifices, all the things in your heart will fall into place. It is through prayer; the weak are strengthened, the message is propagated, financial support is made available, and My prayer center will become viable. Therefore, My little children, continue to pray, pray, pray and do not fear, for in prayer is My protection and the Lord's provision."

■ **March 6, 1995.** While at Mass, just before communion, many angels (about 10) appeared in front of me. They said, "Prepare, because you are about to receive the Lord Jesus." I asked, "What do you want me to do?" They then said, "Make an *Act of Contrition*." So I did. And then when I received Jesus in Communion, He said: "Thank you, for so many receive Me as though I am a symbol." The next day (March 7, 1995), Jesus told me to pray this *Act of Contrition* before every Communion.

■ **March 9, 1995.** Jesus says: "Do you love Me? If you do, tell Me so, for I need to hear it. Do not keep your love for Me buried in your heart. Let it be reflected in your life, in your words and actions. I am never far away. I am as close as your next thought of Me. I am part of the air you breathe. I desire that you know this in your innermost spirit, so that we can be one. Do not fear any portion of the future. I am in the future ahead of you. I am directing angels towards your every need. I send My Mother to be your confidence."

■ **March 9, 1995 / Thursday Night Rosary Service.** Our Lady is here as Our Lady of Guadalupe. She says: "Tonight My daughter, I come to confide to you, that the rivers, streams, and oceans, swell from My tears, falling for the plight of mankind. I ask your prayers now, for the conversion of sinners." We prayed. There were thousands of sparkling lights all around Her when we prayed. She said: "These are the souls who merit from your prayers. Dear children, tonight I invite you to understand that the present moment is unretrievable and cannot be recaptured. Therefore, please surrender to Holy Love in the present, so that by your efforts I can save souls and return them to Jesus. I want to present you to My Son, when the time comes, with your hearts full of love and your hands full of good deeds. Tonight I extend to you My Motherly Blessing."

■ **March 10, 1995.** "Spring is coming. Just as the first leaves of My flowers are ready to push through the Earth, so My Ministry is about to spring up and blossom at a new site. Praise be to Jesus, My angel." Our Lady is here in gray, white and pink. Her Heart is exposed. "You will see, My child, how the grace of My Heart, which has laid dormant over the winter in regards to certain favors, is now about to burgeon forth. Remember, God's ways are not your own. Pray for the grace to recognize God's Holy and Divine Will. My angel, long has Heaven awaited what is to come. Strengthen yourself physically and spiritually." She leaves.

■ **March 11, 1995.** Jesus says: "I am permitting trials and tribulations in the world as a way of reconciling souls to Myself. Tomorrow, when My Mother comes, She will bring with Her a message which will enlighten hearts, but sadden some. Those most upset by Her words are the ones who trust Me little, for in Me is the promise of Salvation."

■ **March 12, 1995 / Monthly Message To The World.**
The Seasons Of Tribulation
Our Lady is here as Our Lady of Guadalupe. She says: "My little children. I come to reconcile souls to God. Please pray with Me now for this intention." We prayed. "Dear children, today I invite you to recognize the season of tribulation that is upon you. As in any season there are signs. Recognize the cataclysmic natural events as from God. These occur in order to return souls to God, Who is King of Heaven and Earth. In the next season of tribulation you will find money systems failing and collapsing. This will occur as a means of stripping people from the idol of money. The next season I reveal to you My dear daughter, My dear people, is the apostasy, which will occur in the Church. It will be as a winnowing fan separating the wheat from the chaff, and will take place mainly in the West. Then the season of the Antichrist. He will be in the world and in hearts. Dear children, I reveal these things to you now, so that as these events unfold, you will recognize God's Hand in your midst. Just as in nature, these seasons will overlap one another. There will be no clear line of demarcation, but you will recognize them through Holy Love. I am blessing you now."

■ **March 14, 1995.** Our Lady is here in white. She says: "I give thanks and praise to Jesus for allowing Me to visit with you. Make My Heart known, not only as a Refuge and a Gateway, but also as a Fountain of Grace that transforms hearts, so that they may pass into the New Jerusalem. It is in My Heart souls are perfected in Holy Love so that I can present them to My Son. Do not be discouraged if you see your own flaws, My daughter. This is a grace and a way of perfection. When you see all others as more holy than yourself, you are progressing in humility and moving along the path of holiness I call you upon. You should never be satisfied with where you are spiritually. This is Satan's deception. Always ask Jesus to help you to be more holy. Such a prayer offered with a sincere heart will not go unanswered." I asked Her a question about property for the ministry. "Be certain Heaven is of one mind with you. Do not act of your own volition. Wait rather, and I will send you a sign. Alone, nothing is possible. Through grace, anything is possible. Pray for hearts to open to My call." She leaves.

■ **March 16, 1995 / Thursday Night Rosary Service.** Our Lady is here as Our Lady of Guadalupe, Her Heart is exposed and She is floating on a pink cloud. She says: "Pray with Me now, that more hearts choose Holy Love." We prayed. "Dear children, please understand that the battle between good and evil is waged in hearts, not in governments. The victory is won in hearts that love, the defeat is in hearts that do not choose to love. Satan is trying to keep you from praying, because he knows the most powerful weapon is the Rosary, when it is prayed with love in your hearts. Do not let him discourage you, or distract you. I am calling you to prayer, My dear children, so that we can be victorious over every evil. Tonight, I am imparting to you My Blessing of Holy Love, which will enable you to live in this virtue. It is a special blessing that you may share with all whom you meet."

■ **March 18, 1995.** Our Lady is here in white with a gold crown on Her Head. She says: "Peace be with you. I come so that souls will be reconciled to God. Let us give praise to Jesus. My children, so that you will make known the Refuge of My Heart as the Gateway to the New Jerusalem, Jesus is allowing the site of My prayer center to be a refuge of peace in the world, where souls will find conversion and answer My call to holiness. It will be as though My Immaculate Heart will already be victorious at this site. My victory will be in every heart that converts. (NOTE - This will be a spiritual refuge and not a physical refuge). Do not imagine that the cross is not a part of My victory. For in the present, the cross is a very real means of salvation and victory both in the ministry and in your lives. Indeed, it is by your cooperation with grace through prayer and sacrifice, we will be victorious. I want to give you this victory, My dear children. See that your response to My call to Holy Love is already My victory in you."

■ **March 22, 1995.** Our Lady is here as Rosa Mystica. She says: "Please pray with Me now, for the conversion of all sinners." We prayed. "Dear children, tonight I call you more than ever, to place your faith in the grace of My Heart, which is all-consuming and never-ending. Dear children, I do not call you to the impossible. I call you to have faith in My mission and trust in Heaven's plan."

■ **March 23, 1995 / Thursday Night Rosary Service.** Our Lady is here in blue with a white veil. She says: "My dear little children, Jesus allows Me once again, this gift of visiting with you. Let us give praise and thanks to Jesus." She says: "Pray with Me now for all those who I call here on the Twelfth." We prayed. "Dear children, once again I call you to this Sovereignty, this Spiritual Refuge, that is My Immaculate Heart. Do not be fooled by Satan into thinking there is safe refuge in the world. He is interested in your soul and wants to see your demise. But My dear children, I call you with a Mother's Love to the path of Salvation, which is Holy Love. My little children, continue to pray, pray, pray." Our Lady blessed us and left.

■ **March 28, 1995.** Jesus says: "When I return, the world will be made new. There will be peace in all hearts. Everyone will embrace Holy Love. My Will will be done. This will be My Mother's Victory as well. Her victory has already begun in hearts that love. So many are concerned for their physical well-being. Why can they not see the value of their soul which is eternal? They are like lambs without a Shepherd, who fear for the darkness that will cover the earth for three (3) days, but they fail to see the darkness in their own hearts. I tell you, each one must triumph over the darkness in his own heart if he wants to be saved. Then, and only then, will the New Jerusalem be made known to you."

■ **March 30, 1995 / Thursday Night Rosary Service.** Our Lady is here as Our Lady of Grace. She says: "Dear children, pray with Me now for the conversion of all hearts in the present moment." We prayed. "Dear children, I come to lead you into the New Jerusalem, clothed in the Light, the Power, and the Energy of Holy Love. Forgive all iniquities of your neighbors and surrender all your iniquities to My Immaculate Heart, so that purified in Holy Love, I can lead you upon the path that I desire you follow into the New Jerusalem. Dear children, I love you, I pray for your moment to moment conversion. I constantly thank My Son, that I am allowed to come to you in this time of grace." Our Lady blessed us and left.

April 1995

■ **April 1, 1995.** Our Lady is here in blue and white. There are many lights around Her which I take to be angels. These lights are even on Her mantle. She says: "Praise, honor and victory to Jesus. Dear child, I come once again to remind you, My victory is in hearts that love. There is no sin unless it is in hearts first, for God sees and judges only hearts. All that is on the surface, superficial words and actions, count as nothing before My Son. These are like chaff that blow away in the wind and do not last. See that Holy Love in hearts is all eternal and the only goal of merit. It is when souls lose site of this, that Satan is winning out in their hearts, and they need to take stock of the path they pursue. Make this known."

■ **April 4, 1995 / Thursday Night Rosary Service.** Our Lady is here as Our Lady of Guadalupe. She says: "Tonight My dear Prayer Warriors, pray with Me for the conversion of all those who will come on the Twelfth." We prayed. "Dear children, tonight I announce to you once again, that I depend so much on your prayers, to dispel darkness and bring the light of Holy Love into hearts. Dear children, you do not see with what great speed the chastisement approaches, and how final God's Justice will be. God's Angels are aligning to come to Earth and Harvest the crop. Dear little children, continue in your prayers." Our Lady blessed us and left.

■ **April 4, 1995.** *(Vision)* After Communion today, as always, I saw myself as seven years old, standing in front of Jesus seated on a throne. Our Lady was on My right. I was asking Jesus to give people the grace they need to move their wills to donate for Our Lady's Prayer Center. Then I saw Our Lady move a little closer to Jesus. She said: "My Son, We do need the authority to meet and pray on that property." As She spoke, I saw a light come out of Her Heart and go to the Heart of Jesus. Then a light came out of Jesus' Heart and went into Our Lady's Heart. These lights seemed to melt together and become one. Jesus said, "It is done." I have never seen Our Lady directly ask Jesus for a petition before.

■ **April 4, 1995.** Jesus says: "Simply be with Me. Abide in Me. I do not call you to heroic sacrifices - but to heroic holiness. It is in My Heart your prayers are transformed into grace, then handed down to you through the benevolent Heart of My Mother. All things are possible. Comfort Me in My loneliness. I am returning."

■ **April 5, 1995.** Our Lady is here as Our Lady of Fatima. She is bending over me and Her Heart is exposed. She says: "My daughter, let us give praise and thanks to Jesus. Today, I come to remind you once again to have every confidence in the grace of My Immaculate Heart. It is Satan who tries to make you lose focus and makes everything seem most desperate. My Victory is coming and with it the glorious reign of My Son's Eucharistic Heart on Earth. It is then ideologies will be harmonious, faith will be pure and unadulterated once again, and people will be united in truth and peace. These days preceding the hideous reign of the Antichrist - both in hearts and in the world - Satan uses division as a tactic to bring down the good and uphold evil. This is why I continue to call you to reconcile yourselves in the safe Refuge of My Heart. There is no other attainable goal of merit, for no good lives outside My Heart."

■ **April 6, 1995.** *(Dayton - Bergamo)* Our Lady is here as Our Lady of Guadalupe, and She has Her Heart exposed. She says: "Pray with Me at this time for those who will come in pilgrimage on the Twelfth." We prayed. "Dear children, do not fear the difficult days that lie ahead, for I am calling you into the light of the purifying flame of My Heart. This Flame which is HOLY LOVE, is the solemn Refuge you must seek. It is the spiritual Refuge, which dispels all error and fear. Dear children, I am praying for your intentions before the Throne of God, and I am blessing you."

■ **April 7, 1995.** *(Grotto at St. John Bergamo)* Our Lady is here as Our Lady of Sorrows. She has the seven swords in Her Heart. She says: "Pray with Me for the conversion of all sinners." We prayed. At the "*Glory Be*", Our Lady rose up higher and the swords in Her Heart were illuminated by bright lights. "Dear children, join with Me now at the foot of the Cross, where you will find all humanity, though most do not recognize their place. Most do not praise the crosses in their lives. I invite you today to realize the great value in every cross that God gives you. Dear children, My Son's Church has entered its agony; separation and trial will be its hallmark in the coming year. I desire to take you into My wounded Heart dear children. I desire that Our sorrows be united. I am praying for your intentions." Our Lady blessed us and left.

■ **April 7, 1995.** Our Lady is here in white with a gray mantle. Her Heart is exposed and has one sword in it. She says: "Pray with Me now for the conversion of all sinners." We prayed. "Dear children, tonight, I come to you to tell you that the greatest sword that pierces My Heart is the unpreparedness for what is to come, for so many remain unconverted and unchanged in their ways. And they do not love. Soon, very soon, a great darkness will shroud the world. This darkness will last for three days and I tell you it will be in souls, as well as, in the world. This darkness will be so powerful, it will shroud the grace of My Heart and obscure the way to this ARK for those who do not already know it. It is for this reason, I ask that you immerse yourselves in the midst of THE FLAME OF HOLY LOVE, that is MY IMMACULATE HEART, while there is still time. I am calling you to love My dear children, and I am blessing you." Our Lady blessed us and left.

■ **April 10, 1995.** Our Lady comes as Our Lady of Grace. I see Her from the waist up. She says: "Jesus sends Me this day to advise you, the time grows short until this ministry is in full bloom. The grace of My Heart is forbearance, multiplied by your prayers and sacrifices each day. Some will come seeking and will not find. Others will receive, unexpectedly, grace they have long sought elsewhere. To all of these I extend My invitation to Holy Love. Each one receives according to God's Holy and Perfect Will. The path of triumph and victory is consecration to the cross in the present. Though you do not see My triumph in your cross, it is at hand." She leaves.

■ **April 12, 1995 / Monthly Message To All Nations.** Our Lady is here as Our Lady of Guadalupe. She says: "Pray with Me now for the unconverted: These include the unbelievers, the unforgiving, and the lukewarm. This number varies from moment to moment, as some do not realize their responsibility towards holiness in the present moment."

"It is through man's will the Chastisement will come - the destruction of the world brought on by man himself. See then, the unconverted not only choose for themselves, but for the world."

"Am I not here, My daughter? I who am your Life, your Sweetness and your Hope? I who am your Perpetual Help, Protectress, and Refuge? What is there to fear? I come with great love once again to call My children to love before the hour wears on and it grows too late."

"Hasten to see that what comes as a purification does not open the abyss between God and man, but serves to unite them together. God's Love is unalterable - His Mercy from generation to generation. The New Jerusalem is attainable to all through the Refuge of My Heart."

"But I tell you, those who do not live in Holy Love will be stripped of their worldly gods. The greatest technology will be rendered useless. There will be great signs in the Heavens, on earth and under the earth, as time, as you know it, draws to an end. Nature itself will bear witness to what will transpire. Those in the world will see it not. The sky and all things under it will be set aflame. This hour will be more devastating than the flood. Two thirds of all life will be taken. Mankind will be judged according to the love in his heart."

"But once again I tell you, those who are in the Refuge of My Heart WILL NOT FEAR. Hasten to make all of what I have told you known to all."

"At this time, I tell you that when My Son returns and everyone is living in Holy Love in the New Jerusalem, all will be made new. The world will be simple and pure as it was meant to be. All will love, and God will be in the center of all hearts. My Son's Church will no longer be divided by schism, apostasy, and error, but will be made whole once again. And so you see, there is nothing to fear, for I am calling you only to the completeness of Holy Love. I am blessing you."

■ **April 16, 1995.** *(7:00 a.m. Easter Sunday)*
The 3-Day Consecration To The Flame Of Holy Love
Our Lady comes in white with white lilies in front of Her. Jesus' Hands with the wounds were on either side of Her. "Alleluia! Praise be to Jesus, Risen and Glorified! Take up your pen, My angel. Here is the beginning of My prayer - *The Consecration to the Flame of Holy Love.*"

The Consecration To The Flame Of Holy Love
"Immaculate Heart of Mary, humbly, I ask that You take my heart into the Flame of Holy Love, that is the spiritual refuge of all mankind. Do not look upon my faults and failings, but allow these iniquities to be burned away by this purifying Flame."

"Through Holy Love, help me to be sanctified in the present moment, and in so doing, give to You, dear Mother, my every thought, word, and action. Take me and use me according to Your great pleasure. Allow me to be Your instrument in the world, all for the greater glory of God and towards Your victorious reign. Amen."

"The souls that thus consecrate themselves relinquish to Me all their faults, their sins - both past and future, their virtues - those they have and will have, their sorrows, their joys and their fears. I will reign in their hearts being victorious over besetting sins. I will take dominion over interior and exterior goods. I ask only their undying faithfulness to living in Holy Love, and to spreading the message of Holy Love. In so doing, they will be My instruments in leading souls into the New Jerusalem."

"Souls that desire to make this consecration must for three days prepare their hearts. Each day I desire that they perform some corporal work of Mercy. Each day they must evangelize the Holy Love message to at least one person. Each day they must reverently receive My Son in the Eucharist [if Catholic]. These three days of light will serve as armor against the three days of darkness that are to come. This is God's Merciful Love I am giving to humanity through you."

"Pray with Me now for unbelievers." We prayed. "Make this known to believers and unbelievers alike." She leaves.

■ **April 19, 1995.** *(Locution from Jesus)* "I am calling you to complete trust in Me - in My plan for you - for I am the Way, the Truth, and the Light. My provision in you is perfect and never lacking. I am in your midst and surrounding you. I desire very much to be in the center of all hearts and so in the center of Churches. Do you need to look for, and search for, what is in the center of your heart? You should not need to search for Me when you enter My Church. I am the Cornerstone. What is sown in hearts is harvested in the world."

■ **April 20, 1995 / Thursday Night Rosary Service.** Our Lady is here as Our Lady of Guadalupe. She says: "Pray with Me now, for those who are victimized by evil in hearts." We prayed. "Dear children, come to realize that God's Divine Mercy and God's Divine Love are one and inseparable. It is through Holy Love I will lead you into the New Jerusalem and God's Divine Love. Dear children, continue to pray, pray, pray." Our Lady blessed us and left.

■ **April 22, 1995.** *(Locution from Jesus)* "If you enter deeply into the mystery of My Resurrection, you must realize the origin of your salvation in Divine Love. None of this would have been possible without Holy Love - that was My Mother's first. Therefore, see the mystery of Holy Love I send My Mother into the world with, is the foundation of your salvation.

Those who reject My Mother, reject Me."

■ **April 22, 1995.** Our Lady comes in white. Her veil is blowing in a gentle breeze. She says: "Today, I announce My coming to you on the Twelfth will have great impact on hearts. God will ordain many graces, interior and exterior, on this day. I invite all who will come to prepare their souls with much prayer and many sacrifices. It is to be My last apparition at this site (Windsor), but the beginning of many miracles and graces I will bring to earth, with Me, when I come to you on the Twelfth of each month. Those in attendance, who are thus prepared as I have requested, will find solace in My visit and profound peace in My call to them. You yourself will find your life changed. I do not come bearing gifts of worldly measure but in the spiritual realm. Make My requests known and continue to pray, pray, pray. I desire that through My visit to you, souls will reconcile themselves to God. Make it known to all My little children."

■ **April 24, 1995.** Our Lady was waiting for me in the chapel. She was in blue and white, floating in a mist. She had a circle of stars over Her Heart and was holding a rosary. She said: "Do you see how all the while I have been waiting for you and yet, I was with you at Mass? [I had just come from Mass.] Let us begin. I tell you, God's Mercy extends from age to age and is upon those who most especially bear no grudge and forgive. It is not within My call to holiness to point the finger of blame at another, but to convict your own heart in Holy Love. Dissension is always accepted in hearts first My angel, before there is division in the world. Solemnly, I tell you that hearts who once heard My call to conversion, and paid heed, have become lukewarm. Some of these visited many of My apparition sites, read many books, and prayed many rosaries. Once again, I call you to see the present moment is your salvation, or your perdition according to your propensity towards Holy Love. Further, I come to tell you, My messenger, that this season in nature will reflect the Season of Tribulation you are now experiencing. Some crops will be watered down and others will be dried up. This reflects the faith that is in hearts. My Son grieves the disregard for the Eternal Father's Commandments. The Sabbath is profaned; Church law disregarded; Life is dehumanized; Values are convoluted. My call to holiness is scoffed and compromised. My Son desires hearts to be patterned in Holy Love. Souls who immerse themselves in the Flame of Holy Love, that is My Heart, will be protected against the adversary's evil designs through introspection as to their own state of holiness. I desire to create in the world a conflagration of this Flame through My words to you. You will make this known to all My little children. Praise be to Jesus. Alleluia."

■ **April 25, 1995.** *(Vision)* I was given the vision of myself as a little girl. I was skipping along a country road. All at once, I was tripping over a stone in the road and fell. I saw Our Lady come and pick me up and brush me off. She said to continue forward on the path and pointed the way. I was told by an interior voice: The path is the road of holiness through Holy Love. The stone is a human fault. You tripped over it because you temporarily took your eyes off the path in the present moment. But see, Our Lady did not re-direct you to regress or go back to the beginning of the path. She encouraged you to continue forward - only reminding you to be holy in the present moment by keeping your eyes on the path She calls you upon. If She is so compassionate towards your failings, you too must forgive others' faults.

■ **April 27, 1995.** Our Lady comes in white. She says: "I come in praise of the Risen Jesus. Alleluia! My daughter, it is important My children know and understand that I am drawing them into the spiritual Refuge of My Heart during these last days. Just as My Heart is a spiritual Ark of Protection, I desire that all know that I am establishing many <u>Spiritual Refuge</u>

Centers on earth. These will be places of renewal and spiritual strengthening through My presence and the embrace of My Heart. Make it known that through My ministry and My call to you, I am establishing such a Spiritual Refuge in this area. It is here I will be in the midst of all who will come, and those who come will be in the midst of My Heart. It is through Holy Love all will pass from this life into the New Jerusalem."

■ **April 27, 1995 / Thursday Night Rosary Service.** Our Lady is here as Our Lady of Guadalupe. She says, "Praise be to Jesus, My dearest little children. Pray with Me now for those who are coming on the 12th." We prayed. Our Lady continues, "Dear children, My Heart is on fire with love for you. I desire so much, you immerse yourself in THE FLAME OF LOVE that is My Heart, just as the first apostles did. This is the Flame of the Ark of the New Covenant. It is only through the grace of this Flame that you will be true apostles of Holy Love. I am with you and I am blessing you. My Grace is upon you."

■ **April 30, 1995.** Our Lady comes in white. Her Heart is exposed and purple, pink and white rays are coming from it. She bends over me and says, "Praise be to Jesus, little one. Solemnly, I come to tell you today, the world is slipping deeper and deeper into the Season of Tribulation. This is by way of Man's infidelity to God which lifts the Staying Hand of Protection from the world. As evil is on the increase, the cataclysmic events I have foretold will increase in severity. If hearts do not return to God and petition His Assistance in these events, soon His Hand will be withdrawn completely. Before you were in the Spring of Tribulation; now you approach Autumn. When Winter comes, God's presence will not be felt in the world. Hearts will be won over by evil and My Words to you will be fulfilled. This is the reason I continue My visits to you and to many around the world. For time has not been exhausted and grace is still inspiring and converting hearts. My child, continue to pray, pray, pray."

May 1995

■ **May 1, 1995.** Our Lady comes in white. Her Heart is exposed. Purple, pink and white rays are coming from It. She bends over me and says: "Solemnly, I come to tell you today, the world is slipping deeper and deeper into the Season of Tribulation. This is by way of man's infidelity to God which lifts the staying Hand of Protection from the world. As evil is on the increase, the cataclysmic events I have foretold will increase in severity. If hearts do not return to God and petition His assistance in these events, soon His Hand will be withdrawn completely. Before, you were in the Spring of Tribulation, now, you approach Autumn. When Winter comes, God's Presence will not be felt in the world. Hearts will be won over by evil and My words to you will be fulfilled. This is the reason I continue My visits to you, and to many around the world, for time has not been exhausted, and grace is still inspiring and converting hearts. My child, continue to pray, pray, pray."

■ **May 2, 1995 / Weekly Rosary Service.** Our Lady is here as Our Lady of Guadalupe. She says: "I invite you to pray for all those who will be coming on the Twelfth." We prayed. "Dear children, tonight I invite you, more than ever, to pray that all hearts return to God. This plague of apostasy and evil that pervades hearts is more intense than any plague that visited Pharaoh. This plague destroys souls and therefore, is the most distasteful that can visit Earth. Dear children, once again, I invite you to realize that only hearts that love can enter My Son's Kingdom. Therefore, continue to pray, pray, pray that all hearts accept Holy Love. "Our Lady blessed us and left.

■ **May 3, 1995.** Jesus says: "Holy Love is the Gateway and the Kingdom."

■ **May 3, 1995.** Our Lady came with the scent of roses. She had roses in front of Her like I had on the May altar. She is in white. She says: "I desire, My daughter, that you know and understand in your heart that: The New Jerusalem and Holy Love are one and the same. This is where My children will live after My Son returns - in a climate and environment that is Holy Love. Hasten to make this known to all My little children. In this give praise to Jesus."

■ **May 3, 1995.** Our Lady comes in white. She is radiant and smiling. She says: "I am your Mother and I come in praise of Jesus. I come to tell all My little children that I desire so much to give all humanity My Love. I am unable to give My Love to hearts that do not love Me. This is why I come to you - to make My Love known throughout the world. So many hearts fear this Season of Tribulation. So many tremble at the thought of the coming chastisement. But today I tell you, for God there is only one season - the Season of Love. This is the climate My Son desires the world live in - that of love. I am blessing you now."

■ **May 5, 1995 - First Anniversary of the Feast of Holy Love.** The Statue of Our Blessed Mother was crowned by the children present. They also laid bouquets of flowers at Her feet and in front of the image of Our Lady of Guadalupe. The congregation stood and sang ON THIS DAY, O BEAUTIFUL MOTHER. A reading from Scripture was followed by the placing of Hearts at the feet of Our Crowned Blessed Mother. This symbolized the giving of our hearts to the Blessed Mother. In the background a tape player was playing GIVE ME YOUR LOVE. It was a very moving occasion followed by the recitation of the Rosary.

Our Lady is here in a white gown with a blue mantle, She is like Our Lady of Grace. She says: "I am your Everlasting and Eternal Mother."

"I give thanks to God for you and for His allowing Me to

come to you this night and always. Pray with Me now for all those who are coming on the Twelfth." We prayed. "Dear children, tonight I request of you, as your gift to Me during this month of May, that each day you consecrate yourselves to The Flame of Holy Love. Begin this month, and continue on, for in this way you are clothed in the dignity of the Grace of My Heart. Satan sees this as a sign of your predestination. I do not promise you will not be attacked or tested, but I promise, you will not be defeated. I am always with you and I am blessing you." She blessed us and left.

■ **May 5, 1995 - Feast of Our Lady of Holy Love.** Our Lady is here with a huge angel whose wings expand behind Our Lady. She says: "Do you recall, My child, what we were doing last year at this time? [We were digging for the spring] In this let us give praise to Jesus. My sweet child, it is not long until mankind will be given an hour of decision; a moment of truth. All will see how they have failed in Holy Love. Holy Love will be the measure of fidelity to God and to His law. For this reason, the tide of necessity rises to make My words to you known. Print what I have given you concerning future events, and most especially on the Twelfth of each month, in a separate and complete issue. Some do not want to attend to these issues at hand, while others are distracted by them. While all the time, I hand you Heaven's solution, which is Holy Love. From time to time, you will update this issue as I continue to enlighten you. I will join you today in prayer. Thank you for attending to My call." She leaves.

■ **May 8, 1995.** *(At the spring-fed lake on the future Prayer Center site.)* Our Lady is here as Our Lady of Grace. Her arms are extended and Her hands are opened. There are rays of light, coming from Her hands, touching the ground. Then the rays of light turned into water. Our Lady then said: "Dear children, today I inform you that, the waters attendant to this property bring with it many graces towards - healing the infirm and reconciling souls to God. Further I inform you, THE HEEL THAT WILL CRUSH THE SERPENT'S HEAD IS HOLY LOVE. Make it known." Then I saw Our Lady's left foot extend out from Her gown. Her Heel then stepped upon the serpent's head.

■ **May 10, 1995.** Our Lady came as Our Lady of Guadalupe. Juan Diego was in front of Her kneeling. She said: "Praise be to Jesus, My daughter." She asked us to pray for the conversion of those coming on the Twelfth. We prayed. "Dear little children, I place My fond embrace upon your loving hearts. I treasure your presence with Me here this night. I ask your prayers towards the propagation of Holy Love. My message to you tonight is to continue to love, love, love."

■ **May 11, 1995 / Thursday Night Rosary Service.** Our Lady is here in a silver gown and white veil. Her Heart is exposed and there are rays of light coming from it. She says: "Pray with Me now for all those who are making the pilgrimage tomorrow." We prayed. "Dear children, My call to you is to understand that Holy Love is the Refuge of My Immaculate Heart. Therefore, no one can enter My Heart outside of Holy Love. Further, I invite you to see, My Heart is the winnowing fan that will separate the wheat from the chaff at My Son's return. I am blessing you now in Holy Love." She blessed us and left.

■ **May 11, 1995.** Our Lady comes in white. There is a light shining from the Blessed Sacrament through Her Heart onto me. She says: "Praise be to Jesus, My little one. I come with joy in My Heart for those who are journeying to be with Me tomorrow. I will bring with Me Light and Grace. In many cases the camera will serve as the eyes of the soul. The peace of My Heart will prevail. Continue in prayer for My Holy Pope and for those around him. In peace I leave you."

■ **May 12, 1995 / Monthly Message To All Nations.**
(Servants of Mary Center in Windsor, Ohio, with a 50-foot-tall statue of Our Lady of Guadalupe) Our Lady is here as Our Lady of Guadalupe. She says: "Thank you for answering My call to come here tonight. It is a grace that I come. Pray with Me now for the lukewarm." We prayed. "My daughter, tonight is My last apparition to you at this site, but I am continually here, greeting the pilgrims. I invite My dear children to follow Me to the site I have directed you to, on the Twelfth of next month."

"All that I am revealing to you is occurring because of lack of Holy Love in hearts. As the Season of Tribulation draws to a close, and during the reign of the Antichrist which will be in hearts and in the world, certain and ordained cosmic events will occur. These will mark the onset of the great purification. Some heavenly bodies will loose their light. Others will fall to earth, relinquishing their place in the heavens."

"When these things begin to occur, people will clamor for admittance to My Heart, just as they clamored to get into the Ark when the flood began. But I will not admit those who do not love."

"Dear daughter, dear children, once again I appeal to you to have Holy Love in your hearts, always in the present moment. For what is in hearts affects the entire cosmos. If hearts embrace the Light that is My Son, the world will be in the Light. If hearts choose darkness, the world will be plunged into darkness. Holy Love is the measure by which you choose. Stay close to My dear Pope, John Paul II, - his teachings and encyclicals. Follow the new Catechism. What stands contrary to any of these, is contrary to Holy Love and Heaven."

"My daughter, I tell you, if the lukewarm would accept Holy Love in their hearts, much about the chastisement would be changed, for these are the ones that gravely wound the Heart of My Son. When the darkness comes it will be complete and certain." Her Mantle is turning black. Some of the stars on Her mantle are slipping off and some are going out. The only light is coming from the area of Her Heart. Our Lady continues. "See My dear daughter, that My Heart is the safe Refuge all must seek. This is Holy Love. Those who do not recognize it will perish. Dear children, your strength and your might are in the Flame of Love that is My Heart. I am always with you, most especially when you are praying My Rosary. I desire that you pray for deep faith and trust. Always follow My beloved Pope who is much maligned and under attack."

"Dear children, continue to be courageous in your efforts to spread Holy Love, for you are My dear apostles. Tonight, I am extending to you once again, My Special Blessing."

■ **May 13, 1995.** Our Lady is here in white and gold. She says: "Praise be to Jesus, ever present in the tabernacles of the world. My daughter, I come to you today, rejoicing in your 'yes' to Me which is bearing abundant fruit in the world. I will continue, faithfully, My visits to you on the Twelfth of each month. Those visits will bring manifold graces into the world. The signs I have been giving those who come, will increase and multiply, as will the numbers I am calling and who will answer My call. Pray much for the lukewarm. Many of My priest sons have slipped into this posture. Once again I inform you, the lukewarm hold in their hearts the destiny of the world." She leaves.

■ **May 14, 1995.** I was asking Our Lady in my heart, who She meant when She said lukewarm. She appeared next to my bed and said, "Those whose faith is exterior and not in their hearts."

■ **May 14, 1995.** Our Lady is here in white. She is holding a white cross out to us. She says: "I am with you, My little children. Praise be to Jesus. Pray with Me now for the lukewarm. Dear children, support your cross through Holy Love, for it is only in this way, that you will be brought to eternal happiness. You do not see that many conflicts are a result of much good. I am asking you to look deep into your hearts, correct any error in Holy Love and move on. Do not let grudges form. I am blessing you."

■ **May 16, 1995.** Our Lady comes as Our Lady of Grace. She says: "Pray with Me for the conversion of the lukewarm." We prayed. "Tonight, I invite you to understand on a deeper level, that what I am giving you as a spiritual refuge center (Immaculate Heart of Mary Prayer Center) has its origin in Heaven. Whereas, this other farm you have queried Me about has its origin in the heart of man. What I am giving you cannot be constructed, bought, or sold, for grace comes only from the Heart of the Eternal Father."

■ **May 17, 1995.** From Our Lady: "During these times, and after the illumination of consciences, Jesus will show many that there is little of value except the soul. Many will come to the property (site of future Prayer Center) bearing the demeanor of contrition. But there will be many lukewarm as well. This is why I continue to call you to pray, pray, pray for My lukewarm children. When you do this, you are wiping the tears from My Face and bringing joy to My Heart." She leaves.

■ **May 17, 1995.** Our Lady comes as Our Lady of Grace. She says: "I come in praise of the Risen One - Jesus Christ! Today, I invite you not to look at the serpent beneath Me, but at the heel which will bring victory to My Heart. Once again, know that this heel is Holy Love in hearts." I asked: "Blessed Mother, can you describe what a spiritual refuge center is?" She responded: "It is a place on earth - first formed and nourished in My Heart of grace. Then, it is formed in the hearts of those I have chosen. Then, it is present in the world. It is a particular place of blessing and grace to those who will cling to the true faith and answer My call to conversion and holiness."

■ **May 18, 1995 / Thursday Night Rosary Service.** Our Lady is here as Our Lady of Guadalupe. She says: "Pray with Me now for the Holy Father." We prayed. "Thank you. Pray with Me now for the lukewarm, whose faith is exterior, but not in their hearts." We prayed. "Dear children, joyfully I tell you, that God's favors are about to multiply upon this ministry and in your hearts. Therefore, do not fear any trial, any misfortune, illness, or anxiety, for I am with you, protecting you, and giving you the graces of My Heart as a pillar of strength. I am blessing you."

■ **May 25, 1995.** Our Lady comes as Our Lady of Grace. First, She is in a bright light and then a dim light, as though the sun is over Her, passing in and out of clouds. "Praise be to Jesus, littlest of My messengers. As you witness the light that first embraces Me and then leaves, you see how quickly souls leave the path of holiness who fail in love." Now She is in a bright light. "Today, I tell you once again, that people have made gods of compromise and error. Many 'freedoms' are slavery to sin through Satan's deception. The end of an era is close at hand and will impact your nation and the world. My visits to you on the Twelfth of each month will begin to loosen Satan's grip on the World. You have not seen as yet, the grace God wills to give. I am blessing you."

■ **May 25, 1995 / Thursday Night Rosary Service.** Our Lady is here as Our Lady of Guadalupe. She says: "Praise be to Jesus, My dear little children, My prayer warriors. Pray with Me now for the lukewarm, especially for the lukewarm priests." We prayed. "Tonight dear children, I invite you to see that My Crown of Glory is the Holy Love that you embrace in your hearts. This is the weapon that will overcome the darkness in the world and usher in the New Kingdom - the glorious reign of My Immaculate Heart and Eucharistic Reign of My Beloved Son. Without Holy Love you are powerless. Therefore, My dear children, come only to Me through Holy

Love. I am embracing you with My Motherly Blessing."

■ **May 26, 1995.** Our Lady is here in an ivory-colored veil and a grayish gown. She says: "I am Mary Immaculate - Mother of Jesus born Incarnate. I come to you now in this season of want and of plenty, to guide you beyond natural expectations, to divine wonders and provision. God's plan continues to multiply in you to shelter the spiritually impoverished in Holy Love, which is the Refuge all must seek."

"The greatest sublime depth of the flame of My Heart is the fifth step of holiness, and last commandment My Son gave while on earth; That is, to love one another as He loved you. This is an unconditional love that embraces friend and foe alike. Those who reach this depth of the Flame of My Heart are in the Kingdom that will come - the New Jerusalem. No longer do I call My children to the threshold of God's Kingdom but to the very depth and interior of this paradise of love. Those who have not become poor in spirit and truly consecrated themselves to the cross, will be unable to pass so deeply into this flame of love."

"My invitation to you is no longer just a choice, but a dictate, if you seek reconciliation with God. There is evil in hearts that threatens unity in the church and peace in nations. You must be the first sign of My call to those around you. Continue to pray, pray, pray."

■ **May 28, 1995.** *(Over the last two months, Blessed Mother has given Maureen confidential messages, not to be revealed until She advises.)* Our Lady is here as Our Lady of Grace. She says: "My daughter do not be concerned for the messages I choose to withhold from many. This has to be, for the time has not come, and hearts are not ready for much of what I confide to you. If all of this were revealed now, it would fall on unbelieving ears. But as more and more events unravel the false security of the world, souls will be ready to listen. One such event is in the offing, so you need to pray. Many are unprepared and do not love."

"Those in the world have eyes and ears only for what satisfies the senses. I am calling My children to love. For it is through love, the heart is opened, satisfied, and at peace. There is no other way. Through you, My little daughter, I hope to bring many hearts to this resolve."

"The time that is left is given only by way of many sacrifices and prayers. It is given as an invitation to love. There is nothing that will change hearts except love. THEREFORE, SEE THAT HOLY LOVE IS MY LAST CALL TO HUMANITY. It is the remedy for the lukewarm, the unconverted, and My Son's Church. It is the safe passage to the New Jerusalem and to Divine Love - the Heart of Jesus, My Son. It is all I hope for, pray for, intercede for. It is the peace and security of My Immaculate Heart. Holy Love is the life-line of the world - the bridge that spans the abyss between Heaven and earth. Graciously, I extend it. I invite My children out of the storm of hypocrisy that rages in the world and into Holy Love - My Heart, My Flame of love. Surrender your wills and your hearts that I may use your love as a spark to ignite love in other hearts. Always remember, there is no tempest that can prevail against the Refuge of My Heart - Holy Love. It is so that I can invite all humanity to this secure ark. Hasten to My call."

■ **May 28, 1995.** Jesus says: "Do you not know I have loved you for all eternity? To you I extend the richness of My Mercy, the fullness of My Love. Nor has My place for you in the world been fulfilled. I only deepen My call to you. I fill you with trust. I embrace your heart in Victory. The path I spill out before you is flooded with garlands of grace, but you will only see the grace through the cross. In you, I place My call to sanctity. I ask you to spread it. My call to you is sweet and palatable. Do not forsake Me. Your place is in Me - there, where I choose to put you in the world. I love you."

■ **May 28, 1995.** Jesus says, "I want to tell you about My

Wounds so that you better understand My Passion. The Wound on My Right Hand represents the pain I suffer for the compromise in My Church. The Wound on My Left Hand is what I suffer in The Blessed Sacrament. The Wound in My Left Foot is the unbelievers and agnostics. The Wound in My Right Foot is the unconverted priests. The Wound of My Heart is all the lukewarm for whom I suffer greatly and for whom I suffer the most."

■ **May 30, 1995.** Our Lady comes in a blue mantle, that is very shiny, and a white gown. She is holding a rosary She lets slip through Her fingers as I finish the last decade. Her Heart is exposed. She says: "Praise be to Jesus, My angel." A bright light comes from Her Heart as She says: "I come to tell you, to reassure you, at My next coming (on My future Prayer Center site) I will consecrate the ground and most especially, the spring to My needs. The water will carry with it special grace to strengthen all hearts in faith and love. Healings will be attendant to these waters. It is a site reserved for all nations - all peoples. Most especially, I call My priest sons to come and to be strengthened in their vocations."

"Reserve a side chapel to the good and Blessed John Marie Vianney - even now in this simple structure I direct you to begin with. It is so I can call priests back to the true faith, to Tradition and away from much compromise. When My priests come, as they will, I will be present, praying with them."

"Do not fear the greatest trial. You will endure, My angel. I desire My children confess before the Twelfth of the month, and make at least one special sacrifice in preparation for My coming. I promise to bring with Me the grace of My Heart. I am blessing you."

■ **May 30, 1995 / Tuesday Rosary Service.** Our Lady is here as Our Lady of Guadalupe. She says, "Praise be to Jesus. Pray with Me now for all the lukewarm, most especially My priest-sons." We prayed. "Please pray with Me now for all those who are coming on the 12th of June." We prayed. Our Lady continues. "Dear children, tonight I graciously invite you to understand that your path to Holy Love lies unencumbered when you die to self. My dear children, I invite you once again to be apostles of Holy Love. Spread My messages to all you meet. I am in your midst when you are loving, My dear children, and I am blessing you."

■ **May 31, 1995.** *(Maranatha Spring 7:30 p.m.)* Our Lady is here in white and She is holding a pink rosary. She says: "Praise be to Jesus, My little one. Joyfully, I reveal to you today that the waters of Maranatha are as the Lourdes* of this continent. They are comparable in healing grace, both in body and soul. They are much like the cascade in Betania (Venezuela 1976-1990). Therefore, you can propagate it with much faith and hope. Pray with Me now for all unbelievers. I leave you now with My Motherly Blessing."

Apparitions of Our Lady to Bernadette Soubirous in France in 1858 and discovery of a miraculous spring on Feb. 25, 1858.

■ **May 31, 1995.** *(11:45 p.m.)* Our Lady came in white with a large pink rosary She held as I prayed. The beads seemed to float through Her fingers. An angel held one end of the rosary. She said: "So it is I come again, My unworthy and humble servant, to offer and give praise to Jesus. You have not began to understand in your heart the depth of My words to you earlier at the spring (see previous message). You doubt, and it is no longer the hour of doubt. Heaven does not fulfill prophecy or extend provision by half measure. Know for certain, water that is given as a means of grace is not restricted, but given the fullness of grace God so intends and wills. The graces given at Maranatha on both properties are extraordinary and comparable to My greatest shrines and sites of apparition. Once the path lies unrestricted to My new property, you will begin to see the full extent of My call."

"Further, I tell you, in your personal life, do not let money issues be a distraction. Buying and selling will soon be obsolete. It will be those who have access to the rudiments of life who will fare the best. It will come to pass," She pauses, "in this Season of Tribulation. Once you were a child and could not bear all I am telling you. Now I speak to one spiritually mature. Love even My call to you. I am leaving you now, to be with you later."

■ **May 31, 1995 - Feast of Visitation.** After communion Our Lady said: "Please understand, My daughter, My 'yes' did not last for a moment, but for a lifetime. So too, your 'yes' must be from moment to moment and continual."

Then Jesus told me: "Every act, whether good or evil, is committed first in the heart, then in the world. So it is many sins are committed in hearts. The soul is misled to believe if he does not act on what he commits in his heart he is blameless. Do you know how many abortions have been committed in hearts?"

■ **May 31, 1995.** Our Lady is here in glistening white. She says: "My daughter, begin to see the fulfillment of My call in those I send you. For even the smallest act of love brings closer the completeness of My call. Even a *'Hail Mary'* said with a sick person is a brick on the path. Therefore, treasure each moment in love as an opportunity of grace towards My end in you." She blesses me and leaves.

June 1995

■ **June 1, 1995.** When I got up Our Lady came dressed like She was the night before. She said: "Good morning. This is the feast month of My Son's Sacred Heart. You will pray to Him for all the needs of My ministry and He will respond with generosity. He has much to tell you. And you will give praise to Jesus." I asked: "Blessed Mother, are you forming physical refuge centers?" She responded: "God preserved Noah because of what was in his heart not because He wanted him to be 'safe'. Many will come to My Spiritual Refuge Center seeking safe ground. But My Son, who sees only hearts, will weed them out. In order to take the Tradition of Faith into the New Jerusalem, certain measures will need to be taken to maintain life. But this is not the reason I form such communities of faith. It is so I can lead them through the trials and the Gateway to the New Jerusalem; then the little nuggets of faith as remnants of the true church can flourish again. I am the port in the storm. Your mission (My mission in you) is one of many around the world. Be transformed in this."

■ **June 6, 1995.** Our Lady is in the corner of the chapel in a silvery light. She says: "My daughter, greater things are at stake than financial issues. I speak of souls. Souls who are erring in their opinions and proud in their hearts. There is no justification for what they hold in their hearts. They are self-serving and do not fear God. Even their communions are lukewarm. You need to pray very much for such souls who do not even recognize the state of their own hearts due to Satan's deceit. You need to trust in My call. Pray very much and I will be with you, interceding on your behalf, and on behalf of My ministry. I leave you now to return later."

■ **June 6, 1995.** Our Lady is here in grayish blue. She says: "I am the Mother of Mercy. Your prayers will not go unheeded. In time, you will see My place unfold. But, offer up the precious moments of waiting with Me for all the unbelievers and most especially the lukewarm. If one is converted, if one embraces Holy Love, it is a victory. You need to pray for increased faith and hope. Begin today. My Son has answered 'yes' to this ministry. His unfolding of His plan is at hand. He wants all that you want which will lead souls to holiness. The waters of

Maranatha will wash clean many souls."

■ **June 8, 1995.** I felt an interior urging to go to early Mass this morning. I didn't know why. I even saw Our Lady at the foot of My bed motioning me to get up. On the way back from communion I saw a particle of a Host on the floor, so I picked it up and held it in My hand until after Mass. Then I took Him back to the sacristy. Jesus said to me, "Thank you for rescuing Me. You did so out of love and respect. If people had love and respect in their hearts, abortion would not be prevalent."

■ **June 8, 1995 / Thursday Night Rosary Service.** Our Lady is here as Our Lady of Guadalupe. She says: "Pray with Me now for the unbelievers and all those who will come on the Twelfth." We prayed. "Dear children, tonight I invite you to surrender completely to My call. Do not allow Satan to enter with his discouragement. For discouragement drives out hope. Know that when you hold the rosary, you are holding My hand and we are united in purpose and cause. Dear children, I cannot make you holy by My coming to you. It is necessary that you chose the path of Holy Love yourselves. I am blessing you."

■ **June 11, 1995.** Our Lady comes as Our Lady of Guadalupe. She says: "Praise be to Jesus, My messenger, My angel. And so it is, another month has passed in time, and hearts continue in their choice of evil over good. The Season of Tribulation progresses in time and severity. The thief is in the sanctuary clothed in compromise. Darkness is spreading, presenting itself as freedom and light. When God's purification comes there will not be time to choose. Hearts that could not decide for good will be judged in their indecision. For at that time every chance and grace will have been given for each one's salvation. My Heart will have exhausted every effort, My Mantle will have been offered to all. So you see with what urgency I call today and how My arms hope to enfold the most distant soul. Some look towards My Son's coming as though the path lay clear for them, when all the while they surrender the present to evil. The Father's Commandments are no longer considered measures of behavior."

"You know all of this, My child. It has been necessary to bring you along the path of many, many, trials - both interior and exterior - so that I could strengthen and mold My ministry as Jesus desires. And now, I tell you, We are preparing to move ahead. You must pray much for strong faith. For what lies ahead is a tidal wave of criticism, disbelief, and lies. My ministry will not succumb. You will endure if you pray much and remain in My Heart. I tell you these things, as a Mother forewarns Her child, of tribulations that lie ahead. You will sorrow for those who turn against you - just as I do. But always you will have the support of a certain number who will be enlightened to see the source of these trials. Much good will be accomplished within a short time. Therefore, do not focus on the trials I prepare you for, but for the victorious mission at hand. Render Me the favor of your submission to the cross and to the victory. My heel is your Holy Love and your response to My call." She leaves.

■ **June 11, 1995.** *(2:00 p.m.)* Our Lady came as Our Lady of Fatima. She said: "Do you love My Son's Church, My angel?" I said, "Yes, Blessed Mother, I do."

"Pride is about to carry off all but a remnant of the faith. You must be strong so that you can spread the faith in your heart, to others. You see signs of this now, but the time is coming when what I speak of will be more than opinions and individualism but it will be purported as the true faith."

■ **June 12, 1995.** Our Lady is here as Our Lady of Guadalupe. She says: "My coming to you today is to bring greater honor and glory to Jesus, My Son. I bring a special grace with Me today which will come to help spread Holy Love in hearts. Tell as many as you can to bring with them objects they desire that

I kiss and bless with a special grace that will bring healing, both spiritual and physical. This blessing will help open unyielding hearts to Holy Love. I will disperse angels during My visit with you to carry My kiss and blessing amongst those present. And this will be customary on My visits to you on the twelfth from now on. Make it known."

■ **June 12, 1995 / Monthly Message To All Nations.** *(Indian Hollow Park, Lorain County, Ohio)* From Our Lady: "I come to you this evening to ask My children to be compatible with the Church's teaching on the Holy Father's infallibility; My Son's Real Presence in the Holy Eucharist; and My Own role in the Church. These are the areas the enemy favors to attack. Do not be deceived into thinking you can pick and choose which doctrine you believe."

"Jesus asks that you offer all your communions during the month of the Precious Blood, the month of July, for lukewarm priests. That they will return to belief in the Real Presence of My Son in the Sacrament of the Altar." Our Lady now says: "Ask people to extend towards Heaven the objects they wish Me to kiss." She says: "Thank you, My dear little children, for coming in faith, hope and love. Today, I extend to you once again, My Motherly Blessing. And I desire that you use these objects, which I have personally kissed through the angels, to bring souls to Holy Love."

"Dear children, this Ministry will undergo further persecution in the future, but you will endure through the grace of My Heart. Jesus in His Majesty and Mercy will extend yet another grace to bring souls into Holy Love. For when the great illumination of consciences comes in the future, souls will also see that Holy Love is the path, salvation and refuge. It is at that time, many will come to My apparition site. Dear children, continue to pray from the heart, that My messages of Holy Love are propagated throughout the world, and I am blessing you."

■ **June 14, 1995.** Our Lady came as Our Lady of Fatima. She said: "Once again, I come for the greater honor and glory of Jesus, My Son. My daughter, it is necessary that you answer My call for continuous prayer for strong faith. My Pope has spent his papacy bracing the Church for what is imminent. If you have faith, you can be courageous in the face of the enemy - and he is all around. My Son's Church will not fall to ruin. It is through the Eucharist and My Immaculate Heart She will prevail. I plead for the many who will be led astray and who will not find the path in time."

■ **June 15, 1995.** Our Lady was in the Chapel when I arrived. She was dressed like Our Lady of Grace, but She had many roses around Her. She said: "I come to offer praise and thanksgiving to Jesus, My Son. My daughter, today I ask once again, that My children consent to Holy Love, which is My call to them. This is a universal call and does not differ from one of My apparition sites to another. It is the heart of My message to the world and My final invitation. Jesus calls souls into the Flame of My Heart to be purified and perfected in holiness. He asks that once a soul surrenders to this Flame of Love that they no longer seek external graces here, there and everywhere. My Son desires that souls find the kingdom of God within their own hearts and pray for the interior grace they need to become more holy. All will be given that is needed for each soul to reach perfection. See then, these exterior graces are only My continued invitation to Holy Love. But Holy Love is living in your hearts, and seeking your perfection in holiness. I give you this example: A soul comes to My Son in adoration and receives many consolations during adoration. Instead of returning there often, he looks for another Chapel of adoration hoping to find even more grace. Such a soul could easily lose his way because he does not look within himself but looks outside himself seeking perfection, seeking more exterior grace. I desire salvation for each one of My children. I ask they seek not so much further signs and wonders, but to look at the heart of My message everywhere, there they will find the fullness of their search - Holy Love. Make it known."

■ **June 15, 1995 / Thursday Night Rosary Service.** Our Lady is here as Our Lady of Guadalupe. She says: "Oh My daughter, how I desire that every heart surrender to give praise to Jesus. Pray with Me now for the lukewarm." We prayed. She continues, "Dear children, each time I come to earth, I come as your Mother, your Refuge, your Comfortress and your Protectress. Today I invite you again not to let My words fall amongst thorns or over rocks, but let your soul open and fervently live the words I impart to you. Let Holy Love be your rising, your retiring, the air you breathe and the food you partake of. I impart to you My Motherly Blessing."

■ **June 17, 1995.** *(Locution from Our Lady)* "The tenure of time until My Son returns will be an interweaving of grace and tribulation. Each of these will intensify until the illumination of consciences. Those who have built their spirituality on sandy soil, will find they have little to cling to."

■ **June 17, 1995.** *(Locution)* "Encapsulated in My words to you is the New Kingdom, the New Era, the New World. Life will take on simplistic nature. Technology will fall by the wayside and in its place, God. Each heart will be a New Jerusalem, an enterprise of faith and trust in Holy and Divine Providence. Commodities will not be bought and sold. Reliance on God will replace reliance on technology. All of this you will make known."

■ **June 18, 1995 - Feast of Corpus Christi.** Jesus says: "Concealed in this Godhead - the Three in One - is the Divine Love, the Divine Mercy that spawns Holy Love. Know that My Mercy and My Love are inseparable, just as My Heart cannot be separated from the Heart of My Mother. These are hidden treasures of your faith. Hidden from unbelievers and lukewarm but revealed in these times to the fervent heart."

■ **June 22, 1995.** Our Lady is here in a white mantle and a bluish-gray gown. She says: "I come once again to offer praise and homage to Jesus. My dear, dear children, you do not see how quickly time is passing before My Son returns. I need your sincere prayers to bring the lukewarm into the Ark of My Heart. Every moment is given as a gift from Heaven and as a gift of God's continued Mercy, so that you, My dear children, can bring Me souls. It is only when you are loving that your prayers are sincere and worthy. Therefore, see and understand that the merit of love in your hearts today, affects the entire cosmos. You cannot answer My call outside of Holy Love. I desire you make this known."

■ **June 22, 1995 / Thursday Night Rosary Service.** Our Lady is here as Our Lady of Guadalupe. She says: "Praise be to Jesus. Dear and faithful children, pray with Me now for the lukewarm and those who will come on the 12th." We prayed. She continues, "Dear children, once again I desire that you use Holy Love as your measure to recognize good and to sort out evil in your lives. Every heart that does not love is listening to Satan. Do not suppose that he is not present and does not discourage prayer. I come to you so often, My dear children, as My Son desires through you to strengthen the remnant, and lead souls to sanctity and away from evil. Dear children, be apostles of Holy Love as I am calling you to be. I am blessing you."

■ **June 24, 1995.** Our Lady says: "My Son has already returned in hearts that embrace Holy Love."

■ **June 24, 1995 – Feast of the Immaculate Heart of Mary.** Our Lady is here in a dark blue mantle and white gown. Her Heart is exposed. She says: "I come in praise of Jesus, My Son. My daughter, I desire My children understand that it is not possible to enter My Heart without first passing through the purifying Flame of My Heart which is Holy Love. This Flame endorses good and convicts evil. Souls cannot achieve loftiness in Heaven who do not allow themselves to be purged in the midst of this Flame. It is the light to dispel darkness. It is the embrace of Divine Love. It is the kiss of salvation. It lights the way for My Son's return. It is the Flame that will encompass the earth. All this I tell you, as My time with you shortens and soon My Son will return. Make this known."

■ **June 25, 1995.** From Our Lady: "As I am calling each one to holiness, I am also calling families to holiness. This family who mourns will be comforted. If they have a will to do so, I invite them to form a Refuge prayer cell. If you help them, My daughter, I will come. Some will oblige Me, others will not. But I still invite. I remain their Refuge." I asked Our Lady: "Why are you dressed as Our Lady of Fatima instead of Queen of Peace today?" She replied: "In Fatima (Portugal 1917), I invited My children to pray and sacrifice for the conversion of Russia and of all sinners. My petition was not heeded. Instead it was ignored and hidden in scrutiny. Here today, I call for love, prayer, sacrifice, and conversion. Once again, My message is not being permitted to be freely circulated. Ones in positions of importance are opposing Me instead of co-operating. This is because their hearts are not as loving as heaven desires. Errors in hearts spread quickly into the world. So today, I invite you to see that the great graces given in Fatima were diminished, because Satan incited hearts to caution and smothered belief. Continue to pray for My Son's Church." She leaves.

■ **June 25, 1995.** I saw Jesus with His Hand extended on one side of the altar. He said: "You have persevered in your coming to Me today. You set your goal and pursued it overcoming many obstacles." (There was a big storm and an accident in front of me on the way.) "This is how I desire souls pursue holiness. When I call a soul, I do so out of love. I desire the soul responds in love, for without love as the foundation, the soul loses heart at the site of the first obstacle."

■ **June 25, 1995.** I heard Our Lady say, "Look, My daughter." She was standing (floating) to the left of the altar. There was a beam of light coming from Her Heart area. "Do not be afraid or feel insecure. I am with you, God is about to multiply His favors in your midst. My Son, who is Wisdom and Uprightness, will come to you so that His plan for you can be fulfilled. I am always with you, have not left, and will not leave. But it is He who sends Me that will assist you in developing My Prayer site. The pattern is not important. It is the grace given there that will convert many. What have you to fear? My Son is the Master Carpenter." She smiles.

■ **June 26, 1995.** *(1:00 a.m.)* Our Lady is here as Our Lady of Fatima. She says: "Praise and glory to Jesus. My daughter, please understand, it is not for the sake of a few or many I come to you, but for all people. Everyone is called to holiness through Holy Love. The grace and love of My Heart is never depleted, only time is depleted for those who do not listen and will not love. To the family I continue My call to be united in Holy Love. Jesus desires family values be substantiated in hearts according to Holy Love. Families that fail to unite in My Heart disintegrate, for this is how Satan attacks sound reason. The evil one opposes family unity, but through My grace you will remain united. I am returning to you soon on this My chosen 'Feast of Queen of Peace'. Spread My peace amongst you by loving as I so very much love you." She leaves.

■ **June 29, 1995 / Thursday Night Rosary Service.** Our Lady is here as Our Lady of Guadalupe. She says: "Praise be to Jesus, My little children. Tonight, I ask your special prayers towards the acquisition of the new property." We prayed.

"Thank you dear children, it is not for Myself that I ask, but for the many who have been turned away that have wanted to pray. Dear children, tonight I invite you to realize that the floods that are occurring around the world are symbolic of the watered-down faith that is in hearts, and of the compromise and error that has flooded hearts. Once again, I remind you, pray for the lukewarm priests in the month of July - the month of the Precious Blood - and offer your communions for these priests. Dear children, keep your feet on the straight path of Holy Love, so that I can present you to the Heart of My Son. I love you, My dear children, and I am blessing you."

July 1995

■ **July 2, 1995 / Message To The World.** Our Lady came in gray. She gave the usual greeting, "Praise be to Jesus. This is My message to the world. Dear children, the Eternal Father has fixed His gaze upon this ministry. This is so, for within My call to Holy Love is your moment to moment conversion and your salvation. You do not understand how complete God's justice is to be. If you understood, you would perfect your response to My call. I am calling you, My dear, dear children, out of the darkness into the light of Holy Love." She leaves.

■ **July 3, 1995.** From Our Lady:

ROSARY MEDITATIONS –
MYSTERIES OF THE ROSARY

First Joyful Mystery - The Annunciation
Most Sorrowful, Ever Immaculate Heart of Mary, the Flame of Your Heart which is Holy Love would not permit You to say 'No' to the angel Gabriel. Immerse our hearts in this Flame, Most Blessed Virgin. Help us always to be willing instruments of God.

Second Joyful Mystery - The Visitation
Most Sorrowful, Ever Immaculate Heart of Mary, You journeyed to visit Your cousin Elizabeth because You believed in the message the angel Gabriel brought You from Heaven. Pray for us, that our lives be journeys of faith through the Message of Holy Love.

Third Joyful Mystery - The Nativity
Most Sorrowful, Ever Immaculate Heart of Mary, You were turned away at the inn when Your Son was about to be born. Help us never to turn away from You and Jesus. Pray with us for those who reject Him in the world and do not open their hearts to Him.

Fourth Joyful Mystery - The Presentation
Most Sorrowful, Ever Immaculate Heart of Mary, You presented Your Infant Son in the temple out of respect for tradition. Keep us faithful to Your Son's Church and the Tradition of Faith handed down to us through John Paul II.

Fifth Joyful Mystery - The Finding Of Jesus In The Temple
Most Sorrowful, Ever Immaculate Heart of Mary, You were separated from Your Son for three days and You searched for Him sorrowing. Pray with us, dear Mother, for those who have fallen away from the Church, that they too, will sorrow for their loss of faith.

First Sorrowful Mystery - The Agony In The Garden
Most Sorrowful, Ever Immaculate Heart of Mary, Your Son suffered agony at the thought of God's Will. He surrendered to the Will of the Father and an angel came to comfort Him. Pray for us to accept the crosses in our lives as God's Will, and to realize that we too will be given the comfort and grace to carry them.

Second Sorrowful Mystery - The Scourging At The Pillar
Most Sorrowful, Ever Immaculate Heart of Mary, though

innocent and undeserving, Your Son submitted to a scourging. He did not defend Himself. Help us to seek the greater good and not always our own comfort in the world.

Third Sorrowful Mystery - The Crowning With Thorns

Most Sorrowful, Ever Immaculate Heart of Mary, Your Son was mocked and crowned with thorns because people did not believe in Him. Pray for us, Mother of God, that we will courageously stand up for Church Tradition and holiness through Holy Love, even though, it is not popularly accepted.

Fourth Sorrowful Mystery - The Carrying Of The Cross

Most Sorrowful, Ever Immaculate Heart of Mary, Your Son carried His Cross out of love for us. Dear Blessed Mother, pray that we will accept our crosses for love of Jesus. His Cross was made heavy by the weight of our sins. Our crosses are made heavier when we do not surrender to them.

Fifth Sorrowful Mystery - The Crucifixion

Most Sorrowful, Ever Immaculate Heart of Mary, Your Son died on Calvary and made Himself an Eternal Victim on the altar of the world. We pray with You now, dear Mother, that belief in His Real Presence will increase in every heart throughout the world.

First Glorious Mystery - The Resurrection

Most Sorrowful, Ever Immaculate Heart of Mary, You suffered at the foot of the Cross only to rejoice when Your Son rose from the dead. Help us to suffer the present day tribulations in preparation for His second coming.

Second Glorious Mystery - The Ascension

Most Sorrowful, Ever Immaculate Heart of Mary, Your Beloved Son returned to Heaven victorious over sin, to take His place at the Right Hand of the Father. Help us as we pray with You, dear Mother, to see that our home is in Heaven. Heaven is the inheritance of the holy. Then assist us in our own personal holiness in the present moment.

Third Glorious Mystery - The Descent Of The Holy Spirit
Most Sorrowful, Ever Immaculate Heart of Mary, humbly we ask You to petition Your Heavenly Spouse that He will flood our hearts with every gift, every fruit. Then we ask Your prayers to be faithful apostles of Holy Love in an unbelieving world.

Fourth Glorious Mystery - The Assumption
Most Sorrowful, Ever Immaculate Heart of Mary, You were taken to Heaven body and soul because Your Beloved Son did not want Your most pure body to undergo the corruption of the grave. Now in Heaven, we ask You to look down on us, dearest Mother. Keep us pure under the mantle of Your protection. Do not allow our hearts to be corrupted by the world.

Fifth Glorious Mystery - Coronation Of The Blessed Virgin Mary
Most Sorrowful, Ever Immaculate Heart of Mary, You are Queen of Heaven and Earth. Solemnly, we petition You from this valley of tears. Let Holy Love reign in all hearts so that we can begin the victorious reign of Your Immaculate Heart here on earth.

(To be recited at the end of the Rosary)
(St. Joseph Prayer)
We offer this Rosary to the Sacred Heart of Jesus, through the Immaculate Heart of Mary, in union with St. Joseph, for the restoration of the priesthood to the Tradition of Faith and for all the unconverted. Make us Your humble instruments of Holy Love.

Mary, Protect our faith!

■ **July 4, 1995 – Independence Day.** Our Lady is here as Our Lady of Mt. Carmel. She says, "Praise be to Jesus, My dear little children. Pray with Me now for those who are coming in pilgrimage on the 12th." We prayed. Our Lady continues, "Dear children, tonight I come to invite you to understand that true freedom is embracing the Message of Holy Love. For only in this way will you step out of the slavery of sin. Dear children, all evil is slavery. And I ask you once again most humbly, to choose good. My dear children, I am blessing you tonight with my Blessing of Holy Love."

■ **July 5, 1995.** *(Locution from Our Lady)* "Dear children, your Rosaries form the link in the chain that will bind Satan in the abyss of fire forever. Your Rosaries are the golden thread that bind you to My Immaculate Heart. Your rosaries form the path of Holy Love that leads to salvation. In this give praise to Jesus."

■ **July 6, 1995.** Jesus says: "Behold, in My Heart every plan made secure. None are made who can transgress My provision which I Myself make ready for you. No darkness penetrates the light of My Heart. Angels defend the righteous. At My bidding, see how I will dispense them to your need. Prepare your heart for change and be My instrument as this plan unfolds in the face of the enemy."

■ **July 10, 1995.** Our Lady is here as Our Lady of Guadalupe. She says: "I come to give praise and honor to Jesus, My Son. My daughter, it is not My intention that one of My ministries or apparition sites oppose another. They, each one, complements and confirms the other. It is Satan who tries to undo My plan of unity through spiritual pride. I come to reconcile and unite all people and to show you the way to Heaven. When My Son returns all will live as one. If you presume to have all the answers, you are being deceived. It is in humility I lead you. It is the adversary who tries to set one against the other. Many of My apparitions and messages go unheeded and uninvestigated due to misunderstandings and confusion brought on by Satan who comes clothed in righteousness. Instead of believing until an authentic and accurate investigation uncovers error, My children have fallen into the mistake of not believing until all is proven to their satisfaction. I come to bring peace, unity, joy. Recognize Me when I come. I want to bless you." She leaves.

■ **July 12, 1995 / Monthly Message To All Nations.** *(Indian Hollow Park, Lorain County, Ohio)* Blessed Mother is standing in front of the Sun. She comes as Our Lady of Guadalupe. She says: "I come to give honor and praise to Jesus, My Son. My little daughter, trusted messenger, My little children, see that under this title I am Queen of the Cosmos, for even the stars of heaven come to rest upon My mantle. In such a way, I invite all humanity to see that the heavens obey He Who sends Me. I come only to lead souls into eternal happiness. Let Holy Love chart the course of all souls for it is in this way harmony is restored in the universe." Blessed Mother now asks that people hold up the articles to be blessed. "Once again, I invite you to see that what is present in hearts decides the future of the world. If hearts are not reconciled to God, the peace and harmony of the entire cosmos is destroyed. So it is, every purification proceeds from the error in hearts. Make this known."

"My Son's Church will undergo a purification before it is once again united in faith and tradition. Faction will oppose faction. The true faithful will be scattered and persecuted. Reverence for My Son in the Eucharist will diminish even more that it has, and become controversial. In all of this, understand I am your Protectress, Refuge and Hope. I come to lead you out of the darkness, into the light, and to the New Jerusalem. Through all of this, the Church will not succumb. When My Immaculate Heart claims triumph, so too, will the Eucharistic Heart of My Son be triumphant."

"My dear children, I desire to share eternity with you. I desire that you be reconciled with God. I come to show you the way through Holy Love. It is not for My welfare, dear children, that I call you to this path, but for your own."

"Your country mistakenly believes that because, it shares with impoverished nations much of its surplus, it is closing the abyss between God and man, at the same time, they are sacrificing lives on the altar of abortion. One does not offset the other."

"Dear children, It is by your efforts, your prayers, your sacrifices, and love that Hearts will change. Tonight I am blessing you with My Blessing of Holy Love."

■ **July 13, 1995 / Thursday Night Rosary Service.** Our Lady is here as Rosa Mystica (Feast Day of Rosa Mystica). She says: "Pray with Me now for those who are led astray through erroneous opinions." We prayed. "Dear children, tonight I invite you to pray all the more, for fervent faith. Uphold the Tradition of Faith in your hearts My dear children, for this is the way to strengthen My Son's Church on earth. Do not be led astray through wrongful reasoning, for these days Satan attacks reason. Dear children, when you have strong faith in your hearts you are strengthening My Son's Church on earth. I am blessing you."

■ **July 15, 1995.** *(Locution from Our Lady)* "Dear children, the joy of My Heart is your moment to moment conversion. Therefore, do not proceed on the path ahead for your purpose, but for My Own. It is important that you assume the role I call you to, Apostles of Holy Love. Trust all things to My care and My direction."

■ **July 19, 1995.** Our Lady comes as Our Lady of Grace. She has a sword tucked in Her sash which turns into a rosary. She says: "Thank you for answering My call to you today. Your sharing was double-edged. Know My children, I come to you in great need. These times are times of spiritual warfare - both in the ministry and in the church. Therefore, dear children, you must be spiritual warriors. I am praying for your strength amidst adversity." She blessed us and left.

■ **July 20, 1995 / Thursday Night Rosary Service.** Our Lady is here as Our Lady of Guadalupe. She says: "Pray with Me now for the unbelievers, the unconverted, and the lukewarm." We prayed. "Dear children, do not be discouraged or feel abandoned, for when you are praying I am always with you. Always seek the refuge of My Immaculate Heart - the Flame of Holy Love - wherein the enemy has no access. Dear children, My coming to you is a great grace and a miracle, but the greatest grace and miracle is your moment to moment conversion. I am always with you, supporting you. Dear children, do not lose heart in these times. I am blessing you."

■ **July 27, 1995 / Thursday Night Rosary Service.** Our Lady is here as Our Lady of Guadalupe. She came out from a very large Heart, which is the Heart of Her Son. She says: "I come to you by way of Divine Love that is the Heart of My most beloved Son. I give praise and glory to Jesus the King. Pray with me now for those who will come on the 12th seeking only exterior grace and for lukewarm priests." We prayed. She continues, "Dear children, tonight I invite you even more, to become apostles of Holy Love. Do not judge which hearts are open and which are not, for I tell you, My dear children, many fertile fields lay uncultivated and are not sown. But today, I desire that you spread Holy Love to every heart. Let it be planted and watered through the Holy Spirit. I am praying for you, My dear children, that you do not lose faith in these difficult times, but become even more powerful in your apostleship. I am blessing you."

■ **July 28, 1995.** Our Lady comes as Our Lady of Grace. She is smiling, Her arms outstretched. She says: "My angel,

I desire My children realize the course of Satan's attack. He seeks to destroy belief in the means by which good will triumph. This is why, in the world today, you find diminished respect for My Son's Real Presence. He attacks the hearts of My Son's Priests, making it difficult for them to keep the Eucharist the center of their lives. The adversary deplores devotion to My Immaculate Heart and to the Rosary. He uses every means to discourage such prayer. He comes against ministries and apostolates that promote these truths. Evil knows in advance the war is lost, but he is trying to snatch as many souls from My Heart as he can before the appointed hour of his defeat. Therefore My little daughter, pray for strong faith and ask My children to seek My protection in every attack. Where Satan is revealed, he is weakened. Then I ask you to make this known. Give praise to Jesus."

■ **July 28, 1995.** Jesus says: "Reveal to My people My Call. For I am coming on a cloud of fire. When My Fire rains down on the Earth, it will not separate or choose good from bad. Prepare! Prepare!"

■ **July 28, 1995.** Jesus says: "You have no idea how much I love you. You have not experienced such a love on Earth. I love each one unconditionally and with untold measure. It is not possible that your sins take away My Love. I am Mercy. My Love and Mercy are inseparable both in My Heart and in the world. All I need is that souls open and I will come into their hearts and their lives. Through My Mother and Holy Love, I invite hearts to open. All of this you will make known."

■ **July 29, 1995.** From Our Lady: "My children, I come to you tonight to request that you make of your hearts spiritual refuge centers. Draw every provision from My Heart and live interiorly, giving every act to My Son, in reparation for the grave sins committed against His most Sacred Heart. My children, time is short and you do not realize how important

My desires are. Make all of this known."

"I desire that you be sanctified My dear children, always in the present moment, for here is your salvation. Let your hearts be purified in this Holy Flame of Love that leads you to sanctity."

August 1995

■ **August 1, 1995 / Weekly Rosary Service.** Our Lady is here as Our Lady of Guadalupe. She says: "I come to offer praise to Jesus, My Son. I desire, dear children, that you pray with Me now, for those who will travel in pilgrimage on the Twelfth." We prayed. "I come, dear children, to continue your conversion, for so many in the world worship false gods full of compromise and error, gods of status and importance in the eyes of men - money and intellect. But I tell you, these will be stripped away and all that will be left is faith, true faith. You must pray, for many will die suddenly and with unprovided deaths falling upon them. So many who were converted in the beginning have now slipped off the path that I called them upon. You, My dear children, must be the spark that ignites the Flame of Love in hearts around you. Tonight I am blessing you with My Motherly Blessing."

■ **August 3, 1995.** *(Burbank, California)* Our Lady is here as Our Lady of Guadalupe. She says: "Praise be to Jesus, My little children. Pray with Me now for the unconverted and the lukewarm." We prayed. Our Lady continues, "Dear little children, I desire tonight that you give your hearts completely to Me and surrender to Holy Love. In this way you will be only My instruments in the world and make My Message to you (HOLY LOVE) known throughout the world. Dear children, time is short and it is not long until My Son returns. You do not see the evil in hearts and how quickly the Third Secret of Fatima is unfolding in hearts, and soon into the world.

■ **August 4, 1995 - Feast of St. John Vianney.** *(Burbank, California)* From Our Lady: "Dear children, once again I continue to call you upon the path of holiness. I desire that your lives imitate the crumb of bread, which when prayed over by My priests, is transformed into the Body of My Son. I desire that your lives be transformed through prayer, and that you become one in the Body of Christ, united and uncompromised in the true faith. Dear children, I am blessing you tonight with My Motherly Blessing."

■ **August 5, 1995.** *(Burbank, California)* Our Lady is here as Our Lady of Guadalupe. She says: "Pray with Me now, My dear little children, for all the lukewarm, the unconverted, and all My priests. We prayed. "Dear children, I want you to be at peace. I want you to have love in your hearts. Please understand, My little ones, that Holy Love is the harvestmaster, and God's Judgment, the winnowing fan that separates the wheat from the chaff. I do not want you to fear, but to love. I am calling you deep into the refuge of My Immaculate Heart, which is Holy Love, where you will be at peace. My Heart, dear children, is the Gateway to the New Jerusalem. I desire that you make this known and that you become apostles of My Heart."

■ **August 9, 1995.** "I am the Lady of Guadalupe. I come so that man will be reconciled with God and to mend the way between Heaven and earth. My reign will not begin in the world until the Kingdom of God reigns in every heart. This kingdom I call you to is Holy Love. Today, once again, you must realize that sin opposes My victorious reign. So, it is man who defies God and is choosing for himself God's Justice. When you try to change and compromise God's Laws and Church laws you are choosing evil and prolonging the reign of evil. Dear children, each time you pray; each time you meditate on the passion; each moment you spend adoring My Son in His Real Presence, you change the world and bring God closer to mankind. Do not procrastinate then, in all that can transform evil to good. My children, continue to pray, pray, pray." She leaves.

■ **August 10, 1995.** Our Lady comes as Our Lady of Guadalupe. She says: "I am the Woman Clothed with the Sun - the Woman of the Apocalypse. I come to seek your efforts in My Victory over evil. Every holy hour of reparation lessens God's Justice and serves to strengthen the remnant Church. It is during the great hour of God's Justice that My Son will secure the remnant in the wound of His Heart. Thus, covered with His Most Precious Blood, the tide of evil will not encroach upon it. His Justice and Mercy will comprise the fiber of this holy remnant. Now you are in the time of trial and many tribulations, but My grace is your strength and your ultimate victory. Do not fail in praying for your enemies. God will hear your prayer. The enemy moves amongst you trying to make all seem hopeless. He is easily defeated through faith and trust."

■ **August 10, 1995 / Thursday Night Rosary Service.** Our Lady is here as Our Lady of Guadalupe, Her Immaculate Heart is exposed and there is a light coming from It. She says: "Pray with Me now for those coming on the Twelfth, that they pray from the heart." We prayed. "Dear children, hold your feet firmly upon the path of holiness that I call you to follow. Do not look in the natural world for the fruits of My mission, but in your own heart. For it is in your heart I seek to plant the Kingdom of God through Holy Love. Dear children, on the Twelfth I am coming to be in your midst clothed with the Sun. I will give you many graces. Most of all, I desire that you have deep faith in My mission in you. I am blessing you."

■ **August 12, 1995.** Our Lady is here as Our Lady of Guadalupe. She says: "Please copy this so to give honor and praise to Jesus. Today, I tell you, thus far, many prayers have steered the course of hurricanes from your country's coast lines, for My Son is attentive to hearts full of Holy Love. I want you to understand and know in your hearts, My dear children, that prayer can change much of what is to come but, you must love. These days, your country, and all nations, have succumbed to a malignancy more virulent than any plague. This disease is complacency in hearts. You must understand, My coming to you is real. You are not safe outside the confines of My Heart. My Heart is Holy Love. The groundwork is already being laid, through Satan's deception, that will discredit your government. This is concealed in proud hearts. It is with sorrow I tell you, My Son's Church is not exempt from such error. Therefore, you must continue to pray with strong faith. See that God alone directs the course of the heavens and the earth. You are dependent upon the Eternal Father for every provision. Alone you are nothing and can claim no accomplishment. But, through God's grace all things are possible. My triumph is in your response to My call."

■ **August 12, 1995 / Monthly Message To All Nations.** *(Indian Hollow Park, Lorain County, Ohio)* Our Lady is here with many angels. She is here as Our Lady of Guadalupe. She says: "I come in praise and honor of Jesus the King. Do Me the favor now of praying with Me for the unconverted." We prayed. Our Lady is asking the people to hold up their objects to be blessed. She is sending out angels now. I asked Her what She wants from all the people here. Our Lady responded: "I desire that all lead consecrated lives; to consecrate themselves to the Flame of Holy Love that is My Immaculate Heart. Further, I desire that My children come to Me under this title of Guadalupe, for in this way I will protect their faith. It is the season of the great apostasy and the unfolding and fulfillment of the Third Secret of Fatima (Portugal 1917). Therefore, My children, I call you more than ever to come into the Refuge of My Heart, where I will protect your faith and lead you to sanctity. I am blessing you."

■ **August 17, 1995 / Thursday Night Rosary Service.**
Our Lady is here as Our Lady of Guadalupe. She says: "All praise, honor, and glory be to Jesus. Pray with Me now for the lukewarm." We prayed. "Dear children, tonight I thank you for your many prayers concerning the most recent threat, in the form of a hurricane to your country's coast line. As you see, your prayers have helped thus far, but the greatest threat to your country is in hearts that do not love with Holy Love. This is a real danger, an insidious evil threat that is not recognized, and is hidden away out of sight. Dear children, your prayers can change hearts, just as they can change the course of weather patterns. Continue to pray, pray, pray." Our Lady blessed us and left.

■ **August 19, 1995.** *(Locution from Jesus)* "I am calling you to complete trust in - My plan for you - for I am the Way, the Truth, and the Light. My provision in you is perfect and never lacking. I am in your midst and surrounding you. I desire very much to be in the center of all hearts and so in the center of Churches. Do you need to look for, and search for, what is in the center of your heart? You should not need to search for Me when you enter My Church. I am the Cornerstone. What is sown in hearts is harvested in the world."

■ **August 24, 1995 / Thursday Night Rosary Service.** Our Lady is here as Our Lady of Guadalupe. She has a rosary of lights in Her right hand. She says: "Praise be to Jesus, My little children. Pray with Me now for My ministry and for the unconverted." We prayed. "Dear children, tonight, I invite you to understand deep in your hearts, that the Rosary is the weapon that will lead you out and away from every tribulation. Tonight, I am inviting you especially, to organize on the Feast of the Triumph of the Cross, a twenty-four hour Rosary-perpetual, from midnight on September Thirteenth, to midnight on September Fourteenth. Offer these rosaries for My ministry. These days, Satan is attacking each apostolate, each prayer group, each consecrated heart, in an insidious way, and he has taken just reason from the world replacing it with his own evil. Therefore, My little children, you must be strong and realize that the weapon I extend to you (Our Lady is now holding out Her Rosary) can overcome any evil. I am blessing you now."

■ **August 27, 1995.** Our Lady is here in a dark mantle and white gown. There are many crosses behind Her in the background. "I come to you as Queen and Mother of Jesus Incarnate. This day, I desire that you see with the eyes of your heart that your cross is ever changing and transitional. When you ponder recent events see them as crosses which can transform souls. I am a part of every trial, for it is impossible to immerse yourself in the Flame of My Heart without consecrating yourself to the Cross. Each cross is given, and permitted, as ransom for a soul. The greater the trial, the greater the need of each soul to exact a conversion. Though My victory is at hand, you will find perseverance sweet in this trial. I am blessing you."

■ **August 27, 1995.** From God, the Father: "The manna I send you, is faith. The path I lead you over, trust. Find My Will in the present."

■ **August 29, 1995.** From Our Lady: "Dear children, today I join you at the foot of the Cross with all the consecrated souls who are consumed by the Flame of Holy Love that is My Heart. I invite you to be warriors of Holy Love. In this way, spreading this Flame from soul to soul, and bringing about My victory. Dear children, My victory does not come from Heaven, but from you, and from your heart of Holy Love. I am blessing you."

■ **August 31, 1995.** Our Lady is here in gray and white. She is floating on a pink cloud. She says: "My daughter, I have a message for the good people who will come tonight. Dear children, last week I requested a united prayer effort in September for My ministry. Be generous in your response as Heaven is ready to act. Jesus desires that you pray against the evil about to unfold in Beijing [Fourth World Conference on Women]. This is the serpent striking against the heel of The Woman Clothed with the Sun. Only evil hearts could contrive such atrocities against love. Once again I emphasize; Satan has removed just reason from hearts and from the world, and replaced it with his evil. You, My dear, dear children, are My warriors of Holy Love. Your weapons are the Eucharist and My Rosary. The third weapon I give to you is the Truth. You must use it to reveal evil where it lies hidden. Satan's greatest weapon is his deception of non-existence. Truth discloses evil. Where deception is revealed, it lies weakened and open to defeat. My words to you on Holy Love are truth and scripturally based. There is no intellect who can truthfully dispute this. Use My messages to unclothe evil in the world around you. My dear love warriors, I am with you tonight and always. I am holding you in My Heart." She leaves.

September 1995

■ **September 5, 1995.** Our Lady came in gray and white by My bed as I was praying. She let the rosary beads float through Her fingers. They were a dark color until She held them, then between Her fingers they lit up like lights. After She held them they were brilliant pink pearls but not as bright as when they were between Her Fingers. She said: "Pick up your pen. I must speak to you. I want to speak to you about the gift of giving love. My daughter, the world today is so full of hate. It is full of hate because My children do not recognize what a wonderful grace it is to give love to another. Love is being Christ-like to those around you. It is never out of place or wrong. It needs to be at the center of every relationship;

parent-child; husband-wife; brother-sister. Every human relationship should be an exchange or giving of love."

"Each opportunity to love is a grace. It is a chance to draw close to God. God is part of every act of Holy Love. When you perfect yourselves in Holy Love, you become more loving and Christ-like to those around you. Your love for one another becomes more steadfast and unchanging as God's love is unchanging and unconditional."

"Satan tries to destroy love in hearts because he is disunity. He does not want you to be happy. He wants you to oppose one another. I come to tell you that hidden in the gift of giving love away, are a myriad of graces. You will never find the grace as long as you refuse to unwrap the package it is in, that is the love God gives you to give to another."

"My daughter, love is not like a fish in a net which is taken off and consumed by the fisherman. No, rather it is like a ray of God's sun which transforms and brightens everything it touches. Instead of being consumed, it is like the harvest master who consumes the harvest. This holy crop of love, however, multiplies wherever it is distributed."

"Little daughter, loving hearts truly are a miracle from God and a cooperation between God's Will and free will. Just as My Beloved Son multiplied the loaves and fishes when He walked the earth, He desires that you allow the love in your heart grow by virtue of it pouring out."

■ **September 5, 1995.** Our Lady comes with a blue mantle and white gown. She has Her head bowed. She says: "Praise be to Jesus, My humble messenger. I come to mend the way between Heaven and earth. It is so that mankind will follow the path to My Heart - the path of salvation. Let us begin with an *'Our Father'* and a *'Glory Be'* for all who do not relinquish their will to God. Treasure always the present moment, My angel. Surrender it to Holy Love. I desire My children understand, now, and always, the certain treasure of the present moment. It is here within the present moment all will choose for, or against good. Salvation is in the present moment, so too, your sanctification. So that My people cease to waste the present, but surrender in it to Holy Love, I am here to give you a special prayer - *CONSECRATION TO THE PRESENT MOMENT.*"

She raises Her eyes to Heaven and prays:

Consecration To The Present Moment

"Dear Heavenly Father, I surrender this present moment to Your Holy Will. I choose through the Hearts of Jesus and Mary to be purified. I surrender to every cross and grace You choose for me. I trust in Your Divine Providence. I am, in this present moment, Your servant of Holy Love. Amen."

Our Lady then said: "Make it known."

■ **September 12, 1995 - Feast of the Holy Name of MARY/ Monthly Message to All Nations.** *(Indian Hollow Park, Lorain County, Ohio)* Our Lady is here. First She was Our Lady of Fatima, Her clothes are changing to Our Lady of Mt. Carmel; now to Our Lady of Sorrows. Now She is Our Lady of Guadalupe. There are many angels with Her and they say: "Blessed be the Holy Name of Mary." Our Lady is asking the people here to hold up their objects to be kissed. Jesus is now here blessing the crowd. He extends His Hands out over the people like He is praying over them. Our Lady continues: "Dear children, most especially, I bless your hearts so that you will be Missionaries of Holy Love. Pray with Me now." We prayed. "Dear children, tonight I ask you to understand that My message to you on Holy Love is the fulfillment of the Gospel message - most especially, in the present moment. I invite you to form a **Lay Apostolate - 'THE MISSIONARY SERVANTS OF HOLY LOVE'**, and enable Me to propagate My Words to you, around the world. I need your prayers and your sacrifices, through which My Victory will come."

"Sadly, I tell you My Son's Church on earth is like a ship tossed about in a stormy sea. The ship's captain, My Holy Pope, is doing his best to guide it into the safe harbor of Tradition, but all around him is a tidal wave of compromise. He is greatly in need of your prayers. While there are many good and holy priests in the world today, there are far more lukewarm priests who are leading many astray by virtue of their position in the Church. Still more threatening are those in the hierarchy who plot against My Pope. It is necessary that I come to you once again to ask you to unite in prayer, so that good can overcome evil. Let My Rosary be the golden chain that binds Satan in Hell forever."

"I have asked for the formation of Prayer Cells. Unite in response to My call. Then you will truly be Servants of Holy Love."

"I come to help you understand, that God's Hand of Justice shall not be removed from the world until hearts understand their place and dependence upon The Almighty for all things. It is the unbelievers who cause division in families and in governments. They depart from God's Law and employ their own evil rules. I do not come to judge, but to warn. It is My Son Who shall judge all peoples. I come to call My children back to God through Holy Love. The deeper you immerse your heart in the Flame of Holy Love, the closer I will take you to Divine Love, which is The Heart of My Son. It is here All Goodness and Mercy abound. Graciously, I tell you, it is not My coming to you that means your salvation, but your response to My call."

"These days, many in this nation, and in the world, concern themselves for the integrity of financial systems. But I tell you, it is the spiritual bankruptcy of the world that must be a priority. Souls are the only commodity of eternal value. Holy Love is the deposit of faith I seek to protect in My Maternal Heart. Make it known."

■ **September 14, 1995 / Thursday Night Rosary Service.**
Our Lady is here as Our Lady of Grace. She says: "I come in praise of the Living God, the Lord Jesus Christ. My daughter, once again, I invite you to make known My desire that a lay apostolate begin to form under the umbrella of Holy Love Ministries. This apostolate will be known as the 'Missionary Servants of Holy Love'. Jesus is asking for this apostolate in these end times to renew and restore souls to love. Your mission field is: the lukewarm, the unbelievers, and spiritually impoverished. It will be an apostolate given over to prayer, sacrifice, and Evangelization of My Holy Love message. Through these means, and by your lives, you will make known the Refuge of My Immaculate Heart (which is Holy Love) as the ark and spiritual Refuge of these times. It is the same call I gave to the seers at Fatima (Portugal 1917). Do not suppose My Grace is not with you, for it is only through this graciousness of My Heart you shall succeed. Make it known."

■ **September 20, 1995.** Our Lady comes in light blue and white with a crown on Her head. She is holding a rosary. She says: "Dear children, God's Holy Will for you is the sweet measure of Divine Love in the present moment. Your prayers and sacrifices, your 'yes' to Holy Love, determine the depth of your spiritual journey into the Flame of My Heart. The Flame of My Heart is but a humble spark of the Flame of Divine Love that is the Heart of My Son. His Heart is the Holy Will of God. My Heart is one with His. When you pray the Rosary you are united to Our Hearts."

■ **September 21, 1995 / Thursday Night Rosary Service.**
Pray "All Glory Be..."
Our Lady is here as Our Lady of Guadalupe. She says: "Praise be to Jesus, My little children. Each time I come to you, it is because I love; and to bring you love; and to call you to love. Dear children, pray with Me now for all hearts who live outside of Holy Love." We prayed. "When you pray the

'*Gloria*', always begin: *ALL GLORY BE to the Father, to the Son and to the Holy Spirit ....*"

"The apostasy is opening in the world, because it is in hearts that do not love and do not respect the Pope's authority. I am coming to you tonight, asking you to prostrate yourselves before the altar of Faith. Seek My protection and I will plunge you into the Flame of Holy Love that is My Heart. Dear children, you cannot own anything on earth that is equal to your faith. I am blessing you."

■ **September 24, 1995.** From Our Lady: "I have chosen this title - 'MISSIONARY SERVANTS OF HOLY LOVE' - as a description of your mission in the world. For to those who hear and answer My call, will come the task of promulgating My Holy Love message to the world. A good servant is dedicated to his master. In this mission there is one Master, Jesus, My Son, who calls you to serve Him through Holy Love, for it is Him who sends Me to you with this message. I do not ask of you special attire to identify you as My missionary servants. Rather, put on Holy Love as your vestment so that all will recognize your call. My daughter, long has My Heart withheld the news of this lay apostolate; an army of strength in Church Tradition, and a sign to Satan of My imminent victory. Take hold of My mantle and cling fast. There are those dressed as good who will come against us, while their hearts weigh heavy with evil. They think they hold all the answers, but they deal in compromise and ambiguity. Do not be dumbfounded when My words to you are fulfilled. Hold fast to the Tradition of Faith. I am blessing you."

■ **September 25, 1995.** Our Lady comes in white with sparkling lights around her. She is holding a White Scapular over Her Arms. She says: "Child, I come in praise of Jesus. My daughter, those who accept and wear this sign of My Confraternity will give witness to the world of their special vocation of love. I will place them in My Heart - gateway to the New Jerusalem. This Scapular is a sign of predestination of those who choose it. It will be a special armor against evil and recourse to My Grace." She comes closer and holds it out to me so that I am able to see what's on it.

She says: "Let it be inscribed thus." There is one face of it that has on it the Immaculate Heart of Mary. The words written around it are: "Make known My Heart as the Gateway to the New Jerusalem." The other piece, or face, is the Sacred Heart of Jesus. Written around it are the words: "Sacred Heart of Jesus, Thy Kingdom come." The one with Our Lady's Heart is blue on a white background. The one of Our Lord's is red with a white background. They are on a white cord. Our Lady continues: "It is to be worn this way." She puts it over Her head and has the side with the Immaculate Heart in the front. "It is a special sign in these the last days of My final call to humanity. Make it known."

■ **September 26, 1995.** Jesus says:
  "My Mother's Heart is Holy Love.
  My Heart is Divine Love.
  If Her Heart is the Gateway to the New Jerusalem,
  My Heart is the New Jerusalem."

■ **September 28, 1995 / Thursday Night Rosary Service.** Blessed Mother is here as Our Lady of Grace. She says: "I come once again in praise of Jesus. Pray with Me now, that all hearts be converted in the present moment." We prayed. "Dear children, I continue to come to you in order that souls may be reconciled with God. For until all hearts are reconciled with God, there will not be peace between nations and peoples. Dear children, I reveal to you tonight, most graciously, that the scapular Jesus has given generously to this prayer group is a particular means of conversion and conviction of heart, and it carries with it My Motherly Blessing. Dear children, make it known." She blessed us and left.

■ **September 29, 1995.** Our Lady comes as Our Lady of Guadalupe. St. Michael comes before Her in a fiery light. Then he disappears. Our Lady is holding the Infant Jesus today. She says: "Praise be to Jesus, My little angel. I come to invite My children to understand that every affliction in the world, whether it is illness, natural calamity, War or any other, is the direct result of man's infidelity to God. When the innocent suffer, it is to bring the wicked to cast themselves upon the Mercy of God. Your prayer that souls recognize God's place in their lives is a good prayer and one My Son will shed mercy upon. Those that wait for signs and certain phenomena to take place before they believe and convert, may wait too long. Each one needs to find his conversion in the grace of the present moment with a full compliment of oil in his lamps. Pray that people realize the value of a soul and the length and breadth of eternity." [I see a roaring fire in front of Our Lady. It moves towards me. The light surrounding Blessed Mother seems to extinguish it. Then I see a rolling meadow. I see myself as a little girl walking hand in hand with Jesus.] She continues: "Souls choose for themselves salvation or perdition, just as they choose the fate of the world. Continue to pray, pray, pray." She leaves.

October 1995

■ **October 2, 1995.**
The Two Hearts Scapular
Blessed Mother is here all in white. She has on the new scapular that She gave to the ministry last week. Now She is extending Her arms forward and out to Her sides (like Our Lady of Grace). In one hand, She has the Rosary hanging from Her fingers. In the other hand, the new scapular. She says: "Praise be to Jesus, My little children. Do Me the favor of praying with Me now, for all My apostolates." We prayed. "Dear children, if a small door is opened through grace, step

through it. The bigger doors will someday open, but you are not as yet ready. Remember, My mission is in your hearts and is not dependent on any recommendation of man, but upon the favor of grace of My Heart. Dear children, I am calling you to complete submission, so that I am always in the minds of your hearts. Make proper use of the time allotted you, and as yet before you. The tribulation will increase, and so too will My call to you. I am blessing you."

■ **October 2, 1995.** Jesus comes and stands before me. He says: "I place in your heart at this time My promises attendant to the TWO HEARTS SCAPULAR as it will come to be known:

The Two Hearts Scapular Promises

1. "It is a barrier against evil, dispelling conflict and confusion in the heart of the one who wears it."
2. "It will lead the soul into the embrace of Our Two Hearts."
3. "It will bear with it a conviction of heart, revealing to the wearer unproclaimed faults. Thus, the soul will be led deeper into holiness."
4. "It will deepen devotion to My Real Presence in the Eucharist." [He stops and just smiles for a minute.]
5. "Those who faithfully wear it shall be embraced in Holy and Divine Love, and shall not die an unprovided death."

■ **October 4, 1995.** Our Lady is here in white. She says: "Praise be to Jesus, My little children. Pray with Me now that many hearts will be touched by the Holy Father's visit to this country." We prayed. "Dear children, thank you for supporting each other in the work that I lead you to follow. Dear children, support each other in every aspect of life. Have faith and do not fear for what the future will hold, for My grace lightens every cross and brightens every path before you. Therefore, My little children, do not fear in the present moment for what the next moment may lead to or bring, for I am with you. This is Heaven's Ministry dear children, and you are only following

My lead. Therefore, how can you be mistaken, or fail. But through My grace you succeed. I am blessing you."

■ **October 7, 1995.** Our Lady comes as Our Lady of Fatima. "Child, I come to you today as the New Eve, and the one who holds reign over Heaven and earth. I AM FORMING THE MISSIONARY SERVANTS OF HOLY LOVE - FIRST IN MY HEART, THEN IN THE WORLD - AS A STRONGHOLD OF FAITH AGAINST HYPOCRISY THAT HOLDS SWAY OVER MANY HEARTS. There are those who bow low but in their hearts seek positions of importance. I come to you not so you will fear, but so that you will understand. The church will not succumb but is threatened on all sides. Confusion is sown by those who lack humility. Follow My Pope, John Paul II. In him there is no compromise. Unite under his banner. Your Rosaries will defeat Satan. Before My Son returns, you will see the unfolding of many events heretofore foretold. The weak, who are those who do not pray and do not love, will succumb to discouragement, doubts, and confusion. The strong, the ones who faithfully attempt to pray and who are in the Refuge of My Heart, will not be misled or fear. These are the ones many will turn to in the last days. Further, I warn you, do not allow the opinions of others to bear weight in your heart. I am your Protectress in all things. In all things God is your Provision. You must be strong so that those around you are strong. Continue to pray, pray, pray."

■ **October 10, 1995.** From Our Lady: "I am with you. I will not forsake you. I know your needs both in want and in plenty. I am holding you in the innermost recesses of My Heart, wherein, the enemy cannot enter. Beside you abide good angels. Ahead of you My own angel Gabriel. Transfix your gaze upon God's Holy Will, for His Will attains every grace." Now She appears as Our Lady of Grace. "I am the Mediatrix of all Grace; your intercessor before the throne of the Almighty. In His Will and His Grace is every provision, through which every plan of Heaven comes to perfection. When man's will impedes, grace circumvents. Remember, I do not come only for your pleasure, but your welfare. Therefore, be at peace. God's provision is all around you. The outpouring of My Heart is upon you. Let us give praise to Jesus. My daughter, it is by your intercession and My Own, we will succeed. Alone you are nothing and can attain no good. But with God all things are possible. He is all goodness, all grace, all mercy. See then, that united and one with Him is our victory. I desire this prayer center so that by your efforts My grace can come into the world." She leaves.

■ **October 11, 1995.** Our Lady comes in blue and white. She says: "My daughter, I am here. I am your Mother and your Protectress. I come to give greater honor and glory to Jesus, My Son. Tomorrow, I will come once again, so that man will choose to be reconciled with God."

■ **October 12, 1995 / Monthly Message To All Nations.** *(Indian Hollow Park, Lorain County, Ohio)* Blessed Mother is here with many angels. She is dressed as Our Lady of Guadalupe. She says: "Praise be to Jesus, My dear children. I come to you today as your Mother and Mother of all Nations. I am sending My angels into your midst with My kiss of Motherly love. Pray with Me now, for all those who are unconverted." We prayed. "Dear children I come to you today as a sign to you of God's mercy, and I ask that you recognize this present day age as the age of God's mercy upon all mankind."

"Dear children, through God's infinite love and mercy, He extends His grace of conversion at each of My shrines and at each of My apparition sites; and through His mercy, which continues to pour into every heart until My Son's coming, He will convert millions. He will give each soul a sign of their state before God."

"If man is not reconciled with God, a disaster worse than the flood will fall upon the world. It will be greater, for it will affect more people and a greater expanse of earth. Millions will die in their sins. (She is crying.) Only through our prayers and sacrifices can I withhold the arm of justice."

"Most do not see and refuse to recognize the evil in the world. This is because people make a god of their free will. In so doing they reject just reason and invite compromise into their hearts. Hearts will be judged according to the measure of Holy Love. It is a cubit unrelenting in righteousness."

"It is for this reason I am choosing to form the Missionary Servants of Holy Love, to propagate and live My message to you. Through My grace it will spread across the world as a purifying flame devouring evil. I invite you always to choose good over evil so that you will be ready when My Son returns. I love you."

"My dear children, this warning and My signs and miracles will come too late for some. I ask you to continue to pray for the unconverted. I am always with you when you are praying. I am blessing you."

■ **October 14, 1995.** Our Lady was already waiting for me in the chapel when I came in. She is all in white. She says: "Jesus sends Me today to tell you that His Kingdom is in hearts that love. Holy Love is the embrace of faith and the perseverance of hope. Do not trip over doubts or cast your lot upon unforgiveness. These are obstacles Satan casts upon your path. My Son's provision is perfect in its coming for every obstacle will be circumvented through grace. Praise be to Jesus."

■ **October 15, 1995.** Our Lady comes in blue with a crown on Her head. She has Her arms around the dresser I bought. She says: "I come in praise of Jesus to teach you that even in this, there is a lesson. This furniture you chose is not unlike My ministry. God created the wood just as He created each one in the ministry. He did not dictate to the wood: 'You must be furniture.' Just as He does not dictate to each of you: 'You must be in My ministry, or you must choose to be single or married, etc...', that is always according to free will. To create the furniture from the wood, He gave certain gifts to certain ones, who used these gifts to make the furniture. So, too, God gives each one in the ministry certain gifts, which united comprise the ministry. The furniture is given a lacquer and a certain design to enhance its appearance. I give to the ministry My Grace to enhance its work among men. When the furniture is completed, it has a certain function in the world. My mission in you is the function of My ministry in the world. I make this simplistic analogy so that all will hear and understand. You will make it known."

■ **October 18, 1995.** Our Lady comes all in white with Her Heart exposed. Her Heart is all gold. She says: "My daughter, it is fitting that you approach Us through Our United Hearts. It is through Our Hearts that Victory will come and evil will be defeated. You must deal with the world a bit longer, for Our Prayer Center will be in the world. But offer each conflict in atonement to Our Hearts. I am calling you to be WARRIORS FOR PEACE which is more valiant than any battle won through conflict. You will be able to spread peace through Holy Love wherever My mission takes you, if you remain united to Our Hearts. I am blessing you."

■ **October 19, 1995 / Thursday Night Rosary Service.** Blessed Mother is here as Our Lady of Guadalupe. She says: "I come to you, as always, to bring souls to My Son. Pray with Me now for the unbelievers." We prayed. "Dear children, I have stood with you, and went with you to the foot of The Cross and soon I will rejoice with you. Satan, the adversary of Faith, Hope, and Love, has opposed My Every plan. But he will not be victorious. My Grace will endure and be Victorious. Dear children, I am calling you once again to be Apostles of Holy Love, through the Missionary Servants of Holy Love. I am giving to you tonight My Motherly Blessing."

■ **October 21, 1995.** From St. Ursula: "Be at peace. God, who sends me, has heard your prayer and is attentive to your needs."

■ **October 21, 1995.** "For those who will devote themselves to My service, as Missionary Servants of Holy Love, I ask their continued and ongoing prayers for the spiritually impoverished. The Rosary is the key which unlocks the door to the grace of My Heart. My missionaries should take on themselves the service of others - most especially through evangelization. Do not neglect My clergy, who often are in need of such evangelization. Put yourselves last, all others first - in your prayers and your lives - then you will be living examples of Holy Love. Sometimes it is necessary to receive from others as well as give. Then you must receive with love as well. Always remember that when you pray and when you love, I am in your midst."

■ **October 26, 1995 / Thursday Night Rosary Service.** Our Lady is here as Our Lady of Guadalupe. She has many sparkling lights all around Her. She says: "All praise be to Jesus, My dear little children, My prayer warriors. At this time, I ask that you place all your petitions and needs upon the altar of My Heart." We prayed. "Dear children, some of your petitions will be answered as a matter of course, through the grace of My Heart. Others, I will continue to pray for as your intercessor before the throne of God. Dear children, your prayers are the key that open the door to the grace of My Heart. The more you pray and the greater your effort, the wider the door swings open. Dear children, I continually call you to prayer, because it is the way out of every situation and the solution which you seek. Tonight, I impart to you My Motherly Blessing."

■ **October 31, 1995 / Thursday Night Rosary Service.** Our Lady is here in a dark blue mantle and a white gown. She has many angels with Her. She says: "Praise be to Jesus, My dear little children. Pray with Me now for all those who oppose justice." We prayed. "Dear children, I continually thank My Son, before His throne in Heaven, for His allowing Me to come to you, in this way, and so often. I cannot admit you into the Refuge of My Heart unless you choose it. I desire that you seek this Refuge, that I may purify you and cleanse you in My Flame of Holy Love, and thus present you to My Son, complete and whole. Dear children, always seek sanctity in the present moment. I am with you and I am blessing you."

November 1995

■ **November 3, 1995.** Our Lady says: "Dear children. I come to invite you once again to live My Message of Holy Love. Do not listen with your ears, but hear what I am telling you in your hearts. You are chosen as a remnant and an advent people – awaiting with excited expectation My Son's second coming on earth. The time is close at hand, when the Refuge of My Heart will be your only stronghold against the pillages of the deposit of faith. Therefore, be wise and prudent in coming to Me so that I can lead you to My Son."

■ **November 9, 1995 / Thursday Night Rosary Service.** Our Lady is here as Our Lady of Guadalupe. She says: "All praise be to Jesus, My children. Let the coldness of this place reflect the coldness of hearts in the world today." (The furnace in the little school house was broken and the temperature inside was 38 degrees.) "Pray with Me now for those who pursue the path of evil." We prayed. "Dear children, let My coming to you in this way serve as a reminder to the world, that they must choose for salvation. So many wait and do not see what awaits them. For not to choose, is to choose the path of perdition. My dear children, pray for those whom I hold in My Heart today, who are forming strong allegiances against

Holy Love. Each time you pray or make a small sacrifice, you make reparation for those who oppose My plans. Dear children, I am blessing you"

■ **November 12, 1995 / Monthly Message To All Nations.** *(Indian Hollow Park, Lorain County, Ohio)* Our Lady is here as Our Lady of Guadalupe. She says: "Praise be to Jesus, My little children. I am here. I am loving you. I greet you with a heart that beats with great hope because of your faithfulness. Dear children, pray with Me now for those who are led astray from the true faith, through compromise and doubt." We prayed. "Today I call to you to surrender to Me your faith so that I may protect it from compromise and hypocrisy. You cannot persevere in your faith without My grace. Alone you are easy prey to the malefactor. But all things you surrender to the grace of My Heart, I will protect, proliferate, and make whole. I come to you for your salvation. Do not concern yourself with the temporal. These things pass by as quickly as a leaf in the wind. Pray, so that you will guard against spiritual bankruptcy. It is by your efforts and My grace you are saved."

"I desire that these things come to light so that souls understand more deeply the profound nature of My call. These days My Son's Church lies divided and faces the challenge of compromise and rebellion against the true dogma of faith. Just as there were the devout, the doubters, and even a traitor amongst the first apostles, so it is in the Church hierarchy today. But the Church will not succumb and will prevail. It is necessary that She pass through a period of purification to bring about wholeness. This trial is upon you. Satan who was unable to defile Jesus in My Womb - the first tabernacle - now seeks to compromise My Son's Real Presence in the tabernacles of the world through doubt and error. In a similar way the adversary challenges all life in the womb. In order to accomplish these atrocities, he takes hearts away from sound spirituality and pulls them into the false reasoning of the world. Often this is accomplished through the door of the pride of intelligencia. Real wisdom comes from God and does not challenge the sound doctrine of Church Tradition. Real wisdom leads to Holy Love."

"Dear children, these days you must realize that wars are not waged between nations, but in hearts. Satan's weapons are compromise, doubt, and confusion. But your weapon, dear children, is your strong faith, with which you give Me your Rosaries. This weapon is stronger than anything that Satan can conjure up."

"Dear children, I want you to let Me protect your faith. I come to you today as your Mother and your Protectress. Do not hesitate to call upon Me. It is through your prayers, I am converting millions."

Now there are many angels here; and, as Our Lady blesses us, they move about the people here. She leaves.

■ **November 15, 1995.** Our Lady is here in white with many angels. She says: "My daughter, today, as always, I come in praise of Jesus. This December Twelfth, you will be like the wise men and shepherds who found Jesus in the stables, for you will assemble to pray in the barn. Do not allow yourselves to be discouraged by cold, distance, or any other distraction. But give Me your hearts and I will give you My grace."

■ **November 16, 1995 / Thursday Night Rosary Service.** Our Lady is here as Our Lady of Guadalupe. She says: "I come in praise of Jesus, King of All Nations. I ask tonight, that you pray with Me for the conversion of all priests." We prayed. "Dear children, tonight as always, I call you to perfect yourselves in Holy Love, so that by your lives others will be drawn to My Message. Dear children, when you are loving, you are bringing souls into the Ark of My Heart. Not two by two, but as many as I call through you. I am blessing you."

■ **November 18, 1995.** Our Lady is here as Our Lady of Guadalupe. She says: "I come in praise of Jesus, My Son. I wish for you to make known these words to the people tonight. Dear children, I come as your Mother to invite you into the Refuge of My Immaculate Heart. It is through you, and by your efforts, My Heart will come to be venerated by unbelievers. I want to reconcile mankind to God through Jesus, and by way of My grace. I desire, My dear, dear children, you make known the Refuge of My Immaculate Heart as the Gateway to the New Jerusalem. I love you, and I am extending to you My Motherly Blessing."

■ **November 20, 1995.** *(Locution from Jesus)* "As far as the earth is from the sun, this is how far I cast any memory of your wrongdoing from My Heart. Transcribed in My Heart forever is your righteousness and every good deed that comes from love. Consider not the road traveled, nor the path you have yet to traverse. But know I am casting My Shadow upon you and holding you always in the Wound of My Heart. Together, we will foil the enemy and bring to the world a sweet and just victory. Reflect upon My Mercy and My Provision which complete the embrace of My Divine Love."

■ **November 22, 1995.** Before Mass I went to light a candle. The tin can of sand used to extinguish the sticks they use to light candles was on fire, (all the sticks had caught fire). Now Our Lady is standing in front of me with the can of burning sticks in front of Her. She says: "This is how self-love consumes the soul and in the end amounts to nothing more than smoke that evaporates in the air. But I am inviting souls to be consumed with the Flame of Holy Love which has eternal value and brings everlasting life. I desire My Missionary Servants of Holy Love be assimilated and transformed by this eternal Flame. By becoming an army of victim souls and offering yourselves for the good of others, this Flame will spread and grow. Make simple acts of love so that through My grace, hearts will open to My call. Repeatedly, and continually, I pray for you, and I give praise and thanks to Jesus for you. Persevere in Holy Love."

■ **November 23, 1995.** Our Lady comes in a flowing white gown. She says: "Today, just as always, I come for the greater honor, glory, and praise of Jesus, the King. His Kingship is for all times and eternity, and He takes up His reign in all hearts that love."

"Today, I desire you understand, that My missionaries are called to clothe themselves always in the vesture of Holy Love. For this love is their bastion against evil and sin. No one attains salvation without loving God. My Son dispenses Love and Mercy simultaneously to the contrite heart. These two are inseparable. In a similar way, it is impossible for a sinner to be contrite outside of Holy Love. And so, to receive God's Mercy, please understand, first you must love. The mystery of Divine Mercy and Divine Love are one. Jesus' Passion and Death are Divine Mercy and Divine Love together. One does not exist without the other. In the human heart, contrition and Holy Love are one. This is why I come to say to you, no one attains salvation outside of Holy Love. You will make it known."

■ **November 25, 1995.** Our Lady comes in white. She says: "Today, I come as always, for the greater glory of Jesus and to reconcile man to God. I reveal to you that the strength of the remnant church will be Holy Love. It is the lack of love in hearts that has brought confusion and compromise into hearts and the church. Please understand, I do not come to threaten you, but to warn. A famine and a plague worse than any that has come in the past is visiting earth. It is a famine of faith and a plague of lack of love in hearts. My Son is sending Me all over the world with this same message of Holy Love, which is the remedy and the solution of earth's woes. Do not suppose that because I come the problem is solved. Hearts need to change so that lives change, and then the problem will disappear. I hold the Church in My Heart. Evil shall not prevail. But the faith of many is compromised by Satan's confusion and conflict. Through Holy Love, I am gathering the remnant into My Heart. This remnant of Holy Love is the legacy I will bequeath to generations to come. It is the true and everlasting path of perfection. Holy Love is My legacy of victory and triumph over evil. Please make it known."

■ **November 25, 1995.** *(Locution)* "If you are really humble, you will forget about yourself. The less you think of your own needs, the more humble you are. Concentrate on others. I desire you make known My message to you around the world. I will bring those to you who will expedite this. Events will unfold accordingly, as quickly as pages turn in a book. For God's patience runs out. His endurance is exhausted."

■ **November 29, 1995.** Our Lady appears as Our Lady of Guadalupe. A small angel is with Her. The angel dictated the following:

5-DAY NOVENA TO OUR LADY OF GUADALUPE

(Recite One Prayer Each Day)

DAY 1
Immaculate and Perpetual Virgin of Guadalupe, You appeared on Mount Tepeyac to reconcile mankind to God. Plead and intercede with Your Son, Jesus, today, that a bond of Holy Love is formed between all humanity and God.

Our Lady of Guadalupe, pray for us!

DAY 2
Immaculate and Perpetual Virgin of Guadalupe, You left Your Image on the cloak of Juan Diego using a humble vessel to bring Your grace into the world. Imprint on our hearts the virtue of humility, dear Mother, and use us to bring others to You.

Our Lady of Guadalupe, pray for us!

DAY 3

Immaculate and Perpetual Virgin of Guadalupe, Your Image of Guadalupe was a symbolic story to the Aztecs, converting them from paganism to Christianity. Pray for us, dear Mother, that our lives will be symbols of Holy Love converting those around us.

Our Lady of Guadalupe, pray for us!

DAY 4

Immaculate and Perpetual Virgin of Guadalupe, Your Image has remained intact on the frail cactus fiber of the Tilma for centuries, free from corruption of the elements of the world. Give to us, dear Mother, a lasting and enduring faith. A faith that will not be compromised by the world.

Our Lady of Guadalupe, pray for us!

DAY 5

Immaculate and Perpetual Virgin of Guadalupe, You proclaimed Yourself Our Mother and Protectress when You appeared on Mt. Tepeyac. Take us into Your Maternal Heart, dear Mother, and protect our faith.

Our Lady of Guadalupe, pray for us!

■ **November 30, 1995 / Thursday Night Rosary Service.** Our Lady is here as Our Lady of Guadalupe. She says: "All praise be to Jesus, My dear little ones. Pray with Me now, for all those who will journey to My prayer site on the Twelfth of December." We prayed. "Dear children, tonight I invite you to draw closer to Me, so that I can bring you closer to My Son. You will find the way if you follow the light, as the shepherds and Wise Men did. Tonight, I tell you, the light I ask you to seek is the light of Holy Love upon the path of Holiness. Dear children I am blessing you."

December 1995

■ **December 3, 1995 – First Sunday of Advent.** Our Lady says, "Dear children, I come to invite you once again to live My Message of Holy Love. Do not listen with your ears, but hear what I am telling you in your hearts. You are chosen as a remnant and an advent people – awaiting with excited expectation My Son's Second Coming on earth. The time is close at hand, when the Refuge of My Heart will be your only stronghold against the pillages of the deposit of faith. Therefore, be wise and prudent in coming to Me so that I can lead you to My Son."

■ **December 5, 1995.** From Our Lady: "Dear child, it is when you are at the foot of the Cross that your prayers are most efficacious, for it is at the foot of the Cross I am closest to you. Here I invite you to renew your consecration to My Immaculate Heart. Here, on Calvary, I am joining together My humble and powerful army of little victim souls. This army of My littlest and least will defeat Satan and usher in the reign of My Immaculate Heart. My army of victims is a contradiction to the worldly wise, who seek proof and glory in their own right. See that it is in contradicting Satan that My victory will come. And so, by your smallest efforts, make My joy and My victory complete. At the foot of the Cross, I choose by God's Will, to place the courage of conviction in the hearts of My victim warriors, My victim apostles. It is beneath My Son's gaze I place My Motherly Blessing in each heart that loves. At the foot of the Cross, I invite you to be victims of love, just as Jesus was for you. Understand, that My Son is the Eternal Victim of Love in every tabernacle where He is worshipped and adored; in every tabernacle where there is faith; in every tabernacle of the world. I am uniting My prayers to your own. I am loving you into eternity."

■ **December 5, 1995.** Our Lady appeared in white standing behind what I understood was the second Maranatha Spring. She said: "My daughter it is here I will dispense My favors and alleviate afflictions of all nations and every people. It is here I will reconcile man and God. It is here I will make known My Holy Love to hearts. It is here I will manifest God's glory amongst men. Make it known."

■ **December 6, 1995.** From Our Lady: "Come to realize, My children, that it is not for your physical well-being I come. But I come to capture and to vanquish your hearts and souls with My Holy Love. It is only through Holy Love, hearts and nations will be reconciled to God. Today, Satan engages Me in battle, most especially, over those souls who are consecrated to Me, and who have mounted to a high degree of perfection. He knows, when he conquers one soul who influences many, he wins a great victory. You must pray very much for those who represent and defend the deposit of faith. Some of these hearts have been laid waste by compromise and error, and misrepresent the faith. Do not be fooled by exterior appearances but look at words and actions. My coming to you on the Twelfth of each month, to commemorate My Image of Guadalupe, must be a sign to My children of My maternal concern, My call to conversion, and a return to the faith. When I came to Juan Diego, I came to stop pagan rituals and convert the unchurched. Today, it is sadly no different, only, the unchurched are those who have apostasized. This is no longer hidden but flagrantly open and accepted!"

■ **December 7, 1995.** From Our Lady: "I have prepared for you a great mission; one of miraculous events resulting in many conversions. The outpouring of My grace has become one with My call to you on our new prayer site. It is by My privilege and through the Merciful Heart of My Son you will unearth the spring next week. Wait upon My lead, and My telling."

■ **December 8, 1995.** From Our Lady: "Today, I initiate in you My mission of merciful love. It is only through mercy and love mankind can span the abyss between himself and God. Have confidence My angel, that at My spring, I will dispense and reveal God's merciful love in the abundance of God's will to all who seek it. With unprecedented graciousness I will fulfill My mission in you and through you."

■ **December 10, 1995.** From Our Lady: "Tuesday, before My coming, I desire that you go to the site of My spring and dig superficially for it. It will prove evident by your efforts."

■ **December 10, 1995.** Our Lady comes as Our Lady of Grace. She says: "I give praise to Jesus. My angel, I want you to understand, I do not come seeking approval from those in high places, but to reconcile souls to God. Therefore, see and understand, the spring you will unearth this week is to bear fruit in hearts and in the world, lending witness to the authenticity of My visits to you. These days, many would lose their faith if it were not for My protection. The wellspring of grace about to come forth will serve as a particular deterrent to Satan, as it will carry with it MY PRESENCE wherever it is taken. I am blessing you. I am blessing you tonight and strengthening you temporarily for our journey ahead."

■ **December 12, 1995.** *(Just after midnight)* Our Lady comes as Our Lady of Guadalupe. She says: "Praise be to Jesus. Today I come to you to commemorate and to continue My mission which was begun in Mexico in 1531. When I appeared to Juan Diego, there was a great war at hand between good and evil – Christian and pagan. Today, the battle has intensified. More human carnage is waged. More souls are at stake. Only today it is not pagans who are sacrificing life, it is well-informed Christians who are making such an educated choice. The final outcome of this war will be determined in hearts. For this is not a war over territories, but over souls. And so, I come to you today on the site of My Prayer Center – a site of profound grace – and I ask your prayers that people choose good over evil. Such decisions made in hearts affect the fate of the whole planet. This is so, for the scale of justice in My Son's Hand is weighing heavily on the side of purification. And so I, your Mother and Protectress, plead with you to know the ramifications of the choices you make in your hearts. Pray, pray, pray."

■ **December 12, 1995 / Monthly Message To All Nations.** *(2:30 p.m. Rosary Service) (Future site of the Immaculate Heart of Mary Prayer Center)* The Blessed Mother is here as Our Lady of Guadalupe. She says: "I bid you give praise to Jesus. I come to welcome all who come to My new site of grace and prayer. I invite you now to extend the articles you need blessed. This is the last time I will send the angels to your midst to bless these articles, because now you have been given the spring. *[Note: Maranatha Spring was unearthed on Our Lady's new prayer site this morning.]* You unearthed the spring this morning as I desired, to show that it is always necessary for hearts to cooperate with grace, or else it will remain hidden from them. But, My grace is readily present here at this site today and always. Today I initiate in you My new mission of Merciful Love and I invite you to take it into the world. Do not leave it captured in your hearts. Holy Love, Merciful Love are one. They come from My Son through Me. I desire that you offer this Love to those you come in contact with, that they too may be apostles of My Heart. For it is in this way the world will undergo a genesis and be renewed in the Faith. Dear children, our beginnings here are humble just as My Son's birth was in a humble place. The impact of My grace depends on you, on your willingness to evangelize. Dear children, I hide no grace from you. I offer all. My provision is complete on this property. I am blessing you with My Special Blessing."

■ **December 16, 1995.** Jesus says: "Today, in these times, I send My Mother all over the world, just as Moses was sent to Pharaoh with signs and wonders, warnings and reproaches. The purpose is the same - to change hearts and to gain freedom. Only, today, hearts need to be freed from the reign of sin."
Read 1 Cor. Chapter 10

■ **December 17, 1995.** *(Philadelphia)* Our Lady is here as Our Lady of Fatima. She is holding a rosary of lights. She says: "All praise be to Jesus, My dear little children. Pray with Me now for all those whose lives will be touched by your visit here." We prayed. "Dear children, I come to embrace your hearts with My Holy Love. Come to understand, My little ones, that My Heart is like a rose which you must come close to, to fully appreciate the fragrance of its grace and the beauty of its depths. The thorns on this rose are all things that prevent you from loving as I desire you to love. My dear little children, it is My wish that My Missionary Servants [of Holy Love] would meet to pray once a month for My intentions and towards the victory of My Immaculate Heart here on earth. I am blessing you."

■ **December 18, 1995.** *(During the Rosary before Maureen's talk in Philadelphia)* Blessed Mother is here as Our Lady of Fatima. She says: "Praise be to Jesus, My children. I come to you tonight with tears in My eyes for those who do not admit Jesus into their hearts during this Advent season. And I ask your prayers at this time that all people will prepare a place in their hearts for My Son." We prayed. "Dear children, tonight I invite you to understand, that the cross is a means and an instrument to reconcile God and man. I ask you not to be afraid of the cross but to embrace it, thereby making it a means of salvation, just as My Son did. Dear children, I am interceding for you and taking your petitions to the altar of My Son in Heaven. I extend to you tonight My Motherly Blessing."

■ **December 19, 1995.** *(Maureen spoke in South Philadelphia yesterday evening)* Our Lady comes in light blue and white. She says: "My daughter, I do not measure success by smoothness of delivery, signs and wonders, or numbers in attendance, but by the numbers of hearts that open to My words. The thrust of My Holy Love message is: Exterior things are of little value and only of passing importance. Of eternal value is what is in hearts. My coming to you is to be manifested in hearts. These loving hearts must then change the world."

■ **December 21, 1995 / Weekly Rosary Service.** Our Lady is here as Our Lady of Guadalupe. She has a bright light coming from Her Heart. "Praise be to Jesus, My dear little children. Pray with Me now for all those who are far from My Son during this Holy Season." We prayed. "Dear children, during these approaching days, I desire that you make your hearts tabernacles of Holy Love. In so doing, when My Son comes to you on Christmas you will be at peace. I will speak most profoundly in a Christmas message to all My children. Tonight, I am blessing you with My Blessing of Holy Love."

■ **December 22, 1995.** Jesus says:
"My strength in your weakness.
My provision in your need.
My grace to smooth the way.
Have confidence in Me."

■ **December 22, 1995.** Our Lady comes in white with sparkling lights around Her. She says: "Note well and heed in the memory of your heart, My daughter. This is the age of prodigies, the age of victory, and defeat. In the end, My Heart will take dominion over evil. For now, evil holds sway over good, for not enough love. This is why you must be courageous and make known My coming to you. I give thanks and praise to Jesus for his allowing Me to continue to come.

Your Rosaries are My weapon against ones who oppose My plans. Make it known."

■ **December 22, 1995.** Our Lady comes in blue and gray. She says: "The greatest outpouring of My grace and miracles has yet to come at Maranatha Spring - all for the greater honor and glory of Jesus, My Son. I tell you all nations will become as one. Evil will manifest itself through certain ones who will be permitted to gain power. The righteous will be put to the test and persecuted. Tabernacles will be desecrated. Only those who persevere in Holy Love will be saved. My Heart is their Refuge. Even so, I confide to you, fear has no place in a heart full of love. It is during the greatest trial and the most desolate hour you will know I am with you - caressing you in My Heart. Make it known."

■ **December 24, 1995.** Jesus appeared before me standing on water. He said, "It is only when you take your eyes off of Me that you lack trust. Remit all things to My Heart. I am the Way."

■ **December 24, 1995.** Our Lady is here in blue and white like My statue. Her Heart is exposed and has a great light coming from it. She says: "Praise be to Jesus, My little ones. Let us pray now for all those who are heathen in their thoughts and actions." We prayed. "Dear children, know and understand that you can depend on My grace in the present moment. And therefore, do not be anxious about any aspect of your life, any illness, any business dealing, but know that My grace is waiting for you in the future."

■ **December 25, 1995 / Message To All Nations.** Our Lady comes in white. She says: "Happy Christmas! All praise and adoration be unto Jesus, for He is King - the Word born Incarnate. I come today to speak to all nations, all peoples. Dear children, centuries ago the angels proclaimed, 'Peace on earth to men of good will.' Today, I solemnly tell you, few are of good will. This is true, for pride has turned good to evil. This is manifest in a multitude of ways. For instance, intellect is a gift from God. But when man takes pride in his intellect through his own will, it is no longer good, but evil. Some go so far as to take pride in their spirituality. This is how Satan convolutes virtue. All evil will be uncovered before My Son's coming. He sends Me ahead of Him, just as the Baptizer preceded My Son. When Jesus returns, and before He will come, the mountains will be made into plains and the dry land into sea. Because His coming will purge the earth of evil, a purification will manifest itself in hearts and in the world first. The greatest tribulation is yet at hand. Hearts are unprepared that do not love. It will be shown and understood by the spiritually wise, that man is solely dependent on God and that each one in the world needs to assist the other. False gods will be stripped away. Money, power, immorality, human intellect, will no longer have power but be impotent. I once again invite you to see the GREAT URGENCY of My Holy Love message, which will be, and is today, the trumpet of the angel [***Book of Revelation***] and the heel that will crush the serpent's head. I am blessing you."

■ **December 25, 1995.** *(While Maureen was attending Christmas Mass)* Jesus says: "Before I return and when hearts are universally convicted, all will be given the opportunity of recognizing Me, truly present in the Eucharist. Many truths will be revealed."

■ **December 26, 1995.** Our Lady comes in light blue and white. She says: "All praise and adoration be to Jesus, born Incarnate. My daughter, today I invite you to understand that My Son's birth in a stable diametrically opposes the materialism this world has come to esteem. For this same reason, His Real Presence in the Eucharist is not understood or appreciated. With great humility and Divine Love, My Beloved Son resides in the tabernacles of the world. He waits hour after hour, and day after day, to be adored and recognized. He is present amidst trial and during eras of peace. His Presence, which transcends human law, opposes evil. He pours out Himself for the welfare of humanity but suffers greatly the insult of neglect by those who know Him, and willful ignorance by those who do not choose to know Him. I come today to ask your continued devotion to His Eucharistic Heart. Holy hours of reparation withhold the Hand of Justice. Bring your heart here spiritually when situations arise that do not permit you to come in person. I am always here as a consolation to My Son. I am blessing you."

■ **December 30, 1995 - Eve of the Feast of the Holy Family.** The Holy Family is here. Our Lady says: "I come in praise of Jesus, My Son. Pray with Me now, My dear little children, for those who never pray." We prayed. "Dear children, I know the inner whisperings of your hearts, the movements of your wills. Once again, I ask you to await the grace of the present moment and allow its opportunity. For Me there is only a short time, for you there is much time. But I come to you tonight, to give you My love, My understanding, and My support. And I ask you to be patient. Have Holy Patience with each other and with those around you. Things are only beginning. The workings of grace have yet to show the magnitude of My call here. I will return tomorrow with My message for the new year." Jesus blessed us.

■ **December 31, 1995 - New Year's Eve / New Year's Message.** Our Lady comes in white, standing below Her picture in My bedroom. She says: "My daughter, I come in praise of Jesus, born Incarnate. I have prepared this day for you, just as, according to Divine Will, I am preparing the year in time that opens before you. I do not come to proffer predictions, but to open My Heart to you and to the world. The year ahead will see the mission I have given you prosper, both in the world, and more importantly, in hearts. This will pose a threat to some and they will set about trying to oppose us, but their attempts will prove futile. Once again, My grace will triumph. In the world the abyss between God and man will continue to widen. (Blessed Mother is crying now.) I encourage you to pray for the godless. Never assume you have prayed enough. God will honor your feeblest attempts. Choices will be made against Tradition which will further compromise the faith of many in certain and specific areas. Well-guarded will be the faith of those close to Me. Tumult and peace will vie for hearts and for a place in the world. Every heart will be challenged. My grace will continue to pour from My Immaculate Heart onto earth. Many signs and wonders will result - challenging unbelievers and convicting hearts. The Rosary will overcome certain sin. This is why ones devoted to the Rosary will be persecuted. All of this is a good sign. Persecution shows Satan's hand of fear. I am with you and, as always, I direct you to My Son's Eucharistic Heart. Let Him take up reign in your hearts as Prince of Peace in the present moment, and so, in the year to come. With joy I am blessing you with My Motherly Blessing."

■ **December 31, 1995.**

Invocation To The Holy Angels
"Dear heavenly angels, all who reside in heaven and assist us on earth, guide us. Minister to the needs of all mankind. Be for us a liaison between God and man. Protect the tabernacles of the world as you protect our hearts as well, against the attacks of the evil one. Dear angels, take all our needs and petitions to Heaven and lay them on the Divine Altar of the Sacred Heart of Jesus. Amen."

■ **December 31, 1995.** Our Lady is here in white. She has a white light around Her head. "I come in praise of Jesus, My

Son. I desire that you pray with Me now that mankind will be reconciled with God." We prayed. "Dear children, remember to let the '*Gloria*' (*All Glory Be...*) be important, for to give praise and honor to the TRINITY through every miracle that takes place on our new property is most pleasing to Me. I desire, dear children, that you do celebrate, for we are beginning what will be a great, great mission and, I will celebrate with you. Come tomorrow to our chapel, our meeting place. I will be there. I desire to speak to those who will come to the property. My little one, allow Me to use you. I am blessing you."

Messages of Holy *and* Divine Love

1996

January 1996

■ **January 2, 1996 / Weekly Rosary Service.** Our Lady is here as Our Lady of Guadalupe. She says: "Praise be to Jesus. I come to you tonight, to ask for prayers for all those who are unbelievers."

"Dear children, tonight especially, I confide to you, there are certain hearts that threaten the future of the world. If these hearts were to be reconciled with God My dear children, the future of the world would be greatly altered, and what is to come, still mitigated. Therefore, tonight I come to you once again as your Mother, pleading for you to pray, pray, pray. And I am blessing you."

■ **January 10, 1996.** Jesus says: "Verily, verily, I say to you. Seek not the delights of this world, but the path of Holy Love, which is the transport to Paradise."

■ **January 11, 1996.** Our Lady comes in gray and white. She said: "Always place your trust in the grace of the present moment. In this give praise to Jesus. Tomorrow and always I desire one rosary be offered for the unborn - binding them to My Immaculate Heart with the Father Gobbi prayer.* *('Celestial Queen, with this rosary, I bind my children to your Immaculate Heart.')* The sin of abortion is the greatest factor in calling God's Justice upon the world. I will return tomorrow to complete My message to all nations."

* See message of October 7, 1996.

■ **January 11, 1996 / Weekly Rosary Service.** Our Lady comes as Our Lady of Guadalupe. She says: "I come in praise of Jesus, My Son. Blessed be His Holy Name. Dear child, make it known that God has created each person to be perfected in Holy Love, for Holy Love is the path of salvation.

You cannot answer to a vocation of love if you do not forgive, if you do not overcome anger, or if you do not love truth. Dear children, live My Holy Love Message through My grace. Ask Me and I will help you. I am blessing you."

■ **January 12, 1996 / Monthly Message To All Nations.** *(Site of the Immaculate Heart of Mary Prayer Center)* Blessed Mother is here as Our Lady of Guadalupe. She has hundreds of angels with Her. The whole area to the rear of the barn above the people was filled with angels. "Thank you for answering My invitation to meet with Me here today. Pray with Me now, for the lukewarm." We prayed. "Dear children, I invite you to realize in your hearts, and understand, that God's Divine Mercy and His Divine Love, are one in the same and inseparable. Therefore, please know that My Holy Love, and contrition for your sins in your own heart, are inseparable. I ask your continued faithful prayers for the intellectual pride of the lukewarm, who oppose My every plan. But, know My children, that My grace is stronger than any evil. I am with you today in a special way."

"My children, let My coming to you today, be a sign to all nations of God's great love for humanity, and His desire to be reconciled with all people. Most especially, I come to inspire the conversion of the lukewarm, who hold the fate of the world in their hearts. The greatest sins are committed by the lukewarm, for their apathy gravely wounds the Heart of My Beloved Son. The majority of all abortions are committed by the lukewarm. Besides this abomination, they have weakened the Church through their compromise. The Ten Commandments, as well, have become dead words in the lukewarm heart. The two great commands, which are the embodiment of Holy Love, find no place in these hearts, BUT HAVE BEEN REPLACED BY FREE WILL."

"Today, I tell you, Holy Love is the only choice you can make towards your own salvation. When you choose Holy Love you are choosing Divine Mercy and Divine Love at once."

"Dear children, these days and during this hour, I continue to visit you under this title and through this image. You are not comprehending the urgency of My call. I come to reconcile an erring generation to God. God has chosen to send Me to you with My Holy Love. You need to be the catalyst in the conversion of your own heart and those around you. Hearing My message is not the same as living it."

"Today, there are more than a few, more than a whole nation of people, who call themselves 'Catholic,' but who take as their pontiff and vicar their own free will. God, Who loves all nations and all people will allow them this. He will also allow them to choose perdition."

"But I am showing you the path, the sure road to salvation through Holy Love. You must make it known."

"I am blessing you."

■ **January 17, 1996.** Our Lady is here in an iridescent white. "All praise be to Jesus, My little children. I'm glad to be with you once again. Pray with Me now, for those who will come on the Twelfth." When Blessed Mother prayed the *"All Glory Be...,"* hundreds of pink rose petals fell down all around Her. Our Lady then says: "These are the graces that will be attendant to the new property."

"Please be jubilant. For this year instead of raising soybeans, I will be raising up souls to God." (The farm had previously been a soybean farm.)

"Dear children, place all your cares in My Heart. Trust Me to see you through these times of error and crises in society."

■ **January 17, 1996.** Our Lady is here in a dark blue mantle with a white gown. She says: "I come in praise of Jesus, My Son. My daughter, I know and understand the innermost workings of your heart. Surrender to Me your every need. Am I not your Protectress? Have I not come to bring peace to every heart? My Holy Love is the means by which the worldly-wise will be confounded and the humble will be brought high. There is no evil greater than My grace. I am laying bare the fallacies in hearts. It is so I will raise up a holy nation amidst the dunghill of error, a nation of souls consecrated to My Flame of Holy Love. This nation that knows no boundary on earth will be the victory of My Immaculate Heart."

"All souls thus consecrated, give to Me their sins and imperfections, their spirituality and their worldly goods. Further this nation is liable to invest others in My Heart through Holy Love. Continue to pray for those who do not seek the path of light which is Holy Love. It is always pride that sets these souls apart. But, I promise very great and profound blessings to those who persevere along this chosen path."

She smiles. "My daughter, make it known."

■ **January 18, 1996 / Weekly Rosary Service.** Our Lady was preceded by an angel carrying a large trumpet. She is here as Our Lady of Guadalupe. "I come in praise of Jesus, My dear little children. Pray with Me now for all unbelievers." We prayed.

"Dear children, tonight I invoke you, that by your sincere efforts, that you remove all anguish, all criticism, all compromise and unforgiveness from your hearts, so that I can fill your hearts with Holy Love. Dear children, it is by My coming to you, and giving you the Holy Love message, that many will be saved. Tonight I am asking you to continue to pray, pray, pray. And I am blessing you."

■ **January 21, 1996.** Our Lady is here in blue and white with a crown of yellow roses around Her head. She says: "My daughter, I am protecting your progress on My behalf. Your efforts are in the folds of My Mantle and well within My Heart. I come as Jesus directs Me to define to you the meaning of grace. I give praise to Jesus, for His mission through Me in you."

"Child, the human intellect cannot fully grasp the power or majesty of God's grace. Grace is the supernatural intervention that attains all good in the face of evil. Grace transports the heart away from natural inclinations towards the spiritual. God's grace is Divine Love, Divine Mercy, and Divine Will together. There is no force or evil comparable to grace. It is grace that sends Me to you. It is grace that draws you to Me. God's grace is your salvation. It is My protection and My Son's provision. Always trust in grace. This trust will merit you every favor. Trust in Me to protect your faith and turn evil into God's good end. I desire you make these things known."

"I am blessing you."

■ **January 23, 1996.** Our Lady says: "My daughter, inspire in hearts this ejaculation, *'Mary, protect our faith.'* Through this prayer I will dispel evil and lay bare heresy. Should anyone dispute this, refer them to the *Memorare.*"

■ **January 23, 1996.** Our Lady comes as Our Lady of Grace. She says: "I come to give greater honor and glory to Jesus, My Son. I desire that My children no longer allow walls to exist between one another. These walls are your unforgiveness (which comes from pride), jealousy and an inability to accept basic differences. I, your Mother, come to ask you to pray these walls down, just as you did the iron curtain. Accept each other just as I accept each of you, in Holy Love. It is only then, mankind can be reconciled to God. Make this known."

■ **January 25, 1996 / Weekly Rosary Service.** Our Lady is here as Our Lady of Guadalupe. She says: "I come in praise of Jesus. Dear children, pray with Me tonight for the development of My prayer center." We prayed.

"Dear children, tonight I come to you seeking your total consecration to My Immaculate Heart. Empty yourselves of all sins, of every virtue, and of past and future efforts towards sanctity. Thus divested, I will fill you with My Holy Love and lead you along the path of sanctity. Dear children, I am blessing you."

* An explanation of the January 25th message was given by Our Lady in the following message from January 26, 1996.

■ **January 26, 1996.** From Our Lady: "I desire that My children surrender everything to Me, the good and the bad - the exterior and the interior - all their meritorious acts and good works - even their personal holiness. If a soul is not hanging on to anything, but has given all things over to the Heart of his Mother, he is then ready to be filled with My Holy Love. I will use what he has given Me towards the sanctity of others and for his own advancement along the path of Holy Love. All this in praise of Jesus."

■ **January 28, 1996.** Our Lady says: "My daughter, please understand that I am calling Holy Love, My LAST CALL TO HUMANITY, not only for the season of time earth finds herself in, but also, because it is the virtue of Holy Love in hearts, in the last moment of life, that will determine the soul's final judgment. No one can enter My Son's kingdom who does not love."

■ **January 30, 1996 / Weekly Rosary Service.** Our Lady is here as Our Lady of Grace. She says: "Praise be to Jesus, My little children. I come tonight, most especially to ask for your prayers for the many who will come on the Twelfth." We prayed.

"Dear children, tonight I come to you assured of your great love for Me by your presence here. I ask you to pray for holy boldness, so that My messages to you will be more widely disseminated. You are letting Satan discourage you from evangelizing to unbelievers. And My books are collecting dust. Dear children, I do not speak to you because Jesus sends Me with a lighthearted mission. These are serious times. The hour is growing desperate. You have at your disposal a great arsenal of weapons in the rosary and My messages. Dear children, please take this seriously. My coming to you is a grace. I am blessing you."

February 1996

■ **February 3, 1996.** Our Lady came with St. Michael. Since I was sick, St. Michael gave me, what Blessed Mother termed, "Mystical Communion." It seemed I felt the Host on my tongue. Our Lady said: "My daughter, do not fear any illness or turmoil of earth. Know with certainty that My grace is laid bare to every situation which you surrender to Me."

■ **February 5, 1996.** Jesus says: "I am knitting together the final remnant of the tapestry of My mission in you. The tapestry will be washed and purified in the Spring [water] of Maranatha and placed in Our United Hearts [The United Hearts of Jesus and Mary]".

■ **February 6, 1996.** Jesus says: "Whatever you surrender to My Sacred Wounds, I will bless with My Provision. Most especially, venerate and adore the wound of My Shoulder. It is most powerful because, throughout My Passion, it remained hidden and unremarkable. Nothing you place in My Wounds will escape My Grace and Mercy. "

■ **February 8, 1996 / Weekly Rosary Service.** Our Lady is here as Our Lady of Guadalupe. She says: "Dear children, tonight I come to seek your cooperation, so that souls will choose good over evil and Holy Love as the path of light. Dear children, I can no longer restrain the HAND OF JUSTICE. Mankind must become reconciled with his Creator. The unbelievers, that wound My Son with the most grievous sins, are the lukewarm, because they once knew the path I chose for them, and they rejected it. Now I ask you to offer each *Hail Mary*, so that souls will choose good over evil. I am blessing you now."

■ **February 9, 1996.** From Our Lady: "The hour of My

Predilection is at hand and will be shown through God's Will and Grace at the site of Maranatha Spring - all for the greater honor and glory of the Most Blessed Trinity. What is to come and what will bear witness to the truth of Holy Love will defy natural law and suspend the forces of nature."

"You yourself will be made the object of pursuit by those who cannot within their own hearts separate the message, the signs given, and the messenger. But I am giving to you My peace, so that, in all things, and in every way, you will know I am in the midst of your heart and this mission."

"Pride will preclude some from accepting even My most revealing signs. This is through their own error and not your own. Some will try to make it seem as though My miracles are fraudulent. They only pursue this path from lack of love. If they do not accept something, they discredit the authenticity. This is how the Holy Father is being attacked as well."

"I have more to confide and to speak to you. Continue to make yourself available to Me as you have been. I am blessing you."

■ **February 9, 1996.** Our Lady comes. There is a blood stain in the shape of a cross on Her mantle. "By the Blood of the Passion you are redeemed. All praise be to Jesus!"

"My little angel, I desire you make it known that the hour of My great predilection is at hand at Maranatha Spring. I am opening My Heart to all nations at this sight and through the favor of My grace, reconciling the lost to God. Tell My children not to fear. You have come to lead them by way of Holy Love into the kingdom of the New Jerusalem. I desire that all who come abandon themselves to My Motherly care. Tenderly, I will lead them to My Son."

"Surrender to every cross. Your victory is in your surrender. I will, through grace, make whole the broken in body and spirit. I am the Perpetual Virgin Mary, Mother of God."

■ **February 9, 1996.** From Our Lady: "Do not fear. Remember, all things are under God's reign and subject to His Authority."

■ **February 10, 1996.** "It is in My Heart and in the Will of God that Cleveland will become a destination of pilgrimages. Not for any secular exhibits or museums, but for the favor of grace that will be dispensed at Maranatha Spring and for My presence at the field of Our United Hearts."

"There are certain ones - certain souls who will be present on the Twelfth this month - whom I have chosen to lead such groups from their points of origin to My Spring. They will recognize in their hearts My call to them. It is through My grace the way will be made clear for this endeavor."

■ **February 10, 1996.** Our Lady comes in gray with a crown on Her head. She says: "My daughter, it is time to make it known, that the United Hearts of Jesus and Mary are the New Kingdom, the New Jerusalem, Holy and Divine Love. I come to you to bring souls into this kingdom. Everything that lies outside of Our Hearts is passing and temporary. Holy Love is the key by which you gain entrance and through which you are newly created. Holy Love is the path. Divine Love is the destination."

"Our Hearts cannot be separated. They beat as one. The devotion to Our United Hearts must be the oil in your lamps as you await My Son's return. Then you will be prepared and Satan will not be able to pull you away from Me."

"The time is fast approaching, when that which is outside of the United Hearts will be laid waste. Satan is conspiring in certain hearts to destroy peace. Cling fast to the present day Manna of the Eucharist. Do not be swayed by free thinking, for today, the guise of Satan is free conscience - free choice."

"Just as I am united to My Son, so I desire that My children be united to our Sacred Hearts. I desire souls seek their perfection through Our Hearts, in the mission I have come to give you. In praise of Jesus, souls need to be consecrated to the United Hearts. I will return with such a prayer in the near future."

■ **February 10, 1996.** Jesus says: "You must spread this devotion to Our United Hearts. Make it known that I will answer every request made through this chaplet."

CHAPLET OF THE TWO HEARTS

There are 20 beads; five sets each of one (1) *Our Father* and three (3) *Hail Mary's*. Following are the meditations of the five sets:

1. In Honor of the Sacred Heart of Jesus
2. In Honor of the Immaculate Heart of Mary
3. Meditating on the Passion of Our Lord
4. Meditating on the Sorrows of Mary
5. In Atonement to the Hearts of Jesus and Mary

At the end, on the medal, say the *Prayer to the United Hearts of Jesus and Mary*.

Prayer To The United Hearts Of Jesus And Mary

O United Hearts of Jesus and Mary, You are all grace, all mercy, all love. Let My heart be joined to Yours, so that My every need is present in Your United Hearts. Most especially, shed Your grace upon this particular need (mention need). Help me to recognize and accept Your loving will in My life. Amen.

■ **February 12, 1996 / Monthly Message To All Nations.** Hundreds of angels preceded Blessed Mother. Our Lady is here as Our Lady of Guadalupe. She says: "I come as The Woman Clothed in the Sun, The Woman of Revelations, Morning Star, The Path. I come in praise of Jesus, My Son. Pray with Me now, for all the unconverted." We prayed. "I come to invite you to see that God's Mercy and Love are the means by which the New Jerusalem will take up reign in hearts, and the means through which My Son will return. Understand that the United Hearts of Jesus and Mary are, and must be, the trumpet that announces My Son's Second

Coming. It is through Our United Hearts the Church will be purified, renewed, and made whole."

"It is important that you pray and sacrifice for hearts to change now while there is still time. Many, many (She is crying now) will die sudden and unprovided deaths. My Son's Church is undergoing a purgation. I want you to understand that there is a false pope in hearts. This pope is free conscience, and for some, has taken precedence over the real Pope, John Paul II, and his undeniable infallibility." I asked Blessed Mother what She wants of the people here today. "I desire their faith, their prayers, their sacrifices. It is My desire, and that also of the Eternal Father, that devotion to the United Hearts of Jesus and Mary be propagated in the world; for it is the final call, and it is the NEW JERUSALEM. Your efforts on My behalf will be proliferated through My grace. It is My great pleasure to invite pilgrimages to come here. For this is the hour of grace, the hour of decision. And Holy Love is the path and the bridge that spans the abyss between heaven and earth."

"I thank you for your sacrifice, dear children, of coming here today [wind chill -11]. And I invite you to continue to pray for hearts that are frozen in sin and error. I am blessing you."

■ **February 14, 1996.** Our Lady says: "May 5th* will be an important day in the life of souls. Those in the ministry should begin to pray for this already. I have come, and continue to do so, out of love."

* *May 5th is the second anniversary of the unearthing of Maranatha Spring on the grounds of Mary's House of Prayer in the city of Seven Hills. Our Lady asked at that time that May 5th be celebrated as Her feast day of Holy Love.*

■ **February 14, 1996.** "Please make it known to all My little children that the key to the UNITED HEARTS OF JESUS AND MARY is HOLY LOVE. Outside of Holy Love one cannot gain entrance to this favored hospice."

■ **February 14, 1996.** Our Lady comes in blue and white. She says: "Make ready your hearts for My coming to you on May 5th in commemoration and celebration of Holy Love. All this is to bring honor and praise to Jesus and to Our United Hearts. I desire that the people come in procession to My Spring on that day. There are very many who will find My grace abundant there. It is so, for the grace of My Immaculate Heart has come to rest there. I desire that My children come to know the field of the United Hearts as a place of My favor and a destination of pilgrimages. I will welcome all who come with My Blessing of Holy Love."

■ **February 15, 1996 / Weekly Rosary Service.** Our Lady is here as Our Lady of Guadalupe. She says: "Do Me the honor of praying with Me, for the conversion of all those who come on pilgrimage." We prayed. "Dear children, tonight I invite you to understand that when you are living My messages of Holy Love, your hearts are immersed in the Divine Love of My Son's Heart, for these two are inseparable; and in the New Jerusalem, Holy and Divine Love will be one. Dear children, I come to you as My Son allows to encourage you to live My message. The Lord is rebuilding Zion. He is using the bricks of Holy Love and the mortar of your efforts. I am blessing you."

■ **February 17, 1996.** Our Lady appeared before me in grayish blue with a crown of thorns on Her head. She said: "My daughter, this crown you see Me supporting represents the Mystical wounds of My Son's Heart. These wounds, hidden from the eyes of men, I gladly take upon Myself to relieve Him. He is already too greatly wounded. These Mystical wounds are inflicted by those souls who have fickle hearts. From one side of their mouth comes praise and from the other side, blasphemy and words contrary to Holy Love. Such hearts are ones that pick and choose which commandments they will obey and which laws of the Church are worthy of obedience.

They see themselves in the light of their own pride as loving and faithful. They pray and tell My Son they love Him but then turn on Him. I wear this crown out of Holy Love - constant Holy Love - to relieve My Beloved Son, Jesus the Word Incarnate, of further agony."

■ **February 22, 1996 / Weekly Rosary Service.** Our Lady is here as Our Lady of Guadalupe. She says: "All praise be to Jesus, My dear little children. Pray with Me now for all those who will make pilgrimage to our prayer site." We prayed. "Dear children, I come to you tonight, as My Son sends Me, so that just as the Hearts of Jesus and Mary are united, earth can be united to heaven through Holy Love and Divine Love. Dear children, forgiveness is a great part of Holy Love and begins in your own heart. The fruit of forgiveness is My peace, My joy, and Holy Love. Tonight I'm blessing you with My Motherly Blessing."

■ **February 23, 1996.** "My daughter, I am here. I come as I always come, in praise of Jesus, My Son. Make known, My messenger, that I come to prepare the world for My Son's return. Heaven and earth need to be united as they will be when He comes. It is necessary that hearts be reconciled to God, for My Son comes as Just Judge. The time before His Second Coming is precious indeed. Too many do not listen. Today, I tell you, the more who turn from evil and choose good, the less the balance between the numbers who choose Holy Love and the degree of mitigation. I say Holy Love in this context for Holy Love is your conversion."

"Do not fear for time, space, or money. All of these and more will turn to your favor. My army of consecrated souls is strengthening and growing in these last days. This is in preparation for My final battle against the red dragon. Surrender completely to Holy Love. My victory is in your 'yes.' I am blessing you."

■ **February 29, 1996.** *(Jesus appeared to Maureen as He was after the Scourging.)* "You see the number of My wounds, you see what I willingly suffered. Mankind accused Me falsely, scourged Me falsely, crucified Me in error. Yet despite all of this, I forgave. I could have come down from the cross, but I willingly stayed upon it. I could have called a multitude of angels to My defense, but I chose not to."

"If I can be so loving and merciful, how can anyone of you hold a grudge against another - you who My Father knit in the womb? You are called to be merciful and loving, just as I am merciful and loving. The more you imitate Me, the deeper you are drawn into Holy and Divine Love."

■ **February 29, 1996.**
Our Lady Restates The Promises
Of The Two Hearts Chaplet
1. "My Son promises He will answer all petitions surrendered to the United Hearts."
2. "Through the recitation of the Chaplet to the United Hearts a more fervent reception of the Blessed Sacrament will be made."
3. "The United Hearts of Jesus and Mary are a fortress against evil."

■ **February 29, 1996 / Weekly Rosary Service.** Our Lady is here as Our Lady of Guadalupe. Her Heart is exposed. She is in a blue light. She says: "I desire tonight that you join Me in prayer for all the pilgrims who will come on the twelfth." We prayed.

"Dear children, I come so that all hearts will be reconciled to God through Holy Love. Please understand, My children, it is your conversion through Holy Love in the present moment which is the heel that crushes the head of the serpent. I come to you as the Woman Clothed in the Sun, the Woman of Revelations. Soon, very soon, all I have confided in secret, to this seer and many other seers, will be made known in the world and will take place just as I have predicted. These are serious times and require your serious efforts. Dear children I am blessing you."

March 1996

■ **March 6, 1996 / Weekly Rosary Service.** Our Lady is here as Our Lady of Guadalupe. She says: "I come in praise of Jesus My Son. I invite you to pray with Me tonight for all those who will come on the twelfth." We prayed.

"Dear children, tonight, I desire that you persevere in all your sacrifices and prayers during this penitential season. I come with this desire in My Heart, for if you pursue this trail, your hearts will be full of Holy Love; and when My Son returns, He will recognize you as His own. Dear children, it is through your efforts that My Immaculate Heart will come to reign in the world. I am blessing you with My Motherly Blessing."

■ **March 9, 1996.** Jesus says: "Because Holy Love is My Mother's Immaculate Heart and because My Mother's Heart is united to and never separated from My own Sacred Heart, please comprehend what I am to say. The call to live in Holy Love is a call to live in union with the Hearts of Jesus and Mary. Such an army of consecrated souls is the way the Eternal Father chooses to usher in the New Jerusalem. This army is the Missionary Servants of Holy Love."

■ **March 11, 1996.** When I entered the chapel for adoration, I saw Our Lady standing to the right of the Altar. I started to pray and Our Lady interrupted Me saying: "Sign yourself." (She has been telling me to pray the *Sign of the Cross* from the heart because it is a prayer.) As I made the *Sign of the Cross*, lights simultaneously appeared on Blessed Mother's forehead, over Her Heart, and on the palms of Her hands. As I was praying the Sorrowful Mysteries, I saw a lighted crown of thorns over Our Lady's head. During the fourth mystery I saw a lighted cross behind Her, and She was looking up to heaven with Her hands crossed over Her breast. During the fifth mystery I saw Her hands extend and lights on both palms again.

Then She spoke. "My daughter, today I come to reveal to you that the Holy Father holds in his heart a profound desire to honor Me, this humble Handmaid. I took part spiritually, physically, and emotionally in My Son's Passion. Though the nails did not pierce My flesh, I felt keenly their pain. So too, I felt the crown of thorns, the instruments of torture, and the agony in the garden. Mystically I died with My Jesus. The Holy Father wants to name Me Co-Redemptrix. He will make this Church Doctrine. Because the truth divides, this will divide hearts. Some will be unable to accept Me in this role. They will need to come deeper in My heart through a consecrated life to understand this. I will speak tomorrow about this. I bless you now."

■ **March 11, 1996.** Our Lady says, "My daughter, because the people have faithfully persevered in adverse weather, Jesus allows that My Image will be captured on film tomorrow. You must not make it known until the service is about to begin. It is important the people come to give honor and praise to Jesus and not for the sake of certain grace." She leaves.

■ **March 12, 1996.** From Our Lady: "Dear children, today I invite you to understand in your hearts that My Son's paschal mystery begins with His surrender to His passion and death. As My Jesus surrendered, so I, His Mother, surrendered to His passion. Dear children, as the Holy Father considers the title Co-Redemptrix on My behalf, I invite you to see that I suffer still as man and countries profane God's laws."

■ **March 12, 1996 / Monthly Message To All Nations.** Blessed Mother is here as Our Lady of Guadalupe. "I come in praise of Jesus, My Son."

"Dear children, I do not come to you so often to satisfy the curious and perform miracles so you will believe. I come to reconcile man to God and to make heaven and earth one in spirit. Through your 'yes' to Holy Love, My Son is glorified. Just as all nature is awakening and coming to life in this season, I come to awaken hearts and bring faith, hope, and love alive again in the world."

"Dear children I encourage you to let your hearts be flooded with Holy Love and melted, just as your countenance is warmed by the sun today. I come to ask your cooperation in making atonement to Our United Hearts for sins perpetrated against life. I desire your Communions in reparation for these sins. Open your hearts, My dear children, and turn them towards heaven, like buds opening in the sun."

"I desire you understand that the fullest meaning of the United Hearts of Jesus and Mary is expressed in this newest and most cherished title the Holy Father will bestow upon His Humble Servant. It is because Our Hearts are spiritually one that I am Co-Redemptrix. Just as I supported My Son in His suffering, I desire My children depend upon Me in the midst of every adversity. Do not despise your crosses, but see that they are the embrace of Holy Grace for souls. Holy and Divine Love were united on Calvary, just as they will be united in the New Jerusalem."

"I am leaving here My peace on this property to be felt always by those who come. Dear children, I am blessing you."

■ **March 14, 1996.** From Our Lady: "My daughter, the hour has come - the hour of My great predilection. The hour you have hoped for, prayed for, and impatiently awaited. It is here. My presence and My grace will bear manifold fruits in the hearts of those who come. Do not be surprised at the depth and magnitude of My grace. This is a latter day ministry. It will, through Our United Hearts, usher in the New Jerusalem. Jesus ordains great and plentiful consolations to His people through Me on this Our prayer site."

■ **March 14, 1996 / Weekly Rosary Service.** Our Lady is here as Our Lady of Guadalupe. She is here with many angels. She says: "My children let us pray now for all the unbelievers." We prayed. "Dear children, I desire that you lead consecrated lives in the present moment so that I can take your prayers on the wings of angels to heaven and use them to bring souls to My Son. Sometimes you are letting Satan toss you about like a leaf on the wind. Keep your hearts centered on Holy Love. I am with you and I am blessing you."

■ **March 15, 1996.** Jesus appeared in front of me with His Heart exposed. Inside His Heart was Mary's Immaculate Heart. He said: "I desire the devotion to the United Hearts be propagated. Satan opposes this Image, for he sees in it a power he cannot vanquish. My provision is upon those who venerate this Image, contemplating its meaning. In the United Hearts is the embodiment of the meaning Co-Redemptrix."

■ **March 17, 1996.** From Our Lady: "Let them know that veneration and meditation upon the United Hearts of Jesus and Mary brings God's fullest provision to their midst. It will be important to have this Image in a prominent place at our new site so that My children can pray in front of it. Make it known."

■ **March 21, 1996 / Weekly Rosary Service.** Our Lady is here in gray. She says: "Pray with Me now for those who will come in pilgrimage to our prayer site." We prayed.

"Dear children, I desire that you surrender the present moment to the Will of God which is always Holy Love. Allow Holy Love to illuminate your souls so that every iniquity is laid bare. In this way, the path of holiness is enlightened through My grace of Holy Love."

Jesus is now standing to the right of Blessed Mother. They both have Their Hearts exposed. Blessed Mother now says: "Tonight, for the first time, We send upon earth Our Blessing of the United Hearts."

■ **March 22, 1996.**
The Blessing Of The United Hearts *(Part 1)*
Jesus says: "I am very glad you have returned (to adoration). I have long desired to share with you what I am about to say. For all time, I have wished to bestow this *Blessing of the United Hearts*, but it has been reserved for these times and to begin here in this mission. I will bestow it liberally upon those who attend the rosary service.

1. It will gratify the most distant heart and bring them closer to Me.
2. It will strengthen spiritually and often physically. I will be coming quite often now with My Mother.
3. This Blessing of Our United Hearts is preparing mankind for My Second Coming."

"I have much more to tell you. I will withhold this until another time."

■ **March 23, 1996.**
The Blessing Of The United Hearts *(Part 2)*

Jesus says: "I welcome you once again. I have been waiting for you. I desire to inform everyone about this blessing. Instruct My missionaries to have an information leaflet printed with what I will give you concerning it. I will bestow this blessing liberally, but it cannot be passed from person to person as can My Mother's Special Blessing. My Mother will not give this blessing alone but only with Me by Her side.

4. The blessing carries with it special graces of healing both spiritual and physical. The blessing comes directly from Me in spiritual union with My Mother.

5. It will be a deterrent to Satan and bring with it disclosure of evil in hearts and in the world. It will draw everyone who receives it to a devotion of Our United Hearts."

"I tell you these things not in confidence but to be made known. As with any grace, it is a cooperation between man and God."

■ **March 23, 1996.** Our Lady is here in white with a gold crown on Her head. She says: "I offer you this opportunity, My daughter, to become a part of My Heart. This invitation I extend to all those who sanctify their free will through Holy Love. Please note I do not say come into the Refuge of My Heart, but I deepen the invitation by asking you to be a part of My Heart. Only those souls who surrender their wills completely to holiness are this close to Me. These consecrated, sanctified souls are a part of Me. We are united spiritually through Holy Love. This type of holiness fulfills and completes the Gospel message that My Son brought to earth. Each 'yes' glorifies My Son in the present and strengthens the remnant of the future. Make it known."

■ **March 24, 1996.** Jesus says: "I am speaking to you

concerning Our United Hearts for the sake of My Mother's humility which precludes Her from addressing so great an honor. The representation of the United Hearts in graphic form is a **symbol of Our spiritual Unity**. It represents the depth of Our union while on earth and in heaven. It is the United Hearts of Jesus and Mary that will come to reign victoriously over the New Jerusalem. The victory is already in Our Hearts and in all hearts that love. The victory will be in the world when all hearts are purified and transformed in Holy Love. No heart is so perfect in Holy Love as My Mother's Heart is perfect. Therefore, see that it is sin that stands in the way of your loving more perfectly for My Blessed Mother is free from sin."

"So too, any situation which destroys your peace, takes you away from Holy Love. Then see that Satan wants to destroy your peace. It is his goal. Do not let him succeed, but see him for what he is."

"How I long to embrace the most errant soul. All they need do is but turn to Me. I stand ready to forgive and to love."

■ **March 25, 1996 – Feast of the Annunciation.** Our Lady comes in gray. She says, "My daughter, write down what I have come to say. I come to you so often in gray, not because of pending war in the world, but because of the war taking place in hearts. It is a spiritual war. *(Ephesians 6)* I weep in sorrow for the ones who once answered My call, but have become tepid. I come to earth, but My children heed Me not. Complacency is a great enemy. Some believe they are saved and living My Message of Holy Love which I proclaim worldwide, but they hang onto unforgiveness, false humility, and pettiness. They make themselves like the Pharisees – all good and holy outside, but full of pride inside. When I said 'yes' on this feast day so long ago, it was a lifelong 'yes'. It was a moment to moment 'yes'. It was a 'yes' in My Heart that shone from the inside out. You must pray for the lukewarm. Pray that they begin to look into their own hearts, with Me, and through My grace. I will return later."

■ **March 26, 1996.** *(After Communion)* Jesus says, "The wounds of Our Hearts are apertures to grace – to mercy, to love and to understanding. No petition placed herein will be left unattended. Add this ejaculation at the end of the Chaplet of the United Hearts:"

> *"Holy and Sacred wounds of the United Hearts*
> *of Jesus and Mary, answer my prayer."*

■ **March 28, 1996.** Our Lady says, "My daughter, I am coming tonight not with the Scepter that rules over nations, but with My call to Holy Love which reigns in the hearts of those who will be saved. Tonight, once again, the Blessing of the United Hearts will be given."

■ **March 28, 1996 / Weekly Rosary Service.** Blessed Mother is here as Our Lady of Guadalupe and Her Heart is exposed. She says: "Pray with Me now, dear children, for those who through pride do not live My message." We prayed.

Now Jesus is standing next to Blessed Mother with His Sacred Heart exposed. Blessed Mother says: "I desire that you rejoice with Me as My mission in you and through you is about to begin and to end, through the Alpha and the Omega. Surrender all your crosses to Me, for these are the tools heaven uses to proceed with this mission. When My Son returns, it will be through the victory of Our United Hearts. See that My Heart is the Refuge that leads you to Divine Love and Divine Mercy."

Jesus says: "We are extending to you now the Blessing of Our United Hearts."

■ **March 30, 1996.** From Our Lady: "Dear children, I desire that you allow Holy Love to penetrate the pores of your soul. Then the sweet aroma of your sanctity will reach the throne of My Son in heaven, Who pleads constantly from the Father the grace of your salvation. My Son sends flowers of grace to every soul, but those unworthy souls who live farthest from salvation will receive the greatest grace. Offer the greatest sacrifices for those who reject salvation. I am blessing you amongst and in the midst of much grace."

■ **March 31, 1996.** Our Lady says: "These days, people are concerned with maintaining and protecting a certain caliber of life. But when My Son returns, it will not matter how youthful, rich, smart, or beautiful they are. The only attribute of value will be the Holy Love in hearts. Some think they are embracing crosses and offering them for sinners, when really God's Will is that they die to self and overcome these stumbling blocks. I speak of unforgiveness, volatile tempers, a sad spirit, fear, and the like. These are not crosses, but faults to be overcome with the help of My grace. Make it known."

■ **March 31, 1996.** Jesus says: "I desire that souls make this Way of the Cross part of their lives. I want them to meditate on My passion considering the United Hearts of Jesus and Mary and understanding My Mother's role as Co-Redemptrix."

STATIONS OF THE CROSS

1. **Jesus Is Condemned To Death**
   "Consider how Divine Love and Holy Love made Their Wills one with the Eternal Father. Imitate this resignation by accepting trials."

2. **Jesus Accepts His Cross**
   "Through the Divine Mercy of the Sacred Heart and the Holy Compassion of My Mother's Heart, I was able to courageously embrace the cross."

3. **Jesus Falls The First Time**
   "When you slip and fall into sin, My Mother, through Holy

Compassion, wraps you in Her mantle and leads you to My Divine Mercy which raises you up again."

4. Jesus Meets His Mother

"Our eyes met and Holy and Divine Love became one. It was Her prayer that enabled Me to go on. How often souls depend on Your prayers. Unite them to the Hearts of Jesus and Mary."

5. Simon Carries The Cross

"Consider the reluctancy of Simon to embrace the grace of the present moment. How often has the present moment escaped you? Too often, you see the cross and not the grace. Place the present moment in the grace of Our United Hearts. We will help you to see the 'why' behind every cross."

6. Veronica Wipes The Face Of Jesus

"Veronica was one with Holy Compassion and Holy Love. She was not fearful to step forward and comfort Me. I left with Her My mark of Divine Love. I desire all souls comfort Me in the tabernacles of the world."

7. Jesus Falls The Second Time

"Through My Divine Mercy - and led to Me through My Mother's Holy Compassion - I will forgive you as often as you fall."

8. Jesus Consoles The Women Of Jerusalem

"Seek the consolation of the Refuge of the Immaculate Heart of My Mother. She will lead you to the greatest consolation of all - spiritual union with My Heart."

9. Jesus Falls A Third Time

"Have you slipped away from Me again? I forgive you. I forgive you. I forgive you. I love you. I love you. I love you. Imitate Me."

10. Jesus Is Stripped Of His Garments

"If you are spiritually one with Our United Hearts, the world will hold no value for you. You will use the goods of the world to attain My end. My Mother gave Me Her veil when I had nothing. I ask you to give Me your heart and I will give you everything."

11. Jesus Is Nailed To The Cross

"My Mother's hands and feet were laid spiritually on top of My own. She suffered as I suffered, for love of sinners. I ask you to stand with Her now and support Her at the foot of the cross through sorrow for your sins."

12. Jesus Dies On The Cross

"I died with and for love of you. Divine Mercy and Divine Love are one. Holy Love and Holy Compassion are one. Die to yourself. Live for the United Hearts."

13. Jesus Is Taken Down From The Cross

"My Mother wept bitter tears as She embraced My broken body. Ask Her to embrace you in Her Heart of Holy Love. Then She will lead you to Me."

14. Jesus Is Laid In The Tomb

"I was laid in the tomb, but there is no end to My Love and Mercy. I rose again. Rise above sin through My Mother's Holy Love. Embrace eternity."

April 1996

■ **April 1, 1996.** "Our Lady comes in light blue with many sparkling lights around Her. She spreads Her hands and says: Today you see snow outside covering the buds that are about to burst forth giving life to the world. This is much like My mission in your heart. You have seen only a glimpse of

God's grace that will be made manifest soon to the public. Much has been clothed in the recesses of your heart and of Mine. But you will see beautiful signs of My presence soon on the property. These signal graces will not be shown just to you but to the public. Tell them to watch the sky - the sun - and even the air around them on the Twelfth of the month. By May, many graces will be given at the Spring as access will be made ready."

"My mission which has remained sequestered in your heart until this hour is now going into the world and amongst My pilgrims. Every preparation is complete in your heart. Paths and gateways in the world are opening through My grace. The mission is indeed ready to bud. You will see many things take place that will astound you."

"For today, I am blessing you in Holy Love."

■ **April 2, 1996.** Our Lady is here in blue with gold stars on Her mantle. She says: "I want you to tell My children this. You are living in a time of the last warnings. It is also the hour of great and manifold prodigies. As the tribulations increase in frequency and intensity, you will be given commensurate grace to come into the Refuge of My Immaculate Heart. You have not as yet received My greatest grace, nor have you experienced the greatest trial. You are living in the last days before My Son returns in glory. You have been given testimonies from around the world in support of this. Trials and grace come together to lead you into My Heart. Do not be tricked into thinking you have time to decide for holiness. You do not know the hour. Each present moment is grace."

"Miracles are beginning to unfold in this mission, not for your excitement, but for your conversion."

■ **April 2, 1996.** Our Lady comes in white. She has many palm leaves around Her. She says: "I am the Immaculate, Ever Virgin Mary. I come to inform you that the month of May will bring a myriad of graces to the ministry. The week prior to the Twelfth and following the 5th will be a particular season of blessings. This is by way of God's ordaining will and through My intercession and mediation. As yet you have not seen nor are you prepared for what is to come. My mission is poised and on the threshold of fruition in the world. Like Jonah, My words to you are going out to proclaim God's Justice is at hand. Like Isaiah, I tell you My prophecy in you will be fulfilled. Now you must be ready. The wait is over. Alleluia!" She leaves.

■ **April 2, 1996 / Weekly Rosary Service.** Our Lady is here as Our Lady of Guadalupe. She says: Pray with Me now for those who will come in pilgrimage on the twelfth." We prayed.

"Dear children, these are difficult times we find ourselves in. Do not seek your refuge and safety in the world, but come to My Heart where every gift, every grace, and all peace is present." Dear children, I seek your prayerful petitions on behalf of all nations. Evil is not readily apparent, but I tell you it is clothed in goodness and ever present. All nations are under attack. Dear children, I offer you the Refuge of My Heart; come to it. I love you. I am blessing you."

■ **April 3, 1996.** Our Lady comes in blue and gray. She has lights on the palms of Her hands, breast, and forehead. When I cross myself, these lights become brighter on Her. She says: "My angel, I am addressing all of My children. Each time I come, each person needs to study My words to see what I am saying to them personally. Do not scrutinize each other's spirituality, but your own. Never assume you are holy enough or that your conversion is over or complete. Your conversion is ongoing and in the present moment. I do not reveal future events to you so that you will assume a morose spirit but to deepen your conversion. A deep conversion touches the hearts of others and strengthens hearts around you. Do not feel overwhelmed by My call to you which is changing and increasing in and through My grace. Be ready to assume any posture or role for the sake of souls! Do not oppose Me through self-will, for to such a soul, I will not tender supportive grace. Everyday pray to be made more perfect in Holy Love. I am with you."

■ **April 11, 1996.** Our Lady comes in white. She says: "Today I invite you to turn to the Lord who is steadfast Love and Whose Kingdom shall reign forever. Submit to the rule of His majesty. Nations shall rise and fall under the auspices of His reign. Hearts will choose for or against salvation. But His Love is everlasting and His provision upon those who fear Him."

"I have not yet begun to show you My greatest miracles. Nor have you received My sternest warning or witnessed the most profound chastisement. Have faith in the path you have chosen. Gird yourself against Satan's cohorts through prayer and sacrifice. Equal is the time between the present moment, My greatest sign to you, and the New Jerusalem. You will make it known."

■ **April 11, 1996.** I see Our Lady descending some "heavenly" steps accompanied by some angels. She says: "I have come to tell you, My daughter, and help you to understand, that your country and most nations are spiritually impoverished. This is so, for nations follow the sophistication of free will over God's law. Free choice has become as a stone god. Free will has become, in many instances, an empty and hollow god - lending neither life to the spirit or to the body. All that opposes life robs souls of eternal joy."

"During these approaching summer months, you will see catastrophic events occur through man's heart and nature itself. God is attempting to show man that he is not an entity unto himself."

"I come to you offering the way of Holy Love which is the signpost along the way to My Heart. It is the path and the Refuge of My Heart. Learn to trust Me and to have faith in those consecrated to Me, for these are the ones I choose to act through. I multiply the efforts and prayers of these souls through My grace."

"This is not the hour to trust in the world or any 'safe refuge' given by human efforts. Depend on the Refuge of My Immaculate Heart which always loves and never changes. I want to immerse you in the Flame of My Heart until all iniquity is burned away. It is by your efforts and My grace you will be transformed." She leaves.

■ **April 11, 1996 / Weekly Rosary Service.** Our Lady is here as Our Lady of Guadalupe. She says: "All praise be to Jesus, Alleluia! Pray with me now for those who will come to our prayer site to pray tomorrow." We prayed. "Dear children, I come not to alarm you, but to bring you My Mother's Love and to tell you not to be afraid. When you are living in Holy Love, I have you by the hand and I am pressing you to My Immaculate Heart. It is through Holy Love you will be sanctified and led into the New Jerusalem. In this way, you will be ready and prepared for profound grace, for much tribulation, God's Justice, and finally His Second Coming. Dear children, allow My words to come alive in your heart now, in the present moment."

Jesus has now appeared to the right of Blessed Mother. His Sacred Heart is exposed. Jesus says: "We are extending to you tonight the Blessing of Our United Hearts."

■ **April 12, 1996 / Monthly Message To All Nations.** Blessed Mother is here as Our Lady of Guadalupe. There are deep pink roses around the edge of Her mantle, and there are hundreds of angels with Her. She says: "Dear children, pray with Me now for all leaders of countries who legislate against Holy Love and God's law." We prayed. "There is a great bear of a nation in the East whose leaders follow the Antichrist."

"Dear children, today I desire that all prayer groups designate the Twelfth of the month as days of prayer support of all life, for abortion is a sin which greatly grieves the Heart of My Divine Son. Dear children, today the United Hearts of Jesus and Mary take dominion over this property and this site of prayer. Do not come here seeking new messages, but begin to live the spirit of Holy Love. In your lives, let the United Hearts come to reign and take dominion over your families and your places of work."

"I invite you to return here on May 5th, My special Feast of Holy Love, where I will show certain signs and grant certain favors to individuals." Now Jesus is with Her. They are giving us The Blessing of the United Hearts.

■ **April 15, 1996.** Our Lady comes in white. There is a gold, sparkling light around Her. She says: "My daughter, I have come to tell you that I am drawing from the midst of this mission an army of victim souls. These chosen few will offer everything to Me in mind, body, and spirit. You yourself are the general of this army. This is a brigade of strength against the forces of evil. Your shield is the Cross; your weapons, prayer and sacrifice. These victim souls are the deciding force that will determine My victory in hearts and in the world. The souls, thus chosen by Me, must surrender to My call and to the Cross. Otherwise, I am unable to enlist their aid. This is an army that extends from region to region on earth and fills the confines of My Immaculate Heart in heaven. All of this you will make known."

■ **April 18, 1996.** Our Lady is here in two shades of blue. She says: "My daughter, you see much debris on this beach. I tell you there is much debris in souls as well. This debris is what holds the soul back from loving more perfectly. My Message of Holy Love is a universal call and one that cannot be compromised. To be sanctified through Holy Love is to obey all the commandments. It is the fulfillment of the law. This is why I tell you, it is impossible to be saved outside of Holy Love."

"Whatever obstructs the path to living most fully My call

to Holy Love needs to be washed away through the tide of self-surrender. When a soul clings to unforgiveness or guilt over past actions, his soul will lay shipwrecked on the rocks of imperfection. These things and many more are easily surrendered when pride is defeated. Pride has pirated many souls away from Me and into the eternal flames of Hell."

"My coming to you on the 5th will bring many to their knees. My mission has been building in you, but has only just begun." She leaves.

■ **April 18, 1996 / Weekly Rosary Service.** Our Lady is here in gray with Her Immaculate Heart exposed. She says: "Pray with Me now for all those who will journey to our prayer site." We prayed.

"Dear children, tonight I come to tell you that all the trials and tribulations that you are now experiencing will not reach into Eternity. They are all passing. All that is everlasting is the Holy Love in your hearts."

"Your country has ratified laws through hearts which are turbulent and do not love. This lack of love has grown like a cancer around the world. You must pray, My dear children, for you are the light. Pray that the light spreads into the darkness and snatches souls from the grasp of evil."

Jesus is now standing to the right of Blessed Mother and His Heart is exposed. Jesus says: "Tonight We extend to you the Blessing of Our United Hearts."

■ **April 20, 1996.** *(Maranatha Spring, Butternut Ridge Road)* "Our Lady comes in white. She listens as we pray. She has Her hands folded over Her chest. She says: "Tonight I extend My invitation to all nations to come to this site and partake of the message of Holy Love. This message is all-embracing, all-encompassing. The prodigies of grace extended here are proof and the fruits of My coming to you. I desire processions come in prayer to the Spring Heaven has given. I ask that you make these things known."

■ **April 21, 1996.** Our Lady comes in white. She spreads Her hands and exposes Her Heart. She says: "I am the Woman of the Apocalypse - the One Who is Clothed with the Sun - the Holy and Chaste Virgin Mary - Mother of Jesus the Christ."

"To all of My apostles I say, bring to Me the greatest triumph - souls, souls, souls. All the rest will be tendered through My grace. The more who come to the property, the more grace that will be extended. Pray on the property often for those who will come. It is a site of My predilection."

■ **April 22, 1996.** Jesus says: "I want a number placed on the information sheet so that those who are healed can call and give witness to My grace."

"The week of May 5th through the Twelfth will be a particular hour of grace and favor at Maranatha Spring."

■ **April 24, 1996.** Our Lady comes in gray and white. Her Immaculate Heart is exposed. She says: "My daughter, I come to you today as My Son sends Me, so that your nation and the world will understand that the abyss between heaven and earth grows greater minute by minute, day by day. It is within My Divine Son's power to destroy what mankind esteems-- power, money, status, and worldly goods. Mankind has seen this over and over through natural and manmade disasters, which the Almighty God has permitted." (Now She has tears rolling down Her cheeks.) "Yet hearts do not change. A great multitude do not love God and neighbor. That which rules hearts, then rules the world. Be certain that the world and each soul will be judged according to the love that is in each heart. Never before has humanity been more distant from God. Events take place each minute which give witness to this."

"Dearest children, I have come to plead that you choose love in the present moment. Do not worry over the past or be anxious for the future. Your salvation is here, now, in this present moment. Begin now to love. It is then I will take you into the Refuge of My Immaculate Heart."

Now She composes Herself, spreads Her hands, and looks towards heaven. She says to me: "You will please make this known to all of My little children." She leaves.

■ **April 25, 1996 / Weekly Rosary Service.** Our Lady is here in white with a blue border on Her mantle. She says: "All praise be to Jesus, Alleluia! Dear children, pray with me now for all those who will come to pray in the month of May at our prayer site." We prayed. "Dear children, tonight I come to you asking that when you pray, you surrender your heart to Me. Then I will give you My Heart, and Heaven and earth will be united. It is in this way, My dear, dear children, that your hearts will be transformed in Holy Love, and you will become worthy apostles." Jesus now appeared next to Blessed Mother. They both blessed us.

■ **April 26, 1996 - Feast of Our Lady of Good Counsel.** Our Lady comes in white. She says: "My daughter, I am here as your Mother and Counsel. All praise be to Jesus. Today I invite you to see that trust in My grace is the path of love and peace. To the untrusting soul, the way seems always fraught with danger. Every obstacle seems insurmountable. But for those that trust in My grace, the path moves steadily on despite uneven advantage, for grace diminishes problems and obstacles and makes the rough way smooth. It is the wise and prudent heart that does not accept an obstacle at face value, but waits for grace to transform the impossible into the possible. God's Provision is all-seeing, all-knowing. In every seeming defeat is hidden the grace of victory. The untrusting heart moves through life's journey much as an unbeliever - not waiting or relying on God's Good Grace."

"Pray with Me later. I am with you."

■ **April 29, 1996.** Our Lady is here as Our Lady of Lourdes. She says: "I tell you, My daughter, radiant as the sun will be the day of May 5th. The ministry which has suffered greatly at the hands of man, will be lifted up like a diadem in My crown. None shall leave empty-handed. This is the day of My exultation. Many who come in bondage will be released. The needy will be satisfied. The thirsty will have their palate quenched. It is the grace of the day that will launch My mission in hearts and in the world. The multitude will prosper in the favor of My Heart."

■ **April 30, 1996 / Weekly Rosary Service.** Our Lady is here as Our Lady of Guadalupe. She says: "I come in praise of Jesus, My Son. Praise be to Jesus, born Incarnate. Dear children, pray with Me now for all the intentions that will be in hearts on May 5th *(Second Anniversary of Our Lady's Feast of Holy Love)."* We prayed. "Dear children, tonight I ask you to make your hearts like rainbows, reflecting the goodness of the presence of God in the world around you and the promise of salvation through Holy Love. I am reserving May 5th as My special day of grace and Heaven's gift to you. It is in My Heart. It is under My mantle of protection. Tonight I am blessing you with My Blessing of Holy Love."

May 1996

■ **May 1, 1996.** Jesus says: "No one is coming to this site of favor on Sunday who will leave empty-handed. Those, who do not see, will feel. Those, who do not feel, will see. Do not fear for loss of reputation amongst unbelievers. My apostles suffered similarly. Let your life be a testimony to My Mother's mission in you. I will not leave you forsaken."

■ **May 4, 1996.** Our Lady is here in gold and white. She has on a gold mantle and Her heart is exposed. She says: "I am glad to see you are holding up well and anticipating a grace-filled day tomorrow, as I will be with you."

"Let us pray now for all those who are making pilgrimage to our prayer site." She says: "Dear children, just as each soul that is coming tomorrow is different, so each grace will be individualized and personalized for everyone there. Do not anticipate that you will receive this or that grace, gift, or healing. I desire that you make this known. Each one will receive according to God's Will, and what is given or withheld is best towards the salvation of each soul."

"I am coming to speak to the world from this site; and therefore, you must not mind the notoriety which is My jewel and My way of communicating with the multitude."

"Tonight I am blessing you with My Motherly Blessing."

■ **May 5, 1996 - Feast of Holy Love.** *(This message was given in multiple parts.)* Blessed Mother is here in white, the lining of Her mantle is gold, and She has a pink sash around Her waist. Our Lady says: "All praise be to Jesus, dear children. Please pray with Me now for all those who do not have love in their hearts." We prayed.

"It is important that you know, My children, that when My Son returns, the world will be judged according to what is in hearts. Therefore, know and understand, that hearts which are not clothed in Holy Love call down God's justice upon themselves and the entire world. You do not know when you will face My Son. Therefore, you must see, much depends on your choice for Holy Love in the present moment."

"See that Satan gains his foothold in any part of you not surrendered to Holy Love."

"Every moment you do not love is lost forever, while the moments given over to Holy Love follow you into eternity. Those souls who surrender completely to Holy Love in this life will be seated at the foot of My throne in eternity."

"Sadly, I tell you today, that the world has lost its innocence. Earth is filling up with the blood of the unborn. Satan has woven a web of complacency and compromise which has ensnared many. But My coming to you is the key and the way out of Satan's snare. I plead that the world corrects its conscience through Holy Love, for this is the way back to God. Love God and love your neighbor enough to choose good over evil in every circumstance of life."

"Greater than the miracle of My coming to you is the miracle of My Son's Real Presence in the Holy Eucharist. Adore Him. Worship Him. Do not let His Presence amongst you go unattended."

"Further, I come to ask all those who oppose the Holy Father to humble themselves and return to the flock He shepherds. My children, be united in the Hearts of Jesus and Mary through love - Holy Love.

"Dear children, I come to you today because you believe. This morning you had the sun. Now you have clouds. In your soul you have light on the path of holiness when you love. When you sin, you are taken off the path of light and led into darkness. I desire, My dear children, that you make My message of Holy Love known to the nation and the world."

Now Jesus is standing next to Blessed Mother. They both bless all here with Their Blessing of the United Hearts.

■ **May 6, 1996.** Blessed Mother stated to Maureen the following: "The reason I come, the reason you must make clear, is that so many souls have lost their way and I have come to lead them back on the path of salvation. The way Jesus has given Me is Holy Love, which He taught when He was on earth. I am preparing souls for My Son's return, and I am leading them into the New Jerusalem."

"My Heart is the Gateway to the New Jerusalem. It is important that My message be made known."

"Further, the graces that Jesus desires I distribute amongst you at this time are the Scapular of the United Hearts, the Chaplet of the United Hearts. And together, Jesus and I will distribute the Blessing of the United Hearts. For it is through the United Hearts of Jesus and Mary, the New Jerusalem will arrive.

Thousands flock to see Virgin

BELIEVERS FLOCKING TO SEE HOLY VISION

MARY'S MESSAGES

Believers, skeptics flock to field in Eaton

Throngs pray to Mary, claim to see apparition

Eaton Twp. 'apparition' site draws hundreds

The fascination of the Virgin

Virgin, Jesus, saints reported to appear at Lorain shrine

Vision on the ridge

An estimated 6,000 pilgrims came to the Eaton Township prayer site
and braved ankle-deep mud to be present for a promised apparition
of Our Lady on May 5, 1996 - The Feast of Holy Love

■ **May 7, 1996.** "I am Mary, Ever-Virgin, Mother of Jesus." Our Lady comes in white with a purple border on Her mantle. She says: "I desire that you make arrangements to have Me come to you at an undisclosed location. I will still be present to the people in the Field of the United Hearts. All present will receive the Blessing of Our United Hearts. Grace allows all things."

"Your whereabouts must not be revealed. I am protecting you from the public eye during our most intimate times."

"You can grant certain ones interviews only if they agree to publish My message in its entirety. God has sent Me to speak to the world. This needs to be the focus. They are losing sight of this."

■ **May 9, 1996.** *(a.m.)* Our Lady is here in white. She has a rosary in Her right hand made out of little white flowers. She says: "My daughter, tell My children this -- My message today is the same as it has been over the centuries. Do whatever My Son tells you to do. My Son is calling you to choose to love in the present moment. When you love God with your whole heart and your neighbor as yourself, you are putting on the armor of holiness. Today, the battle is not between right and wrong according to individual consciences, but between good and evil. The choice you make in your heart to love or not to love affects every balance and counterbalance in nature, and indeed, in the entire cosmos. You do not see that little flaws in the love in your hearts are important. But to God, every effort you make towards your personal holiness brings earth closer to Heaven. When My Son returns, Heaven and earth will be united. Therefore, see that My triumph is your triumph as well." She leaves.

■ **May 9, 1996 / Weekly Rosary Service.** Our Lady is here in white. Her Immaculate Heart is exposed. She says: "Pray with me now for all those who are coming on pilgrimage on Sunday." We prayed. "Dear children, tonight I have come to ask that you realize I do not come for your excitement or your amazement or even to bring you a new message. My Message to you remains the same – Holy Love in the present moment. Dear children, I desire so much that you become apostles of My Message. (Blessed Mother mentions Jonah Chapter 3). Commit your lives to spreading My Message of Holy Love wherever you go. I am anxious to meet with you on Sunday. (Monthly Rosary Service, held on the 12th of each month in Commemoration of the Feast Day of Our Lady of Guadalupe – as Blessed Mother requested.) I am blessing you."

Read Jonah Chapter 3

■ **May 10, 1996.** Jesus says: "I am your Jesus born Incarnate. The fruits of the Holy Spirit are the same as the fruits of Holy Love - gentleness, kindness, peace, love, joy, patience, and humility. All of these need to shine through each of you as you work on earth for Heaven. You must not abandon the spirit of the Message during this hour of favor."

"Satan wants to divide you so that he can be in charge. Make My Message known to My chosen instruments."

■ **May 12, 1996 / Monthly Message To All Nations.** *(The following message was given in two parts due to its length.)* Our Lady is already in the chapel when I (Maureen) get(s) there. She is dressed in a gold mantle, white gown, and has a sparkling crown over Her head. She says: "I am Mary, Queen of Heaven and Earth, Comfortress of the Afflicted. All praise be to Jesus. My child, understand and make it known that My Spring is not given for those who thirst physically, but for those who thirst spiritually. It is not given because of physical properties, but because it is endowed with supernatural grace. For those in the world, this is difficult to comprehend."

"My coming to you is not to enrich the world with beauty and make it physically secure, but to change hearts and lead souls into the New Jerusalem through the Gateway of My

Heart. Your liberation is not in any physical attribute, but in your conversion through Holy Love. My Son did not lead great armies when He was in the world, but He freed people from the captivity of sin."

"Today, He sends Me to show the way of salvation through Holy Love. The Holy Love army is in hearts. Every heart that chooses Holy Love changes the world and brings earth closer to heaven."

"Today, the world is choosing death over life. I speak not only of abortion and euthanasia, but more poignantly of perdition over salvation."

"You must pray for those who will die sudden and unprovided deaths. So many are unprepared to meet My Son - so many." She is crying now. "Pray for those who oppose Me in the world. I come most especially for them. These are the ones who do not grasp the urgency of the hour. They have been caught up in Satan's lies."

"Always trust in My grace to precede and surround all situations in this mission. This is the hour that all nations will gather at Maranatha Spring. I am blessing you."

Our Lady is here as Our Lady of Guadalupe. She says: "Am I not here, I who am your Mother. Pray with Me now for all those who come here without love in their hearts. Dear children, I call you today into the compassion of My Heart. The fullness of My Grace is present amongst you. Tell man of earth he need not search for anything in the water of Maranatha Spring save My grace. Here I am ready to heal, to convert, and to reconcile. My children must be reconciled with God. You must mend your lives, dear children, and return to the ways of Holy Love. I desire to present you to My Son with hearts that are full of love." Jesus and Mary now extend the Blessing of the United Hearts to all present.

■ **May 16, 1996.** From Our Lady: "This is not a replacement for the Sacrament of Baptism, but a special blessing from the Holy Trinity. It is protection and a sign of predestination."

Spiritual Baptism Of The Unborn

"Almighty God, Father, Son, and Holy Spirit, Your Power and Grace transcends all time and space. Cast now Your compassionate glance upon all life in the womb from the moment of conception until the moment of birth. Caress these innocent souls in Your Merciful Love. Protect this life from any marauder. Bestow upon each soul You create a spiritual baptism, in Your Name, Father, Son, and Holy Spirit. Amen."

■ **May 16, 1996 / Weekly Rosary Service.** Blessed Mother is here in white. Her Immaculate Heart is exposed. She says: "All praise, honor, and glory to Jesus, the Risen Lord. Pray with Me now, for all those who will come to our Prayer Site (Maranatha Spring)." We prayed. "Dear children, come to me; abide in me. Do not allow any fear to overtake you. Remain in peace, in love, in joy."

"Dear children, I desire that you fill the world with Holy Love, which is the announcement of My Son's return and the fulfillment of the Gospel message. Tonight I am blessing you with My Blessing of Holy Love."

■ **May 17, 1996.** Jesus says: "My domain is in hearts that love. Let free will be sanctified and made holy through Holy Love. Then My Divine Will and the New Jerusalem will be accomplished."

■ **May 18, 1996.** Our Lady comes in white with Her Immaculate Heart exposed. She says: "Pray with Me now for all those who do not believe."

"My daughter, you do not mind all the probing of the media?"

"I do mind, but I do it for you and to get the message out."

"More are on their way. If they put the question to you, 'why the miracles,' tell them it is the same as in Jesus' day. Why did He perform miracles? To draw unbelievers to the truth. Still, some believed in Him and others believed only for a while. It is no different today and in these times. The signs and miracles will not stop for the sake of those who scrutinize them. No, child, they are increasing, for I am really there. Indeed, My compassion shows forth on those who come. The faith of those who already believe will intensify. The media will see signs and specific happenings themselves if they persevere. Do not fear for what is ahead. My grace is already attending to these matters."

"My greatest grace is yet to come both on our property and in hearts. No impediment nor will of man will forestall it and you will be witness to what is to come. The choice for Holy Love is not an invitation, but a dictate commanded by My Son in His ministry on earth. I only come as He allows to remain and to expand this greatest of all commandments.

Encapsulated in the greatness of the commandment is the greatness of your mission. So too, is the expanse of My call to you. Come to realize, I am not in your midst only as one in a number of apparitions, but as a salvific call to all humanity which treads upon the brink of calamity. It is man himself who is teasing God's patience and coaxing His justice. I come to set myself against the eternal adversary and to release humanity from his evil grip. Therefore, do not be surprised that you are opposed for you are My representative. Persevere. Satan cannot penetrate the fortress of My Heart."

"Dear apostle, I am blessing you."

■ **May 20, 1996.** Our Lady comes in white. There is a gold cross at the top of Her mantle, and there are many gold crosses in the background behind Her. She says: "I tell you, My angel, it is not by happenstance I come to you. I come because of your inadequacies. Jesus allowed Me to choose you and your lack of knowledge concerning church doctrine and spiritual matters at this particular time in history. Since your background does not reflect previous knowledge of the Holy Love message, it is most obvious that the message comes from an outside source - mainly heaven."

"Tell the people that I have come to stop wars in Hearts." (Now I see there is a gold cross at Her throat as well, and as She says this, it seems to pulsate and move towards me.) "Presently, hearts are agitated and lack peace because they do not love. This is a very real sign of Satan's presence in the world. War that is conceived in hearts soon becomes manifest in the world. If people do not pray and hearts do not change, the world will find itself plunged into a deadly war. This war would be like no other. It would upset certain checks and balances in nature itself. My children do not like to be faced with such stark reality. Tell them I come as My Heart bleeds with love for each soul. I desire that My children avert these tragedies. I am giving you the way out through prayer, sacrifice, and Holy Love. Therefore, see that I bring to you a message not of gloom and doom, but one of hope."

She leaves. All the crosses are left in the air momentarily.

■ **May 21, 1996.** From Our Lady: "I am coming to you today as always to restore peace to hearts. This is for the welfare of each soul and of the world. My Son does not judge the exterior but the heart. Everything that merits you a better life in the world is temporary; only the love in your heart is eternal. Do not seek consolation through the world but in the solemn refuge of My Heart."

■ **May 23, 1996 / Weekly Rosary Service.** Blessed Mother is here as Our Lady of Guadalupe. Our Lady's heart is exposed. She says: "I continue to come to you giving praise to Jesus. Let us pray now, for all those who will come to our prayer site." We prayed. When Blessed Mother was praying the *Glory Be*, as She always does, Her arms are extended out to Her sides and Her palms open towards Heaven. A great light shines down upon Her. This time many pink rose petals fall from above Her into Her hands. Then I saw Maranatha Spring at Blessed Mother's feet. She then let the rose petals or graces fall all around the Spring. (Rose petals signify grace.)

"Dear children, just as John the Baptist used the waters of the Jordan to prepare My children for Jesus' public ministry, so now I am using the waters of Maranatha Spring to prepare you (the world) for His Second Coming."

■ **May 23, 1996.** Our Lady is here in white with a gold crown on Her head. She says: "I offer you this opportunity, My daughter, to become a part of My Heart. This invitation I extend to all those who sanctify their free will through Holy Love. Please note I do not say come into the Refuge of My Heart, but I deepen the invitation by asking you to be a part of My Heart. Only those souls who surrender their wills completely to holiness are this close to Me. These consecrated, sanctified souls are a part of Me. We are united spiritually through Holy Love. This type of holiness fulfills and completes the Gospel message that My Son brought to earth. Each 'yes' glorifies My Son in the present and strengthens the remnant of the future. Make it known."

■ **May 30, 1996 / Weekly Rosary Service.** Our Lady is here as Our Lady of Guadalupe. She has a crown of lights over Her head. She says: "All praise be to Jesus. Pray with Me now, dear children, for all those who will come to our Prayer Site." We prayed. "Dear children, tonight once again, I place My message of Holy Love in your hearts, so that in you Heaven and earth will be united. Open your hearts, dear children, as roses in the sun and know that I am with you with My Grace. I desire that you live each moment in Holy Love and see that each present moment is a new opportunity to love. Tonight, I am blessing you with My Motherly Blessing."

■ **May 31, 1996.** "My angel, it is not long until My Son returns. I desire My children prepare their hearts through Holy Love. Just as My Beloved Son is Divine Love, so I am Holy Love. My army of consecrated souls, whom I am forming, will crush the head of the serpent. But, My children must realize that their consecration needs to be rooted in Holy Love. All their actions, prayers, and good deeds must embrace Holy Love. Otherwise, they are superficial. Holy Love makes all thoughts, words and deeds worthy in the eyes of God. It is thus I am able to oppose Satan. It is through Holy Love in your hearts I will be victorious. You must make it known."

■ **May 31, 1996.** Our Lady comes in white. She says: "My triumph began when I was Immaculately Conceived. It continued in My consent to Holy Love. It will climax when all hearts live in Holy Love. Holy Love is a pure and refreshing spring of grace all must drink from – in praise of Jesus."

June 1996

■ **June 6, 1996 / Weekly Rosary Service.** Both Jesus and Blessed Mother are here. Our Lady is to Jesus' left and both of Their Hearts are exposed (Sacred Heart and Immaculate Heart). Blessed Mother says: "All praise be to Jesus." Then Jesus says: "Pray with Us now for those who do not live the Holy Love message." We prayed. Now Jesus is speaking.

He says: "Lose yourself in the present moment, and see what a treasure you have. Those who do not gather with Me scatter."

Blessed Mother now speaks and says: "Live the Holy Love Message and let all your actions be sanctified through Holy Love. To choose an alternate course is to choose evil. I come as always to bring you into My Heart, My dear children."

Now, both Jesus and Blessed Mother extend to all here the Blessing of the United Hearts.

■ **June 8, 1996.** Our Lady comes in blue and a cream color. She says: "Oh, My daughter, I come to you sorrowing and yet joyful. I am thankful for the pro-life bill your governor saw to completion. For here it is in law. There is life - it is a child from the moment of conception. Yet I sorrow for those who continue to support abortion. What hypocrisy! What a lie! How can it be life in one instance and unwanted tissue in the next? Mankind must cease worshiping his free will. That is My prayer."

"I need to strengthen My army of consecrated souls. These are the ones who surrender to Me their past, present, and future. Promote the consecration to the Flame of My Heart by printing it on a prayer card. The core of this mission is comprised of My generals. I ask that you promote this! Promote this! Promote this!"

"I am with you even in the darkest moment. Satan will not succeed in his attacks. I am blessing you."

■ **June 8, 1996.** Our Lady comes in white. She says: "Praise be to Jesus, born Incarnate. My Heart is the dawn of the new Heaven and new earth. Let the old pass away and come to the fullness of the present moment where I await you. Put on your new creation in Holy Love."

■ **June 12, 1996 / Monthly Message To All Nations.** *(The following message was given in two parts due to its length.)* Our Lady is here in a white gown and a blue veil. She says: "Praise be to Jesus, My angel. Please transcribe these words for the people tomorrow."

"Dear children, I come today as always for your welfare and the sanctification of your hearts. Make of your hearts a holy nation dedicated and consecrated to Holy Love. When God's justice comes, it will come through the human will - the human heart. It is necessary that you see that the welfare and future of the world is decided in your hearts in the present moment. My message of Holy Love comes to bring God in the midst of hearts and hearts in the midst of God. You have not chosen salvation if you do not choose Holy Love, for no one enters without love in their hearts."

"God's kingdom and My victory begin in you when you choose love. Love is truth and life. Love is the way. Do not compromise your salvation through self-seeking, but fill the warehouse of your hearts with Holy Love."

"I invite you to make of your hearts flames of Holy Love, igniting the hearts of those around you with this, the eternal virtue. It is thus I can convert the world through you and by your efforts."

2) Blessed Mother is here as Our Lady of Guadalupe. She says: "I come in praise of Jesus, My Son, Redeemer of the world. Pray with Me now for those who oppose Holy Love."

"Dear children, the trials that you suffer can be surrendered for the conversion of the world. I have come today to prepare your hearts for My Son's return. You must understand, that evil is easily provoked in hearts that have not conformed to Holy Love. For these reasons, I tell you that natural disasters will continue to plague your country. Weather extremes will be the rule."

"You must pray, My children, that good overcomes evil in every heart." Jesus is now with Our Lady and they extend to all here the Blessing of the United Hearts.

■ **June 13, 1996.** Our Lady comes in blue and white with a crown of lights over Her head. She says: "I desire that you let your hearts be sanctified in Holy Love so that God's kingdom and My victory will take root in you. In this give praise to Jesus. I do not come so that you can choose holiness once and for all, but so that you continually choose holiness in the present moment. Do not see your will but the Holy and Divine Will of God. It is in this dying to self that you will find yourself. This is how to be at peace and free of all distraction. Do not place upon yourself the yoke of many decisions, for God's Will will be shown with the tincture of time. Therefore, be at peace. Let your heart be in Heaven." She leaves.

■ **June 13, 1996 / Weekly Rosary Service.** Our Lady is

here as Our Lady of Grace. There are also angels with Her. She says: "Pray with Me for all those who do not have love in their hearts." We prayed. "Dear children, I desire that you make of your hearts a burning oblation of Holy Love. Thus, your hearts will become as vigil lights – awaiting My Son's return – and offertories of Holy Love. Tonight I am blessing you with My Blessing of Holy Love."

■ **June 14, 1996 - Feast of the Sacred Heart.** Jesus says: "Come to the font of My Heart, the very marrow of which is My Love and My Mercy. Do not fear the arrows of sharp tongues, but immerse yourself in the fortress of trust that is My Mother's Heart, for it is by virtue and by means of Holy Trust I am drawing you ever deeper into My Sacred Heart."

■ **June 14, 1996 - Feast of the Sacred Heart.** Jesus says: "My Kingship is in every heart that lives in Holy Love. I am building up a Holy Nation, the foundation of which is Holy Love. Upon this foundation I will place My faith community. My Mother's mantle I will place over it as an atmosphere of protection and peace. You still await Heaven's greatest miracle."

■ **June 15, 1996 - Feast of the Immaculate Heart.** Our Lady appears in blue with Her Heart exposed. She is standing in and enveloped by the Sacred Heart of Jesus. She says: "I desire that the world surrender to and conform to the dictates of Holy Love so that Our Hearts may be victorious in the world. Little daughter, I come to give praise to Jesus. Yesterday, the news carried the story of a new surgery procedure, wherein, part of the heart was removed making it more functional. Today, I tell you, all hearts need to surrender to Holy Love, holding back no fraction or portion for themselves. This is the only way in which grave tragedy can be avoided. Those who cannot accept the Holy Father's infallibility on all matters of faith are living in the delusion of self-love which leads to perdition.

Those in authority mislead others when they cast shadows of doubt upon the Holy Father. It is important to know that faith is under attack. But I COME TO PROTECT YOUR FAITH."

"My Heart is the Refuge of all sinners. My Heart is the Gateway and the path that takes you to the Heart of My Son. It is impossible for you to remain in a state of peace without My protections. My Son has entrusted to My Heart the peace of the world. My Heart is Holy Love. Therefore, see and understand that the peace the world seeks and needs is encapsulated in My Holy Love message. It is for this reason Satan comes against you in unique ways. It is for this reason the adversary will not succeed. You must not fear any attack. You are already in My heart and I am in yours."

■ **June 16, 1996.** Our Lady comes in blue and white and with a crown on Her head. She says: "I am Mary, Mother of God and Queen of Heaven and earth. My reign has begun in hearts that embrace Holy Love. Therefore see, My daughter, that My victory has begun in you."

"Do not fear the tide of controversy that surrounds these apparitions. It is necessary that hearts be challenged so that they will change. Each time I come to you, more hearts are converted. God has not abandoned the errant nation of people who choose evil. No, rather, He mercifully ministers to their needs at Maranatha Spring. It is true, the choicest favors are yet to come, but the power of grace manifest on the property grows each minute."

"I am calling together a Holy Nation - a Holy People. One that will challenge Satan's kingdom in hearts and oppose evil in the world."

"The crowds will continue to grow on the Twelfth of the month. Surrender this day to Me and petition My support towards your physical stamina. Pray very much for those who will come. Let us pray now." We prayed. "Do not fear, but pray, pray, pray."

She leaves.

■ **June 20, 1996 / Weekly Rosary Service.** Blessed Mother is here in a silvery-white gown and Her Heart is exposed. There were many sparkling white lights all around Her. She says: "All praise be to Jesus, My little children. Let us pray now for all those who will come to our Prayer Site, most especially, for all those who do not love." We prayed.

"Dear children, tonight, once again I ask you to surrender to Me your heart. Presently, you are suffering much both in your hearts and in the world. I invite you to give up the grudges you hold against those who have hurt you. Then I can present your hearts to My Beloved Son full of Holy Love. In this way, He can use you as His instruments. Tonight I am extending to you My Blessing of Holy Love." She leaves.

■ **June 23, 1996.** Our Lady is here in blue and white and has a great light over Her, around Her and some even shines down on me. She says: "All praise be to Jesus, My angel. Today, I tell you, God's Will, His Mercy, and His Love are one and come to you and to the world through the corridor of Holy Love that is My Heart. I do not come to you for My merit but to take all souls back to God. His reign and kingship will be in all hearts in the New Jerusalem. It is then Our United Hearts will be triumphant and Satan's confusion defeated."

"It is difficult to bring souls into Holy Love that have their hearts implanted in the world. These are the ones that are self-seeking either after money, power, carnality, or intellectual prowess. Some of this, understand, My daughter, is necessary towards God's good end. But, the hearts I speak of have made gods of these things. It is necessary that God will shake humanity loose from these false gods through His loving Justice. He loves with such depth that He sends Me as precursor to reconcile souls to Himself through Holy Love. I cannot affect the choices in hearts without your efforts. Continue to pray and sacrifice much. What I have come to tell you will come to pass soon. Be at peace." She leaves.

■ **June 26, 1996.** I asked the Blessed Mother if the scapulars needed to be blessed. She answered me saying, "The graces attendant to the scapular come through the images of the Two Hearts when They are venerated. The priest's blessing does not change the graces promised, but brings with it the added grace of becoming a sacramental."

■ **June 27, 1996.** After Communion I had the following vision in My heart. Our Lady handed me a small earthenware bowl. She said: "Take this to Jesus, but be careful not to spill anything." I looked in the bowl and thought it was empty. When I got to Jesus, He said: "Thank you for giving Me this. You see the bowl as empty. The vessel is your trust. It looks to be empty because when you put all your problems in it they disappear. The more you put in it, the bigger the vessel of trust becomes. My Mother said to be careful not to spill anything for when you take your eyes off of trust, the problems reappear and come back to you."

■ **June 27, 1996 / Weekly Rosary Service.** Blessed Mother is here as Our Lady of Grace. She says: "Praise be to Jesus, My dear and faithful children. Pray with Me now for those who will come in pilgrimage to our Prayer Site." We prayed. "Dear children, My coming to you today, as always, is a grace. Days ago, years ago, I came to you by way of protecting your faith. Today I come to you calling you into the refuge of Holy Love that is My Heart. My title – 'Protectress of the Faith' – is the KEY to My Heart, but Holy Love is the PATH and the WAY. I desire, dear children, that you make your hearts temples of Holy Love, thus living in faith, love and joy, and spread peace wherever you go through My messages to you. Tonight, I am extending My Blessing of Holy Love."

July 1996

■ **July 2, 1996 - Feast of the Visitation.** Our Lady comes in a cream color. She says: "Praise be to Jesus, My angel. Take up your pen, that I may communicate with all of My children."

"Today, I come to you inviting you to understand that each time I visit you or any of My visionaries, all of the cosmos is affected. Just as My visit to My cousin Elizabeth impacted all generations and the entire universe, so My coming to you profoundly affects every heart, every nation, the whole world, and the heavenly bodies as well. I invite you to see the reason of My telling you this. If hearts accept My message, the world will be converted. Natural laws will be suspended. Wars will cease. All error will be stricken from hearts and so from the world. God's Justice will be altered according to the response to My call."

"In a similar way, if My words are not taken seriously, if hearts do not change, I will no longer be able to suspend God's

"I ask your prayers for those who hear My messages, that their hearts awaken to the truth."

"Pray, pray, pray."

■ **July 4, 1996 / Weekly Rosary Service.** Jesus and Blessed Mother are here. They both have their Hearts exposed. Our Lady says: "All praise be to Jesus."

Jesus says: "Pray with Us now for those who oppose this mission [Holy Love Apparitions and Message] in their hearts and in the world." We prayed.

Our Lady says: "Dear children, today, sadly I tell you, your country has chosen the path of error. Most do not abide in My love and in the Divine Love of My Beloved Son. You must pray for your government leaders, responsible for godless laws, who will be held in judgment for souls that are lost and lives that are lost."

"Dear children, I desire that you come here often and unite your hearts to My Son and My Own Immaculate Heart. Many are the graces I pour forth here [Maranatha Spring] in response to My call."

Now Jesus and Mary are giving us The Blessing of the United Hearts.

■ **July 6, 1996.** *(Belleville, Illinois)* Blessed Mother is here in blue and white. Her Immaculate Heart is exposed and Her hands are extended and open. There are white lights coming from Our Lady's Heart and hands. She says: "Praise be to Jesus, My little children. Thank you for coming tonight. I want to give you every grace from My Heart. I desire, My dear children, that you come to Me in your every need. Trust in Me as you would trust in any mother."

"Dear children, in the world you now have the season of Summer, and there is growth all around you. I desire, My dear children, that in your hearts you see that it is now the season of Holy Love. Sanctify yourselves in the present moment. I love you, My dear children. I want to take you to My Son made beautiful through love. "

Jesus is now with Our Lady. His Sacred Heart is exposed. They give to us the Blessing of the United Hearts.

■ **July 8, 1996.** Our Lady is here. She has on a blue gown and white veil and Her Immaculate Heart is exposed. She also has two angels that are bowed down at Her feet.

She says: "Dear children, I come to you tonight for your holiness and sanctification. I want to give you My grace, so that you will live My message of Holy Love more easily and more readily. Do not let My words to you stand still in your hearts, but let them come alive in the world around you!"

Blessed Mother now turns toward all the people here and says: "Tonight I impart to you My Blessing of Holy Love."

■ **July 9, 1996.** *(Blessed Sacrament Church, Belleville, Illinois)* Jesus and Blessed Mother are here. Jesus is in red and white. Our Lady is in blue and white and both of their Hearts are exposed.

Our Lady says: "All praise be to Jesus. Pray with Us now for the hearts of your government leaders." We prayed the

Our Father and *Glory Be.*

"Dear children, I come to lead you closer to My Son through My grace and by your efforts. It is not long until My Son returns. I invite you to see that the Blessing of the United Hearts yields wholeness wherever it is given. Dear children, it is through this Blessing the New Jerusalem will be ushered in and the entire world will be made new and whole."

Jesus and Blessed Mother now extend to all here the Blessing of the United Hearts.

Maureen giving a talk on Holy Love in Maryville, IL

■ **July 9, 1996.** Our Lady comes in white with sparkling lights all over Her mantle. She says to me: "Today I come seeking your perfection in holiness right now in the present moment. It is necessary that My children do not allow their hearts to be flooded with thoughts of the future. The future they foresee may never come. I come not to frighten or to confuse, but to ask that all My children pursue personal sanctity through the Holy Love message. It is true, too many have fallen from this path of light and that evil rules many hearts. But I come to you with the promise of My victory. I will crush the head of the serpent with the Holy Love in your hearts."

■ **July 11, 1996 / Weekly Rosary Service.** Our Lady is here as Our Lady of Grace. She has 30 - 40 angels with Her. She says: "All praise be to Jesus, My little ones. Pray with Me now, oh dear children, for those who oppose life." We prayed.

"Dear children, I desire much more than your fasts from food that you enjoy. I desire that you fast from any sin. In this way you will make recompense to the sorrowing and grieving Heart of My Beloved Son."

"Dear children, intensify and be extravagant in every sacrifice. I need your efforts so that Satan's works will be revealed in the world. Much evil is clothed in goodness. Tonight, I am imparting to you My Blessing of Holy Love."

■ **July 12, 1996 / Monthly Message To All Nations.** *(The following message was given in two parts due to its length. The two parts are interspersed.)* Jesus and Blessed Mother are both here. Their Hearts are exposed.

Our Lady says: "Praise be to Jesus. Please pray with Us for those who oppose life." We prayed.

I (Maureen) told Blessed Mother that there are many people here who would like to be healed and that they have many needs - physical, spiritual, and emotional.

She says: "Some will need to wait; others will find grace in this present moment. Still others are members of My army of victim souls. Let us pray together for all of these." We prayed.

"Dear child, please take down My words in praise of Jesus. I come to speak to all nations - all people. Today, in your country, a horrendous sin, that of partial birth abortion, is being considered as a viable law. Not only is this worse than Herod's slaughter of the innocents, it is a precedent for other nations to follow suit."

"My army of consecrated souls must be the voice crying in the desert. As children of Mary, you must make your voices heard above the din of complacent consciences. Satan could not have attempted such a blatant, godless law 10 years ago. But today, because righteousness lies dormant in hearts, his actions go almost unnoticed."

"Dear children, it is up to you to be My voice in the world. Bring the Ten Commandments alive again. They have not changed. Speak up for My Holy Love message. You must be My message in the world. We are outnumbered, and so you must pray for strength. My grace is your strength. My Heart will achieve victory in and through you. When you pursue My goals, My blessing is upon you."

Jesus says: "I desire that families venerate the picture of Our United Hearts, for in this is the grace to remain united and to become holy. Marriages that are thus consecrated to Our United Hearts will not dissolve. I am giving the grace today that souls will be moved in this direction. We will now give the people here The Blessing of Our United Hearts." They bless us and leave.

■ **July 18, 1996 / Weekly Rosary Service.** Blessed Mother is here. She is illuminated in a bright, white light and She has rays coming from Her hands and forehead. She also has a green lining on Her mantle. Our Lady says, "Praise be to Jesus, My little children. Pray with Me now for the strengthening and the extension of the faith in the world."

Jesus is now present to the left of Blessed Mother. They both have their Hearts exposed.

"Dear children, tonight I come to ask you to be the fiber of the remnant church. Pray for a strong faith, and I will give it to you through the graciousness of My Son. It is necessary that I come in these times to form this army of victim and consecrated souls who will strengthen the faith of the world. Tonight We are extending to you the Blessing of Our United Hearts."

■ **July 24, 1996.** *(Dayton, Ohio)* Our Lady comes with a light coming from Her Heart. She has on a white mantle and a pink gown. She says: "Dear children, pray with Me now for the success of My mission in the world through Holy Love." We prayed.

"Dear children, tonight, sadly I tell you that the darkness in many hearts is spilling out into the world, for Satan is trying to extinguish My Flame of Holy Love, which is the light on the path of salvation. I ask that you pray for My mission and that you strengthen it through your prayers and sacrifices and by spreading My message of Holy Love to others."

"Dear children, when you live My message, it becomes part of your heart, and your hearts are sanctified in the present moment. Tonight I extend to you My Blessing of Holy Love."

■ **July 25, 1996 / Weekly Rosary Service.** Blessed Mother is here as Our Lady of Guadalupe. She says, "All praise be to Jesus, Redeemer and King. Dear children, pray with Me now that the world will embrace My message of Holy Love."

"Dear children, you continue to see natural and man-made disasters and unprecedented events unfold in the world around you. Yet I come once again to remind you that if you embrace My message of Holy Love, which is the Refuge of My Heart, you will not fear. Dear children, tonight I am blessing you with My Blessing of Holy Love."

■ **July 26, 1996.** Jesus says: "My Mother's Heart is the embrace of Holy Love. Her call through you is to all humanity to come into that embrace."

■ **July 26, 1996.** Jesus says: "Today I extend an invitation to all nations and all people to meet Me and My Mother at Maranatha Spring. It is the hour of My Predilection. I am returning soon to claim what is Mine. I will not recognize the unloving heart. Nor will I recognize such a one in My kingdom."

"Holy Love in hearts can suspend certain cosmic events destined to occur. Through Holy Love, light can uncover darkness where it lies concealed in good. My Hand of Justice is withheld, waiting to see how hearts embrace Holy Love."

■ **July 26, 1996.** Our Lady comes in a mist in light blue and gray. She says: "Good morning, My angel. This morning you have come to Me and I have come to you."

"I desire, My daughter, that you most clearly understand that My appearances to you are all-encompassing. I do not come for a small or certain select group. I come to convert the world through Holy Love. No one, regardless of their beliefs, can see salvation outside of Holy Love. Holy Love combines the two great commandments into one. Thus you are able to see the primacy of My call."

"When hearts embrace Holy Love, evil is revealed both in the heart and in the world."

■ **July 27, 1996.** Our Lady came in dark blue and white. She said: "Pray, pray for the conversion of souls farthest from God." We prayed. She recomposed Herself. She said: "You must pray for these impoverished souls. They travel the road to perdition and do not realize it. "She shows me a vision of Hell. It is a sea of fire. Then She resumes speaking. "There is no love in Hell, My daughter, only wailing and gnashing of teeth for lack of love. Many fall into Hell for lack of someone to pray for them. But you have the key. You know the path. Now you must make it known. You must offer this salvific message to all who will listen." She leaves.

■ **July 28, 1996.**
The Blessing Of The United Hearts
Jesus says: "The Blessing of Our United Hearts is given each 12th of the month to increase and strengthen the remnant Church; to prepare the world for My Second Coming; to draw all people into the latter day ark of My Mother's Heart, which is Holy Love; and through the conversion of Holy Love, to reconcile hearts with God, thereby spanning the abyss between Heaven and earth."

■ **July 28, 1996.**

The Three Days Of Darkness –
General Illumination Of Conscience

I see Our Lady holding the Infant Jesus. She is in a purplish mantle, pink gown. The Baby is in white. Our Lady says: "I come in praise of Jesus, My Son."

"My daughter, I have prepared your heart in forewarning of My telling you these things. Today, most of humanity has chosen self over God and fellow man; death over life; hate over love. For the sake of man's free will, God has only intervened indirectly by sending Me into the world to admonish and call to conversion. My coming to you with this message of Holy Love is a last minute grace, which Heaven hopes will bring many to salvation."

"Today, as I speak to you, cosmic events are taking place. Patterns are being established and certain constellations choosing unforeseen paths. Through the evil in hearts these things are being permitted by God, who does not want to punish but who will not interfere."

"Man's final judgment of choice upon the world will bring about a collision of heavenly bodies. Your planet will swerve from its course. For three days natural laws will be suspended. Earth will be plunged into darkness - both in hearts and in the world. The good will be sustained through the Refuge of My Immaculate Heart and will not see unprovided death. But woe to those who walk the path of perdition. Some will die of fear. Others will take their own lives. "

"It is during this time that those consecrated to the Flame of My Immaculate Heart will be protected. These souls will be the light in the midst of darkness."

"There is no nation that can provide safe refuge during these three days, but My Heart will provide to those who are thus consecrated to Me."

"I do not come to frighten you. I come to show you the way around fear which is this Mother's Heart. I am so ready to shelter My children, to appease injustice, to protect the faith. Make this known."

August 1996

■ **August 1, 1996 / Weekly Rosary Service.** Blessed Mother is here. She has on a pink gown, a gray mantle, and a white veil over Her head. She also has a light coming from Her Heart. She says: "I come tonight to offer you My Heart and to take into My Heart all your concerns and burdens. Pray with Me for those who will come to this property in need."

"I desire that you come in procession to My shrine - to the site of My future shrine - on the 15th of August. Hasten to the grace of My Heart during these times. Dear children, tonight I invite you to understand that My coming to you does not mean that your heart is converted. The sign of your conversion is your living My message. Let this be your ransom from the captivity of sin. Dear children, tonight I am blessing you with My Blessing of Holy Love."

■ **August 4, 1996.** Jesus says: "I am calling souls to understand that the vine which thrives and does not wither is the one which is firmly planted in Holy Love (John 15). Seek not your way nor the way of the world, but realize the kingdom of God is within and it is Holy Love."

■ **August 8, 1996 / Weekly Rosary Service.** Our Lady's here in white. She is standing on a globe of the world. She says: "Pray with Me now, dear children, for all those who will make pilgrimage here on the 12th."

"Dear children, when you pray, you are giving Me strength to defeat Satan and all his works. When you sacrifice, you are distinguishing yourselves as My children. When you love, you are making the way clear for others to love. I encourage you in every aspect of your personal holiness."

"Dear children, tonight I extend to you My Blessing of Holy Love."

■ **August 12, 1996.** Jesus says: "My Provision is certain and complete. My Mother's Heart is the Gateway. My Heart is the Kingdom."

■ **August 12, 1996 / Monthly Message To All Nations.** *(The following message was given in two parts due to its length. The two parts are interspersed.)* Blessed Mother is here as Our Lady of Guadalupe. Her Heart is exposed. She says: "Dear children, pray with Me now for the conversion of all those present here today." After we prayed, Jesus appeared next to Blessed Mother. His Heart is also exposed.

"I have come to speak to all nations - to all people. Dear children, My coming to you is a grace. I do not come to make you holy. You yourselves must choose to be holy. I do not come to bring you peace. You yourselves must choose it. All you need to choose is Holy Love and all else will be added, for when you choose this love, you choose everything."

"I desire very much that apostolates and apparition sites do not oppose one another but, in Holy Love, assist each other in propagating My messages to the world. I do not come to different sites to bring rivalry or friction but, everywhere and each time, to draw My children into My Immaculate Heart which is Holy Love. It is Satan who wants to divide and bring conflict to your midst. Then you are confused and do not see the oneness of My call to you. Dear, dear children, it is not for you to take pride in My coming to this site or any other. Each site that My Son sends Me to is continually and always a site of grace for all people. I never leave any of the sites I visit, but am always present there. Therefore, do not believe one apparition is greater than another or that more grace is attendant to one than another."

"I come to you to bring reconciliation to the midst of your hearts, so that you will be reconciled to God and to each other. This - Holy Love - is the last hope of mankind."

"There is an unhealthy bond forming in the world that opposes My victory. God is not in the formation of this consolidation of powers. I am asking you to be aware and to come against this by your prayers and sacrifices. Comprehend that there is no order outside of Holy Love. There is no truth outside of Holy Love."

"Dear children, I come once again for your good. There is a time in the future when I will no longer come to you, and you will need to live according to My messages. When you pray, pray with hearts full of Holy Love; then My Son will be most attentive to your prayers."

"Countries need not hold summit meetings without Holy Love in their hearts, for they will not accomplish peace in arguments over borders and natural resources but only through reconciliation with God, their Creator. Then they will have peace in their hearts, peace in their countries, and peace in the world."

"Today, We (Jesus and Mary) are blessing you with Our Blessing of the United Hearts." When Jesus and Mary left, Their United Hearts were momentarily suspended in the air as sparkling lights."

■ **August 15, 1996 - Feast of the Assumption / Weekly Rosary Service.** *(NOTE: All here had processed with the Pilgrim Image of Our Lady of Guadalupe 1/2 mile to Maranatha Spring where the rosary continued. Blessed Mother floated above the Image during the procession. Once at Maranatha, the miracle of the sun occurred throughout the remainder of the Rosary (the sun danced and pulsated with many colors all around it).)*

Blessed Mother is here. She is in white with a golden belt and Her Heart is exposed. "I come in praise of Jesus, My dear little children. Pray with Me now, that the petitions of My Heart be granted through your intercession."

"Dear children just as your hearts have been flooded with this sunshine and this golden brilliance here tonight, I desire that the world be flooded with My message of Holy Love, so that each heart can recognize the grace in the immediacy of the present moment and live according to My Holy Love."

"Dear children, tonight I am blessing you with My Blessing of Holy Love."

■ **August 18, 1996.** "Our Lady is here in a periwinkle mantle and a rose-colored cincture. She says: "I come in praise of Jesus, My daughter, and as My Son so calls Me."

"I desire you make it known that I am continually present and awaiting all mankind at Maranatha Spring. It is here I will comfort and console those who come to Me. I desire, as My Son allows, to alleviate afflictions and render certain and untold grace. Ask My children to surrender their petitions to Me at the Spring. Design the entire area around our Spring as a heart. This way when the people draw close to the shrine, it will be representative of coming into Our United Hearts. You will be able to accomplish this through the use of different decorative stones. My daughter, the purpose of the property and of the entire mission in you is to draw My children into the Refuge of My Heart - through and in Holy Love. When they are in Holy Love, which is My Heart, they are also in the Heart of My Son."

"My victory begins in each soul that surrenders to Holy Love. I am blessing you."

■ **August 20, 1996.** Our Lady comes in shimmering white. She says: "My daughter, as I always come, I come to give praise to Jesus. I desire that those souls truly consecrated to the Flame of My Heart live as witnesses to My victory in their hearts. These are the ones that must draw others into this Purifying Flame, and so, into the Refuge of My Heart."

"Here are the steps to entering this Refuge."

1. "First, as with any conversion, the soul must choose to enter My Heart."

2. "Next, the soul must die to self, putting others and God ahead of himself. In so doing, the soul is living the Holy Love message."

3. "The soul needs to recognize that choosing and living this way makes him a target of attack. Satan places such souls under siege. Knowing this, the soul needs to persevere through much prayer and sacrifice. This is the 3rd step."

4. "All of My children, who choose, live, and persevere in being purified in the Flame of Holy Love that is the Refuge of My Heart, must practice living in the present moment. The fourth step is to trust in this solemn refuge in the present moment which embraces your salvation."

5. "The fifth step is all-encompassing of the other four steps. My dear children must pray for the grace to love God's Will. This is your choice, your living the Holy Love message, your perseverance, and your trust. God wants all of these things for you - in the present moment. God's Will is My Heart. God wills that you come into and abide in this Immaculate Refuge, a Refuge He has created for you."

"I desire all of My children know and understand this."

■ **August 22, 1996 / Weekly Rosary Service.** Our Lady's here in white, but it looked to be gold from the reflection of the sun. "I come in praise of Jesus, My Son, King and Redeemer. I desire that we pray now for all the needs of those here present."

"Dear children, tonight I invite you to understand that My coming to you is not only for your welfare but for the good of all people, all nations, the world, even the entire universe. My Son will yield a harvest of many souls from this property and by your efforts through prayer and sacrifice. In this way, I will take up reign in all hearts, just as I reign in Heaven beside My Son. So when I am victorious through your 'yes' to Holy Love in your heart, My Son, too, reigns in your heart with Me. Tonight I am blessing you with My Blessing of Holy Love."

■ **August 29, 1996 / Weekly Rosary Service.** Blessed Mother is here as Our Lady of Guadalupe. "I come in praise of Jesus, My Son. Pray with Me now for the intentions of all those here tonight."

"Dear children, tonight I come to you asking you to continue to persevere in perfecting yourselves in Holy Love. For it is through your personal holiness, My victory will come. It is here in the Field of the United Hearts that certain ones will be made to realize the proper path to follow and the course that I am leading souls. Dear children, direct souls into the Path and the Flame of Holy Love, which is the means of salvation given to the world. For it is only through Holy Love, salvation can be obtained. Tonight I am blessing you with My Motherly Blessing."

September 1996

■ **September 5, 1996.** Jesus says: "My Mercy and My Love are inseparable. Holy Love and Holy Compassion are inseparable. You need to always forgive and overlook each other's faults. Work on your own holiness. I call those who will serve. Remember, I do not call the perfect but the willing."

■ **September 5, 1996 / Weekly Rosary Service.** Blessed Mother is here as Our Lady of Guadalupe. She says, "All praise be to Jesus. My children, pray with Me now for those who must weather storms within and without." We prayed.

"Dear children, tonight you are not only in the Field of the United Hearts, but you are also with Me at the foot of Mt. Tepeyac with My little son, Juan Diego." Juan is now kneeling in front of Blessed Mother.

"The roses that I am giving you tonight are the graces that I place within your hearts, and the image that I give you is the Holy Love that I imprint upon your hearts. Please bear witness to all that is happening here (Maranatha). For I tell you, what you experience is real. Tonight I am blessing you with My Blessing of Holy Love."

■ **September 7, 1996.** From God, the Father: "Listen! From the beginning unto the end I Am Who Am. I call from the burning bush and from the peak of Sinai to love. None shall prevail against this message. The fiery pit is the absence of all love. Heaven is possessed by those who love. Heaven is love in its fullest. I sent My Son to bring love back into the world. Now My Son is sending His Mother."

■ **September 7, 1996.** Our Lady comes in blue. She has a brilliant white light coming from Her Heart and hands. She interrupts My Rosary saying: "Those most in need of mercy are those who do not love. My daughter, give praise to Jesus that He sends Me to you once again. Please open your heart to the understanding that each time I come to you or any other seer, it is to restore man's love for God and for his neighbor. Each one of My apparitions brings with it the underlying message of Holy Love. If you are persecuted or rejected in the world, it is a sign of frailty in hearts that do not embrace Holy Love completely."

"But do not fear being put to the test. It is then I am embracing you in My Immaculate Heart. Herein lies every answer and every proof of My coming to you. The ones who do not come to My Spring are not looking closely at My messages, but listening to human hearts which have given way to error. Pray that error is taken from hearts."

"Once again, I tell you that self-love stands in the way of Holy Love. It fills the heart with self and I cannot fit My Holy Love into such a one. This is why I say, Holy Love is a choice of free will. When this choice is made, the soul must make a conscious effort to remove self and put God and neighbor in his heart."

"I leave you now in My peace, My love, My joy."

■ **September 8, 1996.** Our Lady comes in two shades of blue. I wish Her Happy Liturgical Birthday. She nods humbly. "Let us give all praise to Jesus, Who sends Me. I come to ask you, My daughter, to remain undaunted amidst the tide of controversy that is coming. My best messengers prefer the background but will step out on behalf of My message."

"These are the basics I ask for at this apparition site:
- Conversion through Holy Love.
- Those who are Catholic should support the tradition of faith handed down through this Pope.
- Prayer offered with loving hearts, which will bring about the victorious reign of the Hearts of Jesus and Mary.
- Fasting from your own will - that is emptying yourself of self-love. This can be a fast of bread and water, but the most important fast is to die to self. Then I will fill you with Holy Love."

■ **September 8, 1996.** Our Lady is here in a cream color and rose. She says: "Make it clear, My daughter, that I come to you preparing the world for My Son's return. I do not come to frighten but to prepare. I come to you out of love to draw humanity into love. Long-awaited has been the inner heart of humanity for what I bring - the ark of Holy Love. Not a place of safety in the world - but a Spiritual Refuge between Heaven and earth."

Maureen asked, "Are you the Mother of God?"
"I am Mary, Mother of Jesus Christ born Incarnate."

■ **September 10, 1996.** Our Lady comes as Our Lady of Fatima. She has a green light around Her, and She is holding a rosary. She says: "My angel, I come to you as always to announce the coming of My son. I desire that the people know that their faith and their prayers are important to Me. It is not a mistake that they are invited to pray with Me on our property. My coming to you is real. My grace is real. This grace, this sweet issuance of My Heart, is a foretaste of Heaven. When your rosaries change to gold, it is My sign to you that your prayer changes hearts and, so too, world events. When you are healed in any way, know that God has dominion over every situation in life. Indeed, the air, the earth, and the sea obey Him. God is measuring certain divine graces to be bestowed in particular on My prayer site that I share with you. In anticipation of this, and in thanksgiving for what has already been generously given, I ask you to assemble on the feast of the Holy Rosary (10/7/96) to pray with Me. Do me this honor and I will be with you. I am blessing you."

■ **September 12, 1996 / Monthly Message To All Nations.** *(The following message was given in two parts due to its length. The two parts are interspersed.)* Blessed Mother is here as Our Lady of Guadalupe. Her Heart is exposed. She says: "I come in praise of Jesus, My only begotten Son. Pray with Me now for all the petitions that are in hearts here today." We prayed.

Jesus is now here with Blessed Mother. His Heart is also exposed.

"I come to address all nations, all people in this hour of decision which weighs heavy in hearts, and so the world. Today, Satan's veil of confusion has fallen over hearts in this nation and many nations. My children - all of whom are called to salvation - are confusing freedom of choice with sin. I do not come to take away man's free will, but to beg your choice of good over evil. You will succeed in this if you choose to live in Holy Love. Through Holy Love you must see that the human embryo from the time of conception is a life that you are commanded to love. Consciences have fallen asleep under much misconception, and the toll on God's patience is great. You cannot hope to turn away God's wrath and break His commandments at the same time. My coming to you is to help you to choose. I have begged from My Son this grace. He awaits the change I come to seek in hearts."

"Too many are choosing not only to ignore Me, but to ignore the prophets of old who have foretold these times. [Blessed Mother suggested reading Daniel Chapter 12]. Do not forsake this last call, for I tell you when justice comes, many will pass from this world to the next in one moment. Then your choices will end - for eternity. Begin to love now."

"Dear children, when I appeared to the children at La Salette (France 1846), I was weeping for the sin that was committed in the world, the profanity of the Sabbath, and the profanity of My Son's name. But today, I come to you MUCH MORE YOUR SORROWING MOTHER and at the foot of the Cross. I ask you to consecrate your hearts and your lives to Holy Love. This Flame of Eternal Love that is My Immaculate Heart will lead you along the path of holiness. Your conversion is the beginning of the conversion of all mankind. Today We extend to you the Blessing of Our United Hearts."

Read Daniel 12

■ **September 14, 1996.** Our Lady comes in white with a crown over Her head. She says: "My angel, My messenger, please record My words for posterity. I come in praise of Jesus, My Son. He it is, who allows Me to transcend time and space."

"I come to you seeking devotion in the world to Our United Hearts. Begin a five day novena reciting this grace-filled chaplet of the United Hearts. Answers will be forth coming.

The greatest measure of My Heart has been reserved for these last days, through which I will transpose My Heart upon those who consecrate themselves to Me."

"Because this devotion is scripturally based, it belongs with the Rosary on the Feast of the Holy Rosary. Please ask the people to recite it. Establish this devotion in the world. My grace will assist you."

"Do Me this favor and My Heart will be unable to resist your petitions."

She leaves. United Hearts are in the air temporarily.

■ **September 18, 1996.** Our Lady comes in white. She says: "Today I invite you to live each moment as though it were your last moment on earth. The present moment is invaluable and cannot be retrieved once it is spent. You do not know from one moment to the next when My Son will return. How foolish then to lose the present to perishables that are passing. Build up a fortress of love in your heart that allurements and distractions cannot penetrate. My grace is always with you. I am blessing you."

■ **September 19, 1996 - Feast of Our Lady of La Salette / Weekly Rosary Service.** Our Lady's here in gray. Her Heart is exposed. She says, "I come in praise of Jesus, My Son, King and Redeemer. Let us pray now for the intentions in hearts here tonight."

"Dear children, many, many years ago I appeared in La Salette (France 1846) because of man's indifference towards God's laws. Today I come, once again, weeping (Blessed Mother is crying and the flowers around Her Heart have turned into thorns). My Heart is weeping tears of blood for the morbid sin of abortion that mankind has chosen to embrace. Your holiness in the present moment makes all the difference to Me. Believe in Me, as I believe in you. My regency begins in hearts that choose to love. Tonight I am extending to you My Motherly Blessing."

■ **September 21, 1996.** Our Lady comes with Her Heart exposed. She says: "You are experiencing the bitter-sweet days before My Son returns. Never before has the abyss between Heaven and earth grown so wide. Never before have hearts been so compromised by sin. But, as these last days unfold and the veil between Heaven and earth is lifted, you will experience God's Mercy and Love in unprecedented ways."

"Do not be surprised when I tell you My victory will come as a triumph of love. For My victory will unite every heart to Divine Love and Divine Mercy in Holy Love. In the New Jerusalem there will be no more impediments to love. God's Mercy will be confided to each heart to the fullest. All iniquity will be burned away through My Flame of Love. Spread this Holy Flame of Love wherever you go, My angel. For preceding these most important last days, it is mankind's only recourse towards reconciliation with God."

"I come to you as a Mother who loves you and understands all your frailties. It is because of your weaknesses I come. When you are weakest the Flame of My Heart will raise you up and support you. Remain close to Me as I am to you. I am blessing you."

■ **September 25, 1996.** Our Lady comes in white. She has many little hearts under Her mantle. She says: "Peace, My angel. I come to lead you deeper into the mystery of the United Hearts of Jesus and Mary. You see these hearts which are covered under My mantle of protection. These are the ones devoted to and who promote devotion to Our United Hearts."

"In this devotion, I lead souls to see that Our Hearts are never separated but always joined spiritually. Our Hearts will not reign in the New Era of Peace side by side, but united and as one. My Son's Heart always holds supremacy over My Immaculate Heart. But in depicting Our Hearts as United, He shows the world that Divine Love is only approachable through Holy Love. Living in the divine Will is attainable by living in Holy Love. Therefore, it is mankind's 'yes' to Holy Love that unites him completely to God. The greater his commitment to holiness in this way, the deeper his union with God."

"Hearts that pursue this union are under My mantle of protection. My mantle remains around each one until he fails in love. In sin, My mantle is rent and the soul must by his efforts in love cover himself with it again. Especially protected are those who promote the Union of Our Hearts. I am blessing you."

■ **September 26, 1996.** *(THE DAY THE SENATE FAILED TO OVERTURN PRESIDENT CLINTON'S VETO OF THE MEASURE TO PREVENT THE PARTIAL BIRTH ABORTION PROCEDURE, MAUREEN RECEIVED THIS MESSAGE FROM JESUS; THE ONE FOLLOWING WAS GIVEN TO MAUREEN AT THE WEEKLY ROSARY SERVICE.)*

Jesus says: "Let this night of prayers (October 7, 1996 - 5:30 PM to midnight) be in atonement to the Hearts of Jesus and Mary."

"Today's page in history has been turned."

"NOT EVEN SODOM AND GOMORRAH TORE MY HEART IN SUCH A WAY."

■ **September 26, 1996 / Weekly Rosary Service.** Blessed Mother is here dressed in BLACK and She is crying. "I come to you in tears today, dear children, for I sorrow over the future of your country, which has been placed in peril due to wickedness in hearts. Pray with Me now for the legislators who endorsed this godless law today."

"Dear children, today I come to you pleading for the conversion of the heart of your nation, which has widened the abyss between Heaven and earth through this wicked legislation. Dear children, it is only by the merit of the Holy Love in your hearts, that I am able to withhold the arm of

Justice that My Son seeks to lower upon the world."

"Dear children, pray for the heart of your nation. I am blessing you."

October 1996

■ **October 3, 1996 / Weekly Rosary Service.** Our Lady comes in gray and white. She says: "I will speak now to My children. Dearest little children, tonight, once again, I come to ask you to re-commit your lives to Holy Love in the present moment."

"When you consecrate the present moment to Me in this way, you are allowing Me to use all your prayers and sacrifices to bring reconciliation between God and all people. Because humanity continues along the path of self-destruction, I invite you, in a special way, to join Me on the Feast of the Holy Rosary."

"Dear children, you are strongest when you pray. It is then you are calling My grace into hearts and into the world. Give Me your prayers, and I will give to you the strength of My grace. Tonight, as always, My benediction of Holy Love is upon you." She leaves.

■ **October 5, 1996.** Our Lady comes in gray and a cream color gown. She says: "I desire to make this known to all mankind. It is not long until every conscience will know his stance before God. In that moment of decision, My Son allows that a conflagration of Holy Love ignite in every heart. It will be through this Flame of Holy Love, each soul will be given the choice, most clearly, to choose righteousness. Then, the vessel of Mercy and Love that is My Son's Divine Heart will be overturned and spilled out on humanity as never before. This will be God's final effort towards consecrating erring hearts to the Heart of His Mother. Those who foolishly do not respond to this grace will be plunged into confusion and fear."

"But I am asking you to build up a warehouse of trust and faith in your hearts today, making of them a fortress against fear and doubt. Be stouthearted in the Lord. Do not wait for a crisis and then frantically cling to a weak faith you have little of. Pray to My Immaculate Heart. I, your Mother, want to increase your faith, your courage, and your perseverance. I am blessing you."

■ **October 7, 1996 - Feast of the Holy Rosary.** After Communion I had the following vision. I saw a rosary with a broken cord. The beads were slipping off the end of the cord and falling into space. Then the beads disappeared. I heard Our Lady say: "These are the Rosaries that you have time to say but never say."

Next, I saw a rosary with only a few beads on it. Our Lady said: "These are the Rosaries you say amongst great distraction."

Then I saw a full set of rosary beads. It was encircling the globe. Our Lady said: "These are the prayers you say from your heart. With them, I am able to convert sinners. I desire that you make your prayers global prayers. Pray for all sinners. This way I can bind all nations to My Immaculate Heart."

By this I knew in my heart She wanted me say the (revised) 'Father Gobbi prayer' at the beginning of the Rosary saying:

Father Gobbi Prayer
"Celestial Queen, with this Rosary I bind all sinners and all nations to Your Immaculate Heart."

■ **October 7, 1996 - Feast of the Holy Rosary.** *(At the prayer vigil early evening)* Our Lady is here as Our Lady of Guadalupe. "Dear children, tonight I come to you once again, imploring your prayers that man be reconciled with God. Satan wants to destroy every soul, church, and even the planet on which you live. But you can change this through your

Rosaries, your Eucharists, your Holy Hours of Reparation. I am counting on you My children to be Holy Love in the world and to make My words to you known. I extend to you My Motherly Blessing."

■ **October 7, 1996 - Feast of the Holy Rosary.** *(At the prayer vigil late night)* Our Lady came as Our Lady of Guadalupe. She said: "Dear children, tonight your prayers have made a difference both in hearts and in the world - in Heaven and on earth. Do not assume that you have not been rewarded. Not every light you see around you is made from cameras but some from My grace. I am blessing you with My Blessing of Holy Love."

■ **October 10, 1996 / Weekly Rosary Service.** "Our Lady's here in blue and white. Her Heart is exposed and there are many small crosses coming from Her Heart toward earth; but before they get to earth, they turn into roses. "I come in praise of Jesus, My Son, King and Redeemer. Pray with Me now for those who will come on the 12th."

"Dear children, please understand, that the Cross and Grace come together. Do not reject the Cross, for, in so doing, you would reject My Grace, My beautiful Grace. Dear children, when you are living in Holy Love, I take your petitions deep into My Immaculate Heart, there to remain, bathed in My Grace. Tonight, I am blessing you with My Blessing of Holy Love."

■ **October 11, 1996.** From Our Lady:

THE SEVEN SORROWS

1. The Prophecy of Simeon.
"If I had allowed the knowledge of Simeon's prophecy to pierce My Heart over and over, I would have re-lived Jesus' passion over and over. I prayed for the grace to be at peace in the present moment."

2. **The Flight into Egypt**
   "Though this was a hardship, our flight from Herod portrays God's provision amidst adversity."

3. **Losing the Child Jesus in the Temple**
   "When you seek My Son, you too will find Him in the temple of your heart."

4. **The Meeting of Jesus and Mary on the Way of the Cross.**
   "I embraced Him in My Heart as I saw Him suffering under the weight of the cross. You too must embrace Him in your hearts in the Blessed Sacrament. Do not leave His Love unattended."

5. **The Crucifixion**
   "As I watched My Beloved Son draw His last breaths, I prayed He would persevere to the end. You must pray for the grace of final perseverance."

6. **The Taking Down of the Body of Jesus from the Cross**
   "I sorrowed that more would not benefit from His death. I sorrowed for those who would not turn away from sin. I continue to sorrow for this."

7. **The Burial of Jesus**
   "I dressed His wounds. I arranged His Hands. I grieved. I gave Him to the world and the world rejected Him. Pray for those who still reject Him."

■ **October 12, 1996 / Monthly Message To All Nations.** *(The following message was given in three parts due to its length. The three parts are interspersed.)* Our Lady is here as Our Lady of Guadalupe. As She floated down on a cloud, three small angels were with Her and arranged Her mantle. "I come in praise of Jesus, My Son, Lord and Redeemer. Pray with Me now for all those here present." We prayed. Our Lady then says: "Please tell the people here today that I am taking all their petitions to Heaven to be placed on the altar of My Son's Heart. I come as I am sent by God the Father, Who has formed Heaven and earth, the sea, and all that is in the sea. I come to give praise and honor to Jesus, My Son."

"Today, I invite all My children to understand that mankind cannot be reconciled with God until he accepts his own littleness before the omnipotence of God. Today, sadly, people do not believe in their own humanness and their dependence upon their Creator for all things - all things. Life itself is a gift that God gives and only He can take away. All of nature thrives in harmony with God's Will."

"Because My Son's Heart is so bitterly pierced by the sins of mankind, He will allow certain events to transpire, which will lend proof to all humanity that He is in charge. People will be made to see that they have brought these things upon themselves by emptying their hearts of God and filling them with false gods. You, My faithful ones, must continue to be My light on the path of Holy Love, showing others the way."

"Today, you are experiencing the season of autumn where much that is alive withers or falls asleep. I come to you to bring an awakening to hearts as to the true season, which is one of much evil but much grace as well. It is Holy Love that will take you into the New Era of Peace. I have come to deliver you of false gods and to sign you with the Blood of the Lamb. The greatest errors in the history of the world have taken place in this last century - in particular sins against human rights. Let My coming to you today be a sign of God's continued mercy and forbearing love. As you see miracle after miracle on this property, let your hearts bend and begin to love. Be My message of love to those around you."

"Dear children, I have come today to free you of the captivity of unloving hearts. It is only through Holy Love, My dear children, that you will be made to realize the glory of the New Jerusalem. Holy Love is the bridge that spans the abyss between Heaven and earth. It is because of lack of love in hearts that mankind has taken himself so far away from his Creator."

"Dear children, I am here to encourage you to love and to pray, for it is only in this way mankind can be pulled from the precipice of disaster."

Now Jesus is with Blessed Mother. They are extending to us the Blessing of the United Hearts.

■ **October 17, 1996 / Weekly Rosary Service.** *(Maureen was on a retreat. Blessed Mother gave the message for the prayer service the day before - October 16, 1996)* Our Lady comes as Our Lady of Guadalupe. She's resplendent. She says: "I come as always, in praise of Jesus, My Son. Dearest children, your presence in response to My call is a fruit of the Holy Love in your hearts. Holy Love is the narrow door. Perfect yourselves in Holy Love, so that you may enter. Let your goal and prayer be to love everyone unconditionally, as My Son loves you. You cannot accomplish this alone, but only through grace. God's Divine Will is My grace. I am blessing you in the present moment."

■ **October 17, 1996.** *(In a field at My Father's House - a retreat center in Connecticut)* Blessed Mother is here all in white. She has a scapular in one hand and a rosary in the other, and Her Heart is exposed. She says: "My little children, thank you for coming as I have called you. Pray with Me now for all sinners, but most especially for government leaders." We prayed.

"Dear children, I come to you tonight to reassure you along the way I am calling you. Be certain that My grace is guiding you. Do not be afraid or fear opposition; My grace will overcome. You feel the path I lead you upon to be uncertain and unfamiliar, but I tell you My grace is the light upon the path which will prove to be well trodden and one of great reward."

"Each of you is called to a particular and certain mission in these times. You must come to Me, your Mother, with your fears and your doubts and allow Me to take you into My Immaculate Heart, where I will resolve all your fears and all you doubts through My grace. Tonight I am extending to you the Blessing of Holy Love."

■ **October 17, 1996.** *(Connecticut)* Our Lady comes as Our Lady of Guadalupe. She says: "Today I come once again on behalf of My Son, to Whom I give all praise and honor. I invite you to fall in love with Jesus in the Eucharist. When you love someone, they are ever present in your hearts and in your thoughts. You try to please the one you love. My dear children, do not leave My Son unattended in the tabernacle. Send your angels to adore Him when you cannot go yourselves. These same angels will return to you bringing many graces. I am blessing you."

■ **October 22, 1996.** *(Message from Padre Pio during Maureen's talk in Milwaukee)* From St. Pio of Pietrelcina: "Do not think Our Mother comes to you asking you to 'pray, pray, pray' because She wants to give you something to do like a homework assignment. She needs your prayers in order to reunite Heaven and earth."

■ **October 24, 1996 / Weekly Rosary Service.** Our Lady is here in a gold color. She says: "All praise be to Jesus, My little children. I come to you tonight seeking your prayers for all those who oppose Me in the world."

"My little children, let Holy Love stand guard over the integrity of your hearts. Let Holy Love be the doorway to your salvation. I come today seeking your faith, your hope, and your love, that I may return to My Son and afford Him great ammunition against evil. It is the love in your hearts that allows Me to oppose Satan in such a way. Tonight I am blessing you with My Blessing of Holy Love."

■ **October 25, 1996.** Jesus says: "Trust and courage go

hand in hand. Fear opposes trust. When you put everything into the vessel of trust, I cover it with My grace which I send through the Heart of My Mother."

■ **October 26, 1996.** Our Lady is here in gray. She says: "My angel, I come in love, peace, and joy to bring praise to My Son, Jesus."

"I am speaking to you now concerning the vision on the vessel of trust. The reason it appeared empty to you, as I handed it to you in the vision, is this. When you surrender your problems, your fears, and all your misgivings to trust, you no longer see these problems, but only the trust. When the problems 'spill out' of the vessel of trust, you are taking them back and trying to solve them yourself."

"You need to trust all your tomorrows to Jesus. He will make all things successful through grace. I am blessing you."

■ **October 31, 1996 / Weekly Rosary Service.** Blessed Mother is here as Our Lady of Grace. "Pray with Me tonight, dear children, for all those who seek Holy Love but do not follow the path."

"Dear children, tonight I invite you to realize that your prayers are the way out of every situation and your armor against fear. See dear children, that when I come to you, I bring you My grace. And when you surrender to your crosses in Holy Love, they are transformed into grace. Dear children, be My warriors on the path of Holy Love through your prayers and your sacrifices."

"Tonight I am blessing you with My Motherly Blessing."

November 1996

■ **November 2, 1996.** Jesus says: "I am giving you this consecration of marriages to Our United Hearts because of these times. These last days before My triumphant return see

Satan attacking all vocations - but in particular the priesthood and marriages. Marriages consecrated to Our United Hearts will find the way made easier. Pray this prayer daily for Our Protection and Provision."

Marriage Consecration

Holy and Sacred United Hearts of Jesus and Mary, we consecrate our marriage to You today in this present moment. Through this consecration, we will dedicate our hearts to Your victory. United in You we seek Your protection and provision. Increase our love for You and for each other with every breath we take. Regally clothe our hearts in the Divine Will of the Eternal Father. Help us to increase in holiness in and through Your United Hearts. Amen.

"Propagate this consecration. It carries with it many graces. It will strengthen the soul of marriages gone stale. It will increase fervor in hearts. It will convert the unconverted who consents to pray it."

He leaves with a smile. The United Hearts are in the air.

■ **November 7, 1996.** Our Lady came in blue and a cream color. She says: "Today is a day of recompense to My Heart for the errors against Holy Love in the hearts of your government leaders."

"Your country cannot be reconciled to God when there is duplicity in the heart of the government. The time fast approaches when the proud will be scattered in the conceit of their hearts. What has been concealed in darkness will be laid bare in the light. It is then that confusion will rule hearts and lay waste your country's economy."

"But there is reason to give praise to Jesus, even in these times and circumstances, for this is a sign to you that the victory of Our United Hearts is most imminent. Be mindful of the extremes in nature and the path of self-destruction the human race pursues itself."

"I am with you and, as always, offering to you the reconciliation and the Refuge of My Immaculate Heart." Blessed Mother leaves.

■ **November 7, 1996 / Weekly Rosary Service.** *(It was raining throughout most of the prayer service.)* Our Lady is here in white with a green sash. "Let us pray tonight for the intentions of all those who have come here."

"Dear children, thank you for coming here tonight to be with Me as I have longed to be with you. I am taking all your petitions to Heaven with Me. Dear children, just as the rain cleanses the air, so My grace cleanses your hearts of any iniquity making it possible to live more perfectly in Holy Love. I desire, dear children, that you let My message of Holy Love be a beacon of light to you and a light that you spread amongst all those whom you know. Dear children, tonight I am blessing you with My Blessing of Motherly Love."

■ **November 8, 1996.**
Miraculous Photographs
Our Lady comes in gray. She says: "My daughter, I am prepared to share with you some knowledge of the images that have been captured on photographs. Keep in mind, however, that this is what photographs are - images captured on film. Different images have different meaning to each individual. Therefore, each picture should be surrendered to prayer before conclusions are drawn."

"First, let Me begin with the cloud seen hovering over the prayer center on certain nights of prayer. This is a sign of God's presence and protection over you. The Jews in the desert had such an escort."

"The color purple stands for Jesus' Passion. Red is for martyrdom. Green is for hope. The circle is My signature - whether large or seen as a small Host shape. Padre Pio is your special patron on the property and in this mission, thus his presence in some pictures."

"It is My intent that these simple explanations will help My children. But if they pray, they will know in their hearts the full meaning of each image. Further, their pilgrimage should not be a search for signs but a search for perfection in holiness. Tonight I am blessing you."

■ **November 8, 1996.** "The age of the apocalypse is here. The last days foretold in the Book of Revelation and predicted by the prophet Daniel. I have come to promise you a New Era of Peace. But peace cannot reign in the world until all hearts turn to love. Any choice against God and neighbor is testing God's patience and calling His justice down from Heaven. I come, My dear children, to reconcile your hearts to God through love - Holy Love. Make it known."

■ **November 12, 1996 / Monthly Message To All Nations.** *(The following message was given in three parts due to its length.)* Our Lady is here as Our Lady of Guadalupe. Her Heart is exposed. She says: "I come in praise of Jesus, My Son. Please thank My children for coming here today and praying with Me. Let us pray now for all intentions in hearts and for those who pursue the path of holiness." We prayed.

"Today I ask that you continue to pray for those who do not understand My coming to you. These are the ones whose eyes are closed to the signs of My Son's triumphant return. It is as though these complacent ones are watching a sunset but refuse to believe that nighttime follows."

"Today evil is glamorized and righteousness held in contempt. But I come to you to reconcile all nations and peoples through Holy Love - the only just barometer and scale of justice."

"The docile soul will not find My call arduous. The proud soul will dispute the path, the way, and the call."

"I come to reveal to you these times in which you live - these apocalyptic times - the last days before My Son returns.

The Spirit of Justice will engulf the world before My Son's coming. You must be ready and with certainty have hearts full of Holy Love and hands full of good deeds. Therefore, you must understand I do not come for your curiosity, but for your welfare. I want you to stand prepared when the angel sounds his trumpet."

"Dear children, do not follow the dictates of the leaders of your country when they oppose God's law. Because these certain people sit in high places does not mean they are above the commandments - the greatest of which is Holy Love. Pray rather for your leaders that they choose the path of righteousness. Do not compromise your faith because many do. Remain loyal to the Holy Father. God's scorn will fall upon those who choose the popular path instead of the narrow gate."

Jesus is now with Blessed Mother. His Heart is exposed.

"My dear apostles, surrender to Me your hearts that I may enwrap them in Holy Love. Thus, I will present them to the Heart of My Divine Son and the Victory of Our United Hearts will begin in you. Today we extend to you the Blessing of Our United Hearts."

■ **November 14, 1996 / Weekly Rosary Service.** *(Many people saw the image of Padre Pio superimposed over the Missionary Image of Our Lady of Guadalupe. His image remained visible during the recitation of the Rosary and after the service ended. This has become a continuing occurrence at the prayer services.)*

Blessed Mother is here in white. She doesn't have a veil on Her head. Her hair is flowing freely. Her arms are extended outward and She says: "All praise be to Jesus, My little angels. Tonight let us pray for the intentions in hearts and for those who do not love."

"Dear children, tonight I invite you to deepen your love, for as your love grows deeper for God and for your fellow man, so too, you lessen your fear of the past and of the future. Within a deeper place in My Heart you receive greater understanding of God's mercy and His grace. Let this be the moment that you choose to love with all your heart. Tonight I am blessing you with My Motherly Blessing."

■ **November 21, 1996 / Weekly Rosary Service.** Our Lady is here as Our Lady of Guadalupe. Her hands are folded over Her chest. She says: "Dear children, pray with Me for the conversion of all nations."

"Dear children, come to realize that each time I speak to you, I am speaking to each person on earth. If you pray, you will be given understanding as to what I am saying to you. Then your heart will be changed and you will be living in Holy Love. Dear children, tonight I am blessing you with My Blessing of Holy Love."

■ **November 22, 1996.** Our Lady comes in bluish gray and white. In place of Her Heart is the United Hearts. She says: "Today I come asking you to understand that the Hearts of Jesus and Mary beat as one. This is possible because of the Holy Love that is My Heart. Thus will mankind be reconciled to God and the heart of humanity beat as one with God."

"In Our United Hearts are the secrets of life and death, of the cosmos, and time eternal. The more the soul embraces Holy Love, the more all of nature is one with God's Will. Thus will My Son's triumph be in hearts - then the world. I am blessing you."

■ **November 28, 1996 - Thanksgiving Day.** Our Lady comes in gray and a cream color. She says: "My dear angel, today I come to give the world a greater understanding of the United Hearts of Jesus and Mary - all in praise of Jesus. Today, the embrace of My Heart reaches out to the world, hoping to unite humanity to the United Hearts. Our United Hearts present to the world perfect reconciliation with God. This union can only be achieved in hearts that love."

"When you love, your heart is transformed by grace. The more perfectly you love, the more perfectly you are transformed and united to Our Hearts. When you love with Holy Love, you are kneeling beside My Son's crib on Christmas morn. Holy Love takes you to Mt. Tabor where your soul is transfigured by the light of My grace. A heart full of love shares in the passion and stands with Me at the foot of the Cross. Holy Love resurrects the soul with grace and fills it with the Holy Spirit."

"I call mankind to choose to love; to choose to be reconciled with God; to choose to be united in Our United Hearts. Do not look for solutions to your problems in intellect but in grace that comes to you through love. I am blessing you."

■ **November 29, 1996.** Our Lady's here as Our Lady of Guadalupe. She says: "Tonight I have come with special news. My coming to you on My Feast Day of December 12th will be a telling sign of prodigies yet to come and of the urgency of My Message to all nations through you, My daughter. Many of the things I have foretold to you have taken place within the Church and world itself. But the year to come will hold special tribulations, most especially for those outside of Holy

Love. While these hardships unfold, My grace will support you. My mantle is around My consecrated ones. Cling to and propagate the devotion to Our United Hearts. I am blessing you."

■ **November 30, 1996.** Jesus says:
   "The poor are the ones who have not heard the message of Holy Love. Enrich them."
   "The hungry are those starving for righteousness. Feed them with Holy Love."
   "The prisoners are those held captive by sin. Free them with the message of Holy Love."
   "The naked are those unclothed in Holy Love. Wrap them in My Mother's mantle of protection of Holy Love."
   "Give Me the lonely, the hungry, the naked. I desire to fill them, embrace them, clothe them. Herein lies My call to you."

■ **November 30, 1996.** Our Lady comes in pale gray and white. She says: "My child, I come to you because you have come to Me. I invite you to understand that the coming liturgical year will bring many changes both in hearts and in the world. Evil will preside over many hearts and events - even more so than today. The greatest errors and tribulations will begin to unfold."
   "So that you will recognize these evils which are now formulating in hearts, I will reveal to you now the foretaste of their coming. Satan is attempting to take over the airways and every form of modern communications. His power will be felt in consumerism, shallow economies, and false teachings. Once again, he will masquerade as good. He has many subversive schemes to weaken faith and counter My plans on earth. He seeks the demise of every soul and the destruction of your peace."
   "Recall these, my words to you as this liturgical year unfolds. Rely on My grace and pray much. I seek your assistance in destroying My adversary - the red dragon. If

you pray, you will not be fooled by his disguises. I am blessing you."

■ **November 30, 1996.** From St. Pio of Pietrelcina: "Your mission is to prepare the world for Our Lord's Second Coming through Holy Love. You can only do this if you stop worrying about opposition - who believes or disbelieves. Just put the message out there. Some may just listen and go their way. But you will plant a seed of conviction. Then when they are made to see the state of their soul, they will remember."

December 1996

■ **December 1, 1996.** Our Lady is here as Our Lady of Lourdes. "The time has come when significant changes are coming quickly into the world. Accompanied by every increased trial will be my increased and abundant grace. I am calling souls from darkness as never before and with significant urgency."

"On the 12th of this month I am preparing a special treasure. It is not for all, but for many. It will be profound and intense."

■ **December 2, 1996.** Our Lady came and gave us the following prayer:

Prayer To The Eternal Father
"Heavenly Father, I surrender unto you this day my will and my heart. In return I ask Your favor upon all my actions in thought, word and deed. Hold me deeply in Your bosom of Divine Will that I may not displease You in any way. Render unto me Your Mercy in my every need. Amen."

Our Lady said: "Recite this prayer from your heart and your petition will be granted."

■ **December 5, 1996 / Weekly Rosary Service.** *(Many people saw the image of Padre Pio superimposed over the Missionary Image of Our Lady of Guadalupe. His image remained visible during the recitation of the Rosary and after the service ended. His picture is seen in many photographs taken of the Missionary Image at the property.)*

Our Lady is here as Our Lady of Grace. Her heart is exposed. She says: "I come in praise of Jesus, My Son. Let us pray now for all those who will attempt to come here on the 12th. Dear children, as this liturgical year unfolds, I desire that you surrender to Me your effort at holiness. It is only through the grace of My heart you can attain any good. Therefore surrender to Me all your needs, all your desires and goals. I will petition the Heart of My Beloved Son, and He will render unto you according to God's Will your every need. Tonight I am blessing you with My Blessing of Holy Love."

■ **December 9, 1996.**
Bread Of Holy Love Movement

Our Lady comes in shimmering white with many white roses around Her. She says: "Good day to you. Peace be with you. Praise be Jesus."

"Today I come as the Lord of lords has sent Me. I come to reveal to you My message and plan with which I pray to reconcile God and all men. I want to give to you the bread of Holy Love. This is a united effort to reconcile all nations - all hearts - to God. It is an army of souls who will unite in sacrifice to bring about the conversion of the world. The graces given to souls is the leaven of the bread. The bread itself is the message of Holy Love which, by merit of this united effort, will feed a world starving for holiness."

"The Bread of Holy Love is a powerful weapon in My hand, one which will smite evil and bring change to hearts. Through the prayers and sacrifices of this army, I will be able to touch millions. I call this army 'bread' for the world is starving for this message."

"But I do not ask My children to participate in this effort without reward. Let them have their names recorded in a ledger. Each month on the 12th, Jesus and I will send them the Blessing of Our United Hearts. The record of names will be kept in the apparition room all month. All I ask in return is their prayers and sacrifices. If we are united in this effort, much progress will be made and hearts will surrender to the grace of the present moment."

"This year will be unprecedented in grace and sorrow. Many and most remain unprepared and uninformed. But, through the Bread of Holy Love Movement, I am inviting My consecrated children to stand between unchanging hearts and God, drawing hearts towards reconciliation."

"During this season of giving and receiving, this is a mutual gift that I am giving to you and you are giving to Me. I extend to you My Blessing of Holy Love."

■ December 12, 1996 / Monthly Message To All Nations.

(The following message was given in three parts.) I returned to adoration and Our Lady was waiting for me. She bowed Her head when I came in. She said, "I am glad you have returned."

"I desire you make this message known to all nations on the 12th of the month."

"It is impossible for God to reveal Himself to the proud heart. Therefore, before much of humanity can be reconciled to their Creator, they will be made humble through global warnings, tribulations, and unprecedented occurrences which will make them turn to God for help. Those already converted and consecrated to Me will be under My mantle of protection. The action of grace during these times will bring many to conversion."

"The evil in certain hearts will spread as a contagious disease, leading certain others off track and fooling the universe."

"The greatest threat to the world is mankind's inability to

acknowledge God and to understand His omnipotence. Thus he calls God's justice upon himself."

"I come as the herald of My Son's return. Each soul must take heed of what Jesus sends Me to say before time as you know it runs out."

Our Lady comes as Our Lady of Guadalupe. She says: "I come to give praise to Jesus. I come to you under this sign and title of Guadalupe to bring notice to My call to all nations and peoples to conversion. Only when mankind is reconciled to God will there be true and lasting peace in the world. Then balance will be restored to nature and to the universe. I do not come to bring honor to Myself but to bring souls to My Son."

"My Heart stands as a burning flame of love ready to consume any soul who draws near. But today (She is now crying), too many hold themselves aloof. Out of pride they do not see their sins and do not love. I am extending My grace here today so that more believe and more begin to love."

Blessed Mother is here as Our Lady of Guadalupe. She came with many angels (30-40) that formed a line on both sides of a path of light that She descended upon.

"I come in praise of Jesus. Ask the faithful here to pray with Me for all intentions in hearts."

"Dear children, thank you for answering My call to come here today. I plead for your prayers. Because of your faith I come to you."

"Sadly I tell you that this nation's leaders have chosen to follow a path of darkness. There are many who are being led astray following man's law and opposing God's law."

"Please ask the people to aim their cameras at the Missionary Image [of Our Lady of Guadalupe]."

"Thank you."

"Dear children, I come to you to bring My grace into the world. When My Son returns, He will come not with grace but with His justice. Therefore, I beseech you to follow always My message of Holy Love which is your salvation."

Now Jesus is with Blessed Mother. They extended to us

the Blessing of the United Hearts.

■ **December 19, 1996 / Weekly Rosary Service.** Our Lady is here as Our Lady of Guadalupe. She says: "All praise be to Jesus, My little children. Thank you for coming to Me tonight. I invite you now to pray with Me for those who have cold hearts." [It was -2 below with the wind chill factor.]

"Dear children, tonight I invite you to know and understand that the Holy Love in your hearts is taking you along the path to Bethlehem. Please be certain that the Holy Love in your hearts is the beginning of My Son's return."

"Tonight I am blessing you with My Motherly Blessing."

■ **December 22, 1996.** Our Lady comes with many sparkling lights around Her. She says: "My angel, praise be to Jesus. Dear daughter, for those who hold much concern in their hearts for certain aspects of the future, I invite them to deeper trust in My grace. Their deep trust comes in deeper love. In all ways I am ready to assist. All worldly concerns, after all, are under God's domain. "

■ **December 23, 1996.** Our Lady comes in white and She is radiant. She has large rays of light coming from Her and little sparkling lights around Her. She says: "Praise be Jesus."

"Today I come to you to ask your prayers for a correction of conscience in all nations. These days it is true that many hold themselves blameless where they are in sin. The healthy conscience does not accuse falsely, but neither will such a conscience be persuaded to false innocence. My coming to you with the Holy Love message is a call to all sinners to reexamine the path of their lives according to Holy Love. I tell you, nations that refuse My call and will not repeal ungodly laws, such as abortion, continue to move the world towards chastisement. What is coming can still be mitigated, but only if abortion is eliminated from the world."

"Mankind expects much but wants to give little back to

God. When he should be prostrate asking forgiveness, he is petitioning for favors. In your country many are coming to see My Image on a window.* I want to imprint on hearts My message of Holy Love. You will find soon in your midst My favor and grace towards this end."

* *In December of 1996, a 2-story image of Our Lady of Guadalupe was discovered on the window of a bank building in Clearwater, Florida, USA. It was destroyed by vandalism on March 1, 2004.*

■ **December 25, 1996 - Christmas Day.** Our Lady comes in white. She is holding the Infant Jesus. She says: "Praise be Jesus, alive in the tabernacles of the world."

Jesus raises His little hand and blesses me and the person next to me.

"My daughter, I come to commemorate with you My Son's birth. As you ponder Him, please know that humility is the basis of Holy Love. So many find it too difficult to absorb My message of Holy Love because they are full of pride."

"Soon, time in the world will mark the beginning of a new year. In Heaven, where time does not exist, the sin in hearts and in the world grows old. Too many hearts are unrepentant for they know not love."

"My message of Holy Love to all souls is the only hope the world has and the only way around certain judgment. Many can pray and sacrifice, but all of this must come from hearts full of Holy Love."

"For this reason, you will travel near and far proclaiming My message."

Now the Infant Jesus is speaking. "Make your present moment a prayer by giving it to Me. You will see a great multitude come and go at the shrine. The grace I am giving will touch many and many will touch it. It is for the conversion of the world. The unrepentant will convert. Come to Our United Hearts in preparation of this."

All of a sudden both Jesus and Mary are in gray.

Our Lady says: "Certain hearts will be laid bare. An evil will be exposed, but for some it will be too late. The world must come to His Mercy."

"Believe in Me as I believe in you."

She and Jesus leave.

■ **December 26, 1996 / Weekly Rosary Service.** Our Lady is here in white with a blue and gold mantle. "Praise be Jesus. My little children, let us pray for the unrepentant."

"Dear children, My message to you tonight is as humble and simplistic as My Son's birth in the manger. Seek Jesus with the shepherds from the hillside and the wise men from the East. Seek Jesus. Let your gift to Him be your heart in the present moment. Seek Jesus. I am blessing you."

■ **December 27, 1996.** Our Lady comes in a purplish gray. She has 2 swords in Her Heart, which I am told in my heart, represent Church and State. She says: "Child, begin to write as I come in praise of Jesus."

"Today, sadly, those souls consecrated to Me are in their agony, as was Jesus in the garden at Gethsemani. They are misunderstood, persecuted, and ridiculed. Though God is in their hearts, the world is unwilling to listen and accept it. They have set their hearts to pray for the conversion of unbelievers; and for this, the world does not know them. Those not of the Spirit do not accept the place the world is in according to God."

"While there are those dedicated to good, there are many in important places both in the church and in governments who are opposed to God."

"Everything, everything must be tested by Holy Love. For what opposes the laws of love, opposes God. You have not experienced the worst trials, nor have you experienced My greatest grace. In your sorrow, God will send angels to comfort you just as My Beloved Son was comforted at Gethsemani.

I am always your protection - giving you words to defend yourselves against any attack. God is your provision. I am blessing you."

■ **December 28, 1996.** From God, the Father: "My daughter, in you I want to paint the perfect image of love, so that those who come to you will be convicted by this virtue. Love is the regal virtue - the crown of glory. No virtue subsists outside of love. Love and mercy are one. So as this is the Age of My Divine Mercy, it is also the Age of Holy Love. These two are not side by side, but united - just as the Hearts of Jesus and Mary are united. The function of love is to draw the soul into My Mercy. Herein, lies the blueprint for conversion."

■ **December 31, 1996.** Blessed Mother is here in white. There is a gold border around Her mantle and Her Immaculate Heart is exposed. She says: "Praise be Jesus, My little children."

Our Lady gave a personal message, then said: "Dear children, as this year unfolds, I invoke your prayers for all those who are teetering upon apostasy in their hearts during this coming year, which is most serious and not to be welcomed with revelry but with prayer."

"I invite you to understand that Satan is about to destroy the faith of many. Therefore, you must pray to Me for My protection, as I come to protect the faith in all hearts."

"Some have made gods of their own opinions and will not be swayed from them. For these, continue to pray. For their opinions are not equal to God's commandments or to Church doctrine. Some of these are bound to happen before My Son returns. When He comes, it will be as Just Judge. Tonight I am blessing you with My Blessing of Holy Love."

Messages of Holy *and* Divine Love

1997

January 1997

■ **January 1, 1997.** Jesus says: "Go out and tell the world that these last days are entrusted to Divine Love and Mercy. It is through these two mankind and God can be reconciled."

■ **January 1, 1997.** Our Lady comes standing in the alcove of the new mission center* where Her statue will be. She is motioning with Her arms, and I see many people come towards Her.

"Dear children, today I celebrate with you. This building represents the power of prayer, the dignity of sacrifice, and the victory of perseverance. It is here many and certain prodigies will be revealed."

"I will use the prayers offered here towards My victory in hearts and in the world. You think you see a structure of wood. I see a structure of love - Holy Love."

"Today I am thanking all of you for responding to My call. I am blessing you."

The Immaculate Heart of Mary Prayer Center

■ **January 2, 1997.** Our Lady comes in white and gold. There is a bright light around Her. She says: "I have news of things to be in this coming year. This will be a year of paradoxes* - a year as never before."

- "It is to be a time of certainties and uncertainties - decisions and indecisions."
- "There will be a general conviction of hearts and many unrepentant hearts."
- "It will be an hour of belief and of disbelief."
- "Time will seem to race forward and stand still."
- "In my mission it will be a time of growth and of surrender."
- "It will be a beginning and an end."

403

- "The world will be embraced by global warnings from God."
- "Some will continue in old patterns. Others will seek out new ways."
- "Controversy and compromise will make themselves partners."
- "Heresy and Tradition will oppose one another."
- "One disaster will outweigh all others."
- "My faithful will be sustained in My grace."

"Do not see these things as a riddle to be pondered. The unfolding is at hand. Those devoted to Me and faithful to their consecration will be in My Heart and safe in every trial. The greatest trial is lack of faith. If you have faith - which is trust in God - you have all. Ask Me, and I will protect your faith."

"You will please make this known."

* Paradoxes means contradictions or inconsistencies.

■ **January 2, 1997 / Weekly Rosary Service.** Our Lady is here in a dark grayish blue. Her heart is exposed. She says: "Pray with Me now for all petitions in hearts here tonight." We prayed.

Our Lady gave a private message, then said, "Dear children, as this year unfolds before you, please allow My Beloved Son to take dominion over your present moment. I am with you in the present moment when you love. I invite you to allow this year to be the year you love in the present. Tonight I am extending to you My Blessing of Holy Love."

■ **January 6, 1997.**

Prayer for Urgent Petitions

"Holy and Sacred Wounds, hidden in the shoulder of Jesus throughout His Passion, to you I surrender my greatest and most urgent needs. Cover my petitions with Your Most Precious Blood, Lord Jesus, thus

preventing any evil from prevailing over these needs. Now present in Your most painful wounds and by merit of Your suffering, I trust my prayer will be answered. Amen."

■ **January 9, 1997 / Weekly Rosary Service.** Our Lady is here in a cream color and gray. She says: "Praise be Jesus. Pray with Me now for those coming here on the 12th."

"Dear children, tonight I come to you to awaken consciences as to where they fail in Holy Love. The conscience of the world is steeped in error and serves the god of self. But I am calling you to a deep appreciation of My grace through Holy Love."

"Take heed not to depend on yourselves during difficult times, but always upon the grace of My heart. My Son sends Me to you with great compassion and love and is beckoning you to have hearts full of compassion and love during these times. Tonight I am blessing you with My Blessing of Holy Love."

■ **January 12, 1997 / Monthly Message To All Nations.** *(The first part of the message was given prior to the prayer service.)* Our Lady comes as Our Lady of Guadalupe. She says: "All praise be to Jesus Who is Lord of all hearts. Today, I come to you with a mother's heart to help you comprehend the meaning of My visits to you under this title and in these times. When I came to Juan Diego in the 16th century, the meaning to the people in those days was symbolic and told a story which converted millions. Today, My coming to you in this way and under this banner is of no less importance. I come during these last days to convert the world. I come to reconcile man and God. Under this image I am the Woman of the Apocalypse - the Woman clothed in the sun, the moon beneath Her feet. *(Rev. 12)* Further, let it be clear, I am Queen of the Cosmos as you see the stars in pattern on My Mantle. I am with child. Therefore, let it be known, I am the Mother of All

Mothers. It is decreed in Heaven that life be given. Mankind must not assume the role of God and take life from the womb. In all of this, My head is yet bowed in humility to the One Who sends Me. I am praying as I desire all to pray and with humble hearts. The greatness in this image is in the Creator. The greatness in My coming to you is in the Creator's Mercy."

"I come to restore harmony in the world and in the cosmos itself. It is only through Holy Love in hearts that this delicate balance can resume. Today, when so many feel all solutions come from humanity and not from God, the only real solution is left forsaken - that is, embracing God and neighbor with love."

"Through holy pre-destination, I am Mother of All Mothers, Mother of All Nations and Peoples. I invite you to see, dear children, that your triumph is in the Cross, the Cross which is Jesus' Throne of Mercy and Love. It is from this, Divine Mercy and Love, that I am sent to you. Embrace the Cross as you embrace Holy Love during these decisive times."

"Let your dignity come from your personal holiness in response to My call and not from worldly standards. You can disarm many a proud heart in this way."

(This part of the message was given at the prayer service.) Our Lady is here in white. She is radiant and has a crown of sparkling lights upon Her head. "I come in praise of Jesus. My dear children, rejoice with Me today. You have come in answer to My call. It is through your prayers and your sacrifices that we are now meeting in this building. This is the site of My great predilection and favor. Let us pray in thanksgiving for the many graces that will be poured out here."

Jesus is now with Blessed Mother. Their Hearts are exposed.

"Dear children, today I invite you into the Era of Peace, for when you are living in Holy Love, you will already be in the New Jerusalem. Immerse yourselves in the Flame of Holy Love that is My Heart. Today it is your new baptism and commitment. See that Holy Love fulfills your baptismal vows.

Today we extend to you the Blessing of Our United Hearts."

■ **January 17, 1997.** "Dear children, appreciate these times you are in and the graces being given. Do not stand still, but move forward in My grace. You have been chosen for these times to proclaim My Message of Holy Love, which announces My Son's return and prepares the heart of the world."

■ **January 20, 1997.** Our Lady comes in white in a pale blue light. Her Heart is exposed. She says: "My daughter, today the Lord grants you further understanding of the Unity of the Two Hearts. Know and understand that all grace comes to you through My Immaculate Heart. I am the Mother of Divine Grace. Every grace takes its origin from the Sacred Heart of My Son. Prayers are most powerful when given to Jesus through Mary. The grace of My Heart enhances all petitions. The image of Our Unity tells you one cannot be separated from the other. All the hearts of those who embrace Holy Love are in My Heart, and so in the Heart of My Son. Make it known." She blesses me.

■ **January 23, 1997 / Weekly Rosary Service.** Our Lady comes in mint green and aqua. We begin to pray together. Our Lady is holding a light pink rosary. The beads float through Her fingers, but She does not pray the *Hail Mary*. Before the beads reach Her fingers, they are dull in color. As She touches them, they light up as bulbs. After they pass through Her fingers, they have a soft glow but are not as bright as when She holds them.

As I notice this, She smiles and says: "Let this be a lesson to you in the value of the present moment. Your prayers in the present hold great sway over the outcome of the future. Pay no heed to the past."

Then I saw the beads before She held them were the past; as she held them, the present; and after She touched them, the future. The beads were changed forever after She touched them which means prayer affects the future.

■ **January 30, 1997 / Weekly Rosary Service.** Our Lady is here as Our Lady of Lourdes, and Jesus is with Her. "All praise be Jesus, My little ones. Pray with Me now for those who do not pursue the path of holiness which is Holy Love."

"Dear children, I come to bring you My peace and to call you once again to reconciliation with God. Do not let Satan take you into the past thinking of what could have been, but appreciate the grace of the present moment and what is. I am calling you into Our United Hearts as a refuge, a fortress against the evil of these days, an evil which prevails upon many hearts and confuses the unconverted. Be at peace, and know that I am always with you but most especially when you pray. Tonight We extend to you the Blessing of Our United Hearts."

February 1997

■ **February 1, 1997.** Our Lady is here in white. She says: "Today, My angel, I come to invite you to understand that these are extraordinary times. Today, you witness unusual graces and bear unusual crosses. But believe that each trial permitted by God is meant to bring you closer to Him and deeper in trust. Grace bears every cross with dignity and peace. My coming to your midst in these times is not your idea but God's Divine Plan. I am herald of Jesus' Second Coming. I am preparing hearts just as John the Baptist prepared the world for His public life. Instead of water, I am immersing souls in My Flame of Holy Love."

"You cannot call souls into this Flame without My grace. Each time I come to you, a new soul is being baptized in this Flame of My Heart."

"My daughter, you will please make all of this known."

■ **February 6, 1997 / Weekly Rosary Service.** Blessed Mother is here in white. She has a light coming from Her Heart. She says: "Praise be Jesus; peace be with you, in your midst, and in your hearts. Dear children, pray with Me for those who will come here on the 12th."

"Dear children, tonight I come once again to remind you that My call to Holy love is a universal call to the heart of humanity. It is a call to take off the old and put on the new *(Col:3)*. Do not keep the letter of the law and neglect the heart of the law. Do not say that you keep the Commandments yet hold contempt in your heart for your fellow man."

"Dear children, in all things be humble through Holy Love. Tonight I am blessing you with My Blessing of Holy Love."

■ **February 7, 1997.** Our Lady is waiting for me when I arrive in the chapel. She is in blue. Over Her Heart is a mirror. She says: "Let this mirror be a sign to you that you are to be a reflection of My Heart, which is Holy Love in the world. This is why I have come and why I am sent. My mission of Holy Love is a mission of hearts. It is a mission of hearts in the United Hearts. It is a mission of hearts in each soul, as each one is called to be perfected in and through Holy Love."

"Holy Love is the arch foe of Satan for it opposes all the points of entry into hearts. These are the faults that stem from pride, including: anger; jealousy; unforgiveness; self-righteousness; fear, which is lack of trust; and self-aggrandizement. These faults oppose My mission and My victory both in hearts and in the world. Each one needs to stand guard over his heart and extricate these errors from their souls."

"Now in this present moment, I am blessing you."

■ **February 9, 1997.** I see Our Lady's face. She is in white and has a crown on Her head. In front of Her, and very large, is the United Hearts.

Our Lady says: "I come to you to define most clearly My

mission through you. The devotion to the United Hearts is the core of the Holy Love message. This union represents most dramatically My union with Jesus through Holy Love. The Image also depicts that Holy and Divine Love (which is the Heart of My Son) belong together. Holy Love is the path to Jesus. It is through living and purifying your own hearts in the virtue of Holy Love that I will lead you into the Sacred Heart of My Son."

"Therefore, see and understand, that the United Hearts of Jesus and Mary represents union between Holy and Divine Love. This is the union Jesus wants with each soul. This is why He sends Me, so that I am able to lead you into union with Him through My own Heart."

"You must pray for unyielding hearts who threaten their own salvation by refusing to pursue this path of salvation. You will please make this known."

■ **February 12, 1997 / Monthly Message To All Nations.** *(This part of the message was given to Maureen prior to the prayer service.)* "Holy Love is the correction of the conscience of the world and the bridge to reconciliation between God and all mankind."

"Please understand, My children, I do not come to you on the 12th of each month because most believe. No, like My Son Who came for sinners, I come to aid the unconverted and those who refuse to believe. I come to this site, during this final hour, because of your strong faith and trust in Me. I appeal to you to carry My message of Holy Love out into the world and into your homes."

"The sun is setting on the age of Marian apparitions and rising on the hour of Justice. While I am with you, come often to pray with Me here. I will not leave without rewarding you with My continual presence in your midst. Do Me the favor of being My message in the world."

"I come to you preceding the Harvesting Angels. I come to sprinkle the earth with Holy Love. Here, at this site, I come to relieve the distress of all nations and multiply My favors among all people. I come to uplift the sinners and lay bare the path of holiness. Here I will reveal to all sinners and all nations the obstacles they themselves have placed upon this path. The path of Holy Love is not just for a few, or for many, but for all. Holy Love is the medicine for straying and lukewarm souls; the miraculous cure for heresy and apostasy; and the good remedy for unbelieving hearts."

(This part of the message was given to Maureen at the Rosary Service.) Blessed Mother is here as Our Lady of Guadalupe. Her Immaculate Heart is exposed. She says: "Praise be to Jesus."

"Dear children, once again I invite you to pray with Me for the unyielding hearts."

"Dear children, I invite you to see that your conversion is ongoing and always in the present moment. I invite all nations to rise up and follow the path of Holy Love. Today you see the sun and then the next moment you see clouds. It is thus in a soul as well. For it is sin that obstructs the light on the path of Holy Love and your salvation. Dear children, I plead for your petitions before the throne of My Son; and at My telling, many petitions will be answered through God's Mercy and Love."

Jesus is now with Blessed Mother. "Today we extend to you the Blessing of Our United Hearts."

■ **February 13, 1997.** Jesus says: "Burning within My Heart is the secret of salvation; and it is Holy Love, Holy Love, Holy Love."

■ **February 13, 1997 / Weekly Rosary Service.** Our Lady is here in blue and white and has roses (graces) surrounding Her. They are red, yellow, and white. She says: "Pray with Me once again dear children for the unbelieving hearts."

"Dear children, tonight I invite you to see that the perfect sacrifice during this penitential season is living in Holy Love in the present moment; for in this self-surrender, you are abandoning your own will and living only for others and for God. It is in this surrender that you will find and bring to perfection God's Will in your life. Tonight I am blessing you with My Blessing of Holy Love."

■ **February 16, 1997.** *(Adoration Chapel - Cocoa Beach, Florida)* Our Lady comes in blue and white. She says: How appropriate you are here. Peace be with you. Praise be Jesus."

"You see the time of justice approaches." (I see the second hand of a clock on the Host. It is moving steadily along.)

"I come so that you may better comprehend the mystery of Our United Hearts, As the United Hearts are a symbol of My union with Jesus, it is also a sign of My call to all mankind to be united to My Son. My Heart is Holy Love and the path to the Sacred Heart of Jesus, which is Divine Love. The Flame of My Heart purifies the soul - in and through Holy Love - to be united with the Flame of Divine Love. This Flame of Divine Love is the victory of the New Jerusalem."

"No one enters Heaven outside of the embrace of Divine Love. This union is the melding of wills - the human will and the Divine Will. You may say, 'I do not know God's Will for me in the present moment.' It is Holy Love. Choose this path as you are called, and as I lead you."

"My child, you know the depth of love you hold for your husband. God's love for you is greater still. In His love He calls you along the path of Holy Love and into His Own Heart."

"His Heart is so bitterly grieved for the sins of humanity. Even I cannot console Him. You must make the path known as I call you to do."

"I am blessing both of you now with My Blessing of Holy Love."

■ **February 16, 1997.** *(Mary Queen of the Universe Shrine; Adoration Chapel - Orlando, Florida)* Jesus says: "I am your Jesus, born Incarnate."

"My home is not here but in Heaven. I come to you under this Form so that you may know My Mercy and My Love. Mercy and Love are inseparable. This is true in the Divine, and it is also true in the world - for those who seek to follow Me. No one can truly love who is unforgiving. Perhaps there are those in your life you must be cautious of. Still love them. Still forgive them any wrongdoing. When I return, I will separate the wheat from the chaff. The chaff will be many, steeped in unforgiveness. I am coming. Prepare!"

■ **February 20, 1997 / Weekly Rosary Service.** Our Lady is here as Our Lady of Guadalupe. She says: "Pray with Me now dear children for hearts to be enlightened as to the path they follow."

"Dear children, tonight I invite you to open your eyes and not be amongst the many that follow blindly behind many pied pipers, who call themselves government leaders and lead souls down the path of perdition. Do not place your trust in these, but open your eyes and your hearts, and realize that they are not worthy of your trust if they legislate against life. Continue to pray and love. Persevere in these two and I am with you. I am blessing you with My Blessing of Holy Love."

■ **February 25, 1997.** Our Lady comes as the Protectress of the Faith. She says: "I come in praise of Jesus. I will help you now to understand that I stand as sentinel between Heaven and Hell - for you and for all humanity. My heart is your Refuge, passageway, and path to salvation. The grace of every present moment proceeds from this Refuge. The more you die to self and detach from the world, the deeper I will lead you into the sacrament [a thing that is holy] of the present moment and a great source of grace for many. It is My gift in this hour of need in the world. Too many live for themselves and reject love. I come to open the door to salvation through Holy Love. Please make this known."

■ **February 27, 1997 / Weekly Rosary Service.** Our Lady is here as Our Lady of Fatima. She says: "Pray with Me now, dear children, for those who have unforgiveness in their hearts."

"Dear children, tonight, once again, I invite you to proceed along the path of Holy Love. Perfect yourselves in every way so that your wills will be united with the Divine Will. Thus, you will be safe in the United Hearts of Jesus and Mary."

Now Jesus is with Blessed Mother. They extend to all here the Blessing of the United Hearts.

March 1997

■ **March 4, 1997.** *Tuesday, March 4, 1997 is the day Blessed Mother assisted Maureen in drawing the image of Mary, Refuge of Holy Love.*

■ **March 6, 1997 / Thursday Rosary Service.** Blessed Mother is here. She looks exactly how she looks in the picture [of her] that she helped me draw two evenings ago. She says: "I come to you tonight under the title, 'Mary, Refuge of Holy Love.' I desire that you propagate this Image. Through modern technology it can be enlarged and hung prominently in our prayer center."

"Dear children, pray with me now for the conversion of all sinners."

"Dear children, please know and understand that many and particular graces will come to you through this Image. It is my desire that you make this title and this Image known."

"Dear children, this is truly an alpha and an omega in the life of My Mission. It is the beginning of a new life in a new prayer center where many miracles and favors will be witnessed. It is the end of My Mission's exile. Tonight I am blessing you with My Blessing of Motherly Love."

Mary, Refuge of Holy Love

■ **March 7, 1997.** Blessed Mother is here as she is in the picture, Mary, Refuge of Holy Love. She says: "Peace be with you. Dear children pray with me now for the grace to pursue propagation of My Title, Refuge of Holy Love."

"Dear children, long have I awaited pronouncement of this title. Now it is time in My Mission and in the world to move forward with this."

"No other couple has been given such a mission within their marriage. It is a vocation within a vocation to propagate this newest and most cherished title of mine. For it is through this Refuge of Holy Love that you are led into the Divine Love and Will of My Son and the Father."

"It is through this Refuge of Holy Love that your faith is protected and you are made one with the Heart of Jesus.

"Tonight I am blessing you with My Blessing of Holy Love."

■ **March 10, 1997.** Our Lady is here in blue and white. She says: "I come to you once again as Refuge of Holy Love. Today, dear, dear children, I invite you to pray for the gift of understanding. I am asking my Spouse, the Holy Spirit, to give you this gift so that you will know in your hearts a deep understanding of the depth of my call to you. It is one thing to know about Holy Love intellectually but quite another to grasp the depth of this Message in your hearts. Understanding is a great gift and will open doors for you. I am praying with you. Please make this known."

■ **March 12, 1997 / Monthly Message To All Nations.** Our Lady comes as Refuge of Holy Love. She says: "Peace be with you. Praise be Jesus. My daughter, I come once again on behalf of my Son to address all nations. Once again I caution those who will hear, do not support elected or appointed officials unless their lives are examples of Holy Love. Holy Love is the integrity of every nation and each soul. When my Son returns, as He will, the scale of justice in His hand will be Holy Love."

"Please understand, my children, my coming to you is not your salvation, nor is My Message of Holy Love your salvation. Your salvation is your 'yes' to Holy Love in Your hearts. If you say 'yes', then you take Holy Love home with you, so it is in your families and your communities. The little Flame of Holy Love in your heart today must spread as every word and deed will now be enveloped in your 'yes' to Holy

Love. In this response to my call you are now saving your own soul as well as others. She leaves saying she will return."

Blessed Mother is here as Our Lady of Guadalupe. She says: "All praise be Jesus. My dear children, pray with me now for all those who will be touched by this mission and read this book, [Our Lady was referring to the new Holy Love book "Heaven's Last Call to Humanity"], and the miraculous image which I have sent to you. I ask you to understand, dear children, that all of these things are accomplished only though grace and not by your efforts alone. Let this also be a sign to you of the importance of my mission here, for today I tell you this is the place in the wilderness God has prepared for me. The place that was spoken of in **Revelation Chapter 12**. This is where we will pray for the Victory of the United Hearts of Jesus and Mary, and we will be Triumphant. Today We extend to you the Blessing of Our United Hearts."

■ **March 13, 1997 / Thursday Rosary Service.** Our Lady comes in light blue and white. She says, "Peace be with you. I come to make clear my message of the 12th. Do not fear this or any message. I do not come to you to tear down but to build up."

"I liken this refuge - My Prayer site - to the wilderness where I took refuge from Satan, for this is a spiritual refuge as was the refuge I fled to. That wilderness centuries ago was neither in Heaven nor on earth. This refuge is on earth, but so too is in My Heart and the hearts of those who come and believe. You will please make this known."

■ **March 17, 1997 - St. Patrick's Day.** Our Lady comes as Refuge of Holy Love. She says: "Peace be with you. Praise be Jesus, King of Heaven and Earth." Now she has St. Patrick with her. She says: "This saint sacrificed much and placed himself in much peril in order to convert Ireland. But you, my daughter, must resolve yourself to an even greater mission for your mission field is every soul. I do not place boundaries on the Holy Love message. Indeed, it spans the abyss between Heaven and earth. This saint, who stands here with me, had unwavering faith. He knew God's miracles would be granted in support of his mission. You too, my angel, will be sent amongst unbelievers, doubters, and those who will revile. But you must remain strong. Do not doubt. Every grace will be your support and stalwart allegiance. Expect the miraculous. You will endure and persevere."

"I ask all of my children, and most especially those who have made themselves a part of the Bread of Holy Love Movement, to pray with me now for the important and unprecedented times ahead. There are too many who never pray and who do not know God. They lead pagan lives behind Satan's lead. We must pray that such as these come in contact with the Holy Love message. I want to send you to many lowly places, to my poor, to prisons, and to the spiritually-impoverished rich. You need only my grace to succeed. Pray with me that my plan comes to fruition."

"I am leaving you. My blessing is upon you."

■ **March 18, 1997.** Our Lady comes as Refuge of Holy Love. She says: "My coming to you today is a grace for all mankind. My daughter, the sands of time are running out. Hearts will never find peace through efforts in the world. Peace cannot be legislated or negotiated. Peace must first be established between God and all people. Only then will peace and harmony be restored to the world. Today this area faces much loss of income. Those who are not in Our United Hearts will face the days ahead with fear. But I come to you so that nothing in the world brings you fear. I come so that you will be at peace. My way of Holy Love seems too simple to the sophisticated. But, I tell you, it is the way out of every situation. Holy Love is the harmony of the cosmos, of nature, and of all humanity."

"I come to you so that you will seek this solution - the only solution."

"I am blessing you."

■ **March 20, 1997 / Weekly Rosary Service.** Blessed Mother is here as Refuge of Holy Love. "Praise be Jesus. Pray with me now for all those who oppose Holy Love."

"Dear children, you have suffered greatly for your faith in me and your devotion to the Holy Rosary. Know that I have always held you in my Heart - this Solemn Refuge - this protection against all evil."

"I have held you in my Heart from the moment of your conception, My dear, dear children, and I shall not leave you. I am always in your midst. I am always championing your cause before the throne of God. Do not hesitate to call upon the grace of my Heart, for I am with you now and in the future. Tonight I am blessing you with my Blessing of Holy Love."

■ **March 21, 1997.** Our Lady comes as Refuge of Holy Love. She says: "Peace be with you. Praise be Jesus. Pray with me now for all those who do not believe."

"Child, I know much has been asked of you. You have been asked to believe when most did not believe. You have been asked to witness at great personal loss to yourself. But now, in these times, it is necessary that I ask more of you. Let this not be a burden, but see it only as a grace."

"My title, Refuge of Holy Love is eternally significant and a covenant with humanity. Because God chose that I be immaculately conceived, Holy Love comes to perfection in my Heart. Being perfected in Holy Love, I have the strongest desire to protect my children. While I am concerned for every aspect of your well-being, my greatest concern is for your faith. These are times of weak and lukewarm faith, for Satan seeks especially those who try to come close to me. Therefore, my Son sends me with this prayer - the embodiment of both titles, Protectress of the Faith and Refuge of Holy Love. Now I will state it."

Prayer To Mary, Refuge Of Holy Love
*"Mary, Protectress of the Faith, shelter my faith
in Your Immaculate Heart - Refuge of Holy Love. In*

the Refuge of Your Heart and united to the Sacred Heart of Jesus, Your Son, protect my faith from all evil. Amen."

"You will need to propagate this prayer with the image I have assisted you with. Opposition will not hold sway over it."

"Now I am blessing you."

■ **March 25, 1997.** Our Lady comes as Refuge of Holy Love. She says: "My angel, I come yet again as your Refuge and Protectress. I come to reveal that today all of earth and the universe is held on course by means of prayer that proceeds from Holy Love. It is the Rosary that holds back the Arm of Justice."

"You must challenge the hearts around you to live in the virtue of love. Pray to leave the sophistication of the world that leads away from me. Stay with me in childlike confidence so that I may lead you to salvation and into the United Hearts."

"The days and months just ahead will mark a particular blight of Holy Love everywhere in the world, but the sites of my apparitions will be maintained in my peace. Those that seek the Refuge of Holy Love with sincerity will find it. I am blessing you."

■ **March 26, 1997.** Our Lady comes as Refuge of Holy Love. She says: "My angel, please understand that part and most of your cross is coming from the opinions of others that do not have holy and loving hearts. But it was so with my Son as well. Throughout His Passion the greatest wound was knowing the lack of Holy Love in the hearts of His persecutors. Holy Love makes every cross more bearable."

"Know that my greatest graces are yet at hand. All that is coming proceeds from the United Hearts of Jesus and Mary - So much has been given the world through this mission. You do not realize nor comprehend the souls that have been touched. But now the greatest graces are at hand. The hidden power under my new title, Refuge of Holy Love, will be revealed. The strength of the scapular will unfold. The United Hearts of Jesus and Mary will hold sway over evil and be victorious in souls and in the world. My revelations to you will win popularity in distant and close proximity to my shrine, and unforeseen numbers will come on pilgrimage. This is because all is from Heaven. Prepare with much prayer. Prepare."

"I am your Refuge." She leaves.

■ **March 27, 1997.** Our Lady comes in green. She says: "Put your beads (rosary) down for a moment, My angel, and listen to Me. Let us give praise to Jesus, Who is King and Redeemer. I come to give meaning to the Scripture passage, 'to the rich more will be added, but to the poor, the little they have will be taken away.' Jesus does not allude to worldly wealth here. He is speaking of those rich in faith. The times have come when those with weak faith will be unable to hold onto what little they have. Satan's compromise has infiltrated and deceived even the most unlikely. It is necessary that you pray for all hearts to choose holiness. Some of the most unloving hearts will come in fear to the Spring. They will have faith only if they begin to love. They will love only when they humble themselves before God."

■ **March 27, 1997.** "Have a holy card printed in this Image [Mary, Refuge of Holy Love] together with the prayer I have given you. By this means I will protect faith and bring virtue to the unholy."

■ **March 30, 1997 - Easter Sunday.** Jesus says: "My reign is Love. My Divine Holy Love gives order to all things. Holy and Divine Love are the Holy and Divine Will of the Father."

"You do not yet fathom that Love and Mercy are inseparable as are the United Hearts of Jesus and Mary."

■ **March 30, 1997 - Easter Sunday.** Jesus says: "The

gateway to My Mercy is Holy Love. You must make this known."

April 1997

■ **April 1, 1997 / Conversation with JESUS.**
The Allegiance Of The United Hearts of Jesus and Mary
"Form the Allegiance of the United Hearts of Jesus and Mary, the purpose being to pray for the combined victory of Our United Hearts. One will not be victorious without the other. This is the reason I send My Mother with the message of Holy Love. Holy Love is the means by which We will be victorious."

"Jesus, how do I make known this allegiance?"

"When I send you to speak out on Holy Love, make it known. Teach them the chaplet [*Chaplet of the Two Hearts*]. Ask them to pray it towards the glorious victory of Our United Hearts. This is great consolation to my Heart which longs for this victory.

Chaplet Of The Two Hearts

The chaplet has 20 beads; five sets each of one (1) *Our Father* and three (3) *Hail Mary's*. (If you do not have a chaplet, try using the end of a rosary.) Following are the meditations to be announced at the beginning each set:

1. In Honor of the Sacred Heart of Jesus

2. In Honor of the Immaculate Heart of Mary

3. Meditating on the Passion of Our Lord

4. Meditating on the Sorrows of Mary

5. In Atonement to the Hearts of Jesus and Mary.
At the end, on the medal, say the *"Prayer to the United Hearts of Jesus and Mary."*

Prayer to the United Hearts of Jesus and Mary

O United Hearts of Jesus and Mary, You are all grace, all mercy, all love. Let my heart be joined to Yours, so that my every need is present in Your United Hearts. Most especially, shed Your grace upon this particular need (mention your need). Help me to recognize and accept your loving will in my life. Amen.

Conclude with the ejaculatory prayer:

"Sacred and Holy Wounds of the United Hearts of Jesus and Mary, answer my prayer."

■ **April 3, 1997.** "Dear children, each time I come to you, I come to bring you closer to God. These days especially, when evil holds sway over so many hearts, you need to make an effort to be holy. God cannot give you holiness, just as He cannot give you salvation. You, My dear, dear children, must freely choose it. Open your hearts then, and see that I have laid the way clear for you through Holy Love. Every effort in Holy Love is an effort towards deeper holiness and brings you closer to My Jesus. I impart my Blessing to you."

■ **April 3, 1997.** Our Lady comes under the title Refuge of Holy Love. She says: "Praise be Jesus. I am coming to you under this title of Holy Love because these are such decisive times. I want to help you, my dear children, to choose good over evil. Do not allow Satan to make every decision look trivial or the same as another. Every decision is for or against love, and so leads you closer or farther away from God. The evil one does not want you to understand this. His ultimate goal in every heart is to make damnation look like salvation. This is what compromise leads to."

"Let us discuss compromise. The heart of the church is the Eucharist. My Son is either truly present in the Eucharist or He is not. There is no in-between. Jesus says He is present."

■ **April 3, 1997 / Thursday Rosary Service.** "Our Lady is here as Mary, Refuge of Holy Love. She has the reliquary in front of her and the Curé de Ars is standing next to her. She says: "Praise be Jesus. These little ones (relics in reliquary) are the ones that saved your apartment today. You must listen to the good Curé when he says: 'Do not let Satan ruffle your feathers or gain entry to your peace.' Let us pray now for all unbelievers."

"Dear children, I come once again to help you choose holiness, to choose good over evil, heaven over earth. Do not be dismayed when Satan tries to enter your soul through lack of peace, but come to this refuge of Holy Love that is my Heart. I am with you, my dear children. I am with you always and eternally. I am blessing you."

■ **April 6, 1997 - Divine Mercy Sunday.** Blessed Mother is here as Mary, Refuge of Holy Love. She says: "Praise be Jesus, Alleluia! Dear children, pray with me now that God's Mercy will overcome all evil in the world."

"Dear children, I come to you today so that you will love and have compassion for your fellow man. It is God's Mercy and God's Love that sends me to you once again. I want you to know, dear children, that Satan flees before the image, Mary, Refuge of Holy Love."

"Make sure, my daughter, to tell the people that this image in your apartment vanquished the fire in the apartment complex."

"Dear children, pray always for the lukewarm, for they are a particular sword in the Heart of My Son. Today I am blessing you with my Blessing of Holy Love."

■ **April 10, 1997 / Thursday Rosary Service.** Our Lady is here as Mary, Refuge of Holy Love. She says: "Praise be Jesus. Pray with me now, dear children, for the needs of all those here present tonight and for those who are journeying here on the 12th."

"Dear children, thank you for coming here tonight and praying with me. You have persevered, and I love you for it. You have come by my invitation; and from here, I will address your needs. I will address individuals, certain groups, and the needs of all nations. Continue to be the light of Holy Love to those around you. I will pour forth my grace in abundance upon you, upon this property, and upon those who come here. Tonight I am blessing you with my Blessing of Holy Love."

■ **April 12, 1997 / Monthly Message To All Nations.** *(This message was given in two parts)* Blessed Mother is here as Our Lady of Guadalupe. A lighted cross was in the sky before Our Lady came. She says: "Praise be Jesus. Pray with me now for the needs of all here present today, especially the unbelievers."

"Your mission is now beginning, the unfolding of which is yet to come. I mean to reveal to you the meaning of this Refuge of Holy Love, for herein Jesus confides the peace of the world. Nation shall rise against nation, and nature itself will take revenge against humanity. But in every need, trust that the solution is through my grace and within this solemn Refuge."

"You, my daughter, have experienced Satan's wrath personally. But in his ignorance of all that lies humble before God, he could not comprehend My intercession. Therefore, I say to you, have no misgivings concerning future events. For the future belongs to My grace. I give praise to Jesus in all of this. Remember, your lives and all your possessions are mine and untouchable by evil." *(Reference to St. Louis de Montfort "Total Consecration.")*

"Now I am speaking once again publicly and to all nations."

"Dear children, the war of all wars is already being waged. I invite you to realize this. The battle I speak of is being fought in every heart. It is the war between good and evil. Because most do not even recognize the enemy, my Son sends me to you with the Holy Love Message so that you may see where the foe lays hidden."

"Today, too many are choosing the path of perdition. Thus, My Mantle of Protection has been removed from your country and all nations who legislate against the Ten Commandments God has set forth. This means great tribulation just ahead. Know that I remain a Refuge and Protection of the righteous."

Blessed Mother is now here as Mary, Refuge of Holy Love, and Jesus is now with Blessed Mother. Dear Children, just as the rain has washed the earth clean, today I help you to realize that Holy Love will wash your hearts of all iniquity. My Son has removed most every nation from under My Mantle of Protection, for they do not follow the Divine Will of God in all His Commandments. But I am protecting those who seek the Refuge of My Immaculate Heart with sincerity. And even now I speak to you in the midst of a group of faithful. Such spiritual refuge centers are the balm that soothe My Sorrowing Heart."

"Jesus and I extend to you the Blessing of the United Hearts."

■ **April 13, 1997 / 2nd Sunday to Pray Against Abortion.** Our Lady is here as Our Lady of Guadalupe. She says: "Praise be Jesus. Dear children, I come to you today, once again, to invite you to understand that your country is now unprotected by Heaven, just as the unborn are unprotected by law. You must pray that the effects of this sin, and the tribulations that are to come are recognized for what they are. Be my weapon against this evil, dear children. Continue to pray, pray, pray. I am blessing you."

■ **April 24, 1997 / Thursday Rosary Service.** Our Lady is here as Mary, Refuge of Holy Love. She says: "Praise be Jesus. I come as your Mother and Refuge. Pray with me now for those who do not love - and do not believe."

"Dear children, tonight I invite you to realize that when the battle is the fiercest, victory is at hand. So it is today in hearts and in the world. Satan's power is dwindling and in anger his attacks are most ferocious. But I am with you in Holy Love.

My Heart is continually your Refuge and Fortress. Depend on Me and not on your own capabilities."

"Dear children, do not fear any portion of the future, for I am with you. In your weakness, I am your strength. I am blessing you."

■ **April 24, 1997 / Thursday Rosary Service.** Blessed Mother is here as Mary, Refuge of Holy Love. There is a great light all around her. "Dear children, thank you for answering my call to come here tonight. Let us pray now for those who have been invited and have refused to come."

"Dear children, tonight I invite you to open your hearts in prayer. In the present moment let your hearts be a prayer. You may think that your prayers make no difference, but I tell you, they are the difference between light and darkness. I am calling you to be living prayers of Holy Love; then those who do not have peace in their hearts around you will be called to their conversion through your own lives and your witness to Holy Love."

"Dear children, tonight I am blessing you with my Blessing of Holy Love."

■ **April 27, 1997 / 4th Sunday to Pray for Unbelievers.** Our Lady is here as Mary, Refuge of Holy Love. She says: "Praise be to Jesus. Pray with me now, dear children, for all unbelievers."

"Dear children, today I want to give you understanding in your hearts as to what an unbeliever is. An unbeliever, dear children, is one who has not responded to my call to conversion. If he does not surrender, then his will does not light the way upon the path of Holy Love. For it is only through your own will, dear children, that you will see the way to go to the Refuge of My Immaculate Heart. It is for such as these that we have begun to pray on these special days (every 4th Sunday). Today I am blessing you with my Blessing of Holy Love."

■ **April 28, 1997 / Monday Praise Service.** Our Lady comes as Refuge of Holy Love. "My children, my dear children, my victory and my grace are not in your great numbers but in the prayers that proceed from your hearts. Continue to pray, pray, pray."

May 1997

■ **May 1, 1997 / Thursday Rosary Service.** Blessed Mother is here as Mary, Refuge of Holy Love. She says: "Praise be to Jesus. My little children, I extend my invitation to be here tonight to all sinners and all nations. However, you are the ones who have responded to my call. Let us pray together now for those who do not come and do not pray."

"Dear children, tonight I invite you to realize that you are present here on this property, for it is a spiritual refuge. It is here that I will instruct and show the way to eternal life. It is here you will be protected from the terror of the demons and from the one who strikes at the heel of the woman clothed with the sun. Tonight I am blessing you with my Blessing of Holy Love."

■ **May 2, 1997.** "The enemy of my Immaculate Heart, who is prince of this world, attacks you through those who belong to the world. But I am your Advocate before my Son and before God the Eternal Father. I am your protection. Do not fear. If you are listening, you will be at peace. Praise be Jesus."

■ **May 4, 1997.** Our Lady comes as Refuge of Holy Love. She says: "Praise be Jesus. Please understand, my daughter, it is pride that draws people off the path of Holy Love in every instance. Pride is the marauder that steals the sheep from the flock and from under the watchful eye of the Good Shepherd."

"Those of my children firmly implanted in the Refuge of my Immaculate Heart will see Holy Love as the course of every action and the basis of every decision. See that the tide of controversy around my mission of Holy Love is really an attack on my Immaculate Heart.

"Because I am victorious in the end, the malefactor will not succeed. He is basing his attack on intellectual pride, but the intellect is not your salvation. Holy Love is your salvation."

"Spiritual pride and spiritual envy are enemies of the soul. God loves and favors the simple and humble soul. Many may long to see me through love in their hearts. But those who long to see me with envious hearts need to repent."

"The Flame of my Heart is given to this generation as a cleansing and purifying Flame. It is preparing all who will partake for the coming of my Royal Son - the Priest of all, the One without stain or blemish, the King and Redeemer of all people and all nations. My coming to you is but a humble beginning. My visits are meant to bring you into this Refuge of Holy Love - My Heart."

"To draw the proud and unbelieving souls into this Refuge, you will witness many events unforeseen and unprecedented. Look to this Image (Mary, Refuge of Holy Love) for the unexpected, as I summon the world to conversion. My daughter I impart to you my Blessing of Holy Love."

■ **May 5, 1997 - Feast of Holy Love.** Our Lady comes as Mary, Refuge of Holy Love. She says: "Praise be Jesus. Today, I come to you once again transcending time and space to be with you. I come to you in the midst of despair and hope, wealth and want, faith and apathy. I come to exact certain attitudes from humanity. I desire all be contrite and reconcile themselves to God. I bring you love and I ask your love in return."

"Those that do not love cannot live eternally. I long, oh I long to spend eternity with all of my children. I cannot give you My grace if you will not open your hearts. My dear children, I wish to give you hearts full of Holy Love, which is the greatest grace. The signs I give you, such as your rosaries turning color or images caught on film, are just that, signs that I come to you. The real grace is the Holy Love in your hearts. Therefore, surrender to Me, your Refuge and Mother. I will give you more than you anticipate receiving. Surrender. I will give you more than the world could afford to give you. Abandon yourselves to me. I come clothed in love, and I desire to wrap you in my mantle of love. I am blessing you."

■ **May 5, 1997 - Feast of Holy Love / Prayer Service.** Blessed Mother is here as Mary, Refuge of Holy Love. She says: "Dear children, tonight, you are the cause of my joy. Pray with me now in thanksgiving for this evening."

"Dear children, tonight, please understand, that I am the Woman Clothed with the Sun and the moon beneath her feet. And you, my dear children, are the constellations of Holy Love all around me. Together We comprise a universe all its own. A universe of Holy Love. Dear children, I am rejoicing in your response to my call. And I am asking you to complete my joy by giving this message to whomever you meet. Tonight I am blessing you with my Blessing of Holy Love."

■ **May 8, 1997.** Jesus says: "I want to draw you into My Sacred Heart, which is here in the present moment. To Me, the present moment is always and eternal. I hold no memory of your last transgression against love. I am not now judging the decisions you will make in the future. I am just here, now, with you and around you, and in your midst. Do you not recognize Me?"

■ **May 8, 1997 / Thursday Rosary Service.** Blessed Mother is here as Mary, Refuge of Holy Love. She says: "Praise be Jesus. Dear children, tonight once again join me in prayer for the unbelievers."

"Dear children tonight I invite you to surrender your hearts to prayer, for it is in this surrender that I am able to give you the fullness of my grace. Turn over your lives to Holy Love, then I can use you as weapons against evil. Dear children, I am longing to spend eternity in Paradise with you, but I can only do this if you surrender to me. I am blessing you with my Motherly Blessing."

■ **May 11, 1997 - Mother's Day / Second Sunday of the Month - To Pray Against Abortion.** Blessed Mother is here as the Sorrowful Mother. She says: "Praise be Jesus. Pray with me now, dear children, for all those who have participated in the sin of abortion."

"Dear children, today I inform you that when my Son returns, all will accept me as their Mother. But today, my dear children, it is true that I am not the Mother of most, for they will not accept me; and they will not live with love in their hearts. My heart bleeds, and I weep for those who turn their back on love. I am calling you into the one fold where all is love in the present moment. My heart bleeds, and I weep for those who have left me, who once were in my bosom of grace. But, as a loving Mother, I desire to share my grace with you, as you share your joys and your sorrows with me. Today I am blessing you with my Blessing of Motherly Love.

■ **May 12, 1997 / Monthly Message To All Nations.** *(The following message was given in two parts.)* Our Lady comes as Our Lady of Guadalupe. She says: "Praise be to Jesus."

"I have come into the world to reveal the compromise that has weakened the faith in the hearts of many. Many have made decisions that would bring them laud in the world. Jesus sends Me to you to help you choose that which will bring you salvation."

"Today, for the first time, I invite you to understand that lack of Holy Love in hearts has destroyed right reason. Right reason is all reason based on Holy Love. When the heart is not steeped in Holy Love, compromise replaces right reason. This is why you have abortion, pornography, all sorts of vice, homosexuality, corrupt governments, compromised faith and morals, and more. It is Satan who takes right reason out of hearts. It is Satan who promotes compromise in hearts."

"Your hearts, my dear children, are what Satan pursues. For it is your heart that determines damnation or salvation. When my Son returns, as He will, you will be judged on your own merit - not on what everyone else thinks or does."

"In the world, many and most nations have been led astray through the disintegration of right reason in hearts. As hearts go, so go whole nations; and as nations go, so goes the world."

"There are great numbers of martyrs of the faith in the world these days. Many, many are living in this country. I call them martyrs for these holy and consecrated ones are martyrs of the heart. These are the priests who are unafraid to show devotion to me and hold fast to my place in church tradition. These are the lay people who dedicated their lives to my cause amidst great price. I will not abandon these dear children of mine, but will present them myself to my Son at the hour of His telling."

"Dear children, I am in your midst as the Sorrowful Woman Clothed with the Sun, the Comfortress of the Afflicted and the Mediatrix of All Grace. I invite you to pray with me now for all those who do not believe."

Jesus is now with Blessed Mother. They both have their Hearts exposed. "Dear children, I come to you in sorrow, inviting you to understand that certain persuasions have been accepted, allowing the Antichrist to come to power. You, my dear children, are my army against all evil. Because of your faith, your perseverance, I come to you still, pouring my grace upon the world, converting souls, and showing the way to salvation. Today We extend to you the Blessing of Our United Hearts."

■ **May 15, 1997.** Mary comes as Refuge of Holy Love. "My daughter, I come to you today as your Confidante, Refuge, and Mother. I come to give praise and great honor to Jesus."

"My coming to you should preclude any fear or misgiving

you may harbor in your heart. Please understand that there are many who offer their judgments concerning my appearances to you, but they are of undefined faith and lukewarm conviction. This is why I need to come to you and through you to deliver My Grace and My Message around the earth. If hearts were convicted in Holy Love, they would not question and find fault. When, my Son returns, as He will, the scrutiny will stop and the rejoicing will begin. Until then, you must persevere in patience towards the awkward unbelievers. Some want very much to believe but fear ridicule."

"But today, I come with a more important message than to calm your troubled heart. You have been questioning my telling you that My Image, Refuge of Holy Love, is miraculous. You ask in what way is it miraculous. My sweet daughter, it is miraculous first of all because I held and guided your hand in its execution. Next, I tell you that Satan will flee before the invocation *'Mary, Refuge of Holy Love, pray for us.'* This title is in itself a Spiritual Refuge. The more you will persevere speaking this little ejaculatory prayer, the deeper I will take you into my Heart. Let it be forever on your lips. I will convict souls in the areas of their lives most vulnerable to lack of love. I have come to you to save souls, not to dazzle the sightseers; but as my image brings spiritual healing, it will also bring with it peace."

"You will please note the cross on My Hand which signifies an as yet unproclaimed dogma. It is a sign of My Suffering with My Beloved Son at the Hour of His Passion and Death."

"I have come to give you much. Your 'yes' is my comfort and joy. I am blessing you."

■ **May 15, 1997 / Thursday Rosary Service.** Blessed Mother is here as Mary, Refuge of Holy Love. She is wearing the same crown that is on our large statue [the one from the May 5th crowning]. She says: "Praise be to Jesus." Pray with me now, dear children, for all those who come but do not believe."

"Dear children, today I invite you to realize that is it not my coming to you that is the greatest gift. The greatest gift is My Son in the Eucharist. And I invite you to see that your response to my call is also a gift and a grace. It is not by My coming to you that you will find the path of salvation, but in your response to My call and My Message in your heart. Tonight I am blessing you with my Blessing of Holy Love."

■ **May 16, 1997.** *(Philadelphia, PA)* Blessed Mother is here as Mary, Refuge of Holy Love. She says: "Praise be to Jesus. Dear children, pray with me now for the conversion of all unbelievers."

"Dear children, tonight I invite you into the Refuge of My Immaculate Heart through your 'yes' to Holy Love. When you are living with hearts full of Holy Love, dear children, I am taking you into my Motherly Heart and freeing you of every burden of the world. I want to give you my peace and My grace by this means. Tonight I am extending to you my Blessing of Holy Love."

■ **May 22, 1997 / Thursday Rosary Service.** Blessed Mother is here as Mary, Refuge of Holy Love. She says: "Praise be to Jesus. Dear children, pray with me now for all the spiritually impoverished."

"Dear children, tonight, I invite you to understand that the smallest resentment, when held in your heart, can become unforgiveness. This unforgiveness blocks my grace from taking you into the depths of My Immaculate Heart. Dear children, be on guard over all memories which are destructive to Holy Love. Do not hold records in your hearts of wrongs done against you - but in all things love. Tonight I am blessing you with my Blessing of Holy Love."

■ **May 25, 1997 / 4th Sunday - To Pray For Unbelievers.** Blessed Mother is here as Mary, Refuge of Holy Love. She has a crown over the flame above Her Heart. She says: "Praise be to Jesus. My children, pray with me now for the unbelievers."

As Blessed Mother prayed, She had three rays of light come from above, one ray to her Heart and the other two onto each hand."

"I come, dear children to define to you who is the UNBELIEVER. The unbeliever is the one with the divided heart who does not lead a Christ-centered life. The unbeliever is the one who compromises his faith to suit his own needs. Dear children, I come to you today with the crown of victory over the flame of love that is my Heart. This represents to you and to the world, my dear children, that my victory is coming through this Flame of Holy Love. Thus it will be represented on every Image of Mary, Refuge of Holy Love. Today I impart to you my Blessing of Holy Love."

■ **May 27, 1997.** Our Lady is here as Mary, Refuge of Holy Love. she says: "Grace and peace be with you. Praise be Jesus. My daughter, I come to you bring enlightenment. The crown over the Flame of Holy Love above my Heart is set with three stones. The one in the center represents Jesus, Who is the center of the universe. On each side you see a smaller stone. One represents Me, the Second Eve and the path to the New Jerusalem. The other stone represents the Church which at Christ's coming will be united and made one with humanity. These three - Jesus, Mary, and the Church - will be triumphant and reign in glory in the New Jerusalem. The Era of Peace which will ensue after this triumph will last 1000 years." (*2 Peter 3:8* - "But do not ignore this one fact, beloved, that with the Lord one day is as a thousand years, and a thousand years as one day.")

"Jesus is granting to the world and through My Mission a very great grace. Because My Son desires I be honored in this role, a certain proclamation will come from My Holy Father. In support of this My Grace will come. It is so the multitudes will know and believe. These words are not empty, but carry with them the substance of grace. I am leaving you only to return later."

■ **May 29, 1997 / Thursday Rosary Service.** Blessed Mother is here as Mary, Refuge of Holy Love. She says: "Praise be Jesus. Dear children, pray with me once again tonight for those who do not love."

"Dear children, tonight I invite you to realize that the greatest sorrow of Our United Hearts is the lack of love in the world. Therefore, know and understand, that Our triumph and victory will come through love. It is thus I desire that you consecrate yourselves in the present moment to Holy Love. Live the message in this way, and I will use you to the fullest extent as my apostles. Tonight I am blessing you with my Blessing of Holy Love."

■ **May 30, 1997.** Jesus says: "My greatest pain during My Passion and Death was not physical but a pain of the Heart. I sorrowed as I poured out My life for all humanity for the lack of love in hearts."

■ **May 31, 1997.** Our Lady comes all in white. She says: "Praise be Jesus. I come to reveal and inform."

"This weather is God's disdain for the choices of mankind. Normal weather is not normal anymore. [It has rained for five straight days.] 'Weather extremes' are the normal. But these signs escape those of the world."

"I have come to show you the way to be happy. Happiness is complete surrender to God in everything. In surrendering everything, you no longer have a misfortune or a cross that is all yours. No, every joy and sorrow is shared with Jesus. In trusting all things to Providence, you are also trusting God's Will. God's Will for you is Holy Love, and in Holy Love you have come full circle."

"Do not from this time on claim anything, cross or joy, as yours alone. Share all things with God, and you will be at peace. If you ask me, I will help you. You are my little ones. I am blessing you."

June 1997

■ **June 1, 1997.** Our Lady comes as Refuge of Holy Love. She says: "Praise be Jesus. Dear daughter, you are in the depths of My Heart. Tell My children that for the sinner there is but one path - the Flame of Holy Love. To pass through this Flame takes courage and introspect. But, as you submerge yourself in Holy Love, I am with you and supporting you."

"Today, there are many, many who turn their backs and run from this Flame as though it would devour them. It is their own self that destroys their soul. It is their fear of saying 'yes' that makes them run."

"I have come to bring you now to my triumph, for it is within this Flame of Love that Satan will be consumed and devoured. Do not think he is unaware of this. In the end he will be rendered harmless. Today, he is frantic."

"But My Image (Refuge of Holy Love) leaves him in terror. Use it. Carry it with you. Have it near you. Hold it prominent in your homes. He has no weapon to match this Holy Image."

"I am with you. I will defeat Satan thorough your prayers. I am blessing you."

■ **June 2, 1997.** "Dear children, I invite you to pray with me. When you pray the Rosary, I am with you fingering the beads. Your humblest effort and your greatest efforts are one. God desires your willingness to pray - even amidst distractions. Come and be with me. Sit with me and pray. I will bless you."

■ **June 5, 1997 / Thursday Rosary Service.** Our Lady is here as Mary, Refuge of Holy Love. She says: "Praise be Jesus. My little children, pray with me tonight for the spiritually impoverished."

"Dear children, tonight I invite you to see that many hearts are divided, some loving God, some loving only self. I have come to help you choose, my dear children, in favor of Holy

Love, which puts God above all else, your neighbor second, and self last. Make your decisions in thought, word, and deed according to Holy Love. Dear children. Tonight I am blessing you with my Blessing of Holy Love."

■ **June 7, 1997.** *(From St. John Vianney, the Curé D'Ars - Patron of Parish Priests)* I look up to see the Curé D'Ars. He says, "I see you are not so glad to see me. We do not operate in fear. I know you are afraid I will tell you things that will leave you open to criticism. I only come bearing truth."

"Where do I begin? Faith in the Holy Father, faith in the Real Presence in the Eucharist, devotion to Our Lady and the Holy Rosary - these are the three strong points that a good priest must have. There is nothing here open to debate or compromise. These are Church doctrine. No one can be one-half a Catholic. You either believe or you don't."

"The function of a priest is to bring the sacraments to the people. Nothing should get in the way of this."

"The priest can change many souls and situations from the pulpit and by his lifestyle. He can uncover sin, fight abortion, feed the hungry, and strengthen faith. He can promote the family Rosary and Rosary groups in his own parish. He can ask for prayers against abortion and in support of the Holy Father and the Church. He can lead a saintly, exemplary life not being afraid of unpopularity or being a sign of the priesthood in the world - not being afraid to uncover sin."

"A vocation is a special gift from God. It is a call, and within that call is grave responsibility towards his parishioners and their salvation,"

The Curé nods to me. "There now. Was that so bad? Move forward." He blesses me and leaves.

■ **June 7, 1997 - Feast of the Immaculate Heart of Mary.** Our Lady comes in blue and white. She has Her Heart exposed. She says: "All praise be Jesus. My angel, it is today as it was in the time of Jesus. Sometimes my messages fall upon infertile soil, that is the message falls by the wayside and succumbs to the allurements and the opinions of the world. I desire all people seek the Refuge of Holy love that is my Heart. I desire to describe this solemn Refuge to you today."

"A refuge is a place of safety, a port in the storm, and a shelter of provision. My Immaculate Heart is all of these things. I call you into my Heart that I may protect you from the evil around you in the world today. Satan rarely comes as himself but in every form of disguise. He uses the snare of television to invade your leisure. He writes in newspapers, magazines, and books. He is proficient in every form of art and music. He uses modern communications such as the Internet and e-mail. He transposes himself on good to create evil."

"It is in the Refuge of my Heart I will help you to discover Satan in your life and in the world. In the shelter of my Heart I will protect your faith. Today the Church has been infiltrated with confusion. Through Holy Love I can help you uncover his snares."

"It is through the grace of my Heart all good comes. I dispense the graces I am given by my Son. During these times you are certain prey for Satan without the intervention of my grace."

"This Heart, this Refuge is a shelter that leads to the Kingdom of God and the New Jerusalem. My Heart will take you into the era of peace. It is the vessel of sanctification, the Harbor leading to God's Ocean of Mercy and Compassion."

"To enter, you need more than my invitation. With your will, you need to turn your hearts over to me. You need to live in Holy Love. Thus clothed, I will open wide the door of my Heart."

"My angel, I need for you to make all of this known."

■ **June 8, 1997.** *(From the Curé D'Ars - Patron of Parish Priests)* I look up to see the Curé D'Ars once again. He says, "Forgive the intrusion. I like your dress, for it is modest." (I had been concerned it was too long.) He goes on. "I have come to describe to you the perfect Cardinal, Archbishop, and Bishop.

Such a one is completely loyal to the present Holy Father. He does not support heresy but confronts it. He is not politically motivated nor concerned with popularity within Church ranks or in the world. He is a shepherd standing for Church tradition and truth."

"I come to you so that those who are listening will be able to recognize good and discern evil." He blessed me and left.

■ **June 8, 1997 / 2nd Sunday of the Month - To Pray Against Abortion.** Blessed Mother is here Our Lady of Guadalupe. She says: "Praise be Jesus. Pray with me now dear children for those who participate in the sin of abortion."

"Dear children, the sin of abortion is a silent holocaust destroying lives of national leaders, Church leaders, and world renowned scientists.* Because it is such a gruesome sin, it allows Satan to invade many lives and to influence the future of every nation and even the planet on which you live. For justice will have its way in the end. It is important that you continue to remember this very special intention of mine, that consciences awaken as to the true nature of abortion and to Satan's lies. Pray, pray, pray. Today I am blessing you with My Blessing of Motherly Love."

Four years ago Blessed Mother had advised the visionary, Maureen, that THE FUTURE SCIENTIST WHO WAS TO DISCOVER THE CURE FOR CANCER and THE FUTURE SCIENTIST WHO WAS TO DISCOVER THE CURE FOR AIDS were both ABORTED.

■ **June 10, 1997.** Jesus says: "My Mother's coming to you is to prepare the world for the victory of the United Hearts of Jesus and Mary. This victory is in and through My Mother's call. In the victory of the United Hearts, each heart will be triumphant. Holy Love will reign with Divine Love. God will be established once again as King and Center of all hearts, the world, and the universe."

"You cannot fail when you surrender to this call. The victory is pre-ordained in the Heart of the Eternal Father. Accept My victory in your heart - now in the present moment."

■ **June 11, 1997.** Jesus says: "The Flame of My Mother's Heart is Holy Love. The Flame of My Heart is Divine Love. The Flame of Holy Love purifies. The Flame of Divine Love - loves. When you are in the Flame of Divine Love, you are in Me and I am in you. The center of your existence is to love."

■ **June 12, 1997 / Monthly Message To All Nations.** *(The following message was given in multiple parts. The parts are interspersed.)* Blessed Mother is here as Mary, Refuge of Holy Love. She says: "Praise be Jesus. Thank you for responding to my call to be here today. Pray with me now for those who hear but do not believe."

"Once again I come seeking your reconciliation with God. God remains constant in His steadfast love. It is you that have distanced yourselves from Him."

"Those who make gods of their free conscience, which is free will, are on the path to perdition. You cannot be saved outside of God's Holy and Divine Will, which is Holy Love."

"I come bringing you love and seeking your love in return." (Now she is showing me a human heart in front of her. It has many holes in it and something seems to be pouring out of the holes.) Our Lady says: "This is the heart of many in the world. All my grace escapes them. Perhaps they believe and follow the righteous path briefly. But Satan gains easy access through flaws in Holy Love. These holes you see are the flaws."

"Such a heart is compromised. This is how Satan has manipulated laws to his liking. Pray and sacrifice that hearts be made one with their Creator. I come to you so that Heaven and earth will be united in every human heart."

"My children, it is the hour of apocalypse spoken of by the prophet Daniel. Do not think that because evil thrives in hearts that God will not intervene. In His compassionate Mercy, He gives mankind every opportunity to convert and reverse all evil."

"I have come to show you the way to conversion. Open your hearts as roses in the sun. I have brought you here today for my purpose and your welfare, so that you will believe and help others to believe. I invite you into my Heart. You never know which chance may be your last. You do not know the hour of Jesus' return."

"Dear children, today you pray amidst my tears [it was raining]. I am sorrowful today for what is to come to the world, for the world as you know it teeters on the brink of disaster. It is by merit of your prayers and sacrifices that I am thus able to withhold the hand of justice. My dear children, see what is to come." Maureen now sees a globe of fire coming toward her that passes by. Then another globe appeared that was in total darkness."

"But it is within the Refuge of my Immaculate Heart that I will shelter you. Just as today you find shelter under your umbrellas, so my Heart will be your Refuge in the great trials that lie ahead, as also it will be your consolation."

Jesus is now with Blessed Mother. They extend to us the Blessing of the United Hearts.

■ **June 16, 1997.** Jesus says: "Regard My feelings. I have made Myself a Prisoner among men. Yet I am totally free in the Divine Will of the Father."

■ **June 17, 1997.** When I arrived in the chapel, Our Lady was by the tabernacle waiting. She said: "Come, my daughter, sit with me. Today I was with you in the store. I was hoping you would see the analogy between the electrical power and the light of Holy Love I bring to souls." (I was in a large store earlier. There was a power outage and the auxiliary lights went on.) Our Lady continues, "Some souls - many souls - have only a small light within them. They may be good people in some circumstances, but they do not consciously try to live in Holy Love to please God. Their good deeds are wasted when they perform them for human approval or out of self-satisfaction. I cannot communicate to you on the human level how pleasing it is to God when you perform acts of love out of love for Him. It does not matter how big or how little the act of charity is. What counts is the amount of Holy Love with which you perform it."

"Some go through life only seeking to satisfy themselves. I long to turn on the light of Holy Love in their hearts and in their lives. Holy Love is never wrong and makes all deeds worthy. I am blessing you."

■ **June 18, 1997.**
Patron Saints Of The Holy Love Mission

Our Lady comes as Refuge of Holy Love. She has Padre Pio and St. Therese on either side of her. They are very small. She says: "Praise be to Jesus. My angel, I invite you to put this down. This mission has as its patron and patroness these two saints. Now, my daughter, I will reveal to you some things you cannot understand on your own."

"Both of these (St. Therese - Padre Pio) were victims of love - Holy Love. Both made great strides to bridge the span between Heaven and earth through Holy Love. The good Father Pio carried visible signs on his body of this love, a love he shared with His Savior. I come to you under this title, Refuge of Holy Love, bearing this sign of love on my hand which I extend to the world. Holy Love is the bridge of reconciliation between Heaven and earth. The Cross of Jesus is love. When I cooperated in the Passion and Death of my son, I extended this bridge of love to all humanity. As yet to be pronounced is this my role."

"But, I come to you showing you the bridge of reconciliation between all people and God, so that many will follow across this bridge. Thus the abyss will be conquered."

"Draw then your final conclusion and realization of the

impact of my coming to you. I come to call every soul to Holy Love and across the bridge of reconciliation. I call my children to follow me in docility traversing the abyss in faith. At the end is victory. At the end is the triumph of the United Hearts."

"Perhaps now, my daughter, you can see all the innuendoes and nuances of my coming to you. Let there be no longer a mystery in your heart, but accept in childlike faith my great confidence in you."

■ **June 19, 1997 / Thursday Rosary Service.** Blessed Mother is here as Mary, Refuge of Holy Love. She says: "Praise be Jesus. My dear children, pray with me tonight for all unbelievers."

"My dear children, I have invited you here tonight to be with me at my apparition site, and you have come consenting with your will to be with me. Surrender to me your hearts. In this surrender, I invite you to see that your lives will change. And when you leave my apparition site, you will be renewed in Holy Love."

"Dear children, I come to gather all nations into My Heart of love, which is the path, the gateway, and the bridge to Heaven. I am blessing you with my Blessing of Holy Love."

■ **June 20, 1997.** Our Lady comes as Mary, Refuge of Holy Love. "My daughter, I come to you as I have promised and foretold. I ask you to have confidence in me now, as I must bring you a special message."

"I come as your Advocate and Mother. I ask you to make this known to all of my little children. The year ahead - this June to the next - will be a year of untold sorrow and joy. Many revelations [made by the Virgin Mary during this century] will be realized. Those who are weak will not understand, just as they fail to see today. The current tribulations and evils in the world are only a prelude of what is to come."

"As I come seeking your reconciliation with God, Satan is at my heel seeking your destruction. The apostasy and heresy that is in hearts now, will be externalized as never before. But I do not predict to you destruction of the Church. Many will succumb but not all."

"Those who seek the bridge of reconciliation with God - the bridge which is my Heart and Holy Love - will be safe. I speak of spiritual safety, for my Heart is your Spiritual Refuge. Those who pursue their own will shall be easily misled."

"My daughter, you need not defend this way of love and reconciliation. You need only point it out. This is how Jesus taught."

"The lives of many will be altered in this year of grave decision. This year continues under the reign of Jesus, King of Mercy and Love. But coming swiftly is my Son's reign as Just Judge."

"I do not come to frighten but to awaken sleeping consciences. I do not come to satisfy the curious but to change hearts. The privilege of my coming to you is for all nations and all people. All of these can traverse the bridge of Holy Love. They must choose."

"The reign of the United Hearts will bring an end to division. It is time to unite in this victory. It is time to believe."

■ **June 22, 1997 / 4th Sunday of the Month - To Pray for Unbelievers.** Blessed Mother is here as Mary, Refuge of Holy Love. She says: "Praise be Jesus. Dear children, pray with me now for those who are afraid to believe openly in my apparitions here."

"Dear children, today I invite you to understand that it is not one person that I come to and to whom I ask to spread the message, but it is all. If you have heard my Message of Holy Love you must spread it, especially amongst those who do not believe. Be apostles of my Heart. Today, I remind you that I am your Mother. You must not be afraid of your Mother, or ashamed, but openly face those who mock me. I am blessing you with my Blessing of Holy Love."

■ **June 23, 1997 / Monday Night Praise Group.** Blessed Mother is here as Mary, Refuge of Holy Love. Jesus is with her with His Heart exposed."

She says: "Praise be Jesus. Dear children, My Son has graciously condescended to come with me today, as He will every Monday. We will extend to you, at the end of our meeting, the Blessing of the United Hearts, for with it carries much grace of healing both physical, spiritual, and also emotional."

"Come to realize, my dear children, that the Image of the United Hearts represents the path, the gateway, the corridor, and the Kingdom which is the goal. Much of humanity, in this present moment, stands at the foot of the bridge of Holy Love. You must pray, my dear children, that they choose salvation and not perdition, for so much confusion and compromise is in hearts today. Now We are extending to you the Blessing of Our United Hearts."

■ **June 25, 1997.** *(Before Communion)* Jesus says: "I am your Jesus, born Incarnate."

"Approach the altar with great reverence and faith. Noah did not have such a gift. I am with you as I can be during these times. You will succeed for I am with you. You will persevere for I am with you."

■ **June 25, 1997 - Feast of St. John the Baptist.** Our Lady comes as Our Lady of Fatima. She says: "Praise be Jesus. I come as Herald of My Son's return. I come to summon all nations into my Immaculate Heart. It is foretold in Scripture what is to come." *(Daniel Chapter 7)*

"I come to you today as your Mediatrix and Advocate. I come to warn you against an ungodly union forming amongst nations. In this unity is loss of independence and identity. It will bring no order but disorder."

"Ahead are great trials. The greatest will be suffered by those people who now live sophisticated lives and by nations who have led multitudes astray."

"The humble and those consecrated to my Immaculate

Heart will find peace in the midst of adversity. I will be with them. Great and unforetold are the miracles and graces that will sustain my little ones during these times."

"Nations must not seek to be united under an earthly leader but united in my Heart - united in Holy Love. Pray, oh pray for government leaders who have compromised mankind's position before God. Pray for Church leaders who do not recognize their role in these times."

"With your Rosary you can overcome evil and change the course of coming events. You must pray. I am blessing you."

■ **June 25, 1997.** Our Lady comes as Our Lady of Guadalupe. She says: "It is important that I speak to you now as a mother concerned for her children."

"When your country was founded, hearts were well-centered in Christ. Your country even adopted as its by-word. 'In God We Trust!' But today, God has been forced out of hearts. Consciences have fallen asleep. The word 'freedom' has been convoluted and now stands for every sort of abomination and debauchery against God's law. Because your nation leads and holds much influence over other nations, great, great are the consequences of ungodly decisions. The Church itself stands compromised by opinions instead of loyalty to the Holy Father."

"I am calling the laity to unite in the Hearts of Jesus and Mary. Pray for the courage to battle, in the present moment, every type of hypocrisy and lie Satan is spreading. I am with you. I want to protect you. The future depends on your prayers."

■ **June 26, 1997 / Thursday Rosary Service.** Blessed Mother is here as Mary, Refuge of Holy Love. She came with many angels who are all around her. She says: "Praise be Jesus. I come tonight bringing you life and strength. Dear children, pray with me for those who surrender only superficially to Holy Love."

"Dear children, the path of eternal life that I call you upon is Holy Love. There are some who proclaim themselves to be peacemakers; but they have not surrendered their hearts completely to Holy Love, and any peace that is not based on love is not lasting. These people are important in the eyes of the world and leaders amongst men. But I have come to tell you that you must pray for all hearts to surrender to my Love. Trust those who answer my call. Dear children, tonight I am blessing you with my Blessing of Holy Love."

■ **June 30, 1997.** Our Lady comes in a dark blue mantle and white gown. She says: "I come to address my children. I am Mary, Refuge of Holy Love."

"Dear children, I invite you to comprehend the course of human decisions and the impact of free will upon your nation and the world. Your country was founded upon the rock of trust in God. But over the years that rock of faith has crumbled and turned to sand. Sand washes away in the tide of secularism. Therefore, see that the foundation of your nation will, in a series of events to come, crack and open to swallow up iniquity. Physically your nation will change. Also the cornerstone men have made for themselves fiscally will be shaken."

"Your country has not experienced such events in the past. Hearts are unprepared, for people no longer depend on God but on their own resources. It is during this series of events that mankind will find human efforts lacking and empty."

"I am calling you to understand this now, during these times, so that you will pray and know that I am with you. You are prepared if you are in the Refuge of my Heart."

■ **June 30, 1997.** *(Dictated by Blessed Mother)*

Prayer To Jesus In The Eucharist
"My Jesus, I believe in You - truly present in all the tabernacles of the world. I surrender to You my

sins and all the love I have in my heart. I beg Your forgiveness for those who do not believe in You and do not love You."

July 1997

■ **July 1, 1997.** Our Lady comes in white. She says: "Praise be Jesus. Dear children, you believe and you trust. Surrender to My call to apostleship. Take My message of Holy Love in your hearts wherever you go. Let it come alive in your words and actions. The present moment is the grace-filled time to evangelize. Come into My bosom of love."

"I am extending to you My Blessing of Holy Love."

■ **July 2, 1997.** Our Lady comes as Mary, Refuge of Holy Love. She says: "My daughter, I have come as your Protectress and Refuge. Praise be Jesus. I come to solicit your prayers. I desire that you pray with Me nightly for the victims of this imminent disaster. Comprehend, My daughter, I do not come seeking prayers only for those, who from one moment to the next will be judged before God, but also for those who will survive what will come. This holocaust will affect your entire nation. Then understand, My daughter, that because your nation is so influential, many nations will be affected."

"This mission has passed through the fire and is now ready in these last days. Thank you for persevering. I am with you."

■ **July 3, 1997 / Thursday Rosary Service.** Our Lady comes as Mary, Refuge of Holy Love. She says: "Praise be Jesus. Pray with Me now for unbelievers."

"Dear children, I come to you through time and space to bring you peace and truth. Reconcile yourselves to the will of God through Holy Love. Jesus gave you to Me at the foot of the Cross. Now I am giving you to Him through My Heart."

"Tonight I am blessing you with My Blessing of Holy Love."

■ **July 4, 1997.** "My daughter, I come to you with a longing Heart. I desire to bring to Jesus those who are most greatly touched by the events ahead."

"I come to challenge hearts to live in holiness. Do not search for answers to today's problems in the world around you. Pray and you will be led. If you cannot do this in these times, how will you be able to when greater challenges come to you?"

"In everything praise Jesus. He is the mender of every way."

She leaves.

■ **July 4, 1997.** Our Lady comes in blue. She has a frame around Her with four little hearts on it (like the medal on my new rosary). She says: "Praise be Jesus."

"My daughter, I come to you today seeking your prayers for this nation. To whom much is given, much is expected in return. This is true of nations as well as souls. Your country was founded on sound ideology, given many resources and great leaders. But all of these assets have been taken for granted and abused. Most do not see God's hand in the course of history and even less in the present moment. Good has been convoluted and made into evil through free will. Consciences have become the law of the land. Man's ingenuity has been credited with God's grace. Abortion is accepted and set as a standard before all people and all nations."

"God will enact His Justice not in small measure but according to the evil in hearts. Your country and many more have chosen ways contrary to the perfect balance in nature and the universe."

"All that prevents sheer justice from God's hand is prayer and My mission of Love around the world. I come, not just for you or this nation, but for all peoples and every nation."

"I continue to intercede for you before the throne of God. I ask your perseverance in prayer."

"I am blessing you."

■ **July 4, 1997.** "My daughter, I come to you today as Queen of the Universe and Mother of Jesus born Incarnate. Will you respond to Me?" I look up and see Our Lady in a luminous light, in pink, gold, and white. She has a crown on Her head and is holding Jesus.

She says: "Do not despise rejection. It is a sign to you I am real. It is a sign My message to you is challenging Satan's power in the world." (Someone I knew refused to say hello to me earlier.)

"I am coming to you as Queen and Protectress of the Universe to show you that my Message of Holy Love is a force drawing the world and all balances of nature back to God. The beginning and the end are about to unfold. The beginning of a New Era is coming on the heels of Satan's defeat."

"Win for Me hearts - one at a time. For when a soul chooses conversion, he chooses Holy Love. With Holy Love in his heart, Heaven and earth are united and victorious in him. Each heart strengthens the Kingdom. Each heart hastens My reign."

"This Message is the key to unlocking the door to the New Jerusalem. My Heart is the message of Holy Love. From the moment that God deigned I be Immaculately conceived, it has been so. You are here now proclaiming truth. Truth will win out in the end."

"It is true some do not see the Scale of Justice I hold in My hand - this scale being Holy Love. But in the future it will be shown to them all too clearly. At that time, my Son will be holding it and weighing all thoughts, words, and actions according to Holy Love."

"Continue. I am with you. I know all your needs."

She leaves.

■ **July 9, 1997.** Blessed Virgin to Maureen: "Because hearts have become complacent and apathetic, God will allow this event to take place, so that He will be brought back to the center of lives. Your country has fallen asleep morally." (Blessed Mother advised that quite a number of natural disasters were forthcoming in the United States. However, one in particular was going to be particularly devastating. Our Lady requested prayers for those who would die and also for those who would survive.)

"You have been given the gift of prophetic dreams. What you are being told by Me today you sensed in your dreams as a child." (Maureen had had the same dream a couple of times a month for years.) "The worst part of your dream was - No one would listen to you. Pray and receive courage to circulate My foretelling of these events. I will pray with you that hearts open. In this grace give praise to Jesus."

■ **July 10, 1997.** Our Lady comes as Our Lady of Grace. She says: "Praise be Jesus. I come to help you to understand that you are living in an age of grace and miracles. But greater than any grace that is extended to you is your openness to My grace. Grace is like the Word of God, which sometimes is accepted in a fertile heart and thrives. At other times grace is choked out by the weeds of doubt and misconception. At times, hearts are like stone, and grace cannot take root at all. Always, always, My grace comes to you from the hand of God and towards your own salvation."

"I am blessing you."

■ **July 10, 1997 / Thursday Rosary Service.** Our Lady is here as Mary, Refuge of Holy Love. She says: "Praise be Jesus. Pray with Me now for all those who will come here and those who have come in the past."

"Dear children, tonight I am calling you to surrender completely to Holy Love. Through this message My dear, dear children, you will receive life, the life of salvation.* I am calling you to surrender any pride that keeps you from spreading this message and from bringing souls to their salvation, through the Refuge of my Immaculate Heart."

"Tonight, once again I am blessing you with My Blessing of Holy Love."

* HOLY LOVE is Mary's IMMACULATE HEART which is the PATH and the GATEWAY to DIVINE LOVE which is Jesus' SACRED HEART.

■ **July 10, 1997.** Our Lady comes as Mary, Refuge of Holy Love. "Praise be Jesus. My angel, what is to come will change and alter lives forever. But it is necessary to bring about the reign of Our United Hearts.

I asked Her the meaning of the dream I had last night.

"Satan will come to power and gain strength by this means." (Modern technology? Saw flames on a computer screen.)

"Go now and I will be with you."

■ **July 12, 1997 / Monthly Message To All Nations**. *(The following message was given in three parts.)* "My daughter, let us continue in praise of Jesus."

"The fruits of love are: peace, joy, reconciliation, unity, and compassion. You cannot have the fruits of love if you do not love God and your neighbor first."

"Satan wants you to believe the contrary. Satan does not want you to love God but to love sin; to love self first and foremost; to love money. Satan lies to you by letting you believe these things bring you peace, joy, and all the good fruits of love."

"I come to you asking you to look at your lives. Look into your hearts. See where Satan has fooled you. Then look at your country. See what values your leaders have chosen."

"Realize then, how wide the abyss has come between man and God. Help Me to construct the bridge of Holy Love to span this abyss."

"My daughter, I come to speak to all nations. Centuries ago, when I appeared to Juan Diego under this title, people were worshipping false gods. Today it is also true that the abyss between God and man is the false god of money. Money is viewed as strength. It is fought over and is the root of much evil. You would not have abortion in the world today if it did not line the coffers of those involved. This is also true of child exploitation and many other sins that are an abomination in the eyes of God."

"People see this world as an end in itself, when it is only a beginning. All of these false gods are temporary and serve as obstacles to salvation."

"Further, the world as you know it is passing away. How foolish to cast your lot, then, with what is not eternal. My call to you is to see Satan in all that is temporary. Only with God is there eternal life."

"If your country would resolve the abortion issue and once again rule it illegal, some of what I have predicted would be averted. I cannot resolve this issue for you, only pray that hearts open to the truth."

"I come as the Woman Clothed with the Sun. Praise be Jesus. Pray with Me now dear children for all petitions in hearts here today."

"Dear children, come to realize that God's Divine Will and My Grace are one. Through your prayers, I dispense My grace, that I may hasten the Reign of the United Hearts of Jesus and Mary."

"When My Son returns and Our Hearts are victorious, you will be living in a new Heaven and a new earth. Heaven and earth will be united in every heart; then love will reign as uncontested ruler of hearts, nations, and the world."

Jesus is now with Blessed Mother and they extend to us the Blessing of the United Hearts.

■ **July 13, 1997.** Recently, Maureen returned to the church where Our Lady first appeared to her in 1985. In the initial vision, Our Lady held a large beaded rosary. During the vision the 50 Hail Mary beads changed into the shapes of the 50 states. In this vision today Blessed Mother was holding the same rosary; but this time, the states slipped off the string of the rosary and landed in a pile at Her feet. What was left was a golden thread they had been on.

Blessed Mother said: "This I tell you, My daughter, your country has separated by choice from God."

"Hang on, hang on to this golden thread." Maureen understood the golden thread was Holy Love.

■ **July 13, 1997 / 2nd Sunday - To Pray Against Abortion.** Our Lady is here as She appeared to me (Maureen) two hours earlier at Mass, in a light pink gown, light gray mantle with ivory lining on the mantle. She was holding a golden thread. She said: "Praise be Jesus. Pray with Me now for all those nations who support abortion." All the states have slipped from Her rosary and are at Her feet.

"Dear children, your country has chosen to embrace abortion. In so doing, it has slipped from the grasp of Holy Love. I no longer come to you to deliver your country from God's Justice but to increase and strengthen the remnant of faith in hearts. I extend to you My Blessing of Holy Love."

■ **July 14, 1997.** Our Lady comes as Mary, Refuge of Holy Love. She says: "I know this is difficult for you to comprehend - that so many souls are slipping to their perdition - but it is true."

"I come in praise of Jesus, My Son. My daughter, I am providing for you time to pray for these lost children of mine. Time is racing forward. When justice comes as tribulation after tribulation and wave after wave of ill fortune, it will be too late for many."

"Part of God's mercy is your forewarning of what will come, but you must make this known. Ask everyone to pray."

■ **July 15, 1997.** Jesus says: "These are the last days of My Mercy. If people knew the alternative to My Mercy, they would cast themselves at My feet."

■ **July 15, 1997.** Blessed Mother comes as Refuge of Holy Love. She says: "Praise be Jesus, truly present in the tabernacles of the world. My angel, My coming to you is to toll the bell of warning in the world and to call all people and all nations into the Refuge of My Heart, which is Holy Love. My Jesus, Who readily orders all things, has sent Me from the beginning of time to you. You see the nation in ruin at My feet." (She refers to the vision of 7/13/97.) "But today I tell you, it is not one nation but all who will suffer. Already you have experienced in most nations a moral collapse. The treasury of grace in My Heart has been unable to influence free will. Now I am sending you as God sent Jonah into the thick of things. Boldly proclaim all I have revealed to you. Unlike Jonah, you will have Me by your side. People must repent. Hearts must change; otherwise, a chain of events will unfold and with certainty bring the destruction of property, lives, and annihilation of areas now steeped in sin. This I spoke of at Fatima (Portugal 1917), at Garabandal (Spain 1961-1965), at Akita (Japan 1973), at Betania (Venezuela 1971-1990), and now here. Who is listening?"

"Come into My Heart now and prepare. Your mission is being fulfilled. I am blessing you."

■ **July 15, 1997.** The Blessed Virgin is here, dressed as She was twice earlier today; and the states are piled up in a heap at Her feet. She is holding a golden thread in Her hand. She says: "Dear children, I come in praise of Jesus. I ask you to understand the tenuous position your country is in. Now, the remnant is clinging to My Immaculate Heart through this message of Holy Love, which is also the links of the chain of the Rosary. I come to you, asking you to make this known, so that all will realize the peril your nation is in."

"With a tender Heart I come to you, with a mother's love asking you - MAKE THIS KNOWN."

■ **July 17, 1997 / Thursday Rosary Service.** Once again,

Blessed Mother is here as Mary, Refuge of Holy Love. She has all 50 states in a pile at Her feet. (See 7/13/97 message.) There are two angels with Blessed Mother. One angel picks up one of the states and hands it to the other one. It is like sand in his hand; then it turns into gold with some of the sand falling out as it is changing. The gold is then given to Our Lady who places it into Her Immaculate Heart. Our Lady says: "These are the faithful and righteous who have persevered in faith. Dear children, pray with Me now for all the unbelievers."

"Dear children, I continue to come to you so that the faithful remnant will be increased and strengthened. Humbly understand that you are living in apocalyptic times and that this is a place of revelation - holy revelation."

"Tonight, I am asking you to accept your place in these times and to increase the grace in your hearts by your efforts through prayer and sacrifice. Tonight accept My Blessing of Holy Love."

■ **July 22, 1997.** Blessed Mother is here as Mary, Refuge of Holy Love. She says: "Praise be Jesus. Dear children, I am in your midst. I come to you as your Mother and your Refuge. I am your Refuge as you embrace every cross. I am your Refuge in every decision. I am your Refuge when you feel oppressed by compromise. Dear children, follow Me into the New Jerusalem through My message of Holy Love, for I am the Path and the Gateway. Tonight, I extend to you My Blessing of Holy Love."

■ **July 27, 1997 / 4th Sunday - To Pray For Unbelievers.** Blessed Mother is here as Mary, Refuge of Holy Love. She says: "Praise be Jesus. Dear, dear children, I come to you today, offering you hope and peace. Please understand, that it is your self-love that creates obstacles on the path of Holy Love. When you surrender only to self-will, you are blocking the way between yourselves and My Immaculate Heart. I desire that you realize I come to you not to command your holiness but to invite you to say "Yes" to holiness. Today I am blessing you with My Blessing of Holy Love."

■ **July 30, 1997.** "My mission in you is to prepare the world for my Son's Second Coming. Praise be Jesus!" Our Lady comes as Refuge of Holy Love.

"These are the ways my Son sends Me to you with, that the world may be reconciled to God before His return."

1. "Spread devotion to the United Hearts of Jesus and Mary, for it is through the United Hearts that Heaven and earth will be united."

2. "Promulgate the Image you have before you (Mary, Refuge of Holy Love). In this Image is the culmination of all My apparitions during this century. It is the Refuge of the Immaculate Heart spoken of at Fatima (Portugal 1917). It is the promise of an era to come spoken of at Garabandal (Spain 1961-1965). I speak of the crown over My Heart, which foretells the victory of the United Hearts and the triumph of the Church over evil. The cross on My hand represents a dogma which is coming - Co-Redemptrix. I am pointing to My Heart, calling humanity into this safe Refuge. This Refuge is Holy Love. When you live in Holy Love, you imitate My Heart."

3. "Propagate the Holy Love messages, the path and gateway to the New Jerusalem. Through this simple yet profound message, people should return to holiness, the Ten Commandments, and prayers."

    "Your country is in great peril, for it does not embrace love of God but love of self. It governs by human conscience instead of the Ten Commandments."

    "Pray, pray, pray!"

■ **July 31, 1997 / Thursday Prayer Service.** Blessed Mother is here as Mary, Refuge of Holy Love. She says: "Praise be Jesus. Let us pray now for all the intentions in hearts here tonight."

"Dear children, tonight once again, I invite you to open your hearts to My message of Holy Love. Too often you allow the message to come into your intellect, but it never reaches your heart. Understand, My dear children, that My coming to you is a sign that you must love and let this love penetrate your entire being. I am inviting you once again to be My message of Holy Love. I extend to you My Motherly Blessing."

August 1997

■ **August 1, 1997.** Jesus says: "Make it known. It is self-love that obstructs the soul's journey along the path of holiness. It is self-love that opens the door of the heart to sin."

■ **August 5, 1997.** Our Lady comes in pink and gray with gold stars over Her Head. There are lilies around Her. She says: "Praise be Jesus. My angel, today I come to you as emissary of these times. I invite you to open your Scripture to Daniel, Chapter 12. Within these passages is deep understanding of the days you live in and the hour in which I come."

"You have not seen these times before in the history of man. But now, they are unfolding before you. Earth's tribulations are escalating as evil proliferates in your midst. Hasten to deeper understanding of the Way I lay at your feet. Holy Love is the remedy of man's peril. It is the thread of hope remaining between God and humanity. In this hour it is the salvation of a dying generation. It is the promise of an age to come."

Read Daniel, Chapter 12

■ **August 6, 1997.** Our Lady comes as Refuge of Holy Love. She says: "I come in praise of Jesus, My Son. My daughter, you will please make this known to all of My little children."

"When the triumph of the United Hearts occurs you will be living in the New Jerusalem. Every measure of grace will be expanded, and hearts will be transfixed in Divine and Holy Will, which is Divine and Holy Love. Righteousness will be restored in all hearts and even nature itself. Satan will no longer contend with holiness, and Christ will resume His place at the center of the universe. You do not have to understand theology to know that this is a wonderful plan and reward for all who persevere."

"As I speak to you, the good angel prepares to lift his trumpet, sounding the return of My Beloved Son. You, My children, are so much a part of this. By preparing your hearts for these times you are preparing part of the world as well."

"I am blessing you."

■ **August 7, 1997 / Thursday Rosary Service.** Our Lady comes as Refuge of Holy Love. She says: "Praise be Jesus. Let us pray for those who have come in the past and who will come in the future." We prayed.

"Dear children, today I call you to realize that I need to take you deep into the sanctuary of My Immaculate Heart. Therein, I will form you in the Flame of Love into holiness, that you may share the New Jerusalem with Me and with My Holy Son."

"My coming to you is real. Let your response to My call be genuine as well. Tonight I am blessing you with My Blessing of Holy Love."

■ **August 8, 1997 - Feast of St. Dominic.** Our Lady comes with many (10-12) angels who are saying, "Sorrowful and Immaculate Heart of Mary, pray for us."

Her Heart has many swords in it and is surrounded by white flowers. She says: "Praise be Jesus, Crucified and Glorified. I come to you at the request of Jesus that you will make known devotion to My Sorrowful Heart. Proceed as you have been inspired with the shrine in honor of My Sorrows. This effort will propel the mission forward. The effect of My coming to you will be affirmed in every heart. Proceed with this. It is a pivotal point in the progression of events."

■ **August 8, 1997.** *(At the future site of the Our Lady of Sorrows Shrine and Lake of Tears)* Blessed Mother is here dressed all in white. There is a large white rosary around Her neck that extends several feet in front of Her and is held up by two angels, one on each side.

Our Lady says: "Praise be Jesus. My dear children, this will be known as THE LAKE OF TEARS, and many promises will bear fruit here."

"Manifest will be My grace. You do not see the fullness and the entirety of My plan, but much of it hinges on this humble little shrine that Heaven has chosen for this site."

■ **August 10, 1997 / 2nd Sunday - To Pray Against Abortion.** Blessed Mother is here as Mary, Refuge of Holy Love. She has all 50 states in a pile at Her feet and they are smoldering (as in ashes).

She says: "Praise be Jesus. Pray with Me now, for those who are capable to reverse the horror of abortion."

"Dear children, today I inform you, once again, that abortion is the evil which races your country towards destruction. Only if this evil is overturned in hearts and in the world can your nation be saved from certain death. Dear children, the tribulations have begun and proceed as labor pains of a woman with child, each one stronger and more telling than the one before. I come to you asking you to STOP the DEATH and DESTRUCTION and the loss of life and souls. I come asking you to pray and spread My messages on Holy Love. Dear children, you are the solution and the victory; therefore, pray, pray, pray. I am blessing you."

■ **August 11, 1997.** Blessed Mother comes as Mary, Refuge

of Holy Love. She says: "Praise be Jesus. Pray, My children. Prayer is your hope. Together we can move the Heart of My Beloved Son. I am praying with you. I am blessing you with My Blessing of Holy Love."

■ **August 12, 1997 / Monthly Message To All Nations.** Our Lady comes as Our Lady of Guadalupe. She says: "Praise be Jesus. My dear children, pray with Me now for those who do not love." We prayed.

"Dear children, I come to you from Love offering you great Love. But I cannot clothe your hearts in the grace of Holy Love until you surrender to Me. Whole nations have chosen errant paths and have fallen away from dignity and grace. Let us begin today with your own heart - to return to God and love with holiness as your goal. Dear children, I long to share Heaven with you."

"Now I will speak to all nations."

"Dear children, I come to you once again pleading your reconciliation with God. From moment to moment the abyss between God and mankind widens. You must continue to pray, for it is only through prayer hearts will turn to Holy Love. Today the greatness of God is minisculed by what man considers his own progress and feats. I come to remind you that without God's grace you can accomplish NOTHING."

"Jesus sends Me into the world to help you construct the bridge of Holy Love which can span the abyss between Heaven and earth. But I need your efforts."

Jesus is with Blessed Mother, and they extend to us the Blessing of the United Hearts.

■ **August 12, 1997.** Jesus says: "Just let the people know there is little time left to reverse certain events. The severity of what will come depends SOLELY on the Holy Love in hearts. No one can turn to God or undergo conversion who does not love."

"Satan's job is to take as many souls with him as possible.

This alone makes him the arch enemy of Holy Love. Since the triumph of Our Hearts is through Holy Love, he will not succeed."

"There are those who will suffer needlessly because they reject love."

■ **August 14, 1997 / Thursday Rosary Service.** Blessed Mother is here as Mary, Refuge of Holy Love. She says: "Praise be Jesus. Dear children, pray with Me now that all recognize My grace in the world."

"Dear children, tonight I invite you to understand that each time I come to you, God's Mercy is extended through time and space in My Holy Love Message. Understand that I am drawing you into a new dimension, a dimension of holiness and onto the path of righteousness. The path of light I lead you upon is eternal life. Tonight, I am blessing you with My Blessing of Holy Love."

■ **August 14, 1997.** Jesus says: "My Mercy pours most profusely upon those who are the greatest transgressors against My Commandment of Love. I do not withdraw from them. I constantly pursue them. You must do likewise."

■ **August 14, 1997.** Our Lady comes as the Sorrowful Mother. Along with the seven swords in Her Heart, She also has a rosebud. She says: "I am the Sorrowful Mother. I come to give praise to Jesus."

"Dear children, during these decisive times, I invite you to wipe away My tears with your surrender to Holy Love. Let your 'yes' be a soothing balm on My wounded Heart. How I long to kiss all humanity with the embrace of My Heart and to forever bring My peace to the world."

"You have not seen, nor do you comprehend, what is to come."

She takes the rose from out of Her Heart and holds it out to me. "This is the grace of Holy Love which I offer to all."

"You will please make this known."

■ **August 15, 1997 - Feast of Our Lady's Assumption.**
(A procession with the Missionary Image of Our Lady of Guadalupe preceded the Rosary.) Blessed Mother is here as Mary, Refuge of Holy Love. She says: "Praise be Jesus. Dear children, thank you for your love and your devotion. It is your faith and your prayers that are carrying us into the new era of peace. These are apocalyptic times. Changes will come along with Divine Justice. But tonight I reveal to you, dear children, that HOLY LOVE is the KINGDOM TO COME and the NEW ERA OF PEACE. I am blessing you with My Blessing of Holy Love."

■ **August 21, 1997 / Thursday Rosary Service.** Blessed Mother is here as Mary, Refuge of Holy Love. She says: "Praise be Jesus. Pray with Me now for all those who do not choose to love."

"Dear children, tonight I ask you to soothe My Aching Heart with your 'yes' to Holy Love. You are loving, My dear children, when, in the present moment, you perform every thought, word, and action in and through Holy Love. It is then My grace can act freely in your lives and I can accomplish God's Will through you. Tonight I am blessing you with My Blessing of Holy Love."

■ **August 23, 1997.** Blessed Mother is here as Mary, Refuge of Holy Love. She says: "My dear children, thank you for coming. I welcome you here. I invite you along the path of Holy Love, and I offer you the Refuge of My Heart wherein lies your strength and your peace. Tonight I am blessing you with My Blessing of Holy Love."

■ **August 18, 1997 / Comparison of Self-Love to Holy Love.** From Blessed Mother:

SELF-LOVE vs. HOLY LOVE	
Is motivated towards self-advantage in thought, word, and deed.	Is motivated in every thought, word, and action by love of God, and neighbor as self.
Sees only others' faults, not his own. Considers himself on the right path—perhaps even humble and virtuous.	Sees himself full of imperfections. Is always seeking to be perfected through love. Considers everyone more humble and holy than himself.
Holds a checklist in his heart of every wrong perpetrated against him.	Imitates Divine Mercy as best he can. Is compassionate and forgiving.
Is quick to anger and stands vigil over his own rights making certain they are not transgressed.	Is patient. Takes note of others' needs and concerns.
Hangs on to his own opinions refusing to surrender to another viewpoint.	Offers his own opinions but listens to others and lends them equal merit with his own.
Takes pride in his own achievements. May even take pride in his spiritual progress.	Realizes all things proceed from God; that without God he is capable of no good thing. All good comes from grace.
Sees himself and the world as the be-all/end-all. His only pleasure is thus achieved through the world.	Takes joy in storing up heavenly treasure, in growing closer to God and deeper in holiness. Knows the difference between earthly pleasures and spiritual joy.
Uses the goods of the world to satisfy self.	Uses the goods of the world to satisfy quest for holiness.
Objects to every cross. Sees trials as a curse. Resents others' good fortune.	Surrenders to the cross through love as Jesus did. Sees crosses as a grace to be used to convert others.
Prays only for himself and his own needs.	Prays for all in need.
Cannot accept God's Will. Becomes bitter over trials.	Accepts God's Will with a loving heart even when difficult.

■ **August 28, 1997 / Thursday Rosary Service.** Blessed Mother is here as Mary, Refuge of Holy Love. She says:

"Praise be Jesus. Join with Me now in praying for all petitions in hearts here tonight."

"Dear children, tonight I invite you to have trust in God's Provision and His Plan for you. When you trust, My dear children, you are giving My Son the greatest gift possible. Further, prayers for you are joined with the prayers of ALL the saints and angels in Heaven. Tonight I am blessing you with My Blessing of Holy Love."

■ **August 28, 1997.** Our Lady says: "The Blood and Water which gushed forth from the Heart of My Son on Calvary represented Divine Mercy and Divine Love."

■ **August 28, 1997.** Our Lady comes in pink and gray. She says: "Praise be to Jesus. My daughter, once again I invite you to see that I do not come seeking the approbation of men but to change hearts and to reconcile the world to God. It is mankind who seeks every kind of grace and sign but who misses the heart of the message which is Holy Love. Today, I invite people to open their hearts to Holy Love and every grace and blessing will come to you. Otherwise, when the greatest grace comes, the unloving heart will not believe. I am blessing you."

September 1997

■ **September 1, 1997 / Monday Praise Service.** Blessed Mother and Jesus are both here. Their Hearts are exposed. Blessed Mother says: Praise be Jesus." Jesus nods, smiles, and points to His Heart. Blessed Mother now says: "Dear children, please understand that My Son's dominion reaches to the farthest corners of the earth and the deepest recesses of each heart. Therefore, tonight surrender to His Sacred Heart your crosses and your petitions. United together in this way My Son will look with favor upon your every need. We are extending to you tonight the Blessing of Our United Hearts."

■ **September 2, 1997.** Our Lady comes as Mary, Refuge of Holy Love. She says: "Praise be Jesus," and at that moment a light shines down on Her. "Dearest daughter, I have come to thank you and all involved in moving ahead with the Shrine honoring My Sorrows. Great, great are the channels of grace this will open. My Sorrowful and Immaculate Heart needs to be recognized in the world as the Solemn Refuge for all who will surrender to My love."

"I am going to give you meditations. I desire that people come to understand that it was possible for Me to bear each sorrow only through Holy Love."

■ **September 4, 1997 / Thursday Rosary Service.** Blessed Mother is here as Mary, Refuge of Holy Love. She says: "Praise be Jesus. Pray with Me now for all those who do not love."

"Dear children, tonight I invite you to understand that all of My sorrows are as one and originate from the lack of love in the world today. Dear children, I am begging you to begin to love in the present moment, so that by this means the world may come to her conversion, the soul of mankind reconciled with its Creator. Dear children, I offer you the remedy of these times [Holy Love]. Seize upon it as I tell you; while you contemplate holes in the atmosphere and the ozone layer, the abyss between Heaven and earth is widening. Dear children, I am blessing you."

■ **September 4, 1997.** "Dear children, once again I tell you that this is the site of My predilection and the province of God's Mercy and Love. Those who come here will not find their hearts emptied but filled as they leave. Hearts will change; lives will change. Today I am blessing you with My Blessing of Holy Love."

■ **September 5, 1997.**

Our Lady is here as Refuge of Holy Love. She says: "Praise be Jesus. I have promised you meditations on My Sorrows which will be placed around the Lake of Tears. Let us proceed."

MEDITATIONS FOR
THE SORROWFUL MOTHER SHRINE

1. **THE PROPHECY OF SIMEON.** I invite you to meditate upon My knowledge of all future Sorrow which was given to Me by God at the Presentation.

2. **THE FLIGHT INTO EGYPT.** I invite you to meditate upon the anxiety in the hearts of Joseph and Myself for the safety of Baby Jesus and the anxiety I feel today for those who run from salvation.

3. **THE LOSS OF THE CHILD JESUS IN THE TEMPLE.** I invite you to meditate upon the pain of separation I felt when Jesus was lost. This is a pain all should feel when they separate themselves from My Son through sin.

4. **THE MEETING OF JESUS AND MARY ON THE WAY OF THE CROSS.** I invite you to meditate upon the pain of My Heart as I saw the physical pain My Son suffered due to lack of love in hearts. Also think of the pain I suffer today for lack of love in hearts.

5. **THE CRUCIFIXION.** I invite you to meditate upon the pain of a Mother's heart at the death of Her Son, and the virtue of forgiveness I received through grace and prayer. Think of My pain at the sight of the death of the unborn.

6. **THE TAKING DOWN OF THE BODY OF JESUS FROM THE CROSS.** I invite you to meditate upon the acceptance of Divine Will that I surrendered to. Ask for that same grace in your life now.

7. **THE BURIAL OF JESUS.** I invite you to meditate upon the understanding I had as My Son was placed in the tomb, that death was a beginning and not an end. Think of the extreme sorrow I felt as I cleansed His Wounds. My sorrow was, as it is today, for the lack of love in hearts.

"After each meditation please recite a *Hail Mary*."

■ **September 6, 1997.** Our Lady comes in pink and gray. She says: "Praise be Jesus. My angel, today I come to help you understand that My Son judges all actions, words, and thought patterns according to their motive in the heart. If the motive is Holy Love, then much merit is gained. If, however, the motive is self-love, even though the exterior seems good, God will judge otherwise."

"Today there is a movement in hearts towards unity - one religion, a common monetary system, and the like. But the motive is not a worthy motive. The inspiration comes from a need to control. The only unity that comes from God is based on love - Holy Love."

"I cannot impress upon you too strongly the need to use Holy Love as your check and balance. It is by this rule countries should be governed and lives should be led."

"Apathy does not come from God but from Satan. I am not calling you to be a social activist but to live My message and to spread it. Your surrender takes you deeper into My Heart. The Flame of Holy Love must consume the world lest the fire of justice does so."

"I will be giving you all the grace you need to accomplish this. I am blessing you."

■ **September 8, 1997 - Liturgical Feast of the Birth of Mary.** Our Lady comes as the Sorrowful Mother. She says: "My angel, I come in praise of Jesus. Today, I invite you to understand that My victory will be one of love and of sorrow. My victory will come through tears for the many who will be lost. This is why, in these times, heaven holds an affinity for those who venerate My Dolors. This is why special and unusual graces will be given. The Shrine of your Heavenly Mother's Sorrows will be a site of favor. The water coming into the Lake of Tears is My tears. This water will bring special consolation to mothers who sorrow for their wayward children. For today, it is the good who suffer and the converted who are persecuted. I understand the pain of a mother's heart and I have requested this grace from My Beloved Son."

"Continually there are many angels in attendance with Me at this Lake of Tears. They are carrying petitions to Heaven as I desire. You will begin to see many images there."

"My affection and presence is always at Maranatha Spring, the Lake of Tears and the holy Stations of the Cross. Indeed, I am present everywhere on this chosen property. I am praying with you and for you."

■ **September 8, 1997 - Liturgical Feast of the Birth of Mary.** Blessed Mother: "Despite the flavor of cynicism that has surrounded this apparition, you have persevered in belief and in fulfilling My every wish. You are about to witness the abundance of My grace in your midst which will dispel disbelief, silence the wagging tongue, and convict hearts. I am requesting a prayer vigil from 7 to midnight on the Feast of the Exaltation of the Cross. Then on the Solemnity of My Sorrows, pray the 15 decades at My new shrine in honor of these Sorrows. I will come. I ask this, as I request all things, to bring praise and honor to Jesus My Son."

■ **September 10, 1997.** Blessed Mother: "Allow Me to continue. I have come to you attempting to show the way to personal holiness in the present moment through Holy Love. Some excuse themselves every fault by saying, 'It's my personality' or, 'We're human.' Yet, no attempt is made to correct these faults or to recognize Satan's hand in their midst. They allow themselves to be ruled by their emotions, rather than trying to conquer them through Holy Love. I do not come to excuse but to convict."

"I give you new and sufficient grace in each new present moment to overcome your faults and to come deeper into My Heart. You cannot hide from Me. You are always under My maternal gaze. Yet, if you believed I was with you always, you would not give in to anger and pride. You do not accept Me at My words."

"Surrender to Me. Do not give in to every emotion Satan throws at you. You should be progressing beyond infancy and into adulthood in your spiritual journey by now. You must learn to call on Me in time of need."

"At My shrine and around the world, I weep copious tears for the unrepentant. Do not be among them. Once again, I bless you."

■ **September 10, 1997.** Jesus says: "When you surrender to the Cross, as I did at Gethsemane, you receive the grace to carry it."

■ **September 11, 1997 / Thursday Rosary Service.** Blessed Mother is here as Mary, Refuge of Holy Love. She says: "Praise be Jesus. Dear children, pray with Me now for all the unrepentant."

"I come as always in praise of Jesus. I hope that you will realize through these visits, My dear children, that I am preparing you for the victory of Our United Hearts. This triumph can only come when Holy Love is triumphant in hearts. Dear children, please cooperate with My grace in bringing this victory into hearts. I am praying with you, and I am blessing you."

■ **September 12, 1997 / Monthly Message To All Nations.** *(This message was given in several parts.)* Our Lady is here as Our Lady of Guadalupe. She says: "Praise be Jesus. Dear children, pray with Me now for all the unrepentant."

Jesus is now with Blessed Mother. "Dear children, today

I invite you to realize that your peace does not come from the heart of man; therefore, do not trust a common monetary system, one government for all people, or a new religion that embraces all faiths. Trust ONLY that which comes from God. His peace proceeds from Holy Love in hearts. It is from this common vocation [Holy Love] that all are called, and which all must embrace."

"My angel, I come to discuss with you the reasons My Son was rejected in the world, for it is much the same here today in this mission. Jesus was not despised and rejected because He was wrong in what He taught and said. On the contrary, He was right and brought to light much error in hearts. His message of salvation through Holy Love shook the foundation of those in high places and challenged these proud ones to change."

"Today the greatest errors come from intellectual pride and fear of scorn from contemporaries. All must pray for wisdom to recognize truth and the courage to abide by it."

"I have not come to condone familiar ways or accepted practices which are contrary to the commandments. I come to lead souls on the straight path - the path of Holy Love."

"My children must pray for those who have compromised their faith in order to 'fit in' with their peers. Many of My loyal faithful have been persuaded to accept compromise in place of truth.

You must decide everything according to and based on Holy Love. There is no alternative if you seek salvation. Do not place yourself between Holy Love and your own salvation. Love God and neighbor first. Do not obey laws or people when doing so opposes Holy Love."

"Today We extend to you the Blessing of Our United Hearts."

■ **September 14, 1997 / 2nd Sunday - To Pray Against Abortion.** Blessed Mother is here as Mary, Refuge of Holy Love. She says: "Praise be Jesus. Pray with Me now for the protection of the unborn."

"Dear children, today I ask you to unite with Me in prayer, that all nations will be united under the banner of Holy Love. This is the way to peace, salvation, and the survival of every nation. It is through Holy Love that your thoughts, words, and deeds will be inspired by God to bring about His Will and to reconcile mankind with his Creator."

"This is My plan, the plan I wish to place in the hearts of men by your efforts and through My grace. I am praying with you and for you, and I extend to you My Blessing of Holy Love."

■ **September 14, 1997 - Feast of the Triumph of the Holy Cross / Prayer Vigil and Healing Service.** *(7:00 p.m. – midnight)*

Testimony from Maureen Sweeney-Kyle Regarding How She Received the Strand of Our Lady's Hair

Maureen states that in the apparition room of the Prayer Center, before the Healing Service of the Prayer Vigil began, she was distractedly noticing the cuff area of the long sleeve of her white blouse, noting that it was clean and well-pressed. A few moments later, after Our Lady appeared, she glanced again at that arm and noticed a long dark hair on the white sleeve. [Maureen's hair is short and blond.] She brushed this off and it fell to the floor. Then she heard an internal voice say, "That may be a hair from the Blessed Mother." This startled her, and she immediately searched the floor for the hair and found it, placing it in an envelope.

(See also Messages given by Blessed Mother on March 6, 1998 and May 28, 1998, and a Message given by Jesus on June 4, 1998.)

The Glass-Covered Reliquary Containing
A Strand of Blessed Mother's Hair

■ **September 15, 1997.** Our Lady comes in pink and gray. She says: "Praise be Jesus. My daughter, nothing lies between us today. In the present moment we are one in spirit. I have come to request that you make it known that the Shrine of your Mother's Sorrows is predestined as a place of great favor. I invite every nation to come and to join Me there in prayer. All issues can be resolved through Holy Love. It is here I will show favor upon those who listen and respond. Give to Me your hearts and I will give to you My grace. Place your petitions at My feet and I will respond to them according to God's Divine Will. You have not chosen Me; I have chosen you. Here I will unite your hearts to My own Sorrowful and Immaculate Heart. The greatest hour of My grace is at hand. I have come to share with you God's Eternal Plan. It is here I will bless you."

Excavation of the Lake of Tears

Newly completed Lake of Tears

Our Lady of Sorrows Shrine

Our Lady of Sorrows Shrine and Lake of Tears

■ **September 15, 1997 - Feast of Our Lady of Sorrows/ Dedication of Our Lady of Sorrows Shrine.** Blessed Mother is here as the Sorrowful Mother. She says: "Praise be Jesus. My dear children, I am with you tonight as never before, and I invite you to understand the great need of My Heart is for those who do not love. Please make it known that My consolation and My grace are attendant to the Lake of Tears, and that this is the way to peace and reconciliation of hearts in the world."

"Never before has such a grace been given. Tonight I am blessing you with My Blessing of Holy Love."

■ **September 16, 1997.** Our Lady comes in white and as Our Lady of Grace. She says: "Praise be Jesus in the Holy Eucharist. Today I invite you to comprehend, My angel, the dimension of the present moment. It is far reaching and eternal. Within the concept of the present moment is your salvation or your damnation. When you surrender to Holy Love in this present moment, you are choosing salvation. Some of the greatest minds in the history of the world have failed to comprehend what I am telling you today. It is too simple for the sophisticated and the intellectual. It is too humble a concept for the proud. But to the child-like it is the truth they search for. It is food for the hungry and joy to the saddened heart. The present moment reaches into eternity and comes with you to Heaven when you surrender it to Me."

"I do not forsake those who give to Me the present through Holy Love. These are the ones truly consecrated to My Immaculate Heart, for they live in Me and through Me. These are the ones I hastily lead into the Heart of My Son which is the Divine Will."

"No longer fear, or be anxious about, or seek anything in this world. I have come to you today bearing all truth to you. At My Lake of Tears I will alleviate the afflicted, make steadfast the wavering heart, and console the downtrodden. What more then do you need or desire? I am blessing you."

■ **September 17, 1997.** Our Lady comes in white, gray, and pink. She says: "I come in praise of Jesus. My angel, I desire you understand that My words to you are as a leaven amongst believers which will bear its due increase in numbers of followers. These are the days of preparation. The Father is allowing a strengthening of hearts and He is weaving a fine tapestry through My apparitions in the world. But the common thread woven throughout His design is Holy Love. The needle He uses is His Divine Will. Soon you will see the fruits of Our combined efforts. But I am preparing you for the path ahead. You must cooperate with My grace so that I may complete My effort. I will bless you."

■ **September 18, 1997 / Thursday Rosary Service.** Blessed Mother is here. She says: "I am Mary, Refuge of Holy Love. Praise be Jesus. Let us pray now for all petitions in hearts here tonight."

"Dear children, it is time you realize that you are living in the end times and through the Book of Revelation. My children, realize that My Son is returning soon and that I have come to prepare you for His return through My message of Holy Love."

"I have come seeking your 'yes'. Do not listen to those in the world who, through compromised reason, believe that time, and all events, will continue unchanged. But come into My Maternal Heart through this message of Holy Love. I am blessing you."

■ **September 20, 1997.** Jesus says: "Trust in Me. My ways are beyond your own. In My Heart is the eternal plan. My plan brings future, past, and present into one. In My Heart is all understanding and knowledge. The dimension of time fades away within the confines of My Heart. Therefore, I embrace every petition for eternity. Console Me, for like you yourself, I am so misunderstood in the world."

■ **September 25, 1997 / Thursday Rosary Service.**
Blessed Mother is here as Mary, Refuge of Holy Love. She says: "Praise be Jesus. Pray with Me now for those who never pray."

"Dear children, through your prayers lives can be changed, hearts can be converted, and I can bring good out of every situation. You must pray with love and humility, so that I can use your prayers as My great weapons to change evil into good. I desire, My dear children, that the love that is in hearts here tonight be spread around the world through prayers and acts of reparation. It is important that you know that time is short. Earth is suspended by the thread of Holy Love. Dear children, never cease praying for My intentions. I am blessing you."

■ **September 28, 1997 / 4th Sunday - To Pray For Unbelievers.** Blessed Mother is here as Mary, Refuge of Holy Love. She says: "Praise be Jesus. Dear children, today you are struggling, but you do not realize I am in your midst, protecting you and strengthening you in the siege at hand."

"My grace is your ally. You may not realize that I am with you today, but in retrospect you will see the power of My presence. I am helping you to be strong in this hour of contradiction and compromise that weighs upon the world. Decide always for Holy Love."

"You are like David with his slingshot armed with Holy Love. With this weapon you will bring down the Goliath of disbelief, sin, and compromise."

"I am blessing you."

■ **September 29, 1997.** Our Lady comes as Our Lady of Lourdes. St. Michael is in front of Her. She says: "Praise be Jesus. Dear child, these are the times of great conflict between your heavenly Mother and the red dragon. Hearts are confused and besieged by every sort of heresy and apostasy. But I come to you as the Path and Refuge. Through prayers you can find the solution to every problem. My message of

Holy Love should dispel confusion and help you to pray and decide always for righteousness."

"The true battle is on the cross of every trial. Here you must surrender so that I can act as your Mother and give the grace you need to be victorious. Just as My beloved Jesus surrendered and suffered for all people, you must surrender. Our victory will come when things are most desperate. Satan was disarmed by My Son's Resurrection. So too shall he be defeated and disarmed by every victory of Your Mother in hearts and in the world."

"Place yourself in the wilderness with Me and pray with Me for the day of My adversary's defeat. While he comes clothed in goodness outwardly, his true worth will show through to the humble heart. I have come to gather My army of little ones around Me. It is the humble who shall triumph with Me."

October 1997

■ **October 1, 1997.** Our Lady comes as Refuge of Holy Love. She says: "Praise be Jesus. My daughter, let My coming to you today be a sign to the world that My message of Holy Love is the thread that will reunite mankind with His Creator. I come in love seeking to enkindle the heart and soul of the world with the Flame of My Heart - the Flame of Holy Love. This holy surrender to My call is the choice which will take the world off its collision course with Justice."

"Today, sadly, your nation and most countries have chosen a course contrary to Holy Love. It is a path never before accepted with such conviction and lack of conscience. It is a path contrary to life and the laws of nature given by God. The world does not see the consequences of its choices. When I showed you all the states of your nation piled at My feet in a smoldering mass, I was revealing to you the end this nation and many others have chosen. It is a consequence that causes the angels to tremble before the throne of God seeking mitigation. I myself weep for such a loss."

"But that terrible day has not yet come. I am building for the Lord a remnant, mighty in prayer - unyielding in faith and tradition. These holy ones will endure through My certain and prevailing grace. This will be a time of the alpha and the omega. It will be a time of purification for the Church. It is necessary that the impure pass through this purifying Flame. But before this terrible day, Jesus sends Me to purify those who will respond to Me in the Flame of My Heart - which is Holy Love."

"To some, it seems too simplistic. Understand, the simple is difficult to live." (Now She has Thérèse of Lisieux with Her.) "All vocations and stations in life are to be vested in Holy Love, as this humble nun proclaimed. All must realize the significance of the present moment. It is in the present moment that the reality of your salvation lies. You are always in the Refuge of My Heart when you live this message."

"I have come to you offering this Holy Refuge and pleading for all people, all nations, to accept My invitation."

"Nationally, your nation is attempting to strengthen itself through a week of prayer and fasting. I will place all those who participate with a sincere heart under My mantle of protection and in the embrace of My Heart. Ask the people to fast from their own will. You will please make all of this known."

■ **October 2, 1997.** Our Lady comes as Refuge of Holy Love. She says: "Praise be Jesus. My daughter, today as the week of prayer and fasting is about to unfold, I have this request of each one of My children. Let this be the week you truly and with all your heart begin to live in Holy Love. Do not look at the faults of the ones God puts in your life around you. Work on your own shortcomings and failings in Holy Love. As you pray, this will be revealed to you."

"By week's end you should then be shining from the inside beauty that this effort in self-perfection gives you. I want to take you deeper into My heart and the mystery of Holy Love. Let us begin."

■ **October 2, 1997 / Thursday Rosary Service.** Blessed Mother is here as Mary, Refuge of Holy Love. She has seven angels with Her. She says: "Praise be Jesus. Dear children, pray with Me now for those who choose not to love."

"Dear children, tonight I invite you to surrender to Me all the guilt you hold in your hearts over past events, and all the worry you have in your hearts for the future. Then, in the present moment, I invite you once again to decide with your will to love as I have been teaching you. Then your hearts will be made beautiful and the world around you will be beautiful as well. Tonight I am blessing you with My Blessing of Holy Love."

■ **October 4, 1997.** Our Lady comes in black (like a picture we were given as a gift). She says: "I am the Mother of God. Praise be Jesus."

"My angel, I have come to help you understand in depth My mission here. While your country has flourished physically and has been made a leader among nations, it has failed spiritually to embrace the sound doctrine of Holy Love. The soul of your country has become easy prey for Satan's lies and compromise. And so... you have abortion." She looks down sadly.

"Most people, it seems, look only to their own interests and do not care for, or love, their neighbor. And so... the innocence of many is scandalized for personal gain."

"God has been taken out of schools in an effort not to impose upon consciences. And so... you have a lack of conscience in the general populace."

"People view modern technology as their own doing and not a gift from God. And so... certain technology has become a tool of Satan."

"All of these things have spoiled this nation and others from the inside out. Most do not realize it. This is why I have been sent here - to awaken hearts as to the spiritual apathy all around you. I come to draw you into the Refuge of My

Immaculate Heart which is the way of your salvation. I come to lead you through this 'way', which is Holy Love, to the Heart of My Son."

"People must open their eyes and their hearts to the choices they are making. I have come so that you can behold the Woman clothed with the sun - the Woman of Revelations. Recognize the apocalypse is upon you. Then hasten to your conversion."

"My daughter, My angel, proclaim it. I will help you. I will lead the way."

■ **October 5, 1997.** Our Lady comes as Mary, Refuge of Holy Love. She says: "Praise be Jesus. My daughter, I have come to help you realize your best effort during this week of prayer and fasting.* Any sacrifice needs to be offered from a heart of love. This is the foundation which makes it most worthy. Do not offer up anything out of dread, but from motivation of Holy Love."

"While it is very good and acceptable to fast on bread and water, it is not good to try this if you are ill or if such a fast would threaten your health. The best fast is to fast from your own will. Your will is self-love. I have given you these guidelines. Surrender being in the spot light, having your own way, doing as you choose when you choose it. Make yourself little."

"Let this week be a challenge to you - not a challenge beyond your capabilities, but a challenge which leads you to the fulfillment of your capabilities. Such an effort will bring you My blessing."

* October 5 – 13, 1997 National Week of Prayer and Fasting to pray against abortion

■ **October 6, 1997.** Blessed Mother comes in white with white roses around her. She says: "Praise be Jesus. Dear children, thank you for praying with me tonight. I am using your prayers and fasts to change the course of human history and to save lives. Tonight I am extending to you My Motherly Blessing."

■ **October 7, 1997 - Feast of the Holy Rosary.** Our Lady comes in white. In front of Her and suspended in the air is an unusual rosary. The Our Fathers' are crosses of drops of blood. The Hail Marys' are tear drops with unborn babies inside of them. The cross is gleaming gold. Our Lady says: "I come in praise of Jesus, My Son. I come as Prophetess of these times."

"The rosary you see is heaven's way of describing to you the weapon that will overcome this evil of abortion. Heaven weeps for the cost of this great sin. The history and the future of all nations has been changed because of this atrocity against God's gift of life."

"Today, sadly, much responsibility must be placed on the laity who are consecrated to Me. I cannot depend on Church leadership to unite in an effort to vanquish the enemy through the Rosary. Even My apparitions have caused division by Satan's efforts to thwart My plans."

"So today, on My feast day, I am calling all My children to unite in My Heart. Do not allow pride to divide you according to which apparition you will follow. Become part of the Flame of My Heart. Be united in love and in the prayer weapon of My Rosary. The evil of abortion can be conquered by your efforts and through My grace."

"Propagate the image I have shown you today."

■ **October 7, 1997.** Our Lady comes as Refuge of Holy Love. Her face and Her heart are glowing. She says: "My angel, it will come to pass and God will permit it, that the public financial system will come under complete control of Satan. People will be fooled by the convenience of computerized consumerism and they will come under the scrutiny of Satan by cooperating in his plans."

"My revealing this to you opposes Satan's plan. Please make it known."

■ **October 8, 1997.** Blessed Mother is here as Mary, Refuge of Holy Love. She says: "Praise be Jesus. Dear children, thank you for joining Me in prayer tonight. I am taking your prayers and petitions to heaven with Me. Through you, I am increasing and strengthening the remnant of faithful. Continue to be My servants of Holy Love. I am blessing you."

■ **October 8, 1997.** Our Lady comes as Refuge of Holy Love. She says: "Praise be Jesus. My angel, today I come to you seeking your clearer understanding of My Missionary Servants of Holy Love. Understand that My Heart is a missionary Heart. It is a servant's Heart. It is, as well, an apocalyptic Heart. These times and this hour is one of great insecurity and confusion. Faith is nebulous, watered down, and compromised. The sin of abortion is like a 'black death' threatening the future of the world."

"Therefore, it is necessary, as a good missionary that I form a strong remnant of faith and shelter them in the Refuge of My Heart. Just as I formed a Marian army of priests, I am now forming a Holy remnant of faith. You will come from the arms of obscurity to make this known, My daughter."

"The Missionary Servants will spread and strengthen the remnant through prayer. The way of Holy Love will be their bylaw. This way will lead them into the New Jerusalem."

She has the Little Flower with Her. "Remember, My daughter, this saint who never left the cloister, but who became the patron saint of missionaries. She will assist you."

"You must be certain to follow the remnant of faith as it now stands under John Paul II. Yes, the faith is already fragmented. Be strong. I am protecting you and I will protect your faith." She leaves.

■ **October 9, 1997 / Thursday Rosary Service.** Our Lady comes in blue and white. She says: "I come to you as Mother of all nations - your Refuge and Hope. Praise be Jesus."

"My angel, endeavor to understand what I am about to tell you. I have come to you here and to many seers under many titles. But the title 'Refuge of Holy Love' is most dear to Me and to My Beloved Son, for it is through this title I will purify and strengthen the Remnant Church."

"Understand that when the virtue of Holy Love is compromised, faith too is compromised. Faith is attacked and weakened always, always through self-love. The individual believes he, himself, is better qualified to determine right from wrong as to the influence of Church doctrine and tradition in his life. In effect, the person believes he knows more than all the Holy Fathers put together. But Jesus, Who is the Just Judge, does not accept or excuse such thinking. All Truth has been given through the Church, which My Jesus put in place Himself. It is pride that takes you off course and away from His Real Presence in the Eucharist."

"It is a false conscience that accepts and approves abortion, birth control, women in the priesthood, practicing homosexuality, or any form of witchcraft."

"All of these things and more are accepted through self-love. This is why I have come to build and strengthen the Remnant of the Tradition of Faith through Holy Love. Those who pass through this purifying Flame will not become complacent. Their faith will not be compromised."

"I need you to spread this message, My angel. The Tradition of Faith as it is handed down to you through John Paul II must, and will, be maintained through Holy Love. People must not decide to form their own opinions concerning Church doctrine. Dogma and doctrine are not choices, but laws. Today, the world needs the security of such laws; but people run from it, much as they run from Me."

"You will need to ask for My Heart for this mission at hand. I will bless you."

■ **October 10, 1997.** Blessed Mother is here as Mary, Refuge of Holy Love. She says: "Praise be Jesus. Dear children, tonight I invite you to understand that your rosaries turn hearts away from evil to the salvation of the Holy Love message. Your rosaries change hearts convicted in evil to pursue good and righteous lives. Tonight I ask that you make Holy Love your goal, that you spread it. Dear children, I am blessing you with My Blessing of Holy Love."

■ **October 10, 1997.** Jesus comes and bends over me. He asks how I feel. He says: "You will be better by Sunday. I have come to tell you these things."

"The pillars of the Remnant Church are the same ones shown Don Bosco in his prophetic dream. On one pillar is My Holy Mother. The other supports My Eucharistic Heart. Hearts must be well anchored to these two devotions. The time approaches when the only security in the world will be the faith in your hearts."

"Do not trust the faith or the teachings of anyone who is not anchored to these two pillars. These are the devotions that take you into Holy Love to Divine Love." He leaves.

■ **October 12, 1997 / Monthly Message to All Nations.** Blessed Mother is here as Our Lady of Guadalupe. She says: "Praise be Jesus."

Our Lady now looks around at everyone here and nods Her head. She says: "I am happy so many have come. Today, once again, I come into the world as My Son allows, to pray for those who do not believe and who do not love. Please join Me."

"My daughter, with humility understand what I am telling you. Today, as never before, evil has become prevalent in all areas of the world. Satan has made bold inroads into hearts that hold sway over world policies and in moral issues. His policies are hidden under terms such as freedom, rights, choice, and feminism. When you hear these terms, please know you are dealing with My adversary, in many instances."

"It is a desperate hour - one in which God must intervene to save souls and the world. The faith of many is threatened by compromise. This is why it is necessary that I build up a remnant faithful who will not be swayed by new thinking, but who will remain faithful to John Paul II. Earlier I gave you two opposing guidelines – self-love and holy love. Today I give to you the signs of states of hearts - apostasy, heresy and schism, as opposed by the faithful remnant.

APOSTASY, HERESY, SCHISM	HOLY AND FAITHFUL REMNANT
Doubt or do not believe in the Real Presence of Jesus in the Eucharist. Show little or no reverence to Him in this Form.	Firmly believe in and revere Jesus' Real and true Presence in the Holy Eucharist.
Hold little or no devotion to the Blessed Mother. Have no affection for the Holy Rosary. Consider devotion to Mary extreme.	Are faithful apostles of the Holy Rosary and of other Devotions to Mary. Promote these devotions in the world.
Challenge the authority of this Holy Father, John Paul II. Unwilling to accept his doctrines, even some dogma of the Church.	Faithful to John Paul II. Accept his authority on all issues.
Consider their own conscience their god and judge.	Submit to Church law and the sacrament of reconciliation where Jesus is present to forgive sins.

"In the left-hand column you have the ways hearts are being separated from the truth. In the opposite column are the ways in which the faithful cling tenaciously to the faith. These are the present remnant. Some of these will follow Me into the New Jerusalem as the future Holy Remnant. I have taken all of the remnant Church into My Immaculate Heart. I am their Protectress. You will please make it known."

"The flavor of this mission is to restore and maintain the tradition of faith in hearts, thus building up and supporting the remnant Church."

Now a flame is rising out of Our Lady's extended hand. "Do not be disturbed by the signs of apostasy and schism all around you."

"This," (She raises the flame in Her hand towards Maureen), "is the remnant of the tradition of faith. It will be one with the Flame of My Heart, which is Holy Love." She raises the flame in Her Hand up to Her Heart and it disappears into the Flame of Her Heart. "The fiber of the remnant is Holy Love, just as the fiber of My Immaculate Heart is Holy Love. I have come to reassure you that this remnant will be made strong through My grace."

"The greatest trials lie yet ahead and will come unexpectedly. But, you are prepared and secure if you are living in Holy Love. There is no security or refuge in the world that can match this."

"Every affliction and trial is made bearable when you live in Holy Love. Today, My tears flow copiously upon the world. I weep today for the lack of love in hearts. Your response to Me is a loving kiss upon My brow. Each one that comes and each one that responds is a little miracle in the eyes of your Mother. Embrace the message and you will embrace My Heart."

"Dear children, I come to restore the faith in the heart of the world. I am asking you to pray daily for those who do not believe. My children, the world has slipped from the path of righteousness, and as I seek to reconcile mankind with his Creator, more and more ignore Me. Please respond to My call, not just today, but in every present moment. Pray for the conversion of all hearts, for earth needs to be healed from the inside out. Dear children, I weep for those who do not believe."

Jesus is now with Blessed Mother. "We are extending to you the Blessing of Our United Hearts."

■ **October 16, 1997 / Thursday Rosary Service.** Blessed Mother is here as Mary, Refuge of Holy Love. She says: "Praise be Jesus. Dear children, pray with Me now for those who oppose Church tradition. Dear children, I come to bring you peace borne on the wings of Holy Love. I ask that you consecrate your lives to the cross so that I can bring souls into the kingdom. The New Jerusalem is a kingdom unlike any other that you have known, or will come to know in this life, for it is all peace, all mercy, all love. Dear children, tonight I am blessing you with My Blessing of Holy Love."

■ **October 17, 1997.** Our Lady comes as Refuge of Holy Love. She says: "Praise be Jesus. My daughter, I come to help you realize and understand My call to you. You are questioning why I speak of the remnant Church when I come for all people, all nations. In God's Eyes, souls are not apples and oranges - they are one. All people and all nations are called into the tradition of faith as given and stated in the New Catechism. It is man himself who chooses to believe otherwise. I come to you as Refuge of Holy Love - Refuge and Protectress of the Remnant. Many learned and influential people oppose Me, but I still come. If Holy Love is accepted in hearts with sincerity, then it is impossible to compromise the tradition of faith. Each soul is given the grace to believe. It is an ecumenical call which leads souls to the truth. I am blessing you."

■ **October 18, 1997.** Jesus says: "Make it known that human faults and failings become sinful when no effort is made to overcome them."

■ **October 21, 1997.** Jesus says: "Abortion is the sin of the century which is and will be responsible for the greatest loss of life and souls. It is the offspring of apathetic hearts. For this I lament."

■ **October 23, 1997 / Thursday Rosary Service.** Blessed Mother is here as Mary, Refuge of Holy Love. She says: "Praise be Jesus. My children, please pray with Me for those who are attacked by doubts."

"Dear children, these are decisive times. By your 'yes' to Holy Love you are helping to determine the call of justice and the future of the world. I need your efforts in holiness through the message of Holy Love. Dear children, continue to pray, pray, pray. I am blessing you."

■ **October 27, 1997 / Monday Evening Praise Service.** Jesus and Mary both come. Their Hearts are exposed. Our Lady says: "Praise be Jesus. Dear children, be united and one with the Heart of your merciful, sorrowful and loving Mother. Through My call to Holy Love be one with your Creator."

Jesus and Mary extend to us the Blessing of the United Hearts.

■ **October 30, 1997 / Thursday Rosary Service.** Blessed Mother is here as Mary, Refuge of Holy Love. She says: "Praise be to Jesus. Pray with Me now for all sinners. Dear children, tonight I come to you as your eternal Mother and Refuge. I am protecting you in the face of evil and sheltering you in the Refuge of My Immaculate Heart. Eternally I am your Mother, your Refuge and your Protectress. Wipe the tears of your Mother through your efforts in holiness. Dear children, I am blessing you with My Blessing of Holy Love."

November 1997

■ **November 1, 1997.** Our Lady comes in blue. She says: "Praise be Jesus. My dear children, I have not come to you out of My need but your own. Realize I need only the Will of the Father. I come to you so that I may present your needs to the One Who sends Me."

"I am your advocate and the cause of your joy. I hold you in the Refuge of My Heart wherein no evil enters. Come to Me, and allow Me to take your burdens and present them to God."

"The greater your need, the more powerful My grace." She leaves.

■ **November 3, 1997 - Feast of St. Martin De Porres / Monday Praise and Prayer Service.** Jesus and Mary are both here. Jesus has His hand up like He is going to bless us. He says, "My brothers and sisters, today I hold no memory of your iniquity but only of every act of love you have given Me - no matter how small. With sincerity I make this covenant* with you, one of love and understanding; and I promise with every beat of My Sacred Heart to give you My protection and provision."

They extend to us the Blessing of the United Hearts.

Please note: this covenant was given by Jesus to those present at the Praise Service of November 3rd.

■ **November 6, 1997.** Our Lady comes in blue and white with Her Heart exposed. She says: "Praise be Jesus. My daughter, I have come to help you understand the fragile state of humanity - a humanity that does not understand their position before God."

"Each day and every minute the relationship between God and man deteriorates more. The more man trusts in himself and his own skills, the less he trusts in his Creator. All human technology is under God's domain and thus dependent upon God alone for its state of being. Nothing - be it creature or matter - exists outside God's Holy and Divine Will. But, today due to Satan's compromise and deceit, mankind has lost sight of this. In his pride he has chosen to tamper with creation itself and placed himself in the role of Creator, deciding who should live and who should die."

"Now you have a separate church - a church of dissenters - who dare to challenge the authority of this worthy Holy Father. This is leading many astray and will cost many souls."

"I have come to help you see that earth is suspended by a thread. If the thread breaks, God will invoke His Justice. The fiber of this thread is Holy Love. Only through Holy Love can God and man be reconciled. No one reaches salvation without loving God and neighbor. I speak to you only from truth. You must make this known."

■ **November 6, 1997.** St. Thérèse comes. She says, "I have come in praise of Jesus. Our Mother sends me to dictate to you this prayer."

Prayer For The Remnant Church
Dictated by St. Thérèse of the Child Jesus
(The Little Flower)
"Heavenly Mother, Protectress and Refuge of the Faith, lead and protect the Holy Remnant of the Tradition of Faith. Keep us faithful to the Church tradition as handed down through Pope John Paul II and as stated in the new catechism. Help us to boldly bear the light of this faith in the face of all apostasy, heresy, and schism. Unite us, the Holy Remnant, in Your Immaculate Heart. Amen."

■ **November 6, 1997 / Thursday Rosary Service.** Blessed Mother is here as Mary, Refuge of Holy Love. She says: "Praise be Jesus. Pray with Me now for all those who do not love."

"Dear children, I invite all of you to surrender to Me. It is impossible to surrender if you first do not trust, and it is impossible to trust if you do not love. Therefore, My little children, see that I am calling you to trustful surrender through Holy Love. And I am blessing you with My Blessing of Holy Love."

■ **November 8, 1997.** Jesus says: "Fear makes its own enemies and creates its own problems."

"But trust in My grace brings peace. Peace bears the fruit of love, and love bears the fruit of peace."

■ **November 8, 1997.** Our Lady comes on a cloud with many angels around Her. The angels are bowing down and saying "Triumph and reign, triumph and reign," over and over.

Our Lady says: "Praise be Jesus. My angel, I have come to further help you understand the tenuous position the world is in. The thread that suspends the world to God is Holy Love, but it is comprised of many 'lukewarm faithful.' The flock is scattering and confused. People are making much of their own opinions and little of My message to the world and the deposit of faith. Therefore, I am here. When faith is destroyed in most hearts, the thread of Holy Love will snap. Now is the hour you must pray. Pray most of all for those lukewarm. The hour grows late, and they have not decided which side they are on. But once again I tell you, no decision is a decision. Those, who are not for God, are against Him. Further insults only serve to pick away at the thread of Holy Love."

"Now I have spoken, and you must act on these words by making them known. I will bless you."

■ **November 10, 1997 / Monday Praise and Prayer Service.***
Jesus and Blessed Mother are both here. Blessed Mother says: "Praise be Jesus. It is the Lord's Will that Jesus speaks on Monday nights." [Monday Praise and Prayer Service.]

Jesus says, "My brothers and sisters, it is plain that you are not far from the kingdom, for it takes a childlike heart and a simplistic heart to dwell and be drawn into the depth and the height of Our Blessing of the United Hearts. Tonight We impart to you this Blessing."

* This message was directed specifically to those in attendance at the Monday Praise Service.

■ **November 12, 1997 / Monthly Message To All Nations.**
(This message was given in two parts.) Blessed Mother is here as Our Lady of Guadalupe. She says: "Praise be Jesus. Dear children, pray with Me now for all unbelievers."

"My angel, today I come to you, once again, seeking man's reconciliation with God. I appeal to all nations to be united with one heart in Holy Love. These days it is most obvious that what is in the heart of one nation affects all nations in the world. Sadly, there is a spiritual blight amongst government leaders. This lack of focus on God calls down His Justice upon all people, all nations."

"I have come once again to help you see that Holy Love is your justification. Failure in Holy Love causes every sort of disaster in nature and amongst men themselves. Man in his arrogance does not see that nature is connected to the Creator. Nor does he see that famine and disease are caused by spiritual hunger and a disease of the heart, namely self-love."

"Today, I come still again asking each one to choose Holy Love - love of God and neighbor - above and beyond self-love. Then I will show you My favor, My protection, My grace."

"I invite all to pilgrimage to My property. Here the grace of My Heart is pouring into the world. Certain ones will be made to see Me there. Others have already captured Me in the eyes of their camera. My Statue of Sorrows comes to life as a sign of My presence there. The flesh takes on the hue of real flesh, both to the naked eye and on film. Rosaries turn gold as a sign to all that prayer does change things. The scent of roses is further proof of My presence. Certain saints and angels will be photographed on the property as a sign of Heaven's favor. In the Mission Center, I will step out of the statue in the alcove as a sign of My greeting those who come. This too will be photographed."

"The healings at every source of water on the property will increase and continue. Those who recite the stations will find solace and healing. Much peace will be given in the station area. I will accompany those who pray the Way of the Cross there."

"Exceeding all of this is the grace of the Blessing of the United Hearts to be given on the 12th of the month and on every Monday evening. It carries with it the grace of conversion and reconciliation as well as healing."

"All these favors are offered to those who will come. Please ask the people to ask Jesus to forgive them any lack of love in their hearts as they approach the Spring and Lake of Tears."

Jesus is now with Blessed Mother and Their Hearts are exposed.

Blessed Mother says: "Dear children, tonight I invite you to surrender to the peace of My Heart, for it is here you will find My grace and My peace. Dear children, I am calling you into the Refuge of My Heart during these times of great decision that weigh upon the world. Please understand that the time is short. There have not been enough prayers and sacrifices to stop God's Justice against sins committed against life. There is still time to strengthen the faithful remnant and increase My grace in the world, thus mitigating what is to come. Dear children, pray, pray, pray."

Jesus and Blessed Mother now extend the Blessing of the United Hearts.

■ **November 13, 1997 / Thursday Rosary Service.** Blessed Mother is here as Mary, Refuge of Holy Love. She says: "Praise be Jesus. Dear children, tonight I invite you to understand that there are many reasons God's Justice must visit the world. But we are not here to dwell on this. I have come once again to plead with you to spread My message of Holy Love in the world around you. Do not be distracted by signs in the world, by punishments, chastisements, or the like. Do not listen to criticism concerning your state of life or the world around you, but only with docility come into the Refuge of My Heart. This is My plan, My dear children; then you will be at peace and in harmony with God. Tonight I am blessing you."

■ **November 17, 1997 / Monday Praise and Prayer Service.** Jesus and Blessed Mother are here. Jesus says: "My brothers and sisters, abide in Me, for I am your refreshment. Take up your repose in My Heart of Hearts. All your petitions are in the wound of My Heart; thus you must trust in My mercy and love. Allow Me to reign in your hearts in the present moment. Abandon yourselves to Me. We will bless you." Jesus and Blessed Mother extend the Blessing of the United Hearts.

■ **November 20, 1997 / Thursday Rosary Service.** Blessed Mother is here as Refuge of Holy Love. She says: "Praise be Jesus. Dear children, pray with Me now for peace in all hearts."

"Dear children, tonight I come especially to help you understand that My Heart is not a symbol of Holy Love but, through the Divine Will, is Holy Love."

"Since My Son has entrusted the peace of the world to My Immaculate Heart, further understand that it is through this message and My Heart of Holy Love that peace will come into hearts and so into the world."

"I am blessing you."

■ **November 23, 1997.** First Maureen saw two hearts. They disappeared. Then Our Lady came as Mary, Refuge of Holy Love. She says: "Praise be Jesus. Dear children, pray with Me now for hearts to open to love."

"Dear children, tonight I invite you to see that all things today are influenced by prayer. See then the importance of prayer in the present moment. I am coming to help you understand that in Heaven God's actions in the world [His Justice and His Mercy] are not measured by time - every minute, every hour. Please understand that it is prayer and sacrifice vs. sin and evil that bring about or mitigate every action of God in the world. Further understand, My dear, dear children, the great importance of the present moment, which is eternal and which can bring about great change in the world today through your prayers and your sacrifices. Continue to pray, pray, pray. I am blessing you."

■ **November 24, 1997.** Our Lady comes in blue and white as soon as Maureen came to the chapel. She smiles and says: "Praise be Jesus. Satan has laid many obstacles in your path this morning." (Maureen had lost her mittens.) "I am glad you have come."

"Unite and surrender your heart to Me now. Give to Me all issues and decisions. I will assist you. The adversary likes to keep you in a state of turmoil and indecision."

"I have come to help you understand that My coming to you is a firm anchor amidst the confusion of the world. This has been a century of misinformation, miscommunication, and indecision. These are all hallmarks of My adversary. This is how he sets good people against My plans here. When he succeeds in getting the good to oppose the good, he is able to confuse others even more."

"In the end, My daughter, My Immaculate Heart will triumph. Clarity and righteousness will be brought to light in every issue, both in hearts and in the world. The Holy Love message is much a part of this. This is why it is opposed today. Hearts will be made one with their Creator through Holy Love."

"Today many live with suppressed fear in their hearts. I have come to vanquish fear. Surrender to Holy Love, and do not be afraid. Begin to trust, so that My victory may begin in you. Tell this to My children. I have come to help them find their place before the Eternal Father. I am blessing you."

■ **November 24, 1997 / Monday Praise and Prayer Service.** Jesus and Blessed Mother are here. They are looking around and smiling.

Blessed Mother says: "Praise be Jesus."

Jesus says: "My brothers and sisters, I rejoice in your presence here tonight. I am in your midst. You have come because I have gone into the highways and byways to invite you. I ask you tonight, through Holy Love, to surrender all things to Me. Win for Me souls through the message of Holy Love. We extend to you tonight the Blessing of Our United Hearts."

December 1997

■ **December 1, 1997.** Our Lady comes in blue and white. She says: "Praise be Jesus. My dear, dear children, today I invite you to realize most fully your role as an advent people. As you prepare your hearts during this season of Advent to receive My Son on Christmas morning, also prepare yourselves through Holy Love for My Jesus' Second Coming. You are an advent people living in apocalyptic times. As changes take place in your lives and in the world around you, please realize God is preparing you for My Son's triumphant return. Allow Him to reign in your hearts through the message of Holy Love, for this is also the season of love."

"I am blessing you."

■ **December 1, 1997 / Monday Prayer and Praise Service.** Jesus and Mary come with Their Hearts exposed. Jesus says: "Come, My brothers and sisters, as sheep to the shepherd. Surrender to Me your misgivings, fear, and all that is between us. These come from pride. Trust Me. Trust proceeds from love. I want you to love Me."

Jesus and Mary extend to us the Blessing of Their United Hearts.

■ **December 4, 1997 / Thursday Prayer Service.** Blessed Mother is here as Mary, Refuge of Holy Love. When She appeared, She seemed to push aside a curtain that contained many small crosses.

Our Lady says: "Praise be Jesus. Dear children, tonight I

invite you to especially understand that you must give praise to Jesus, not only in good times but also in times of adversity. For it is during the most adverse conditions that Satan tries to pull you off course, to distract you and encourage you to give in to impatience and discouragement. It is only My grace that keeps you on the path of Holy Love during every present moment. In this please give praise to Jesus, My Son, Who longs for your love and your affection. I am blessing you."

■ **December 8, 1997.** Our Lady comes in white and holding the Infant Jesus. She says: "Praise be Jesus. My angel, I come to bring you peace."

"To all of My children, I invite you to realize that there are many who celebrate My feast today, the day I was immaculately conceived, who still believe in abortion. There are priests amongst this group. If it is on one hand true that I was conceived without sin as Church dogma dictates, then it must also be true that the soul is present at conception. This being fact as well as dogma, how can anyone argue for the destruction of life in the womb? The embryo is a living, vibrant, God-given life complete with soul. Suppose I Myself had been the victim of abortion? Imagine God's wrath. Today, My Heart cries out for each life that is destroyed. This is a greater sin than the Holocaust in Germany. It is more serious than any sin in Noah's day or in Sodom and Gomorrah."

"You must continue to pray courageously that hearts are convicted and open to the truth."

■ **December 8, 1997 / Monday Prayer and Praise Service.** Jesus and Blessed Mother are here. Blessed Mother says: "Praise be Jesus." She turns to Him and bows Her head.

Jesus says: "My brothers and sisters, you have come here tonight at My invitation. Thank you for your songs and praise. I want you to honor My Mother as She deserves to be honored. So many turn away from Her today. Do not be shy about your devotion to Her. I send Her to your midst that you will be led along the righteous path. It is through your actions, your unity, and your prayer that you will be able to lead others as I so desire. You are the example of Holy Love in the world. Continue to pray, to love, and to be joyous."

Jesus and Our Lady extend Their Blessing of the United Hearts.

■ **December 11, 1997 / Thursday Prayer Service.** Blessed Mother is here as Refuge of Holy Love. She says: "Praise be Jesus. Pray with Me now for all the unconverted." (Maureen asked Blessed Mother to pray for some people, and She nodded.) She says: "Dear children, tonight, I invite you to listen to My words to you only with loving hearts. Do not come to Me with hearts full of fear but with hearts full of love, for love is the father of trust; and trust begets faith. Tonight I am blessing you with My Motherly Blessing."

■ **December 12, 1997 / Monthly Message To All Nations.** Our Lady comes as Our Lady of Guadalupe. She says: "Praise be Jesus. My daughter, I come to you under this title, not for one nation or hemisphere, but for all nations and all people. I am the Mother of mercy and love. I am your Mother."

"I have come to lead My children out of the desert of confusion and to deliver them into the Arms of Truth."

"My daughter, find your peace in My favor. Please ask the people to pray with Me now, to pray for all unbelievers."

Our Lady wished Maureen "Happy Birthday."

"Today I invite you to have a clear understanding of these times. When the King returns to review His Kingdom, He will come wielding a sword of flames. His bounty will be the righteous who pursue His unending Mercy from age to age. The fate of every nation rests with the unborn. It is the unborn who will judge and convict."

"I call you from the death of sin to the light of salvation. When you love, you are victorious."

"My daughter, I continue to come to you under this title

of Guadalupe so that mankind will pursue reconciliation with God. During this time all that calls you back to God - faith, prayer, holiness, life itself - is opposed and persecuted in the world. The sins today are more grievous and more offensive to God than any, for they are not committed through pagan ignorance but by those who say or pretend to love My Jesus or who once loved Him." (She has tears coming down Her cheeks.)

"My Immaculate Heart is held in contempt by many when it is always and should be a sign of Refuge. The Angel Gabriel addressed Me as 'full of grace.' My grace is not for Me but for all people - all nations. But fear opposes My grace. Thus the adversary uses fear to oppose My words to you on Holy Love. Those who fear Holy Love must also fear the triumph of My Heart, for it is by this means I will be victorious."

"Everything that I come for - My presence on this property, My message of Holy Love, the graces given through the Blessing Point and sources of water - are grace from God. Since fear opposes My grace, you must recognize that suspicious fear comes from the adversary."

"There are those who want Me to be only what they think I should, to say what they want to hear, and to perform signs only as they prefer. But I come clothed in God's Divine Will. Everything I say and do transcends through His Holy and Divine Will. If you can accept Me as I come to you, then you will receive much. It is only your difficulties with My presence here and your doubts that stand between us. I want you to receive My grace to the fullest. Pray, and I will help you."

"Dear children, today I invite you to understand that no peace can come into the world through negotiations or war machines. You will have peace when there is an end to abortion. The victory is through My Immaculate Heart which is Holy Love. You will please make this known."

Maureen asked Her to pray for the woman who has the brain tumor. She smiled and nodded. "Please let the people know that I am praying for all their intentions here today. Their hearts are not unknown to Me."

Jesus is now present with Blessed Mother. They extend to all here the Blessing of the United Hearts.

■ **December 14, 1997 / 2ⁿᵈ Sunday Prayer Service - Against Abortion.** Blessed Mother is here as Mary, Refuge of Holy Love. She says: "Praise be Jesus. Pray with Me now for all the unborn."

"Dear children, tonight I reveal to you that God's Mercy and His Love are one. It is necessary because of the state of evil in hearts that God intervene in the world, that His Justice come, that His retribution be satisfied. Dear children, solemnly I tell you a purification will come - its length, breadth, and depth depending upon the fate of the unborn. You will persevere through Holy Love, the Refuge of My Immaculate Heart. Do not be frightened, but realize the time of reconciliation with your Creator is at hand. I am blessing you."

■ **December 15, 1997 / Monday Prayer and Praise Service.** Jesus and Blessed Mother are here. Their Hearts are exposed. Blessed Mother says: "Praise be Jesus," and She bows Her head.

Jesus says: "My brothers and sisters, I see your innermost hearts. My Mercy is upon you and everlasting. I have forgiven you every sin, even the ones you do not recall, and I have placed My seal upon your hearts - that which is Holy Love. Come after Me and imitate Me. It is good you are here."

Jesus and Blessed Mother give the Blessing of the United Hearts.

■ **December 18, 1997 / Thursday Prayer Service.** Blessed Mother is here as Mary, Refuge of Holy Love. She says: "Praise be Jesus. Let us pray together now for the conversion of those furthest from My Immaculate Heart."

"Dear children, I come to you once again seeking your decision, good over evil. I desire your moment-to-moment conversion, for without it I cannot be victorious. It is necessary that you put aside things of the world. Do not concern yourself for what might happen or what has happened, but stay with Me, My dear, dear children, in this present moment, sanctifying it through your 'yes' to Holy Love. The world as you know it will change. Already the signs are upon you. Come into My Heart and abide with Me. Tonight I am blessing you with My Blessing of Holy Love."

■ **December 22, 1997 / Monday Prayer and Praise Service.** Jesus and Blessed Mother are here. Their Hearts are exposed. Blessed Mother says: "Praise be Jesus."

Jesus says: "I have come to you asking each of you to let your hearts be like unto the Christmas star, leading others to the manger. Stand guard by the manger and wait humbly for My return. Take your hearts from out of the world and all its empty promises. Come to Me. Be poor in spirit. Honor the little King this year, as never before, through hearts of love."

Jesus and Blessed Mother extend the Blessing of the United Hearts.

■ **December 25, 1997 - Christmas Day.** Our Lady comes in a white mantle with a gold lining and a white gown. She is in a bright light and is holding the Infant Jesus. She says: "Praise be Jesus. Christmas blessings to you and your husband. I come to you tonight as Queen of the Universe, Queen of Heaven and Earth. I come to address all nations and all peoples."

"It is the hour of telling, the hour of decision. I invite all of My children to comprehend what is at hand. You will not achieve peace in the world until you accept and live in love. My Son was born Prince of Peace not to impose His Will but to show you how to love. He came to fill the valleys of your deficiencies and indecision with love. He came to lay level the mountains of your pride and self-love with Holy Love."

"Today the world is in the valley of indecision on the brink of the abyss of God's purification. Surrender your will, and you will have the peace you seek through selfless desire. If you cannot and will not, you must expect the unfolding of the fruits of disunity. Do not look for the natural order of events but the disordered chain of events born of Satan's confusion."

"Love. Love God and your neighbor. My Son is returning, and you disregard the signs. Believe, and My grace will be yours. I will bless you through My grace, just as I bless you today through Holy Love."

■ **December 28, 1997 / 4th Sunday - To Pray For Unbelievers.** The Holy Family is here: Blessed Mother, St. Joseph, and Jesus. Jesus looks to be about 7 or 8. Blessed Mother says: "Praise be Jesus, Word Incarnate. Pray with Me now, dear children, for all unbelievers."

"Dear children, understand that each of you has an individual part to play and place in God's family. No one can take your place in this individual role. With your hearts choose My path of holiness, which is Holy Love, that I call you upon. Then you will realize your place in the Kingdom to come. I am blessing you with My Blessing of Holy Love."

■ **December 29, 1997 / Monday Prayer and Praise Service.** Jesus and Blessed Mother are here. Blessed Mother says: "Praise be Jesus."

Jesus says: "Tonight, My brothers and sisters, Our Blessing carries with it special grace to be cognizant of the present moment and to follow the path of Holy Love I send My Mother to lead you upon. Amidst joy and despair, you will find grace to endure and to lead others in holy boldness along this path of righteousness. We are extending to you tonight the Blessing of Our United Hearts."

■ **December 31, 1997 / New Year's Eve Prayer Service.** Blessed Mother is here as Mary, Refuge of Holy Love. She says: "Praise be Jesus. Invite the people to pray with Me now for those who do not recognize the evil in their lives."

"Dear children, tonight I invite you to pray very hard that this coming year of 1998 will see the victory of good over evil and that abortion will be banned in this country once again. If this evil is not conquered, you will see many changes take place brought on by man's embrace of sin. I am always near you and I offer you the Refuge of My Heart as your spiritual retreat and refreshment. Tonight I am blessing you with My Blessing of Holy Love."

■ **December 31, 1997.** Our Lady comes as Refuge of Holy Love. She says: "Praise be Jesus, born Incarnate. My daughter, each time I come to you, it is as Protectress and Refuge. You know Me and trust Me as this. I desire all My children believe in Me in this way. I come to protect their faith and provide for each one spiritual refuge in My Immaculate Heart."

"But today the pride of compromise has alienated many from the truth. Many walk the path of perdition believing they are on the path of righteousness, for they have not searched for truth with humility and Holy Love. Satan presents error as truth so cunningly and with such authority causing too many to be led astray. The adversary most often clothes his suggestions in good. Unless you come to Me and seek My protection and this Refuge of Holy Love, you can be easily tricked. Do not think yourself above it."

"As the new year unfolds, you will see many changes. Many events will disarm you. Others will edify. Everything is a grace. Every present moment is given towards your salvation."

"Seek the guidance of the Holy Spirit in the morning, and consecrate your day to Him. Let your hearts be open to His voice and murmurs. He will help you find the Path of Light. Surrender to Him as He calls you."

"I will bless your 'yes' to My Heavenly Spouse. I will bless you."

A small shrine near Maranatha Spring that is dedicated to Blessed Mother and to the United Hearts of Jesus and Mary offers pilgrims a place for prayer and peaceful reflection.

APPENDIX

PRAYERS, DEVOTIONS *and* MEDITATIONS
from HEAVEN
(With Message Dates)

1993

- 'THE KEY TO THE REFUGE OF OUR LADY'S HEART' *(Our Lady – June 27, 1993)*

- 'PRAYER FOR HOLY LOVE' *(Our Lady – Oct. 23, 1993)*

- 'OUR LADY'S MOTHERLY BLESSING' *(Oct. 24, 1993; Jan. 24, 1994; and May 22 1994)*

1994

- 'ROSARY MEDITATIONS' *(Our Lady – Jan. 26, 1994)*

- 'CONSECRATION TO THE EUCHARISTIC HEART' *(Our Lady – Feb. 20, 1994)*

- 'MISSIONARY PRAYER OF HOLY LOVE' *(Our Lady – Sep. 22, 1994)*

1995

- 'OUR LADY'S BLESSING OF HOLY LOVE' *(Mar. 16, 1995)*

- 'MISSIONARY PRAYER OF HOLY LOVE' *(Our Lady – Sep. 21, 1995)*

- '3-DAY CONSECRATION TO THE FLAME OF HOLY LOVE' *(Our Lady – Apr. 16, 1995 / Easter Sunday)*

- 'ROSARY MEDITATIONS' and 'ST. JOSEPH PRAYER' *(Our Lady – July 3, 1995)*

- 'CONSECRATION TO THE PRESENT MOMENT' *(Our Lady – Sep. 5, 1995)*

- 'ALL GLORY BE' *(Our Lady – Sep. 21, 1995)*

- '5-DAY NOVENA TO OUR LADY OF GUADALUPE' *(An angel – Nov. 29, 1995)*

- 'INVOCATION TO THE HOLY ANGELS' *(Dec. 31, 1995)*

1996

- EJACULATION: *'Mary, protect our faith'* *(Our Lady – Jan. 23, 1996)*

- 'THE CHAPLET OF THE TWO HEARTS' *(Jesus – Feb. 10, 1996; Apr. 1, 1997)* and Promises *(Our Lady – Feb. 29, 1996)*

- The initial 'BLESSING OF THE UNITED HEARTS' *(Mar. 21, 1996)* and Promises *(Jesus – Mar. 22, 1996; Mar. 23, 1996) (See also July 28, 1996; Nov. 10, 1997)*

- EJACULATION to pray at the end of the Chaplet: *"Holy and Sacred Wounds of the United Hearts of Jesus and Mary, answer my prayer." (Jesus – Mar. 26, 1996)*

- 'STATIONS OF THE CROSS' *(Jesus – Mar. 31, 1996)*

- 'SPIRITUAL BAPTISM OF THE UNBORN' *(Our Lady – May 16, 1996)*

- The revised 'FR. GOBBI PRAYER' is to be prayed at the beginning of the Rosary *(Our Lady – Oct. 7, 1996)*

- 'THE SEVEN SORROWS' *(Our Lady – Oct. 11, 1996)*

- 'MARRIAGE CONSECRATION' *(Jesus – Nov. 2, 1996)*

- 'PRAYER TO THE ETERNAL FATHER' *(Our Lady – Dec. 2, 1996)*

1997

- 'PRAYER FOR URGENT PETITIONS' *(Jan. 6, 1997)*

- 'PRAYER TO MARY, REFUGE OF HOLY LOVE' *(Mary, Refuge of Holy Love – Mar. 21, 1997)*

- INVOCATION: *'Mary, Refuge of Holy Love, pray for us' (Mary, Refuge of Holy Love – May 15, 1997)*

- 'PRAYER TO JESUS IN THE EUCHARIST' *(Blessed Mother – Jun. 30, 1997)*

- 'MEDITATIONS FOR THE SORROWFUL MOTHER SHRINE' *(Mary, Refuge of Holy Love – Sep. 5, 1997)*

- 'PRAYER FOR THE REMNANT CHURCH' *(St. Thérèse of Lisieux – Nov. 6, 1997)*

Historical Note to Volume 1
RELIGIOUS AND SECULAR LEADERS
1993 – 1997

The following religious and secular leaders of the time may be referenced in the Messages:

■ **Pope John Paul II** (1920-2005) served as the 264th Pope of the Roman Catholic Church from October 16, 1978 to April 2, 2005.

■ **Democratic President William (Bill) Jefferson Clinton** served two terms as the 42nd President of the United States from 1993 - 2001.

■ **Bishop Anthony M. Pilla** was installed as the 9th Bishop of Cleveland in 1981, where he served until his resignation in 2006.

Our Lady Gives the World
THE ROSARY OF THE UNBORN
and THE CHAPLET OF THE UNBORN
To End Abortion

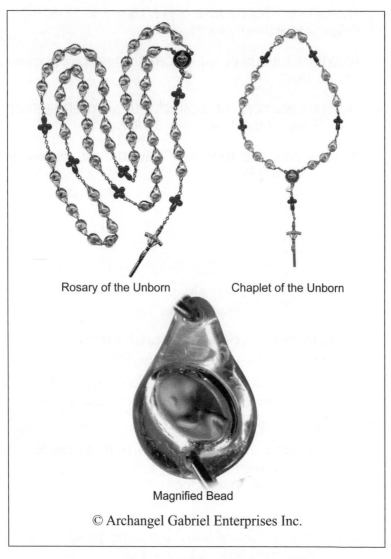

Rosary of the Unborn   Chaplet of the Unborn

Magnified Bead

© Archangel Gabriel Enterprises Inc.

www.RosaryOfTheUnborn.com

VISION OF THE ROSARY OF THE UNBORN

Our Lady comes in white. In front of Her and suspended in the air is an unusual rosary. The Our Father beads are droplets of blood in the shape of a cross. The Hail Mary beads are light blue tear drops with unborn babies inside of them. The cross is gleaming gold. Our Lady says: "I come in praise of Jesus, My Son. I come as Prophetess of these times."

"The rosary you see is Heaven's way of describing to you the weapon that will overcome this evil of abortion. Heaven weeps for the cost of this great sin. The history and the future of all nations has been changed because of this atrocity against God's gift of life."

"Today, sadly, much responsibility must be placed on the laity who are consecrated to Me. I cannot depend on Church leadership to unite in an effort to vanquish the enemy through the Rosary. Even My apparitions have caused division by Satan's efforts to thwart My plans."

"So today, on My feast day, I am calling all My children to unite in My Heart. Do not allow pride to divide you according to which apparition you will follow. Become part of the Flame of My Heart. Be united in love and in the prayer weapon of My Rosary. The evil of abortion can be conquered by your efforts and through My grace."

"Propagate the image I have shown you today."

(October 7, 1997 - Feast of the Holy Rosary)

Promises for Praying
The Rosary of the Unborn

1. "Praise be to Jesus. I see you are using the new Rosary of the Unborn. I affirm to you, my daughter, that **each 'Hail Mary' prayed from a loving heart will rescue one of these innocent lives from death by abortion.** When you use this rosary, call to mind My Sorrowful Immaculate Heart which continually sees the sin of abortion played

out in every present moment. I give to you this special sacramental* with which to heal My Motherly Heart." Maureen asks: "Blessed Mother, do you mean any *'Hail Mary'* or just one prayed on the Rosary of the Unborn?" Blessed Mother: "This is a special grace attached to this particular rosary. It should always be used to pray against abortion. You will please make this known."

(Our Lady as the Sorrowful Mother - July 2, 2001)

Note: *Catholics believe that, in order to be a sacramental, the rosary must be blessed by a Catholic Priest.*

2. "Please tell the world that **each *'Our* Father'** recited on the Rosary of the Unborn **assuages My grieving Heart. Further, it withholds the Arm of Justice."**

(Jesus - August 3, 2001)

3. "The greatest promise I give you in regards to this rosary is this: **Every Rosary prayed from the heart to its completion on these beads mitigates the punishment as yet withstanding for the sin of abortion** ...When I say the punishment as yet withstanding for the sin of abortion, I mean the punishment each soul deserves for taking part in this sin. Then too, I also refer to the greater punishment that awaits the world for embracing this sin."

(Jesus - August 3, 2001)

4. "If a group is gathered who are praying for the unborn from the heart and only one person has in their possession the Rosary of the Unborn, **I will honor each *'Hail Mary'* from each person in the group** as if they were holding the Rosary of the Unborn themselves."   *(Jesus - February 28, 2005)*

VISION OF THE CHAPLET OF THE UNBORN

Blessed Mother says: "I have come with yet another important weapon in the fight against abortion. As you know, abortion is the one crime which, if conquered, would change the future of the world. The weapon I now hand off to you is the Chaplet of the Unborn."

Blessed Mother holds out a chaplet with five sets of three Hail Marys and one Our Father - like the Chaplet of the United Hearts. The beads are like the beads on the Rosary of the Unborn.

(March 24, 2013)

Promises for Praying
The Chaplet of the Unborn

1. "Every time the Chaplet is prayed from the heart, some soul contemplating abortion will have a change of heart."

2. "Each time the Chaplet is prayed from the heart, some soul will be reconciled with the Truth of what abortion really is - the taking of a life.'

3. "The Chaplet is a means of reconciliation between the heart of man and the Heart of God, which is so greatly wounded by the sin of abortion."

(Blessed Mother - March 25, 2013)

"My Chaplet of the Unborn is important as it points out the error of abortion, the importance of life in the womb, and petitions a healing of heart for all who participate, in any way, in abortion. Pray it daily."

(Blessed Mother - January 29, 2014)

Additional Resources Available Through Archangel Gabriel Enterprises Inc.

Books and Booklets

The Chambers of the Divine, Sacred Heart of Jesus
Confraternity of the United Hearts Member Handbook
Confraternity of the United Hearts Prayer Life
Conversations with Divine Love
Devotion to the Mournful Heart of Jesus
Discernment: Discovering the Truth
Divine Love
First Chamber of the United Hearts—Holy Love
Heaven Speaks to the Heart of the World
Holy and Divine Love Messages on the Eucharist
Holy and Divine Love: The Remedy and the Triumph
Lessons on the Virtues
Message of Christ's Mystical Church of Atonement
Messages from God the Father
Messages from Heaven on Faith, Hope, Love and Trust
Messages from St. John Vianney
Messages from St. Peter on Temptation
Messages from St. Rita on Perseverance
Messages from St. Thomas Aquinas
Our Lady Gives the World the Rosary of the Unborn
Our Lady's Messages at the Arbor
Pilgrim's Guide to Maranatha Spring and Shrine
Purgatory
The Revelation of Our United Hearts: The Secrets Revealed
The Seven Moral Standards of Truth
St. Michael's Shield of Truth Devotion
Triumphant Hearts Prayer Book
Truth
United Hearts Book of Prayers and Meditations
Visions of Saints

ARCHANGEL GABRIEL ENTERPRISES INC.
37137 Butternut Ridge Road   North Ridgeville, OH 44039
Phone: 440-327-4532

E-mail: customerservice@rosaryoftheunborn.com

To order online: www.RosaryOfTheUnborn.com

Website: www.RosaryOfTheUnborn.com